T0341099

Crisis in Higher Education

A Customer-Focused, Resource Management Resolution

Series on Resource Management

RECENT TITLES

Crisis in Higher Education: A Customer-Focused, Resource Management Resolution
by Mark A. Vonderembse
ISBN: 978-1-138-03253-8

A Healthcare Solution: A Patient-Centered, Resource Management Perspective
by Mark A. Vonderembse and David D. Dobrzykowski
ISBN: 978-1-4987-5875-8

Supply Chain Construction: The Basics for Networking the Flow of Material, Information, and Cash
by William T. Walker
ISBN: 978-1-4822-4046-7

Directing the ERP Implementation: A Best Practice Guide to Avoiding Program Failure Traps While Tuning System Performance
by Michael W. Pelphrey
ISBN: 978-1-4822-4841-8

Building Network Capabilities in Turbulent Competitive Environments: Business Success Stories from the BRICs
by Paul Hong and YoungWon Park
ISBN: 978-1-4665-1575-8

Principles of Supply Chain Management, Second Edition
by Richard E. Crandall, William R. Crandall, and Charlie C. Chen
ISBN: 978-1-4822-1202-0

Supply Chain Risk Management: An Emerging Discipline
by Gregory L. Schlegel and Robert J. Trent
ISBN: 978-1-4822-0597-8

Supply Chain Optimization through Segmentation and Analytics
by Gerhard J. Plenert
ISBN: 978-1-4665-8476-1

Vanishing Boundaries: How Integrating Manufacturing and Services Creates Customer Value, Second Edition
by Richard E. Crandall and William R. Crandall
ISBN: 978-1-4665-0590-2

Food Safety Regulatory Compliance: Catalyst for a Lean and Sustainable Food Supply Chain
by Preston W. Blevins
ISBN: 978-1-4398-4956-9

Driving Strategy to Execution Using Lean Six Sigma: A Framework for Creating High Performance Organizations
by Gerhard Plenert and Tom Cluley
ISBN: 978-1-4398-6713-6

Crisis in Higher Education

A Customer-Focused, Resource Management Resolution

MARK A. VONDEREMBSE

CRC Press is an imprint of the
Taylor & Francis Group, an **informa** business

CRC Press
Taylor & Francis Group
6000 Broken Sound Parkway NW, Suite 300
Boca Raton, FL 33487-2742

Printed on acid-free paper

International Standard Book Number-13: 978-1-4987-9952-2 (Hardback)
978-1-1380-3253-8 (Paperback)

Library of Congress Cataloging-in-Publication Data

Names: Vonderembse, Mark A., 1948- author.
Title: Crisis in higher education : a customer-focused, resource management resolution / Mark Vonderembse.
Description: Boca Raton : Taylor & Francis, 2018. | Includes index.
Identifiers: LCCN 2017025432 | ISBN 9781138032538 (hardback : alk. paper)
Subjects: LCSH: Education, Higher--United States--Finance. | Educational change--United States.
Classification: LCC LB2342 .V88 2018 | DDC 378.73--dc23
LC record available at https://lccn.loc.gov/2017025432

Visit the Taylor & Francis Web site at
http://www.taylorandfrancis.com

and the CRC Press Web site at
http://www.crcpress.com

To my wonderful wife, life companion, and best friend, Gayle

In memory of our loving parents: Paul Edward Vonderembse, Ruth Mary Vonderembse, Robert L. Bauer, and Pauline M. Bauer

To our children and their spouses and significant others: Leisje and Dan, Tosje and Ted, Anthony and Lindsey, Vanessa and Don, Talia and Jake, Elaine and Greg, and Maryke and Jeremy

To our grandchildren: Dax, Perry, Koen, Milo, Aubriella, Stella, Trevor, Logan, Lillia, Ava, and Jack

Love to all.

Contents

Acknowledgments

There are many people to thank for their contributions to the creation of this book including teachers, mentors, and colleagues who, over the years, have taught me and provided important insights about higher education. A special thanks to Dr. Thomas Sharkey, faculty colleague, administrator, and friend for the many discussions I had with him about higher education as well as for reading an early draft of the book. Dr. Thomas Gutteridge, former Dean of the College of Business and Innovation at the University of Toledo, was a role model for what good administrators must be so that faculty and more importantly students can be successful in the classroom and in the job market. A big thank-you to both of them for stimulating conversation and ideas that became part of the analysis of the problems and elements of the solution.

A special thank-you to William T. Walker CFPIM, CIRM, CSCP, a resource management series editor for CRC Press/Taylor & Francis Group, who guided me through the writing and creative processes, giving me valuable comments as well as reading the manuscript and providing excellent feedback; Michael Sinocchi, publisher for Productivity Press, who saw potential in these ideas; Alexandria Gryder, editorial assistant for Productivity Press, who provided important insights about the writing and editorial aspects of the book; and Judith Simon, production editor for CRC Press, who guided me through the completion of the manuscript.

Finally, I want to express my thanks and love to my wife, Gayle, who was a constant source of encouragement, support, and advice. Her insights as a professional educator and school psychologist helped me to stay focused on the important issues. She gladly accepted additional responsibilities so that I could focus on the book.

Author

Mark A. Vonderembse earned a PhD in Business Administration from the University of Michigan, an MBA from the Wharton Graduate Division of the University of Pennsylvania, and a BS in Civil Engineering from the University of Toledo. In addition to holding the rank of Professor at the University of Toledo (UT), he has held important leadership positions, including Founding Director of the Intermodal Transportation Institute and Founding Director for the School of Healthcare Innovation and Excellence. In addition, he served six years as Chair of the Information Operations and Technology Management Department and three years as Chair of the Finance Department.

Dr. Vonderembse has taught courses in Germany, India, and China and traveled extensively, giving presentations on operations and supply chain management in China, Hong Kong, Japan, Korea, Singapore, India, Morocco, South Africa, Spain, England, Germany, Greece, and Canada. He and another faculty member led efforts to design and build UT's PhD program in Manufacturing and Technology Management, and he served as its Director for nine years. He chaired or co-chaired twenty-two PhD dissertations at UT and served as a member of nineteen other dissertations, including eleven from outside the United States.

He is widely published, including thirteen articles in the *Journal of Operations Management*, which is widely regarded as the best journal in the field. Dr. Vonderembse has also published in *Management Science*, *Decision Sciences*, *IIE Transactions*, *International Journal of Production Research*, and *European Journal of Operational Research*, among others. He has nearly two dozen awards for his research, including Outstanding Researcher at UT. He has held more than forty research grants from various sources, including the U.S. Department of Transportation, U.S. Department of Education, and the National Science Foundation. He has received more than $4 million in grants as the principal investigator and another $10 million as co-investigator.

About the Book

Higher education in the United States is at a tipping point. For decades, it has been regarded as the best in the world and for good reason: The United States gained worldwide economic and technologic stature through its incomprehensible feats of production during World War II and its achievements in computer and information technology, space travel, biotechnology, and other fields. Fredrick W. Taylor, the father of industrial engineering; Chester I. Barnard, the author of *The Functions of the Executive*; and Peter F. Drucker, Douglas M. McGregor, and Herbert A. Simon are just of few of the scholars who set the stage for the success of U.S. business in the twentieth century. The United States enhanced its educational arsenal by passing the GI Bill at the end of World War II, which created a generation of scientists, engineers, educators, and others, who continued the extraordinary achievements in economic performance and technological advancements.

Their sons and daughters (baby boomers) had access to a growing public college and university network in the 1960s and 1970s that offered high-quality education at an affordable price. During this era, students could hold a part-time, minimum-wage job during the school year and a full-time job in the summer, and they could pay their tuition, fees, and books at a public community and technical college or public university. If they lived at home, they probably had enough left over to buy a used car. With a little help from their parents, they could afford to live in a dormitory or an apartment. People who were motivated to earn a college or university degree were not held back by money. These were the halcyon days for higher education.

A primary cause of the pending crisis is out-of-control costs that restrict access to higher education, even for students from middle-income families, and create mountains of debt. High costs and fear of debt may cause some students and their parents to give less consideration to higher education or avoid it altogether. For graduates and even for students who start but drop out of school, student loan debt curbs their lifestyle and restricts U.S. economic growth because they postpone purchasing homes, cars, and other goods and services. The culprits are high costs for tuition, fees, and textbooks, which for decades have risen much faster than the rate of inflation. In fact, the rate of increase for tuition, the largest of these costs, is nearly twice the rate of increase in healthcare costs and three times the rate of increase in inflation from 2003 to 2013. It should be noted that community and technical colleges have much lower average tuition than public or private universities, and, as mentioned later, are not the primary focus of this book.

Although the international ranking of U.S. universities is still strong, especially for elite universities, other countries are improving their higher education systems and closing the gap. Past success may have led to complacency among U.S. universities. In addition, increasing enrollment and a lack of pushback on tuition hikes may have caused universities to focus less intently on ways to improve learning. One result is that instructional methods have not advanced substantially in a very long time, unless the transition from chalk and blackboards to overhead projectors and marking pens to PowerPoint presentations and video projectors is considered substantial. In many ways, these tools have made life easier for faculty, but it is not clear if they have enhanced student learning in meaningful ways.

There are also three quality-related questions that concern parents. They may not come to the minds of students, but they should: Will students drop out? How long will it take? Will they get a good job at graduation? Unfortunately for too many universities, graduation rates are low; completion times are too long; and job placement rates in some fields of study are poor. Part of the explanation may be that students are poorly prepared and not capable of doing the work, or they may not put forth enough effort. Another part, possibly a big part, is that universities are not offering knowledge in ways that students learn best, that is, student-centered learning, where knowledge is presented in different ways using different formats so students can pick the ones best suited to their learning style. In addition, universities place roadblocks in students' paths, which postpone graduation and increase dropout rates. High costs can be one of those impediments. Or universities may offer majors and recruit students to majors where there are not enough jobs for the number of graduates or the jobs that are available do not pay well.

These underlying problems have a set of root causes, which include a lack of understanding about customers, escalating administrative spending, limited productivity, and a lack of student preparation. These issues must be addressed in order to resolve the problems. The relationships between the root causes and the underlying problems are summarized in Table 4.3. A comprehensive and integrated solution with nine different elements is developed and presented to address the root causes. The relationships between the elements of the solution and the root causes are summarized in Table 5.1. Thus, it is possible to trace each element of the solution back to the underlying problem. Chapters 6 through 14 discuss each element and provide a list of recommendations that make up the element. A compilation of the recommendations is given in Appendix A.

To describe these underlying problems, root causes, and the elements of the solution, this book uses data from undergraduate degrees programs offered by state-supported, public, universities, which represent more than 60% of undergraduate enrollment. Although the problems, causes, and solution are described with public universities in mind, the book expands the discussion as appropriate to include community and technical colleges, which offer two-year degrees, and private universities, which can be not-for-profit or for-profit institutions. The problems and root causes faced by the different types of institutions are similar, often differing only by the order of magnitude. The elements of the solution are likely to be common as well.

There are many views on how to fix the problems. At one extreme, people suggest that public higher education should have zero tuition, as it was for some state-supported, public universities 50 years ago. The difficulty with this approach is that government subsidies simply cover up the problems and there is little if any reason for universities to change their behavior. They will gladly accept the subsidies and ask for more. At the other extreme, some suggest that governments eliminate subsidies for higher education, which would make it even more difficult for many students from low- and moderate-income families to earn an advanced degree. Plus, the future of the U.S. economy and its standard of living depend on having a highly educated workforce. There are shortages of engineers, scientists, physicians, and technologists, and the United States relies on foreign nationals to immigrate and fill many of these good-paying jobs. Under these circumstances, it seems reasonable to incentivize students to pursue advanced degrees.

Neither of these extreme options is appropriate to deal with the underlying problems. These problems must be understood and resolved directly and as quickly as possible because the problems are already acute and will likely take several years to resolve. Focusing on public universities is a good place to begin because state governments have leverage to motivate corrective action. Private universities, at least some of them, may be forced to take similar actions to remain competitive. Community and technical colleges may also gain some insights from these discussions and recommendations.

Mark A. Vonderembse

1

The Higher Education Conundrum

For thousands of years, the world evolved from a place where success/survival was determined by physical strengths, running speed, and hand–eye coordination to a place where intellectual ability, knowledge, and creativity are key success factors. Admittedly, strength, speed, and coordination are still essential for professional athletes and a few other professions, but this group is a very small portion of the population in the developed world.

Manufacturing jobs, which are considered manual labor, are a declining portion of the U.S. labor market. In 2013, manufacturing employment was only 12 million workers or less than 9% of the U.S. workforce.[1] In addition, many manufacturing jobs are held by supervisors, engineers, and managers who engage in intellectual work such as scheduling, designing, and planning. Even the mundane, repetitive jobs on an assembly line often have automation and power assistance to cope with the physical dimensions of work. Plus, assembly line workers are expected to identify and solve problems related to workplace safety, equipment reliability, process improvement, and maintenance. This may not require education beyond high school, but it does require thought, knowledge, and creativity.

As the United States and other countries continue the march toward jobs that require intellectual work, the need for more and better education becomes obvious. A hundred years ago, graduating from the eighth grade was celebrated as high school graduations are celebrated today. At that time, an elementary school teacher often had only a high school diploma. In 1940, only 25% of the population aged 25 years and older had completed high school and only 5% of adults held a bachelor's degree or higher.[2] World War II began a big push for higher education by emphasizing the importance of innovation and technology as well as high-output, efficient manufacturing systems. The United States entered the war with weapons, especially airplanes, that were inferior to its enemies in both capabilities and quantity. In a short time, it dramatically improved both, becoming the "arsenal of democracy."

In 1944, a grateful nation passed the Servicemen's Readjustment Act better known as the G.I. Bill, which provided a series of benefits to World War II veterans, including cash payments for tuition and living expenses to attend institutions of higher learning. By 1956, roughly 2.2 million veterans used this benefit,[3,4] which is still in place today. In 1964, the leading edge of the baby boomers graduated from high school and sought college degrees in record numbers. In 1965, President Lyndon Johnson signed the Higher Education Act that provided massive federal support for students through tuition grants, guaranteed student loans, and work-study funds.[5] As a result, institutions of higher learning benefited from decades of growth—enrolling just over 2 million in the early 1950s, 13 million in 1987, and more than 21 million in 2010.[6,7] By 2015, 33% of the U.S. adult population held a bachelor's degree or higher.[2]

This background information is important because it provides a context for understanding higher education. During this time, it was common for institutions, especially public colleges and universities supported by state and local tuition subsidies, to double in size and double again in response to:

1. Pent-up demand from nearly 16 years of the Great Depression and World War II
2. Recognition that higher education is needed to advance science, technology, and business
3. Veterans taking advantage of the G.I. Bill
4. Baby boomers seeing the value of higher education and demanding it
5. Low out-of-pocket costs for tuition, as a result of federal, state, and local subsidies.

During this rapid growth phase, the concern of higher education leaders tended not to be about planning, cost control, and workforce productivity, on which for-profit manufacturing and services firms focused intently. These resource management concepts took a backseat to concerns about meeting what appeared to be an insatiable demand for quality programs. Faced with these circumstances, most organization would have acted similarly. If customer after customer bought a Tahiti vacation and did not ask the price, why would the travel agent be concerned about keeping costs low? Higher education was heavily subsidized, so out-of-pocket costs were low.

There were other factors that reinforced this "meet demand for higher education" mindset. Many higher education leaders were and are today faculty members with PhDs in subjects like history, medicine, and science, so their inherent interest was investigating problems and providing a quality education with small classes. In addition, investing in higher education was an easy choice for politicians because they could boast to their constituents about educational opportunities for their children, plus it was thought to be a driver of jobs and economic growth. Furthermore, recent high school graduates had little experience in buying goods and services, and their parents often had no experience with higher education, so students and their families did not push back as cost increased. In combination, these factors help to explain why the cost of higher education grew much faster than the rate of inflation.

In the global economy, the country with the best educated population should have the best innovation, most entrepreneurs, strongest economy, and highest standard of living. Combining brainpower with a supportive environment for transforming ideas into useful and innovative goods and services creates a winning economy. The United States accomplishes this in two ways. As technology increases in complexity, and new products require innovative design capabilities and production processes, and organizations become larger and require sophisticated management, higher education responds with comprehensive, in-depth programs of study to meet these needs. In a knowledge-based economy, higher education plays a key role in building wealth for society as it provides the educated actors who participate in the value creation process. This process transforms inputs, including labor, materials, energy, and capital, into outputs—goods and services—that are worth more to society than the costs of these inputs. In the not-for-profit arena, higher education delivers a high-quality workforce for organizations involved in healthcare, education, and public service.

Second, building a highly educated and motivated workforce is facilitated by an immigration policy that

1. Encourages scientist, engineers, and highly trained professionals from other countries to immigrate to the United States in order to meet this growing demand.
2. Draws high-quality students from other countries to U.S. graduate programs and eventually entice them to work in the United States and become U.S. citizens and permanent residents.

3. Offers pathways to success for immigrants who come to this country legally searching for a better life for themselves and their families. The first generation may not be well educated, but they work hard and encourage and support their children to succeed. These children are highly motivated to make a better life for themselves and their children.

1.1 UNDERSTANDING HIGHER EDUCATION

Institutions of higher learning are often seen as a set of buildings made of brick and stone where people go to earn a degree. In fact, these institutions are by design collections of faculty scholars who have as their mission the creation and dissemination of knowledge. To accomplish this, they engage in the following:

1. *Research and innovation:* Faculty participates in discovering and developing new thoughts, ideas, and processes across a wide variety of topics from basic science, to sociology, to economics and business. It might involve advances in medical testing, power generation, or philosophy. The results of these efforts are disseminated through journal articles and books.
2. *Teaching and learning:* Knowledge is also disseminated as faculty designs and delivers curricula to undergraduate and graduate students who are seeking to become better citizens and have a better life. Curricula are the content in courses that students must grasp to earn a degree.
3. *Service to the academy:* Here, academy is a society or organization of distinguished scholars that promotes and maintains standards in their fields. Faculty members support various academic society and journals that critique and publish research, and they seek to understand how people learn and improve teaching techniques. In addition, they participate in governing institutions of higher learning through committees that design curriculum and evaluate promotion and tenure as well as through service as institutional leaders and administrators.

Institutions of higher learning come in different forms, offer different levels of study, and usually have Boards of Trustee, which are the final decision makers. Faculty members are the principle employees, and there are different types with vastly different compensation and responsibilities.

1.1.1 Types of Institutions

Some entities are called universities, others are called colleges, and still others are called community and technical colleges. There are two-year associate, four-year bachelor's, and graduate degrees.

1. *University:* Can be a public or private entity that offers four-year bachelor's degrees in multiple fields of study. These fields are typically organized as colleges within the university (sometimes called schools) such as engineering, business, and education. Universities usually offer graduate degrees and engage in research as part of their mission. Most universities, both public and private, are not-for-profit entities, but some operate on a for-profit basis. These universities build cost structures and set pricing policies to generate a surplus of cash that represents a profit, which is returned to shareholders. A few universities offer two-year associate degrees.
2. *College:* As time passes, this designation is becoming less common. In the nineteenth century, higher education was dominated by liberal arts colleges that offered a "gentleman's" education in classical literature, art, economic, language, and similar subjects. Today, these institutions serve as many or more women than men. They still offer an excellent liberal arts education, but many have succumb to the demand for degrees in subjects such as business and nursing that lead more directly to jobs. These institutions are usually smaller than universities, especially state-supported public universities. In some cases, these institutions have changed their designation from college to university in order to reflect their growing diversity of programs.
3. *Land grant colleges and universities:* The land grant system began in 1862 as a result of the Morrill Act that provided public lands that could be sold or used to establish institutions of higher learning, which focused on agriculture and the mechanical arts. This was a response to the emerging Industrial Revolution and was complementary to liberal arts colleges. Although their origins may be different, many of these universities are no longer easily recognizable as land

grant institutions—Cornell, Pennsylvania State, and Mississippi State are three examples. The Morrill Act of 1890 provided additional funding and resulted in the establishment of land grant colleges for black Americans, giving rise to institutions like Florida A&M and Tuskegee University. A 1994 Act of Congress conferred land grant status for Native American colleges that were part of the American Indian Higher Education Consortium.[8]

4. *Community college:* This designation covers two-year (mostly public) institutions that grant certificates, diplomas, and associate degrees. After completing an associate degree, graduates can transfer to a four-year college or university to complete their undergraduate degree. Community college tuition is typically much lower than tuition at a university or a traditional liberal arts college. States often have more community colleges than public universities, and they tend to locate the former in or near population center, providing students easy access to the first two years of post–high school education. As a result, students can commute to campus daily, so community colleges may not have campus housing or may have only a limited supply.
5. *Technical college:* This is also a two-year (mostly public) institution that grants certificates, diplomas, and associate degrees. It is similar in structure to community colleges, but its programs focus on specific, job-related subjects such as information technology, legal assistant, or industrial engineering technology. Usually, graduates seek jobs in their chosen fields rather than pursue a bachelor's degree. It is common to combine the offerings of a community college and a technical college to create one entity, which is typically labeled a community and technical college.

As shown in Table 1.1, there are big cost differences among these institutions. For 2015–2016, the average total cost for public, two-year, in-state community and technical colleges was $16,833 per year for a full-time student. Low tuition was the key to low costs. This cost would have been reduced by almost half if students were able to live with their parents or other responsible adults and avoid the cost of room and board. Students who attended public, four-year, in-state colleges and universities and stayed on campus paid $24,061 per year on average. This cost would have been reduced by more than $10,000 if students lived with their parents or someone else who supported them. For out-of-state students at public universities, the cost jumped to $38,544 per year, and the entire difference

TABLE 1.1

Estimated, Average, Annual, Undergraduate Expenses for Full-Time Students (2015–2016)

Expenses [a]	Public, 2-Year, In-State, On-Campus	Public, 4-Year, In-State, On-Campus	Public, 4-Year, Out-of-State, On-Campus	Private, Not-for-Profit, 4-Year, On-Campus	Private, For-Profit, On-Line
Tuition and fees	$3,435	$9,410	$23,893	$32,405	$15,610
Room and board	$8,003	$10,138	$10,138	$11,516	$12,960[b]
Books and supplies	$1,364	$1,298	$1,298	$1,249	Included[c]
Transportation	$1,774	$1,109	$1,109	$1,033	NA[b]
Other expenses	$2,257	$2,106	$2,106	$1,628	NA[b]
Total expenses	$16,833	$24,061	$38,544	$47,831	$28,570

[a] The costs in the table, except those described in points b and c, are from the College Board website. (*Source*: College Board, *Trends in Higher Education: Published Prices—National*, 2016. http://trends.collegeboard.org/college-pricing/figures-tables/published-prices-national#Published Charges, 2015–16.)

[b] Students attending private, for-profit universities such as the University of Phoenix, even if attending classes online, have room and board, transportation (although not to attend class), and other expenses. They may avoid some of these costs if they live with their parents or others who can support them. The estimated amount for these services from the University of Phoenix website is $12,960 per year. This amount is used in the table. University of Phoenix provides no breakdown, so all the costs are listed under room and board. (*Source*: University of Phoenix, *Tuition and Expenses*, 2016. http://www.phoenix.edu/tuition_and_financial_options/financial-plan-services/review-tuition-and-expenses.)

[c] Private, for-profit universities, such as the University of Phoenix, often include books and other learning materials in tuition and fees.

was higher tuition. Students who attended private, four-year, not-for-profit colleges and universities and stayed on-campus paid $47,831 per year.[9] Nearly all of the difference was higher tuition.

Private, for-profit universities, which often operate over the Internet using "distance learning," cost $15,610 per year for tuition and fees.[9] Students who use online learning tools may avoid purchasing textbooks. Estimates for room and board, transportation, and other expenses were obtained from the University of Phoenix's website and were estimated at $12,960.[10] It may be possible for students to avoid a substantial part of these costs by living with parents or others who support them. If not, the total cost for a private, for-profit university was estimated at $28,570 per year.

There are big differences in enrollment by institution type. Table 1.2 shows that public institutions had a dominant market share in 2009 with 14,810,642 students or 72.5% of the total. Enrollment in private, not-for-profit institutions was 3,765,083 students or 18.4%, while private, for-profit institutions had 1,851,986 students or 9.1%. These figures combine full- and part-time enrollment in two-year and four-year institutions. Despite large enrollment differences between public institutions and private, not-for-profit institutions, there are approximately 1,650 of each type. This number is largely unchanged since the late 1980s and has increased only slightly since 1975. On the other hand, private, for-profit institutions have increased from a handful in the late 1970s to nearly 1,200 by 2010.[6,7]

With respect to four-year degrees, public institutions enrolled 7,709,197 full- and part-time students in 2009, whereas private institutions enrolled 5,197,108. For two-year degrees, nearly all enrollments were in public institutions with 7,101,445 students. Private, two-year institutions, both not-for-profit and for-profit, enrolled only 419,961 students.[6,7] A likely explanation for the dominance of public institutions is that state and local subsidies keep tuition low, which negates the small class-size advantage of some private institutions. The dominance of public, two-year institutions may be further explained by the inability of private, two-year institutions to claim elite status as private, four-year institutions tend to do.

1.1.2 Types of Faculty

When most people hear the term *faculty*, visions of scholarly, thoughtful, somewhat befuddled tenured professors come to mind, but this is a shrinking part of higher education. Faculty who teach the majority of courses at community and technical colleges and in undergraduate programs are full- and part-time contractual faculty as well as graduate teaching assistants. A description of the different types follows:

1. *Tenured and tenure-track faculty:* Generally speaking, this group holds the intellectual capital of institutions of higher learning. In addition to teaching, they are responsible for conducting research and serving the institution and the academy in various roles such as curriculum design, governance, and support for academic journals that publish research. In almost all cases, they are full-time employees, and they either have tenure or are in the process of earning it. If they are successful, they

TABLE 1.2

Enrollment in Higher Education by Institution Type, 2009

Institution Type	Enrollment Full-Time	Enrollment Part-Time	% Enrollment Full-Time/ Total	% Enrollment Part-Time/ Total	Total Enrollment	% Total Enrollment
Public 2-year	2,880,631	4,220,814	14.1	20.7	14,810,642	72.5
Public 4-year	5,649,713	2,059,484	27.6	10.1		
Private, not-for profit 2-year	23,483	11,284	0.1	0.1	3,765,083	18.4
Private, not-for-profit 4-year	2,783,162	947,154	13.6	4.6		
Private, for-profit 2-year	344,609	40,585	1.7	0.2	1,851,986	9.1
Private, for-profit, 4-year	1,041,184	425,608	5.1	2.1		
Total	12,722,782	7,704,929	62.2	37.8	20,427,711	100

Source: United States Department of the Treasury and Department of Education, *The Economics of Higher Education*, 2012. https://www.treasury.gov/connect/blog/Documents/20121212_Economics%20of%20Higher%20Ed_vFINAL.pdf.

are granted tenure typically at their seventh year of employment. They progress through the ranks from assistant professor, which they are granted at the time of hiring, to associate professor when they earn tenure, and to full professor when they have met the standard, which is typically five or six years beyond earning tenure.

2. *Full-time contractual faculty:* Contracts with these faculty members can vary significantly, but generally speaking, they are divided into two groups: instructional faculty and professional faculty.
   a. Instructional faculty, which often holds the rank of instructor or lecturer, may have some experience in the field in which they teach. They usually have one-year contracts with renewability based on the needs of institutions. Most of their teaching is done at community and technical colleges or in undergraduate programs. They earn substantial less than tenured faculty—half as much or even less, plus they have teaching loads that are twice as high as tenured faculty because they have no or very limited research and service commitments. Lower wages and higher teaching loads make them doubly attractive.
   b. Professional faculty members typically have many years of high-level work experience. A well-known musician, former vice president of marketing, or founder of a computer technology company may be selected. Although they may have one-year contracts and hold the rank of instructor or lecturer, it is also possible that they have three- to five-year contracts and are called professors of practice or adjunct professors. They often teach upper-level undergraduate courses and masters-level courses in their professional specialty. Their compensation could be much higher than instructional faculty and their teaching load much lower. They may be involved in research and are likely to have a very active role in working with organizations that hire graduates of the program.
3. *Part-time contractual faculty:* This faculty type has course-by-course contracts, and their sole responsibility is to teach. They typically make a few thousand dollars per course and receive no or very limited fringe benefits, so they are the cheapest source of teaching labor.
4. *Graduate teaching assistants:* Colleges and universities with graduate programs often use these students to teach undergraduate courses. Most PhD programs require their graduate assistants to teach as preparation for careers as tenured faculty. These students typically receive free or reduced tuition and a stipend.

Specifics about faculty salaries are given later in the chapter. Moving forward, the term *faculty* is used to reference all faculty members in the institution, and the term *tenured faculty* refers to faculty members who have earned tenure as well as those in tenure-track positions who are seeking to earn it.

1.1.3 Role of Technology

Looking backward, institutions of higher learning have been late adopters of communication and information technologies for both managing the institution and instructing students. It seems odd that organizations that pride themselves on research, innovation, and developing disruptive product and process technologies would be reluctant to invest in technology. This conflict seems to indicate that institutions of higher learning do not understand or are not concerned about the value that technology can bring to their business. When management problems arise or better student services are needed, the preferred action seems to be to hire more people to fix the problem. This has caused administrative costs to grow much faster than enrollment. This will be described in greater detail in Chapter 2. In the past, top administrators had little education or experience with information technology and were hesitant to use it for various reasons, including a fear of appearing inexpert. With unwillingness to invest and faculty's resistance to change, the application of technology to teaching moved slowly over the past five decades from chalkboards to overhead projects and transparencies to power point slides and video projectors.

Looking forward, technology must be a key part of the solution. It can help institutions improve management practices and enhance student services while reducing the costs of administration. Technology is also needed to improve the quality of instruction as well as the productivity of faculty.

1.2 A FRAMEWORK FOR HIGHER EDUCATION: UNDERSTANDING DIFFERENCES

Higher education is different from manufacturing and other service providers in subtle, yet important ways. Yes, it offers a service, has customers and competitors, generates revenue, and acquires resources (mostly labor and capital) to provide its service. Like other organizations, the customers of higher education pay for access to the services, including payments for tuition, special fees, books, room and board, and miscellaneous expenses such as entertainment and smartphone access. Some of these payments go to the institution, whereas others go elsewhere. Revenues to the institutions are used to assemble resources including faculty, facilities, technology, administrators, support services such as financial aid and advising, and ancillary services including on-campus housing and sports programs. There is a competition among institutions for the best students, which can lead to extensive discounting of costs through scholarships offered by the institutions. These aspects of higher education are similar to ways other organizations produce and sell their goods and services.

However, a close examination of the framework in Figure 1.1 shows key differences between higher education and other organizations. These items are discussed in the following sections.

1. *Two demand–supply relationships:* There is one demand–supply relationship with applicants who desire to attend institutions of higher learning and another with organizations who want to hire their graduates.
2. *Multiple payers:* These relationships are confounded by the fact that higher education has multiple payers: students, parents, other family members, friends, and governments, as well as scholarships from various sources and donations from foundations and other entities.

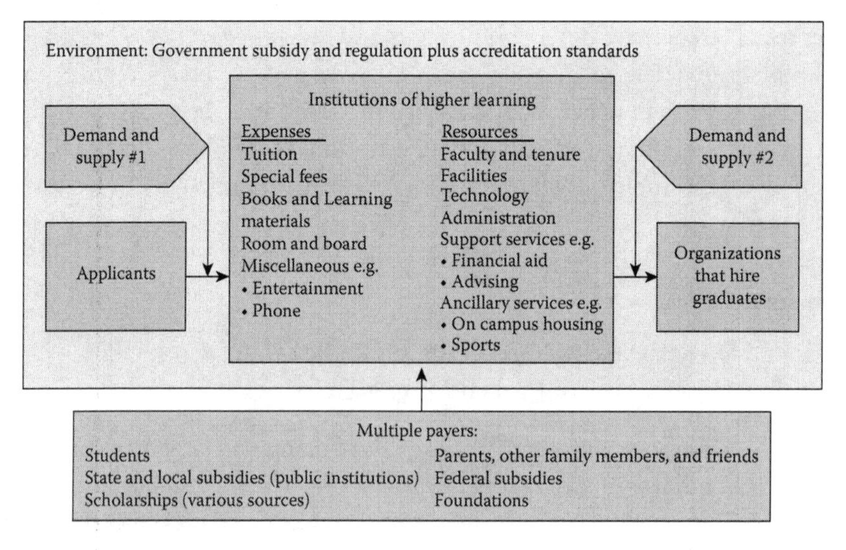

FIGURE 1.1
Framework for higher education.

3. *Uncertainty about customers:* Because there are multiple demand–supply relationships and third-party payers, questions arise about who the customers really are and how they should be treated.
4. *Regulation and accreditation:* Higher education operates in an environment of government subsidy and regulation and a wide variety of accrediting agencies that assess quality and examine performance.
5. *Tenure:* It can be granted to tenure-track faculty usually after six years on the job. Tenure provides specific rights of due process and requires that universities show cause for dismissal.
6. *Conglomerate:* Institutions of higher learning have ancillary services such as sports and student housing that require vastly different resources and capabilities and whose outcomes are not related to the institution's primary mission.

1.3 MEDIATING TWO DEMAND–SUPPLY RELATIONSHIPS

As shown in Figure 1.1, higher education sits astride two important demand–supply relationships. First, applicants seek admissions to schools, which often have a limited number of slots available. There is competition to gain admission to elite colleges and universities for programs with strong national and international reputations. Some students seek special programs, others want the small school experience with small class size, and still others make the choice based on sports or extracurricular activities. Having selection criteria like these is typical for customers who purchase other goods and services, but the difference is the back end, where students become graduates who seek employment.

This second demand–supply relationship is important because institutions should feel responsibility to educate graduates who can work for biotech companies, elementary schools, engineering firms, governments, and other organizations. When demand and supply are in balance, graduates begin their working lives with opportunities for success, including paying back loans and living comfortably. So both students and organizations that hire graduates are customers, and higher education is the matchmaker that mediates this critical relationship. This point is discussed in more detail later in the book. There are some graduates who seek advanced degrees in fields such as medicine or law, but ultimately they seek employment, and after the work employment their first degree is a stepping-stone to that end.

1.4 HIGHER EDUCATION HAS THIRD-PARTY PAYERS

Higher education is similar to healthcare in that customers do not pay all or even most of the costs. Employers and governments pay the lion's share of healthcare costs. In higher education, Figure 1.1 shows that the costs are shared. Students pay a portion of the cost, and so do parents, other family members, and friends. Publically supported colleges and universities receive payments from state and local governments that subsidize tuition, and the federal government offers grants, guaranteed student loans, and work-study jobs for students who qualify. Institutions of higher learning award scholarships that help students pay for their education. Scholarships and donations are available from various organizations such as unions, churches, fraternal organizations, and foundations.

A study conducted by Ipsos Public Affairs for Sallie Mae estimates how the typical family paid for higher educations in 2014–2015 (see Figure 1.2). It may be surprising that the largest share was paid by parents from income and savings, 32%, and borrowing, an additional 6%, which totals 38%. Other family members and friends chipped in 5%. Scholarships and grants were second at 30% with a substantial amount coming from institutions

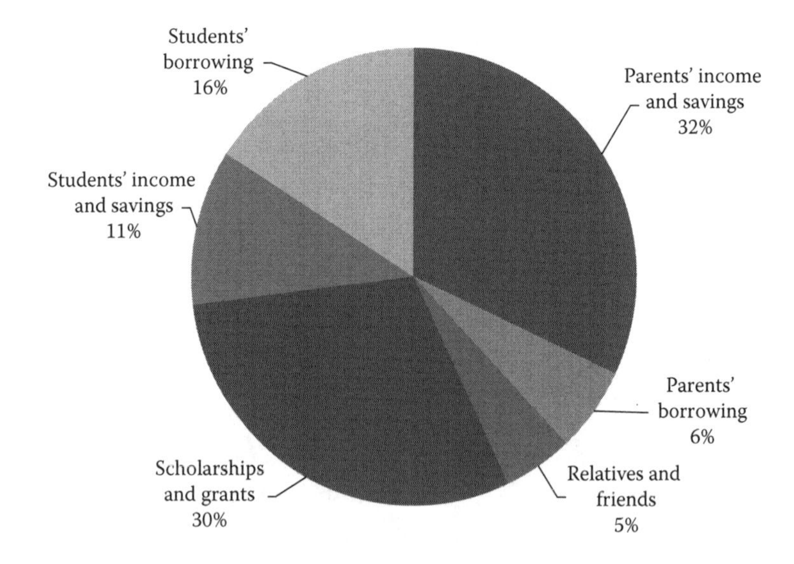

FIGURE 1.2
How typical family paid for higher education in 2014–2015. (Courtesy of SallieMae, How America Pays for College 2015, 2015. http://news.salliemae.com/files/doc_library/file/HowAmericaPaysforCollege2015FNL.pdf)

of higher learning. Students' income and savings totaled about 11%, and students' borrowing was 16%, so students contributed 27% of the costs. Federal subsidies show up as student loans, grants, and student earnings through work-study programs.[11]

It should be noted that the respondents to this survey were family members, so these data do not include the subsidies that states and local governments provide for their public colleges and universities. These subsidies have declined over time but are still substantial. The contributions to higher education from state and local governments for 2013 were $72.7 and $9.2 billion, respectively. State support represents about 21% and local support less than 3% of the budgets for public colleges and universities.[12] This support explains why these institutions have lower tuition than private ones.

1.5 WHO IS THE CUSTOMER OF HIGHER EDUCATION?

In most relationships, customers are usually easy to identify. They pay for goods or services, and they gain benefits from their use. Higher education is different because there are two critical demand–supply relationships to address, and students pay only 11% of the cost at the time of purchase. Student loans, which are deferred to a future time, represent another 16%, and these loans may actually be paid in total or in part by parents or others. This means that higher education faces a trifurcated customer:

1. *Students:* They participate in higher education and gain knowledge in the process. If successful, they benefit by living better, including higher incomes and more job satisfaction.
2. *Third-party payers:* Parents, other family members, friends, governments, scholarships providers, and foundations pay most of the costs without receiving any direct benefits. Parents, other family members, and friends are doing so for unselfish reason; they want the student to succeed. Governments hope to support and stimulate the economy by providing a highly educated workforce. As part of their mission, institutions of higher learning offer scholarships to applicants in financial need and/or who are well qualified. Foundations usually have mandates to do good as described by the philanthropists who established them.

3. *Organizations that hire graduates:* They are major beneficiaries of higher education. They hire and compensate the graduates for the work they do, which allows the graduates to repay their loans and "make a living." In effect, applicants to institutions of higher learning must look through the educational process and see the lifetime of possible benefits that await them.

1.5.1 Customer Confusion Leads to Poorly Articulated Goals

With a trifurcated customer, there is no clear and strong "voice of the customer" to guide tenured faculty (who control curriculum content) and high-level administrators (who typically share faculty values and hold faculty rank and tenure). Tenured faculty and administrators often feel they know best and step in to fill the void. Many tenured faculty still hold the view that the primary purpose of a bachelor's degree is to grow personally and intellectually, understand complex issues and problems, and create better members of society—that is, to become a more refined and thoughtful person. The vision, mission, core values, and goals of most universities usually reflect the dominance of this "better member of society" attitude. Job placement, career success, and meeting the needs of business and industry are usually not prominent in vision and mission statements.

This approach may have worked decades ago when students were primarily from well-to-do families who wanted their children to be prepared to assume their rightful place in society. But it does not work today for the single mother of five with a full-time job who is attending a university on a part-time basis to improve her life and the lives of her children. There is value in creating a better person as part of the higher education experience, and universities should try to contribute to this end, but preparing people for successful careers must have top priority for several reasons.

1. *Graduates:* They may not understand the value or purpose of their education while attending, but they certainly understand its importance as they pay back their student loans, buy a home or condominium, and save for retirement. They do not want to live in their parents' basements.
2. *Parents, other family members, and friends:* They want the best for their graduate, which means, among other things, a successful career and a good job. Even if they have a basement, they do not want the graduate to live there.

3. *Governments:* Federal, state, and local governments want economic prosperity and jobs that are facilitated by a well-educated workforce.
4. *Companies that hire graduates:* They want well-educated employees who begin working immediately without substantial on-the-job training.
5. *Society:* It needs people with good jobs and bright futures because they are more likely to stay out of trouble and contribute to society in positive ways. Society wants a strong economy, so there are tax receipts to support government, including helping those who need assistance.

1.5.2 Customer Confusion Leads to Misaligned Actions

There is a three-way tug of war over curriculum.

1. Students have multiple demands on their time, and they may not fully appreciate the long-term nature and value of their education. As a result, they may not be motivated to perform as well as they should. They may find it difficult to appreciate the importance of learning some subjects because they do not see how these topics can be useful. Are students, who pay only a small part of the cost (11%, see Figure 1.2) while they are pursuing their education, good consumers who seek the best value and demand to learn more? Do they put pressure on institutions to be more cost conscience, and are they motivated to work hard, finish early, and perform well in class?
2. Tenured faculty members prefer to focus on theory and concepts, and they use this perspective to determine what is important. They want graduates to understand the big ideas and be prepared for a lifetime of learning. This often leads to aggressive learning objectives that demand careful thought and substantial amounts of time.
3. Organizations that hire graduates want the "top students" with practical, hands-on education so their entry-level employees can begin work immediately.

This narrative indicates that institutions of higher learning face substantial problems as they try to meet the needs of multiple masters. Figure 1.3 shows a contrast between for-profit providers of goods and services and institutions of higher learning. For-profit organizations begin with clearly defined and easily measurable end goals such as sales, market share, profits, and return on invested capital. The seller and its customers are closely

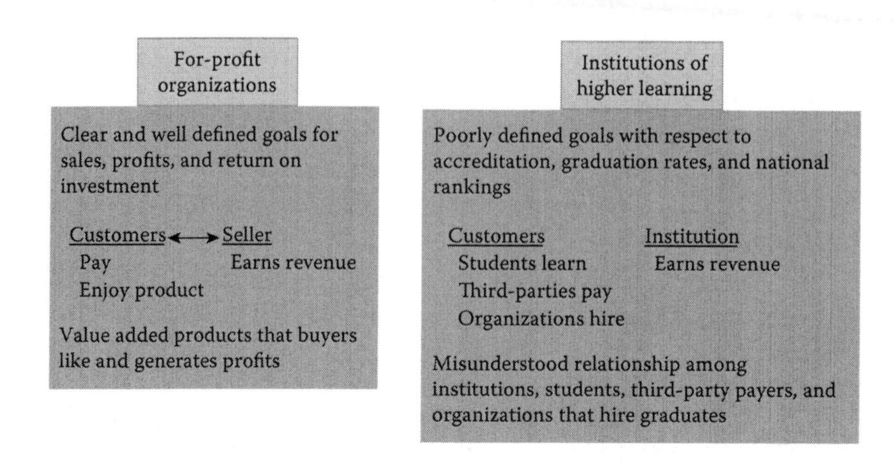

FIGURE 1.3
Differences in end goals, and customer and seller relationships between for-profit organizations and institutions of higher learning.

linked, as illustrated by the double-headed arrow, because customers, who pay for the good or service, extract value from it. The value they receive is commensurate with the price they pay. The price is more than the sum of the costs for the good or service, so the company makes a profit and societal wealth is created. On the other hand, institutions of higher learning often have disconnected and poorly defined end goals such as gaining or maintaining accreditation or achieving a national ranking in one subject or another. There is no well-defined and easily measurable goal such as market share or return on investment that enables these institutions to focus actions on improving outcomes. When institutions of higher learning fail to recognize the trifurcated customer, they are challenged to make good decisions about product/program develop and resource allocation as well as understand the important role of the organizations that hire their graduates.

1.6 HIGHER EDUCATION FACES GOVERNMENT REGULATION AND A MULTITUDE OF ACCREDITATION AGENCIES

As suggested by Figure 1.1, institutions of higher learning are regulated and subject to review by various accreditation organizations. All universities that accept federal subsidies, including student loans—and nearly all universities do—must comply with federal regulations and reporting requirements, and this creates substantial administrative costs. In addition, publicly supported colleges and universities are subject to state oversight and reporting requirements, which come in the form of State Boards of Regents or Departments of Education. These oversight groups usually require financial reporting, establish operating policies and guidelines that institutions must follow, and create complex mechanisms to review and approve new programs. Public colleges and universities comply because the state legislator approves funding for these institutions. Private colleges and universities may participate in some parts of this process, even though they receive no state funding. On top of this, a small number of public colleges and universities receive funding from local governments, which adds another level of oversight.

In addition to regulation, nearly all institutions of higher learning face accreditation from external bodies, which occurs at two levels: the institution overall and parts of the institution, including colleges, schools, and individual programs and majors. Although the length of time between accreditation reviews is a variable, a common length seems to be five years. Accreditation tends to examine three factors.

1. *Input:* The quality and sufficiency of the resources that support the institution and its programs, including the qualifications and number of faculty and advising staff, quality of applicants, classroom space and functionality, computer technology, and library access.
2. *Process:* Assesses an institution's ability to design and deliver high-quality programs, foster an environment that encourages learning and creates tools to assess it, implement methods to improve programs and learn continuously, and plan for future opportunities and threats.
3. *Output:* Validates the quality of the program by assessing achievements, including graduation rates, job placements, admissions to graduate programs, results from licensure or certification exams, and others as defined by the mission of the institution or program.

The Higher Learning Commission (HLC) is an independent corporation found in 1895 as one of six regional accreditors. It accredits degree-granting, postsecondary institution in the north-central portion of the United States. It mission is to assure and advance the quality of higher education. A description of the HLC's criteria goes on for several pages and is organized around the following five main points. Broadly speaking, these are typical of the standards set by many accreditation bodies.

1. *Mission:* The mission of the institution of higher learning is clear and guides its operations.
2. *Integrity—ethical and responsible conduct:* The institution acts with integrity, and its conduct is ethical and responsible.
3. *Teaching and learning—quality, resources, and support:* The institution provides high-quality education, wherever and however its offerings are delivered.
4. *Teaching and learning—evaluation and improvement:* The institution demonstrates responsibility for the quality of its educational programs, learning environments, and support services. The institution evaluates the effectiveness of its programs for student learning through processes that lead to continuous improvement.
5. *Resources, planning, and institutional effectiveness:* The institution's resources, structures, and processes are sufficient to fulfill its mission, improve the quality of its educational offerings, and respond to future challenges and opportunities.[13]

For consumers, accreditation provides a reasonable level of assurance that institutions are meeting basic standards for higher education. The downside is that institutions must dedicate a large team of faculty and administrators to oversee the process and prepare detailed reports about inputs, processes, and outputs. They can spend eighteen months or more and prepare reports of more than 1,000 pages in the process, consuming large amounts of time and critical resources.

In addition to institutional accreditation, there are dozens of accreditations processes for specific degrees and programs. Business schools seek accreditation from the Association to Advance Collegiate Schools of Business (AACSB), which assesses all business programs offered by an institution as well as provides special accounting accreditation.[14] Through its four commissions, ABET reviews and accredits programs in applied science, computing, engineering, and engineering technology.[15] The Council on Social Work Education develops accreditation criteria that describe knowledge standards and ensure that social work programs are in compliance.[16] These are just a few examples.

Like institution-wide accreditation, college- and program-specific accreditations provide assurance of quality, and they require considerable time and effort on the part of tenured faculty and program administrators, generate lengthy reports, and carry significant costs. These accreditations can be a source of conflict between the programs/schools/colleges and central administration. The educational units want accreditation because it gives them standing in the academic community, which gives them bragging rights and is helpful in recruiting faculty. It also provides opportunities to brand and market their programs to potential applicants and their parents as accredited and therefore of the best quality. As budgets in higher education become tighter and tighter, educational units look forward to these visits because the findings can be used as levers to pry more resources from "tight-fisted" administrators who are looking to save money. The accreditors' reports may identify faculty and other resource deficiencies that must be addressed if accreditation is to be granted. Central administrations are learning to dread these visits and accuse their educational units of using accreditation as a vehicle to "blackmail" the institution for resources that it does not have and the educational units do not need. As with most disagreements, the truth lies somewhere in the middle.

To show the magnitude of the problem with regulation and accreditation, consider the following. The Higher Education Compliance Alliance, which provides information about federal compliance, found more than 250 separate federal compliance regulations for U.S. colleges and universities.[17] A report from Hartwick College, a small liberal art college with 1,500 undergraduates students in upstate New York, shows how significant this problem can be. Hartwick is regulated by 28 different federal agencies and department, 15 different state agencies, 4 local governments, 7 accreditation agencies, and 4 private entities. It must comply with three athletic associations, including the NCAA, which has 94 annual compliance requirements. It is required to comply with rules and regulations from several hospitals and medically related organizations for its nursing program. There are hundreds of statutes and regulations with which it must comply.[18] The time and cost of compliance are significant.

1.7 TENURE

It is a right to due process, meaning that an institution cannot fire a tenured professor without presenting evidence that the professor is not competent, behaves unprofessionally, or is a member of a department that is going to be closed or a school that is in serious financial difficulty. Nationally, about 2% of tenured faculty are dismissed each year.[19] Dismissing a tenured faculty member is not as easy as many administrators would like it to be, but it can be done. The primary purpose of tenure is to prevent administrators, who usually have tenure and hold faculty rank, from firing faculty who disagree with them on theory and concepts, have slighted or criticized them in the past, or have a history of personal differences. Tenure is intended to create an environment where freedom of thought and expression are not only tolerated but encouraged.

For years, tenure has been a lightning rod, used to explain what is wrong with higher education. In the minds of many, eliminating tenure is a problem solver, but consider the following. Tenured faculty make up less than 30% of the faculty at colleges and universities.[20,21] Table 1.3 lists the percent of faculty by the type of institution. In 2007, across all institutions, tenured faculty was 27.3%. There was a big difference between two-year community colleges, which teach primarily foundational and hands-on courses, at 17.5% and public, four-year institutions, which have no or very small graduate programs, at 39%. For public, doctoral granting institutions, only 28.9% of faculty had tenure because these institutions used many graduate assistants to teach undergraduate courses. At private, four-year and private, doctoral institutions, only about 29% had tenure.[21] Therefore, the impact of tenured faculty is much smaller than what most people believe, and moving forward, the impact will most likely be less as the portion of tenured faculty continues to decline. From 1978 to 2014, administrative positions have increased by 369%, part-time faculty by 286%, and full-time, non-tenure-track faculty by 259%. During this period, full-time, tenured positions have increased by only 23%.[22,23]

It is difficult to blame the rising costs of higher education on greedy faculty. The median salary for part-time faculty at a public research university was $3,200 per course. It was only $2,250 at community colleges.[24] In 2013–2014, full-time instructors and lecturers, which are usually non-tenured positions, earned $48,388 and $53,343 at public institutions, respectively. At public institutions, earnings for assistant professors, associate professors, and professors, which is the normal progression for tenured faculty, were $69,100, $80,448, and $112,897, respectively.[23]

The salaries for tenured faculty are not exorbitant when one considers the time it takes to earn a PhD. At a minimum, it requires five years of

TABLE 1.3

Distribution of Faculty Positions in Higher Education by Institution Type, 1997–2007

	1997	2007	1997	2007	1997	2007	1997	2007	1997	2007	1997	2007
	All Institutions		Public Doctoral		Public 4-Year		Public 2-Year		Private Doctoral		Private 4-Year	
Full-time, tenured, or tenure track	33.1%	27.3%	34.1%	28.9%	51.0%	39.0%	20.6%	17.5%	34.9%	29.2%	39.3%	29.0%
Full-time, non-tenure track	14.2%	14.9%	14.1%	14.4%	9.0%	10.9%	13.4%	13.8%	17.3%	17.9%	15.6%	17.2%
Part-time	34.1%	36.9%	14.3%	15.8%	33.6%	43.9%	64.7%	68.6%	29.9%	31.3%	42.3%	52.2%
Graduate assistants	18.6%	20.9%	37.5%	41.0%	5.7%	6.3%	1.2%	0.0%	17.9%	21.6%	2.9%	1.6%

Source: Jaschik, S., The Disappearing Tenure-Track Job, *Inside Higher Education*, 2009. https://www.insidehighered.com/news/2009/05/12/workforce

study beyond an undergraduate degree, and in some disciplines it takes 10 years or more, plus there is no guarantee of a job. In some disciplines, like.business, there are shortages of PhD-qualified faculty, whereas in others there are large surpluses. Physicians, who have similar educational requirements, earn more than two to three times the amount of a public university professor: $221,000 for primary care physicians and $396,000 for specialists.[25]

A closer look at administrative salaries provides additional insights about pay increase. From 2000 to 2010, the median salary for top administrators at public universities rose 39% with presidents' salary increasing by 75%, whereas full-time professors gained only 19%. At private colleges and universities, top administrator salaries increased by 97%, presidents by 171%, and full-time faculty by 50%. It is clear that faculty salaries have lagged.[22,23] From this discussion, it is reasonable to ask the question: What percent of an institution's budget is faculty instructional costs? It is common to pay about 30%–35% for instructional costs, with the lion's share of the remainder going for administration.[20] This supports a claim that there is more to the high costs in higher education than having tenured faculty.

1.8 MANY INSTITUTIONS OF HIGHER LEARNING ARE UNWIELDY CONGLOMERATES

A conglomerate is a single entity that owns multiple businesses, which serve entirely different markets. The parent company is often referred to as a holding company. The theoretical advantage is that different businesses should have different customers, streams of earnings, and risks. When diverse businesses are combined, fluctuations in earning should offset, so the holding company will have strong and steady earnings, which should be rewarded with a high stock price. Conglomerates became popular in the 1950s and 1960s, resulting in holding companies that might own the following subsidiaries: glass container maker, forest ownership and papermaking, nursing home manager, real estate marketer, and digital display developer. During the 1970s and 1980s, many conglomerates were dismantled because there were no synergies among these diverse businesses, so cost rose and corporate performance suffered. On top of that, the smoothing of earnings was largely ineffective.

Although most people would agree that the primary purpose of higher education is to engage in teaching and research plus the services that directly support these activities, most colleges and universities have a diverse set of ancillary businesses that generate revenue:

1. *Sport franchise:* For most colleges and universities, this has become a multi-million-dollar operation. For large universities the athletic budget can be more than $100 million.[26,27]
2. *Student housing:* Dormitories and other types of on-campus housing were built for and are owned by the institution of higher learning. In the case of public universities, state and local governments provided capital dollars to build the facilities.
3. *Hospitals and clinical enterprises:* A relatively small percent of universities have hospitals and clinical services, but when they are present, their size and scope are staggering. Many of these facilities have revenue in the billions of dollars, which makes them as large as or larger than the "academic" side of the university.[28]
4. *Other revenue-generating services:* Institutions may offer other services, including food preparation, book stores, and parking. These tend to be smaller in scale and in some cases have been outsourced, so other companies own the assets and run the operations.

Important questions for leaders of institutions of higher learning are as follows: What are the synergies among these activities? How do these activities relate to the institutions' mission? Do the institutions have the knowledge to manage these activities successfully? How do the institutions, their faculty, and students benefit by maintaining management responsibility? When this list of ancillary services is examined, there appears to be limited synergy. The commonality between hospital care and higher education is minimal, and the links between housing and high education or between sports programs and higher education seem to be nonexistent. Leaders of institutions of higher learning know little about running hospitals, on-campus housing, or athletics. Ownership of these assets does not facilitate resource sharing or create economies of scale. When a service is fundamentally different from the mission of the institution and it has its own revenue stream, it may be time to consider outsourcing. Outsourcing is also sensible when the services do not have a separate revenue stream, such as janitorial and campus security. Outsourcing is discussed in Chapter 11.

1.9 FOCUS OF THE BOOK

So far, the discussion provides basic information about institutions of higher learning and attempts to describe the different participants. Higher education is vast and complex with many different factors to consider. To stay on track, this book focuses on state-supported, public universities that have undergraduate and graduate programs. Public universities have the largest portion of the enrollment in higher education at 37.7%, according to Table 1.2. In addition to being the largest part of higher education, it is likely that more information is available because these are public entities. Public, two-year colleges also have large enrollments, 34.8% of the total. These institutions tend to have different cost structures and much lower tuition than four-year, public universities. It is likely that many of the ideas discussed and the solution proposed can be applied to these institutions.

Large, private, not-for-profit universities are often insulated from the problems faced by public universities because they have large endowments, which provide hundreds of millions or even a billion dollars in earnings that can absorb unexpected expenses. These institutions are less transparent than public universities and often have very supportive and wealthy alumni who want their children to attend the same school. So enrollment management is a process of picking the students they want from a long list of applicants. Because demand exceeds supply, these institutions can increase tuition and fees with little resistance. Small private colleges have a different set of problems because they often lack the economies of scale necessary to offer all of the programs and services students want, so they offer small classes but charge much higher tuition than public universities. Private, for-profit universities typically offer programs online, and this presents another set of problems. These differences do not mean that the solutions described in this book will not work for private colleges and universities; in fact, it is likely that many of them will.

There will be times when the discussion expands to include two-year community and technical colleges and not-for profit and for-profit private universities, but the data, where available, and the ideas focus on the undergraduate programs at four-year, public universities.

1.10 USING THE BOOK: UNDERLYING PROBLEMS, ROOT CAUSES, AND A COMPREHENSIVE, INTEGRATED SOLUTION

When faced with serious problems, managers and politicians often craft solutions based on a high level understanding of the problems without taking the time and putting forth effort to fully understand their causes, which are typically multifaceted. The result can be an unworkable, ineffective solution. For example, when tuition costs are growing too quickly at state universities, common solutions that governments impose are freezing tuition, limiting hiring, and/or cutting state subsidies, but these ideas rarely address the fundamental causes; that is, what factors are driving costs higher? This book makes a serious effort to understand the root causes of the problems before creating a solution.

This chapter describes important facets and special characteristics of higher education that are vital for understanding the problems and their causes. As shown in Figure 1.4, two stages are needed to develop and implement a comprehensive and integrated solution. The journey begins by identifying and discussing the underlying problems (Chapters 2 and 3). As illustrated by the curved arrows moving from right to left, this understanding is essential to identify the root causes (Chapter 4), and the root causes, in turn, provide the basis for creating a comprehensive and integrated solution (Chapter 5). Stage 2 begins with developing

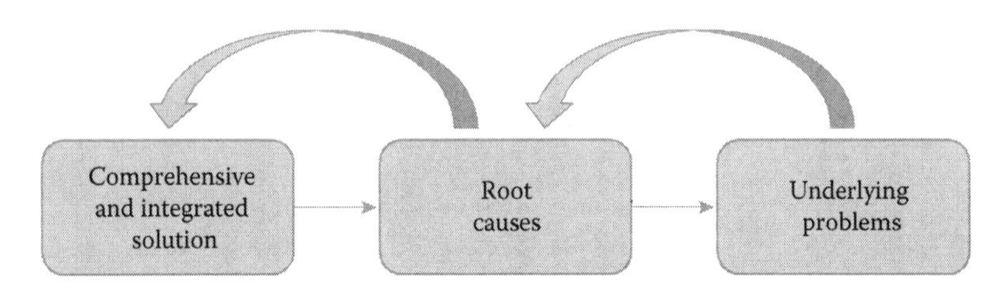

FIGURE 1.4
Resolution methodology: A comprehensive and integrated solution addresses the root causes of the underlying problems.

and implementing the elements of the solution, which are described in Chapters 6 through 14. Each element has a series of recommendations that are summarized at the end of each chapter and compiled in Appendix A. The elements of the solution address the root causes, which resolve the underlying problems. Figure 1.4 represents this with the straight arrows from left to right.

The elements of this comprehensive and integrated solution must work together, reinforcing one another to create the desired outcomes. Table 4.3 provides an overview of the relationships among the root cause and the underlying problems. Table 5.1 shows the relationship between the elements of the comprehensive and integrated solution and the root causes. These tables complete the picture, allowing readers to trace elements of the solution to the underlying problems.

REFERENCES

1. Scott, R. E. 2015. The Manufacturing footprint and the importance of U.S. Manufacturing Jobs. *Economic Policy Institute.* January 22. http://www.epi.org/publication/the-manufacturing-footprint-and-the-importance-of-u-s-manufacturing-jobs/ (accessed June 14, 2016).
2. U.S. Census Bureau. 2016. *Educational Attainment in the United States: 2015.* https://www.census.gov/content/dam/Census/library/publications/2016/demo/p20-578.pdf (accessed June 23, 2016).
3. Military.com. 2016. *An Overview of the GI Bill.* http://www.military.com/education/gi-bill/learn-to-use-your-gi-bill.html (accessed June 14, 2016).
4. Wikipedia. 2016. *G.I. Bill.* https://en.wikipedia.org/wiki/G.I._Bill (accessed June 14, 2016).
5. Selingo, J. J. 2015. Baby boomers and the end of higher education. *The Washington Post,* November 12. https://www.washingtonpost.com/news/grade-point/wp/2015/11/12/baby-boomers-and-the-end-of-higher-education/ (accessed June 14, 2016).
6. United States Department of the Treasury and Department of Education. 2012. *The Economics of Higher Education.* https://www.treasury.gov/connect/blog/Documents/20121212_Economics%20of%20Higher%20Ed_vFINAL.pdf (accessed June 23, 2016).
7. Gumport, P. J., Iannozzi, M., Shaman, S., and Zemsky, R. 1997. *The United States Country Report: Trends in Higher Education from Massification to Post-Massification.* http://citizing.org/data/projects/highered/Trends%20in%20HE%20from%20Mass%20to%20Post-Mass.pdf (accessed June 27, 2016).
8. Committee on the Future of the Colleges of Agriculture in the Land Grant University System. 1995. *History and Overview of the Land Grant College System. In Colleges of Agriculture at the Land Grant Universities: A Profile,* pp. 1–17. Washington, DC: National Academy Press.

9. College Board. 2016. *Trends in Higher Education: Published Prices – National.* http://trends.collegeboard.org/college-pricing/figures-tables/published-prices-national#Published Charges, 2015–16 (accessed June 20, 2016).
10. University of Phoenix. 2016. *Tuition and Expenses.* http://www.phoenix.edu/tuition_and_financial_options/financial-plan-services/review-tuition-and-expenses (accessed June 20, 2016).
11. SallieMae 2015. *How America Pays for College 2015.* http://news.salliemae.com/files/doc_library/file/HowAmericaPaysforCollege2015FNL.pdf (accessed June 16, 2016).
12. The Pew Charitable Trusts. 2015. *Federal and State Funding of Higher Education: A Changing Landscape.* http://www.pewtrusts.org/en/research-and-analysis/issue-briefs/2015/06/federal-and-state-funding-of-higher-education (accessed June 16, 2016).
13. Higher Learning Commissions. 2016. *Accreditation.* https://hlcommission.org/ (accessed June 21, 2016).
14. AACSB International. 2016. *AACSB Accreditation.* http://www.aacsb.edu/ (accessed June 22, 2016).
15. ABET. 2016. *ABET Accreditation.* http://www.abet.org/accreditation/ (accessed June 22, 2016).
16. Council of Social Work Education. 2016. *Accreditation.* http://www.cswe.org/Accreditation.aspx (accessed June 22, 2016).
17. The Higher Education Compliance Alliance. 2015. *Compliance Matrix* (last update December). http://www.higheredcompliance.org/matrix/ (accessed June 24, 2016).
18. Zack-Decker, K. 2012. *Compliance at Hartwick College: A Special Report to the President of the College.* http://www.naicu.edu/docLib/20130315_Compliance-HartwickColl-12-12.pdf (accessed June 24, 2016).
19. National Education Association. 2016. *The Truth about Tenure in Higher Education.* http://www.nea.org/home/33067.htm (accessed June 24, 2016).
20. June, A. W. 2012. Adjuncts build strength in numbers. *The Chronicle of Higher Education.* November 5. http://chronicle.com/article/Adjuncts-Build-Strength-in/135520/ (accessed June 24, 2016).
21. Jaschik, S. 2009. The disappearing tenure-track job. *Inside Higher Education*, May 12. https://www.insidehighered.com/news/2009/05/12/workforce (accessed June 26, 2016).
22. McNutt, M. I. 2014. Why does college cost so much? *US News World Report*, September 22. http://www.usnews.com/news/college-of-tomorrow/articles/2014/09/22/why-college-costs-so-much-overspending-on-faculty-amenities (accessed June 24, 2016).
23. American Association of University Professors. 2014. *Losing Focus: The Annual Report on the Economic Status of the Profession*, 2013–2014. https://www.aaup.org/reports-publications/2013-14salarysurvey (accessed June 24, 2016).
24. Wiessmann, J. 2013. The ever-shrinking role of tenured college professors. *The Atlantic*, April 10. http://www.theatlantic.com/business/archive/2013/04/the-ever-shrinking-role-of-tenured-college-professors-in-1-chart/274849/ (accessed June 24, 2016).
25. Japsen, B. 2012. Doctor pay rises to $221k for primary care, $396k for specialist. *C Forbes.* June 12. http://www.forbes.com/sites/brucejapsen/2013/06/12/doctor-pay-rises-to-221k-for-primary-care-396k-for-specialists/#4553fc3c69c9 (accessed June 24, 2016).

26. Tuscaloosanews.com. 2013. *Alabama's Athletic Budget, Revenue on the Rise.* http://www.tuscaloosanews.com/sports/20130727/alabama-athletic-budget-revenues-on-the-rise (accessed October 3, 2016).
27. The Record. 2014. *Michigan Athletics Presents Fiscal Year 2015 Budget.* https://record.umich.edu/articles/michigan-athletics-presents-fiscal-year-2015-budget (accessed October 3, 2016).
28. Ohio State University. 2015. *Fiscal 2016 Operating Budget.* http://www.rpia.ohio-state.edu/cfb/docs/FY16%20Operating%20Budget.pdf (accessed October 3, 2016).

2

Underlying Problem: Higher Education Costs Are Out of Control

When most radio and television pundits discuss the problems with higher education, the dominant theme is student loan debt, which is really a surrogate for the simple fact that it cost too much to get a university degree. They may mention that tuition costs are rising faster than inflation without much detail about how much faster or the reasons for the increase. Others mention that government should do more, which usually means providing additional funding, so higher education costs less for students.

During the primary season for the 2016 presidential election, Senator Bernie Sanders made political hay, especially among millennials, when he suggested that public colleges and universities should have zero tuition. Unfortunately, increasing federal and state funding does not answer the underlying questions: *Are the costs of higher education out of control?* (Sections 2.1–2.6), and *Is higher education a good value?* (Section 2.7). Providing more subsidies allows academic leaders to continue the status quo and avoid facing difficult problems such as how to reform higher education so it is more affordable, more accessible, and higher quality. The following sections break down the cost of higher education into its components and describe how these costs have increased. Chapter 3 examines the underlying problems related to quality, access, completion time, graduation rate, and job placement.

2.1 RISING COST OF A FOUR-YEAR, PUBLIC UNIVERSITY EDUCATION

The crisis in higher education is, in large measure, out-of-control costs. Tuition and fees are growing much faster than the rate of inflation. For one year of on-campus education at a four-year, public university, tuition and fees are about 40% of the total ($9,410 for tuition and fees divided by $24,061, 2015–2016 data). For students attending private, not-for-profit universities, tuition and fees are about two-thirds of the cost. These data are from Table 1.1 in Chapter 1.[1] High cost has driven students and their families into debt or has limited access by putting an advanced degree out of reach for many people.

Although tuition and fees usually get the bulk of the attention, there is more to the cost of a university degree. For on-campus students at a public, four-year university, the other 60% of the costs are books and learning materials, room and board, and other living expenses. The cost categories are listed and described briefly here with elaboration in the sections that follow.

1. *Tuition:* This payment is designed to cover instructional cost except books.
2. *Special fees:* The intent is to cover services that are not directly related to education. For many years, institutions have charged a student activity fee for things like attending sporting events, sponsoring homecoming, building and operating student unions, supporting clubs, sustaining student government, and building and operating recreation centers.[2]
3. *Books and learning tools:* For nearly every course, there have been reading materials and/or other learning aids. For decades, these were primarily printed textbooks, workbooks, and study guides. Today, other things like e-books and online learning tools are available.
4. *Room and board:* All students need a place to live and sustenance. In some cases, this is a university dormitory and meal plan. In other cases, it is an apartment with cooking facilities or living and dining at home.
5. *Miscellaneous living expense:* Students need locomotion, the ability to communicate, entertainment, and other items to live in reasonable comfort.

Each university provides estimates for these costs so applicants and their families can prepare budgets and plans to secure funds for these expenses. These estimates are also needed when students apply for federal financial aid. Even though many universities combine tuition and fee when estimating costs, tuition and fees are separated here because they have different purposes and uses.

2.2 TUITION COSTS

The cost of higher education, especially tuition, is rising much faster than the rate of inflation. When President Lyndon Johnson signed the Higher Education Act in 1965 to expand federal support, tuition and fees at public universities for in-state residents were very low and in some cases zero.[3] Until 1970, California residents paid zero tuition to attend public universities in pursuit of a four-year degree, although there were modest fees. In 1968, the fee climbed from $84 to $300 per year for state residents.[4] For 2014–2015, undergraduate, in-state tuition for schools in the University of California system such as UCLA and UC Berkeley was $11,220.[5] Many states like Ohio had very low tuition. Ohio University charged no tuition in the 1960s, although it did charge a comprehensive fee of about $200 per semester or about $400 per year for in-state students. By 2015–2016, its tuition was about 11,500 per year.[6] Tuition at the University of Toledo, which had municipal and state support, was $17 per semester hour in 1966, so a full-time undergraduate student paid $255 per semester (15 credit hours) or $510 per year plus $92 per year in fees for an annual total of $602.[7] In 2015–2016, its undergraduate tuition and fees were about $9,550 per year.[8] Tuition and fees for public universities in California increased by about 3,600% since 1968. Tuition and fees at Ohio University and the University of Toledo increased by about 2,800% and 1,500%, respectively. During this period, the Consumer Price Index (CPI) climbed only 641%, so what cost $1.00 in 1966 costs $7.41 in 2016.[9] The University of Toledo, which has the lowest tuition and fees among the three, still grew at more than twice the rate of inflation.

It is important to go beyond these anecdotal data points. Data from The College Board's Annual Survey show that published tuition and fees at public, four-year universities, after *adjusting for inflation*, increased substantially from a baseline of 100 in 1985–1986 to 322 in 2015–2016.[10]

So \$1.00 spent on tuition and fees in 1985–1986 would cost \$3.22 in 2015–2016, after *adjusting for inflation*. If tuition and fees had increased at the same rate as inflation, \$1.00 spent on tuition and fees in 1985–1986 would cost \$1.00 in 2015–2016 after *adjusting for inflation*. So it is clear that tuition and fees grew much faster than the rate of inflation during this period.

More recent data show that the cost of public higher education continues to increase faster than the rate of inflation. According to the Department of Labor, the price index for tuition has increased by 79.5% from 2003 to 2013, nearly doubling the rate of increase in medical care at 43.1% and growing three times faster than the Consumer Price Index (CPI) at 26.7%. During this time, women's and men's apparel increased by 5.6% and 6.9%, respectively, housing was up by 22.8%, and the food and beverage category increased by 31.2%. These data are summarized in Figure 2.1.[11] By comparison, the federal minimum wage was \$5.15 in 2003 and \$7.25 in 2013.[12] The minimum wage increased by 40.8%, which is faster than inflation but slower than the rate of increase in tuition and fees, making it more difficult for students to work and earn enough money to pay for their education.

This rate of increase in tuition cannot and must not continue.

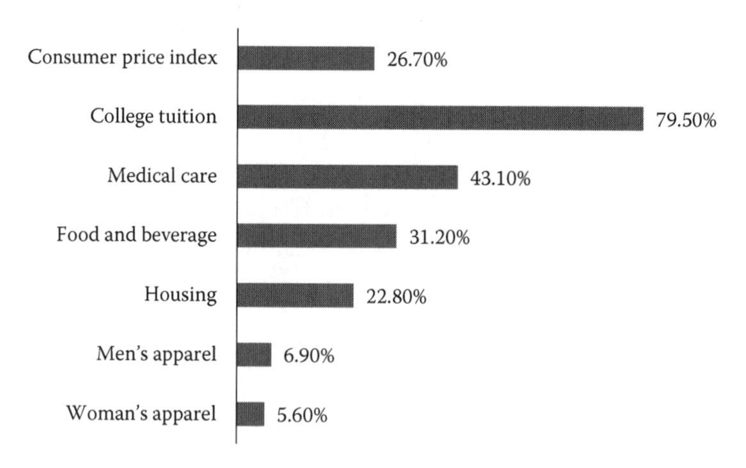

FIGURE 2.1

Percent change in Consumer Price Index (CPI) and various components of CPI, 2003–2013. (From Kurtzleben, D., *Charts: Just How Fast Has College Tuition Grown? US News World Report*, 2013. http://www.usnews.com/news/articles/2013/10/23/charts-just-how-fast-has-college-tuition-grown.

2.3 SPECIAL FEES

Why do colleges and universities have tuition and fees? The glib answer might be to lessen the impact of sticker shock when parents and students consider the cost of an education. The more honest answer is that tuition was intended to cover all learning aspects of higher education except buying books. Initially, fees tended to be for student activities that covered admissions to football games, student clubs, and intramural sports. Over the years, student activities fees increased to build student unions, offer healthcare, build large and well-appointed recreation centers, and even provide legal services.

Over time, fees were added to support laboratory classes in disciplines like science and engineering—buying things like test tubes and chemicals for chemistry lab or equipment and cement for concrete lab. This put a toe on the line between instruction and extracurricular activities because lab fees supported instruction and learning. The logic may have been that these items were like books in that they are important learning tools. As computer access became a bigger part of higher education, fees were added to build computer labs for students and support access to software. This took another stepping over the line separating instruction and extracurricular activities. This line was obliterated when some universities began adding fees in the form of surcharges when students enrolled in certain courses. As an example, a student taking an advanced undergraduate course in finance or accounting might have to pay an additional amount per credit hour to attend this course. These surcharges were often used to circumvent rules established by state government to limit tuition increases at public universities.

Digging deeply into the amounts and types of student fees is challenging because most data sources combine and report the cost of tuition and fees as a single number. Even when fees are reported separately, there is limited detail about the specific uses and the amounts of fees. Data are available for individual universities, but aggregated data showing overall trends are lacking. So it is not clear how much is spent across all universities to support sports teams, the recreation center, or student activities.

In 2010, the Office of the State Auditor for Colorado prepared a detailed performance audit on fees in higher education at state-supported, public colleges and universities. The audit was conducted in response to a legislative request for a review of student fee policy and student input into the process of determining fees. Although the results apply only to Colorado, it is not unreasonable to assume that other states have similar issues and concerns. The audit provides specific data on tuition and fees from 2006 to 2010 for the state's public colleges and universities. Table 2.1 shows that fees rose steadily and substantially from $89.3 million in 2006 to $216.3 million in 2010, which is a 142% increase. During this same period, tuition increased by a not-so-modest 69%.[2]

There are three factors about the data that should be discussed. First, the assumption is made that the mix of resident and nonresident students was approximately the same across the five years shown in Table 2.1. This is important because nonresidents pay higher tuition than residents, so if a higher percentage of nonresidents enrolled in 2010 than 2006, the increase in tuition would be overstated. However, it seems reasonable to assume that the mix of residents and nonresident students did not change substantially during this time.

TABLE 2.1

Resident and Nonresident Tuition, Fee Revenue, and Enrollment for Colorado's Public Higher Education Institutions (Revenue in Millions)

	2006	2007	2008	2009	2010	% Change
Tuition	$879.3	$918.3	$1,001.2	$1,180.4	$1,483.9	69%
Fees	$89.3	$95.6	$110.8	$132.0	$216.3	142%
Total	$968.6	$1,013.9	$1,112.0	$1,312.4	$1,700.2	76%
Fees % of Total	9%	9%	10%	10%	13%	
Enrollment	157,152	155,664	158,157	163,410	179,656	14%
Tuition (EA)	$879.3				$1,276.2	45%
Fees (EA)	$89.3				$186.0	108%
Total (EA)	$968.6				$1,462.2	51%
Fees % of Total (EA)	9%				13%	
Tuition (SFA)	$879.3				$1,075.0	22%
Fees (SFA)	$89.3				$155.9	75%
Total (SFA)	$968.6				$1,230.9	27%
Fees % of Total (SFA)	9%				13%	

Source: Office of the State Auditor, State of Colorado, *Higher Education Student Fees, Department of Education: Performance Audit*, 2010. http://www.leg.state.co.us/OSA/coauditor1.nsf/All/BCE425B0727916C18725777D00766A3D/$FILE/2046%20Higher%20Ed%20Fees%20July%202010.pdf

Note: Enrollment Adjustment (EA): Used the base data and adjusted for change in enrollment. State Funding Adjustment (SFA): Used the enrollment adjusted data and adjusted for decline in state funding for higher education.

Second, there was a 14% increase in student enrollment from 2006 to 2010, so total tuition and fees grew by 14% because of higher enrollment, so this overstates the increases if the intent is to compare the changes in costs between 2006 and 2010.[2] This can be adjusted by including only 86% of the tuition and fee costs and recalculating the 2010 numbers. When tuition, $1,483.9 million, for 2010 is multiplied by 86%, the result is $1,276.2 million. In a similar manner, the fee expense for 2010 is reduced to $186 million. When this enrollment adjustment is made, tuition and fees jumped by 45% and 108%, respectively, and these are still very large increases. See the enrollment adjusted (EA) data in Table 2.1.

Third, in response to the great recession, many states cut funding for public colleges and universities, and these institutions responded with larger than normal increases in tuition and fees. Colorado cut state funding for higher education substantially from $555.3 million in fiscal year 2006 to $324 million in 2010, a decline of $231.3 million. To cope with this cut, it is assumed that public colleges and universities in Colorado increased tuition and fees to cover this shortfall.[2] So as not to penalize these institutions because of a state-mandated funding cut, the 2010 amounts for tuition and fees are further reduced by a total of $231.3 million. Because tuition is 87% of the costs of tuition and fees, $201.2 million ($231.3 million multiplied by 0.87) is subtracted from the already reduced 2010 tuition revenue in Table 2.1. Similarly, 13% of $231.3 million, or 30.1, is subtracted from the already reduced 2010 fee revenue. See the state funding adjustment (SFA) data in Table 2.1.

These assumptions and adjustments seem fair and reasonable, and they provide data to assess how public colleges and universities in Colorado managed underlying cost pressures during this period. The results in Table 2.1 show that tuition increased by 22% and fees increased by 75% from 2006 to 2010 after these adjustments were made. These increases are much faster than the rate of inflation as CPI increased by only 8% during this period.[9] The adjusted data also show that fees rose faster than tuition. Whereas tuition increased nearly three times faster than inflation, fees increased more than nine times faster than inflation. The more rapid increase in fees is further illustrated by data in Table 2.1 showing that fees as a percentage of total costs went from 9% in 2006 to 13% in 2010.

In addition to examining how student fees have changed over time, the Office of the State Auditor's Report dug deeper and considered important factors about the governance and use of these fees. Following is a listing and brief discussion of their findings.

1. *Student inputs on fees:* Students did not have consistent opportunities to offer inputs regarding the amount of the assessment or its use.
2. *Fee amount:* Some fee amounts seemed to be higher than needed to cover expenses.
3. *Fee use:* Approximately 30% of the student fee expenses reviewed by the Legislative Audit Committee appeared to have expenses that did not match their stated purpose or violated policy of the Colorado Commission on Higher Education (CCHE). An additional 9% appeared to have questionable usages of funds: (1) funds were commingled with other revenue sources so it was not clear what the fees paid for; (2) the purpose of the fee was undefined or broadly defined so the universities could spend the fee revenue on virtually anything; and (3) the expense was not consistent with the university's guidelines.
4. *Fee disclosure:* Neither the Department of Education nor the institutions always provided students, parents, and others with clear, easily accessible, and complete information on the existence of fees and their amounts.
5. *Review process:* Nearly all of the institutional fee plans (21 out of 25) did not contain all of the components designated by the policy of the CCHE. Since at least 2006, the Department of Education has not submitted required reports to the General Assembly of Colorado that assess the consistency of institutional fee policy with policy of the CCHE on Higher Education. Finally, some institutions incorrectly reported some fees as academic or academic-facility fees.
6. *Fee framework:* There is no clear distinction between expenses that should be paid from tuition versus fees.[2]

Based on the Office of the State Auditor's Report, three important factors regarding the size, governance, and use of student fees emerge. The causes for these problems and means for resolving them require further examination.

1. Although fees are much lower than tuition, they appear to be growing more rapidly than tuition, which in turn is growing much more rapidly than the rate of inflation.

2. If fees are intended to offer services for students, students must have more say in their enactment, amount, and use.
3. There must be a clear distinction between tuition, which should be spent for things that are related to and essential for learning, and student fees, which may be useful but not required for learning. Recreation facilities and intramural sports, which are supported by student fees, may be relaxing and relieve stress, but requiring students to pay for these denies them the options to spend their money on other things. For example, downloading music or engaging in yoga may be more effective for improving their mental attitude and enhancing learning.

2.4 COST OF TEXTBOOKS AND LEARNING TOOLS

For decades, textbooks have been a primary learning tool. They are usually authored by tenured faculty and published by companies that specialize in or have parts of their organization that specialize in textbooks. Over time, these books have become very expensive. As an example, a new hardbound copy of *College Algebra* by Beecher and Penna, 5th edition, is listed online at Amazon.com for $204.05; *Managerial Economic* by Samuelson and Marks, 8th edition, is listed for $187.62; and *Operations Management* by Krajewski and Malhotra, 11th edition, is listed for $290.70.[13] For textbooks, production costs are both very high and fixed whereas sales volumes are low compared to traditional markets for books like novels and biographies. As a result, textbooks must cover these high fixed costs with low sales volumes, which lead to high prices and limited economies of scale. The last textbook in the example is substantially more expensive than the other two because it fills the need of an even smaller market. (As an aside, textbook authors earn a small commission per book, typically 15% of the price paid to the publisher by the bookseller, which is substantially less than the retail price.) If students take four or five courses each term, they could pay $700 to more than $1,000 each semester for new books. The costs per book in the 1960s would have been about $10 each with an entire term costing about $50.[7]

These specific examples are buttressed by data showing that prices for textbooks have grown much faster than inflation. Between 2003 and 2013, the increase in prices was 79.4%, almost matching the increase in tuition, which is listed in Figure 2.1 at 79.5%.[11] The bottom line is that textbook inflation is about three times more than inflation measured by the CPI, which was 26.7%.[9]

Like most people, students are rational decisions makers, so they find ways to spend less. They search for used books, which can cost half the price of a new book, possibly less. This causes companies who publish textbooks to create new editions every three or four years to eliminate the used book market. Aggressive students respond by seeking out the older editions, which can be purchased for very little. Often, the changes between editions are not substantial, so students can make it work. As technology advances, options exist to rent hardcopy textbooks for the semester or to purchase or rent e-books. In some cases, two or more students share one copy of the textbook. In other cases, students try to find a copy of the book in a library or simply not buy the book and hope to get by. Usually, the students' educations suffer.

A way must be found so that students can take advantage of their expensive education by learning as much as possible, yet keep the costs of books and other learning materials low. Part of the answer is new ideas that use computer technology and the Internet to gain access to a warehouse of information and interactive videos. Course materials from a variety of sources should be available to students electronically and "printable on demand." Some book publishers and new startup companies are breaking ground in this area. Universities as well as their administrators and faculty must become active and enthusiastic supporters of these ideas.

2.5 COST OF ROOM AND BOARD

Basic living expenses such as shelter and food are required for all students. Students can reduce the cost of their education substantially if they live close to a public university, want to save money, and have parents or someone willing to provide them with "free" room and board. The downside is that students miss the transitional maturation process of living away from home. Table 1.1 in Chapter 1 shows that in-state students at public universities would save about 40% by living at home.[1] Because most of the board costs and a large part of the food cost, such as preparation, do not change if one more person lives in a household, the out-of-pocket costs to the parents or person(s) providing the "free" room and board are modest. The good news is that room and board costs at universities have not increased at the same blistering pace as tuition, fees, and textbooks.

Table 2.2 provides CPI data that apply across all colleges and universities and illustrate that tuition, fees, and books have risen much faster than the

TABLE 2.2

Comparing Prices Changes among Components of Higher Education

Category	1982–1984	May 2016	Average for 2000
Books and supplies	100	666.3	279.9
Tuition and fees	100	702.5	324.0
Shelter	100	298.9	201.3
Food and beverage	100	247.6	168.4

Sources: Bureau of Labor Statistics, CPI Detailed Report: Data for May 2016: Consumer Price Index for All Urban Consumers (CPI-U), 2016. http://www.bls.gov/cpi/cpid1605.pdf; Bureau of Labor Statistics, *Annual Average Index for 2000: Consumer Price Index for All Urban Consumers (CPI-U)*, 2016. http://www.bls.gov/cpi/cpid00av.pdf, 2016

Note: All CPI values in the table are based on 1982–1984 = 100 expect shelter, which is based on 1982 = 100. The difference in basis is small and does not significantly impact the comparisons.

cost of shelter and food. The baseline for these data is 1982–1984, so the value for this time period is set at 100. As of May 2016, Table 2.2 shows that "Education Books and Supplies" are at 666.3, which means the cost in May 2016 is 6.663 times higher than the cost was in 1982–1984. Using the same logic, the cost of "Tuition and Fees" in May 2016 is 7.025 times higher than the cost in 1982–1984. "Food and Beverage" cost and "Shelter" cost, which are used as surrogates for apartment and dormitory living, have increased by factors of 2.476 and 2.989, respectively. A caveat about these data is that the baseline for "Shelter" is 1982 rather than 1982–1984. This small difference does not materially impact the data or the conclusions.

Table 2.2 also provides data from the year 2000, which is approximately halfway between 1982–1984 and May 2016. These data illustrate that increases for "Education Books and Supplies" and "Tuition and Fees" from 1982–1984 to 2000 are 279.9 and 324.9, respectively.[14,15] So the price for these items increased 2.799 and 3.249 times, respectively. These values represent less than half of the price increase from 1982–1984 to May 2016. Therefore, inflation for "Education Books and Supplies" and "Tuition and Fees" has been a long-term, continuing problem. In fact, these data indicate that the rate of inflation for these items has accelerated since 2000. On the other hand, more than half of the price increase for "Food and Beverage" and "Shelter" occurred from 1982–1984 until 2000. Thus, the price increases for these items decelerated (meaning they increased at a declining rate) from 2000 to May 2016.

The primary reason for a much more subdued price increase for "Food and Beverage" and "Shelter" is competitive and free markets. If dormitory rates at universities skyrocket, students have other options such as living at home, in off-campus fraternity houses, or in apartments or condominiums. In many instances, these markets are highly competitive so university residence halls must be comfortable and up-to-date and must be close to the prices for these other options. In addition, meal plans have changed in response to competition. In the past, dormitory students were assigned to a dining hall with limited options. Today, universities offer a variety of meal plans and may allow students to eat at private establishments. In some cases, universities attempt to control what students do by mandating that first-year students live on campus. But even so, if the quality is low and/or prices are substantially higher than living off campus, parents and students would and should revolt.

2.6 MISCELLANEOUS LIVING EXPENSES

In addition to attending classes, studying, and being involved in school activities, students have basic needs that must be met, such as transportation, communication, and entertainment. Once again, Table 1.1 in Chapter 1 indicates that these expenses are much smaller than tuition and fees, typically about $2,700 to $3,200 for students who live on campus. Students, who commute like many students attending two-year community colleges, pay more for transportation. This is also shown in Table 1.1.[1] These expenses are subject to free market pressure, so the cost of a smartphone, a night out with friends, or deodorant and toothpaste has increased modestly over time compared to tuition, fees, and books. This fact does not preclude these expenses from scrutiny and possible reductions.

2.7 IS HIGHER EDUCATION A GOOD INVESTMENT?

The response to this question has at least two perspectives: society's and students'. For society, the answers seem clear, in fact obvious. The United States must invest in education if its goals include the following:

1. *Prosperous economy:* for example, designing automobiles and airplanes
2. *High levels of mental and physical health:* for example, creating new diagnostic equipment and treatment regimes

3. *Strong national defense and cyber security:* for example, developing military hardware and Internet firewalls
4. *Sustainable environment:* for example, creating and implementing new ways to reduce the consumption of resources and make existing power supplies cleaner
5. *Equal opportunity:* for example, creating a society where everyone has the same chance for success by providing access to good primary and secondary schools and helping people overcome the physical, mental, and emotional obstacles they face.

These important activities rely heavily on the knowledge gained from associate, bachelor's, and graduate degrees as well as technical skills like welding and electrical work. The United States has no choice but to invest. The challenging question is: How much of this investment is the responsibility of government? There is no definitive answer, but Chapter 7 attempts to discuss the role of government in higher education. For now, the thought is that the investment in higher education would have a much better payoff if its cost declined, while the number and quality of graduates increased. This would be a productivity increase for universities and a cost decline for payers, which would free resources for other uses. Individuals could save more for retirement, donate more to charity, or spend more on entertainment. Governments could invest more in new highways and medical research.

From the student's perspective, the decision to earn a bachelor's degree is personal, but the financial impact is measurable. Data from the National Center for Educational Statistics claim that the median income of adults ages 25–34 in 2014 was $49,900 with a bachelor's degree and $30,000 with a high school degree.[16] If this gross difference is maintained for the working life of college graduates (22 to 65 years old, or 43 years), the university graduate earns $855,700 (43 multiplied by $19,900) more than the high school graduate.

However, the university graduate must pay four years of tuition, fees, books, and so on, which could have cost $60,000 (a public university education with the student living at home) up to $200,000 (a private, not-for-profit university with the student living on campus).[1] These data are from Table 1.1 in Chapter 1. There are a few ways to spend less than $60,000 such as taking the first two years at a community college, and there are ways to spend more than $200,000 with the most obvious ones being to fail and repeat courses, change majors, and change universities. Assuming an investment of $100,000 in university expenses over a four-year period, the $855,700 advantage is down to $755,700. Also, high school graduates have a four-year head start on earnings. Assuming they earn $30,000 per year for four years, high school graduates earn an extra $120,000. Now, the advantage is down to a still sizable $635,700. In the following list, there are a number of caveats regarding this simplified analysis.

1. *Feelings:* Some decision makers come from families where attending college is expected; it is the natural step after high school. For others, the career they want requires a college degree, and return on investment is not a consideration. Parents or other family members, who did not have the opportunity to earn a bachelor's degree, may strongly encourage their high school graduates to pursue an advanced degree, regardless of economics.
2. *Time value of money:* The prior calculation does not consider the fact that a dollar earned today is worth more than a dollar earned in the future because the dollar earned today can be invested and earn over time a return, making it more valuable. University graduates forgo earnings from the ages of 18–22 and must pay for their education. When the time value of money is applied, these lost wages and education costs reduce the benefit from a university degree further; that is, the benefit is less than $635,700, but it does not eliminate the benefit.
3. *Greater savings:* On the other hand, university graduates have an opportunity to save more because they have higher earnings. In addition to more savings, they receive a return on investment each year, which can grow their savings dramatically.
4. *Other assumptions:* There are many other explicit and implicit assumptions. For example, students may take more than four years to graduate, shortening their earning lives. As they progress in their jobs, the salaries of university graduates may increase faster than the salaries of high school graduates. If this happens, the advantage for university graduates is understated.
5. *Scholarship:* Many students earn scholarships, which reduces the cost of their education and increases their return on investment for a university degree.
6. *Reducing the cost of a university education:* If the United States is able to reduce the cost of higher education, the return on investment from a university degree improves.

7. *Bucking the trend:* For decades, in reality for centuries, work has moved from manual to intellectual. For bright and capable high school graduates to choose not to attend a university or a community and technical college and pursue work with little skill or intellectual content seems to be the wrong choice.
8. *Changing job market:* Two or three decades ago, there were many more unskilled jobs that paid well and required a high school degree or even less education. Looking forward, competition from developing countries like China and Mexico is likely to keep a lid on wages for jobs requiring limited skill and education—in fact, wages may actually decline. If this trend continues, two or three decades from now the return on investment for a bachelor's degree will be much higher. Students and their parents should consider this possibility as they evaluate an advanced degree.

It seems clear that a university degree should be a good investment.

REFERENCES

1. College Board. 2016. *Trends in Higher Education: Published Prices—National.* http://trends.collegeboard.org/college-pricing/figures-tables/published-prices-national#Published Charges, 2015–16 (accessed June 20, 2016).
2. Office of the State Auditor, State of Colorado. 2010. *Higher Education Student Fees*, Department of Education: Performance Audit, July. http://www.leg.state.co.us/OSA/coauditor1.nsf/All/BCE425B0727916C18725777D00766A3D/$FILE/2046%20Higher%20Ed%20Fees%20July%202010.pdf (accessed July 8, 2016).
3. Selingo, J. J. 2015. Baby boomers and the end of higher education. *The Washington Post*, November 12. https://www.washingtonpost.com/news/grade-point/wp/2015/11/12/baby-boomers-and-the-end-of-higher-education/ (accessed June 14, 2016).
4. Vega, L. 2014. The history of UC tuition since 1868. *The Daily Californian*, December 22. http://www.dailycal.org/2014/12/22/history-uc-tuition-since-1868/ (accessed July 5, 2016).
5. CollegeCalc.org. 2015. *California In-State Tuition Ranking.* http://www.collegecalc.org/lists/california/most-affordable-in-state-tuition/?start=41 (accessed July 7, 2016).
6. Ohio University Archives and Bursar's Office. 2016. *Ohio University Fall Tuition and Room Since the Civil War.* https://www.ohio.edu/instres/Factbook/tuitroom.html (accessed July 7, 2016).
7. The University of Toledo. 1966. *Financing Your Higher Education at the University of Toledo.* Provided by Barbara Floyd, University Archivist on July 18, 2016.
8. College Tuition Compare. 2016. *University of Toledo: Tuition and other Expenses.* http://www.collegetuitioncompare.com/colleges/OH/Toledo/University-of-Toledo.html (accessed July 5, 2016).

9. Bureau of Labor Statistics. 2016. *CPI Inflation Calculator.* http://www.bls.gov/data/inflation_calculator.htm (accessed July 5, 2016).
10. College Board. 2015. *Published Tuition and Fees Relative to 1985–86, by Sector.* https://trends.collegeboard.org/college-pricing/figures-tables/published-tuition-and-fees-relative-1985-86-sector (accessed July 8, 2016).
11. Kurtzleben, D. 2013. Charts: Just how fast has college tuition grown? *US News World Report*, October 23. http://www.usnews.com/news/articles/2013/10/23/charts-just-how-fast-has-college-tuition-grown (accessed July 5, 2016).
12. United States Department of Labor. 2016. *Changes in Basis Minimum Wages in Non-Farm Employment under State Law: Selected Years 1968 to 2016.* https://www.dol.gov/whd/state/stateMinWageHis.htm (accessed July 5, 2016).
13. Amazon.com. 2016. *Search Words, Operations Management.* https://www.amazon.com/s/ref=nb_sb_noss_2?url=search-alias%3Daps&field-keywords=Operations+Management (accessed July 10, 2016).
14. Bureau of Labor Statistics. 2016. *CPI Detailed Report: Data for May 2016: Consumer Price Index for All Urban Consumers (CPI-U).* http://www.bls.gov/cpi/cpid1605.pdf (accessed July 14, 2016).
15. Bureau of Labor Statistics. 2016. *Annual Average Index for 2000: Consumer Price Index for All Urban Consumers (CPI-U).* http://www.bls.gov/cpi/cpid00av.pdf (accessed July 14, 2016).
16. National Center for Educational Statistics. 2016. *Annual Earnings of Young Adults*, May. http://nces.ed.gov/programs/coe/indicator_cba.asp (accessed September 8, 2016).

3

Underlying Problems: Quality, Access, Graduation Rate, Completion Time, and Jobs

Out-of-control cost is a critical problem for higher education because it contributes significantly to other problems. High cost (1) increases barriers for applicants from middle- and low-income families, (2) puts pressure on students to work more while in school, which takes time away from studying, reduces student learning so education quality declines and graduates are less qualified for jobs, and increases the likelihood of failure or dropping out, and (3) lengthens completion time because students take fewer courses in a semester to save money or leave school for a semester or longer to earn money. But there is more than just high cost; other factors affect quality, access, graduate rate, completion time, and job placement.

When most people examine higher education in the United States, they see a strong and highly effective system that is envied by other countries, and there is evidence to back this up.[1] For decades, large numbers of students from other countries have come to the United States seeking undergraduate and graduate degrees and many have stayed to find jobs and raise families. Often, this infusion of talent is from underdeveloped and developing countries where educational infrastructure and capabilities are not as strong as in the United States. Foreign applicants see opportunities here that may not be available in their home countries. However, as countries develop and mature, their higher education systems improve, so the universities in developed countries have closed the gap on U.S. universities.[1] The crisis in higher education is not predominantly a quality problem, but there are identifiable improvements that can and should be made to enhance the quality of higher education and maintain its status as the best in the world.

Limited access to higher education is a problem that has been only partially addressed. For decades, access was limited by four factors. Some people were

1. Unaware of higher education and its value
2. Shut out because they lacked the financial resources to attend
3. Poorly prepared or did not graduate from high school making higher education impossible without substantial remedial education
4. Victims of discrimination based on race and other irrelevant factors.

Over time, communication systems improved, including newspapers, telephones, radio, television, and the Internet, so more people became aware of higher education and it value. The barrier created by racial discrimination changed with affirmative action, which is a set of laws, policies, and guidelines that are intended to correct the long-term effects of discrimination. Although the idea of affirmative action has been discussed and debated in the United States for more than 150 years, the concept gained legislative backing and took flight with the passage of the Civil Rights Act of 1964.[2,3] Regardless of a person's view of affirmative action, the plight of minority students improved because race is now used in a positive manner when colleges and universities make admission decisions. Unfortunately, rapidly increasing costs and declining quality in primary and secondary schools, especially in large cities, are combining to increase barriers to higher education. Middle-income families are also feeling the pinch from high prices.

Too often, applicants who are well prepared, have resources, and gain admission do not graduate. The National Center for Education Statistics reports a six-year graduation rate of only 59% for first-time, full-time students who began pursuing a bachelor's degree at a four-year college or university in Fall of 2007 and completed it at that institution by Spring of 2013. Students attending two-year colleges did far worse as only 29.4% of first-time, full-time students, who began in 2010, completed their degree at that institution within three years. Students who graduate are taking longer to complete their studies. At public universities, only about one out of three students graduate in four years.[4]

Another problem is that many students graduate but are unable to find a job or are unable to find one that pays enough to sustain them and repay their loans. It is difficult to find precise data to substantiate what is often anecdotal tales of recent graduates who live with their parents because they cannot find good jobs or work two or three part-time jobs to make ends meet.[5,6] Quality, access, graduation rate, completion time, and job placement are discussed in the following sections.

3.1 QUALITY OF HIGHER EDUCATION

U.S. higher education is generally regarded as the best in the world, but other universities are gaining ground. The World University Ranking for 2015–2016 uses international performance measures to assess universities on teaching, research, knowledge transfer, and international outlook. The methodology employs 13 performance indicators that provide a comprehensive evaluation. The ranking includes performance indicators that are relevant for students and their families such as student–faculty ratios, resources, links to business, and global reputation. The United States has 6 of the top 10 universities, 17 of the top 25, and 63 of the top 200, which shows the dominance of its top universities. But the United States is losing ground, as institutions in Europe improve their performance, including those in the United Kingdom, Germany, the Netherlands, and Switzerland. The United States and United Kingdom have dominated the top spots, but things are changing as Singapore's National University is in 26th place, and China has 2 universities in the top 50.[1]

3.1.1 System-Wide Quality

Universitas 21 has the only ranking of national higher education systems. It began in 2012 as an effort to meet a long-standing need to shift the discussion from the best universities to the best overall higher education system so governments have a tool to benchmark their country's performance. The study examines 50 countries, using four overarching areas (resources, environment, connectivity, and output) as well as 25 specific measurements across these areas. The United States is ranked first overall.[7] Following is a brief explanation for each area and the U.S. ranking.

1. *Resources:* This is 20% of the evaluation, and it is measured by various types of expenditures for education as a percent of gross domestic product (GDP), which normalizes to some degree for country size and wealth. The United States ranks third behind Denmark and Singapore.

2. *Environment:* This is 20% of the evaluation, and it is measured by female participation both as students and faculty, diversity, data quality, a supportive policy environment, and how well the university system meets the needs of a competitive economy. The United States ranked first, followed closely by several countries.
3. *Connectivity:* This is 20% of the evaluation, and it is measured by the proportion of international students, joint research with faculty from other countries, open-access articles on the Web, and knowledge transfer and joint research with industry. The United States ranked 14th in connectivity, falling behind in collaboration with international researchers. This lag may be explained by the fact that the United States is a research leader in many areas of science, technology, engineering, and business, and it may not see collaboration as beneficial.
4. *Output:* This is 40% of the evaluation, and it is measured by several items that assess research output, enrollment and graduates as a percent of the population, and the unemployment rate for graduates. Most of these items are adjusted for population size. However, the total number of research articles published by higher education institutions, which is one quarter of the 40%, is not per capita. This helps to explain why the United States achieves first place in the Output area by a wide margin. The United Kingdom, which is second, trails by more than 30%.[7]

The Universitas 21 study goes further and adjusts its ranking for the stage of economic development of each country using GDP per capita. This provided an expected value for each variable, given a nation's level of income, which effectively reduces the ranking of countries like the United States (16th place) and elevating countries like China (5th place) and India (15th place). In this overall adjusted ranking, the United States is also behind the United Kingdom (1st place), Serbia (2nd place), Finland (6th place), South Africa (7th place), Portugal (8th place), and New Zealand (9th place).[7]

3.1.2 Instructional Quality

When drilling down on quality, students have one overwhelming complaint: this or that faculty member is a poor teacher. The problem is often, although not always, associated with inexperienced faculty. After all, teaching is not an innate skill, but a learned activity that requires considerable thought to understand the problems and effort to improve continuously. On top of this, many universities fall short in providing the training, support, and feedback that new faculty members need. It is not uncommon for new faculty to receive a teaching contract, a copy of the textbook and the course outline, and an offer to stop by and talk to the department chair if they have any questions.

When most university faculty members were tenured, these complaints often focused on newly hired assistant professors with limited teaching experience. These faculty members were motivated to enhance their teaching ability because earning tenure required a strong teaching performance, so they sought help from senior faculty and others in order to improve. As they became better teachers, their problems dissipated. Today, less than 30% of the faculty holds tenure, whereas the others fall in three groups: full-time contractual faculty, part-time faculty, and graduate teaching assistants. According to Table 1.3 in Chapter 1, the percentages for these three groups in 2007, across all types of institutions, were 14.9%, 36.9%, and 20.9%, respectively.[8] This total is 72.7%, and it is most likely higher today.[9–11]

Today, most institutions have high faculty turnover because these groups are transient. Full-time contractual faculty members are the most stable because their contracts are for a year and are likely to be renewed if they teach well. Even so, it is unlikely they will stay for more than a few years. The more transient groups, part-time faculty (36.9%) and graduate assistants (20.9%), made up 57.8% of teaching capacity for all institutions in 2007.[8] Again, see Table 1.3 in Chapter 1. Part-time faculty members have one-semester contracts and a very high turnover rate. Although it is true that some may teach the same course for several semesters or even a few years, they are the exceptions. Graduate teaching assistants likely teach for one, two, or three years before graduating. Colleges and universities constantly recruit these faculty and graduate students to fill these positions. Universities must institutionalize a process to train and support teachers because dependence on these transient faculty is unlikely to change.

3.2 LIMITED ACCESS TO HIGHER EDUCATION

Although it may be difficult to get hard data to support a direct link between the runaway cost of higher education and limited access, making this link is intuitive and logical. Economics 101 claims that a good or service that costs more is likely to have fewer buyers, in part, because they cannot afford it. Over the years, as higher education costs grew faster than the rate of inflation, access became more limited. A report by *Science Daily* claims that in the 1980s financial constraints did not determine who attended universities, but today family income and parental wealth make a big difference.[12] In addition, students are unable to earn enough money through summer jobs and part-time work during the school year to pay for their education. This has made it more difficult for students from middle- and low-income families to earn a university degree even from a publicly supported university.

Here are some hard numbers to clarify the point. What percentage of tuition and fee costs could a student who attended a public university earn by working a minimum wage job in 1966 and today? Assume the student can work 40 hour per week for 15 weeks in the summer and 16 hours per week for the rest of the year with 2 weeks of vacation. With these assumptions, the student works 1,160 hours per year. In 1966, the student would have earned about $1.25 per hour[13] or a total of $1,450. As noted earlier, tuition and fees in California's public universities, Ohio University, and the University of Toledo were $84, $400, and $602 per year, respectively. Taking the highest cost, $602, students would have earned 2.41 times the cost of the tuition and fees, which would have made their education affordable. If they live at home, they could have graduated and put money in the bank. With dormitory expenses and modest help from parents, it is possible for students to graduate without any student loans. Today, the student would earn $7.25 per hour[13] or $8,410 for the year, which is 0.89 times the average tuition cost for public four-year universities, which is $9,410. These higher costs make it impossible to pay for their education without significant help. This tuition data point ($9,410) is taken from Table 1.1 in Chapter 1.[14]

A report from Vice President Biden's Middle Class Task Force offers statistics to support claims that access and success in higher education are impacted by its high costs. Family income is an important determinant of college enrollment and graduation. Although 78% of high school graduates from high-income families enroll in college and 53% graduate, the numbers for middle-income families are 64% and 25%, respectively. Students from middle-income families start out 14% (78% minus 64%) behind students form high-income families in enrolling, and they end up 28% (53% minus 25%) behind in graduating. Part of the reason may be financial. Many low- and some middle-income families routinely eliminate a university education as an option because of high costs.[15] Government's response to affordability problems is to push a robust package of policies that expand grant and loan programs. However, a solution that provides more government support and does not reform the system guarantees that wasteful activities will continue and costs will increase faster than inflation.

There is more to access than the cost of higher education. Many students are simply not prepared. Intelligent students, especially inner-city, minority students, drop out of primary or secondary school for a wide variety of reasons. The average graduation rate for urban high schools is only about 50%, and it is lower for African American males.[16] Without a herculean effort in the pursuit of a General Educational Development (GED) certification, they have no access to a university degree.

Then, there are students who graduate from high school but did not take the right courses for higher education. There are others who took the right courses but did not learn as much as they should have. In the Programme for International Student Assessment (PISA) for 2012, the United States ranked 26 out of 34 countries that are part of the Organisation for Economic Cooperation and Development. PISA focuses on mathematics with some science and reading. One out of four U.S. students did not reach baseline level 2, which is where students begin to show the ability to participate effectively in day-to-day activities.[17] In 2012, a state representative in Florida claimed that 50% of the state's high school graduates cannot read at grade level. According to the representative, that level is not difficult. There is no reading test in twelfth grade, but there is evidence to support his claim. On the statewide, tenth-grade exam scoring a 3 or higher is considered reading at or above grade level. Only 39% of tenth graders scored that well.[18] Poor reading skills are worse than poor math skills because if students cannot read well, it is difficult to learn anything requiring reading, which is most everything.

Even when students have learned what they need to learn and have access to government funds, they may not be aware of their ability or do not know how to proceed. These students do not have the information about the process and are unaware of which schools are affordable and a good fit academically.[15] They do not have the relationships or networks with people who encourage pursuit of a university degree, and they lack role models and mentors, who can help them succeed or at least get them to someone who can help.

3.3 LOW GRADUATION RATES AND EXTENDED COMPLETION TIME

Students who are admitted to colleges and universities often face a high dropout rate, and many who graduate are likely to spend more than four years earning their degree. The reasons are many and include the following:

1. Students are not well prepared or have trouble learning so they must take remedial courses, which increases their completion time and encourages them to drop out.
2. Students do not have the funding and leave school for a semester or two so they can earn money, and sometimes they decide not to return.
3. Students work part- or full-time for financial reasons, which allow less time for studying and causes them to take fewer courses each term, thereby extending their completion time.
4. Students may not be strongly motivated and not put forth full effort, or they may choose not to take a full load of courses each term so they have more free time.
5. Students hold scholarships with a minimum grade point average. Poor performance may cause them to forfeit their scholarships and drop out.
6. Tenured faculty members create curricula that cannot be completed in four years, which may discourage some students and cause others to take more than four years to graduate.

The extent of the problem regarding low completion rates and extended time for earning a bachelor's degree is shown in Table 3.1. Data for 2007 from the National Center for Education Statistics show that the percent of students completing a four-year degree in four years is poor at 39.4% for all types of institutions offering a bachelor's degree. Public universities are at 33.5%, which is a dismal showing, whereas private, not-for-profit universities are significantly higher, but still a poor showing of 52.8%. Private, for-profit universities have a miserable 22.5% completion rate in four years. As expected, the six-year graduation rate is higher at 59.4% for all four-year institutions. The rates for public universities, private, not-for-profit universities, and private, for-profit

TABLE 3.1

Percent Completing a Bachelor's Degree in Four Years and in Six Years

Cohort Starting in	% Completing 4-Year Degree in 4 Years				% Completing 4-Year Degree in 6 Years			
	All	Public	Private Not-for-Profit	Private For-Profit	All	Public	Private Not-for-Profit	Private For-Profit
1996	33.7%	26.0%	48.6%	21.8%	55.4%	51.7%	63.1%	28.0%
2000	36.1%	29.0%	50.3%	25.7%	57.5%	54.8%	64.5%	32.6%
2002	36.4%	29.9%	51.0%	14.2%	57.2%	54.9%	64.6%	22.0%
2003	37.0%	30.7%	51.6%	14.8%	57.8%	55.8%	65.1%	23.5%
2004	38.0%	31.4%	52.6%	20.6%	58.4%	56.1%	65.5%	28.6%
2005	38.3%	32.0%	52.2%	20.0%	58.6%	56.6%	65.2%	29.1%
2006	39.0%	32.8%	52.9%	22.8%	59.2%	57.2%	65.5%	31.5%
2007	39.4%	33.5%	52.8%	22.5%	59.4%	57.7%	65.3%	31.9%

Source: National Center for Education Statistics, *Graduation Rates*, 2015. https://nces.ed.gov/fastfacts/display.asp?id=40

Note: Graduation rates are from the first institution attended for the first time. These rates are for full-time students seeking a bachelor's degree at a four-year postsecondary institution.

universities are at 57.7%, 65.3%, and 31.9%, respectively.[4] Following are important points about the data.

1. The 2007 cohort is used because some students may not graduate until 2013, which is a six-year lag.
2. Graduation rates are from the first institution attended for the first time. These rates are for full-time students seeking a bachelor's degree at four-year postsecondary institutions.
3. An overall graduation rate of 39.4% in four years is a very poor showing. It seems reasonable for universities to admit students with the ability to do the work and do the work in a reasonable time. To have a completion rate of less than 40% is not acceptable. When comparing private, not-for-profit and public universities, there is a 19.3% difference in four-year graduation rates (52.8% minus 33.5%). When six-year graduation rates are examined, public universities close the gap on private, not-for-profit universities to 7.6% (65.3 minus 57.7).[4] The difference in performance between public universities and private, not-for-profit universities is likely caused by private, not-for-profit universities having, on average, higher admission standards.

4. Private, not-for-profit universities have the best performance. Although these institutions tend to have much higher tuition and fees, their applicants' families tend to have higher incomes so students do not have as many concerns about financing their education or holding a job while attending school. Second, the applicants' parents are more likely to have earned at least a bachelor's degree, so the parents and students know their way around institutions of higher learning. Third, these institutions tend to have higher admission standards and are more selective, so their students tend to be better qualified.
5. Many public institutions have very high standards, standards that are comparable to elite private schools, but there are public institutions that are labeled "open enrollment," which normally means these institutions accept anyone with a high school degree. It is possible to graduate from high school with less than a C average and attend a public university. So a student with a 1.3 high school grade point average (GPA) may be admitted and is expected to graduate with a 2.0 GPA from a university. As expected, open-enrollment, public institutions have poor six-year graduation rates (32.9%). Universities that admit 90% or more of their applicants have a slightly better six-year graduation rate of 46.9%. Table 3.2 shows that the graduation rate increases substantially as public universities become more selective. The six-year graduation rate for public institutions that admit less than 25% of their applicants is 84.8%.[4]

TABLE 3.2

Six-Year Graduation Rate for Public Universities by Percent of Applicants Admitted

Admission Rate	Public University Six-Year Graduation Rate
Open enrollment	32.9%
90% or more accepted	46.9%
75 to 89.9% accepted	53.7%
50 to 74.9% accepted	61.4%
25 to 49.9% accepted	61.4%
Less than 25% accepted	84.8%

Source: National Center for Education Statistics, *Fast Facts*, 2015. https://nces.ed.gov/fastfacts/display.asp?id=40

6. Table 3.1 shows that private, for-profit universities have a four-year graduation rate of 22.5%, which is abominable, and the six-year rate is only slightly better at 31.9%.[4] Something must be done to resolve this because these institutions are taking advantage of students as well as government programs that support higher education.
7. The raw data used to create Table 3.1 show that the trend in graduation rates from 1996 to 2007 has been upward across university types. This is also true across gender and race.[4] The reasons are not clear, although state legislatures have put pressure on public universities to reduce dropout rates. Many have established an "Office of Retention" to determine the reasons for dropping out and to find solutions.

3.4 LOW JOB PLACEMENT RATES

Higher education seems to feel little responsibility for verifying that enough jobs exist for the quantity of graduates being produced in some fields of study. Most universities offer job placement services for graduates but that is only a search for existing jobs. What is needed is a "best effort" from universities to align the number of graduates with the pool of available jobs. Furthermore, there appears to be limited concern whether salaries for entry-level positions are sufficient to (1) justify the investment made by students, parents, and others or (2) repay student loans without living in poverty. Applicants should have the right to make career choices, but they need good information to make those decisions.

Newsweek claims that millennials are lagging in the workplace and are often unemployed, underemployed, or working two jobs to make ends meet. Millennials, typically age 20–36, will soon be the largest and best educated generation in the United States, but many faced sky-high tuition and now face staggering student debt.[6] Citing Bureau of Labor Statistics data, the Center for College Affordability and Productivity reports that 48% of employed university graduates in the United States hold jobs that require less than a four-year degree. About 5 million graduates are in jobs that require less than a high school degree.[5]

The duty of the university, at a minimum, should be to provide historical data, current data, and projected data for job availability and salary. This allows students to make informed decision about what major to select.

Universities must become better at placing graduates in good jobs, including building strong relationships with organizations that hire their graduates and using their alumni networks to secure jobs.

REFERENCES

1. Times Higher Education. 2016. *World University Rankings 2015–2016*. https://www.timeshighereducation.com/world-university-rankings/2016/world-ranking#!/page/0/length/25/sort_by/rank_label/sort_order/asc/cols/rank_only (accessed July 4, 2016).
2. National Archives. 2016. *Teaching with Documents: The Civil Rights Act of 1964 and the Equal Employment Opportunity Commission*. http://www.archives.gov/education/lessons/civil-rights-act/ (accessed July 5, 2016).
3. Wikipedia. 2016. *Affirmative Action in the United States*. https://en.wikipedia.org/wiki/Affirmative_action_in_the_United_States (accessed July 5, 2016).
4. National Center for Education Statistics. 2015. *Graduation Rates*. https://nces.ed.gov/fastfacts/display.asp?id=40 (accessed July 5, 2016).
5. The Center for College Affordability and Productivity. 2013. *Underemployment of College Graduates*. http://centerforcollegeaffordability.org/research/studies/underemployment-of-college-graduates/ (accessed July 5, 2016).
6. Goodman, L. M. 2015. Millennial college graduates: Young, educated, jobless. *New York Times*, May 5. http://www.newsweek.com/2015/06/05/millennial-college-graduates-young-educated-jobless-335821.html (accessed July 5, 2016).
7. Universitas21. 2016. *U21 Ranking of National Higher Education Systems*. http://www.universitas21.com/news/details/220/u21-ranking-of-national-higher-education-systems-2016 (accessed July 14, 2016).
8. Jaschik, S. 2009. The disappearing tenure-track job. *Inside Higher Education*, May 12. https://www.insidehighered.com/news/2009/05/12/workforce (accessed June 26, 2016).
9. Wiessmann, J. 2013. The ever-shrinking role of tenured college professors. *The Atlantic*, April 10. http://www.theatlantic.com/business/archive/2013/04/the-ever-shrinking-role-of-tenured-college-professors-in-1-chart/274849/ (accessed June 24, 2016).
10. American Association of University Professors. 2014. *Losing Focus: The Annual Report on the Economic Status of the Profession, 2013–2014*. https://www.aaup.org/reports-publications/2013-14salarysurvey (accessed June 24, 2016).
11. June, A. W. 2012. Adjuncts build strength in numbers. *The Chronicle of Higher Education*, November 5. http://chronicle.com/article/Adjuncts-Build-Strength-in/135520/ (accessed June 24, 2016).
12. Science Daily. 2011. *Limited Access to Higher Education May Harm Society*, December 15. https://www.sciencedaily.com/releases/2011/12/111214102926.htm (accessed July 14, 2016).
13. United States Department of Labor. 2016. *Changes in Basis Minimum Wages in Non-Farm Employment under State Law: Selected Years 1968 to 2016*. https://www.dol.gov/whd/state/stateMinWageHis.htm (accessed July 5, 2016).
14. College Board. 2016. *Trends in Higher Education: Published Prices—National*. http://trends.collegeboard.org/college-pricing/figures-tables/published-prices-national#Published Charges, 2015–16 (accessed June 20, 2016).

15. Middle Class Task Force: The Vice President of the United States. Circa 2010. *White House Task Force on Middle Class Families STAFF REPORT: Barriers to Higher Education*. https://www.whitehouse.gov/assets/documents/MCTF_staff_report_barriers_to_college_FINAL.pdf (accessed July 14, 2016).
16. Guryan, G., and Ludwig, J. 2014. Why half of urban kids drop out. *CNN*, March 12. http://www.cnn.com/2014/03/12/opinion/ludwig-guryan-chicago-education/index.html (accessed July 14, 2016).
17. Ryan, J. 2013. American Schools vs. the world: Expensive, unequal, bad at math, *The Atlantic*, December 3. http://www.theatlantic.com/education/archive/2013/12/american-schools-vs-the-world-expensive-unequal-bad-at-math/281983/ (accessed July 14, 2016).
18. Sherman, A. 2012. Half of Florida's high school grads can't read at grade level, say Bill Proctor. *Politifact Florida in partnership with the Tampa Bay Times and Miami Herald*, February 23. http://www.politifact.com/florida/statements/2012/feb/23/bill-proctor/rep-proctor-says-half-high-school-grads-cant-read-/ (accessed July 14, 2016).

4

Understanding the Root Causes

Parents want what is best for their children, and today many parents believe "the best" is an opportunity to earn a two-year or four-year degree that provides the financial and intellectual foundation for a long and happy life. Many of these parents went directly from high school graduation to work on the factory floor, in clerical and staff positions that led to middle management jobs in large corporations, or in service businesses at a time when good jobs were plentiful and these jobs paid enough to own a home, have a comfortable life, and build a good retirement. These jobs often required minimal training, and in some cases they did not even require a high school diploma. Many of the parents who took these jobs did well in high school and could have opted for advanced degrees. Instead, they chose to avoid the expense and delay of more formal education and earn a good living immediately out of high school, thereby getting a jump on their high school classmate who went to college. Besides, a factory job in that era, even without overtime, paid more than many college graduates would earn after four years of studying to become teachers, business persons, social workers, and others.

What changed this sentiment over the past few decades? There are two primary reasons for the decline in "good" jobs that require limited education or training and no particular skill or talent.

1. "Free trade" deals, such as the North American Free Trade Agreement (NAFTA) and favored nation status for China, have opened U.S. markets to less expensive imports. Even if these deals are fair to all participating countries, the impact is different for different segments of the economy. By its nature, free trade creates a global price for goods and services that can be traded and, by implication, a global wage rate for those who produced these products. Free trade allows unskilled workers with minimal education in Mexico, China, the United States, and other

countries to do the same work. Because the wage rate for this type of work is much higher in the United States, these jobs naturally migrate to other countries, causing this portion of the U.S. workforce to suffer in terms of fewer jobs and declining wages. On the other hand, because the United States has strength in designing and building complex equipment, creating new and innovative technologies and products, and providing sophisticated services, this part of the economy grows. For the most part, these jobs require advanced education or specialized skills, so wage earners in this segment of the economy benefit. As jobs requiring low skill and low education leave the country, unskilled and undereducated workers migrate toward jobs that cannot be exported, such as those in fast food restaurants and landscape services.

2. Second, open borders, guest workers, and illegal immigration expand the workforce. In some cases, immigrants have special skills and strong educational backgrounds, which the United States needs. In other cases, the immigrants are unskilled and undereducated, so they compete in this already crowded segment of the job market. This additional supply keeps wages low in many service businesses like lawn care and housekeeping; some construction work, especially homebuilding; and low-skill manufacturing jobs that have difficult working conditions.

Therefore, millennials and future generations face difficult choices. On one hand, they can seek jobs that pay well and require limited education and skill while knowing that these jobs are becoming fewer and more difficult to land. Or, on the other hand, they can pursue a degree in higher education, which is expensive because the costs of tuition, fees, and books have grown much faster than the rate of inflation, leading to crippling student loan debt. Plus, if they graduate in the wrong field, they may not find a job or they may find one that does not pay enough to repay their loans and live comfortably. For these reasons and others, higher education must address its underlying problems so everyone, including millennials, is better off.

Evidence to support the dilemma faced by millennials is provided by The Economics of Higher Education report prepared for President Obama. The 2011 data show that the unemployment rate for workers with less than a high school diploma was 14.1%, and their median wage was $451 per week. With a bachelor's degree, the unemployment rate was only 4.9%, and the weekly earnings were more than double at $1,053.

With a PhD, the unemployment rate was only 2.5% and the weekly earnings were more than triple at $1,551. For each step up the education ladder, the unemployment rate is lower and wages higher with only one small exception.[1] See Table 4.1 for the full data.

The path to success in the United States seems to require either knowledge beyond high school or skills such as welding or electrical. If the United States is to educate a larger portion of its population, it must find ways to reduce the cost and improve the outcomes of higher education. This chapter begins the process as it describes the root causes of the problems and discusses the links between the causes and the problems. The next chapter and the balance of the book describe a comprehensive and integrated solution to address the causes, thereby providing millennials and generations to come a higher education system with lower costs, higher quality, better access, higher graduation rates, on-time completion, and better job opportunities.

4.1 SUMMARIZING THE UNDERLYING PROBLEMS WITH HIGHER EDUCATION

When people discuss the problems with higher education, they normally focus on its high cost, which is a significant problem. However, a focus on cost may cause people to miss the fact that high cost contributes to other

TABLE 4.1

Unemployment Rate and Median Weekly Earning in 2011

Education	Unemployment Rate 2011	Median Weekly Earnings in 2011
PhD	2.5%	$1,551
Professional degree	2.4%	$1,665
Master's degree	3.6%	$1,263
Bachelor's degree	4.9%	$1,053
Associate degree	6.8%	$768
Some college, no degree	8.7%	$719
High school diploma	9.4%	$638
Less than high school diploma	14.1%	$451

Source: United States Department of the Treasury and Department of Education, *The Economics of Higher Education*, 2012. https://www.treasury.gov/connect/blog/Documents/20121212_Economics%20of%20Higher%20Ed_vFINAL.pdf

important problems such as limiting access, increasing dropout rate, and extending completion time. Before describing the root causes, the underlying problems are summarized.

1. *Costs* are too high: For decades, the costs for tuition, fees, and books have risen much faster than the rate of inflation, making it more and more difficult to earn an advanced degree without incurring substantial debt.
2. Other countries are closing the *quality* gap: The United States has been and continues to be regarded as the best or at the very least one of the best places to earn a university degree. But it is clear that other countries are getting better.
3. Limited *access*: Access has improved because (1) more people are aware of the opportunities for and the advantages of degrees in higher education and (2) affirmative action requires institutions to consider race as a positive factor for minority applicants. However, access is worse because high costs for tuition, fees, and books put an advanced degree out of reach for many students from middle- and low-income families. Plus, too many students, especially in urban areas, do not complete high school or graduate and are poorly prepared.
4. Low *graduation rate*: Too many students who meet the admission qualification start college but drop out before graduating. A four-year completion rate of 39.4% and a six-year completion rate of 59.4% for students seeking bachelor's degrees are not acceptable. See Table 3.1 in Chapter 3.
5. Extended *completion time*: Students are taking too long to complete a bachelor's degree, which should be finished in four years. The data in point 4 show that a significant percentage of the graduates take up to six years to complete their degree.
6. Low *job placement rate*: Too many graduates are unemployed and underemployed. Institutions have a responsibility to balance the size of an academic program, the number of students admitted, and the number of jobs available by providing information to students and working with them to select fields of study where jobs are available and compensation is good.

These problems cannot be fixed by passing laws, setting price controls on tuition and fees, or establishing new government regulation. These simplistic solutions do not work because they do not address the root causes of the problems. Creating an effective solution requires identifying these causes and understanding how they helped to create the problems. Before proceeding, it is essential to have a clear understanding of the customers and their expectations.

4.2 UNDERSTANDING THE CUSTOMERS OF HIGHER EDUCATION

As with other parts of the economy, any attempt to solve the problems faced by institutions of higher learning should begin with full knowledge of their customers and what they expect from the institutions. As described in Chapter 1, colleges and universities are key players in two demand–supply relationships: one with students and the other with organizations that hire their graduates. People familiar with supply chains might argue that many and possibly all companies have two sets of relationships. Typically, a company acquires inputs such as materials, information, and knowledge from its suppliers and transforms those inputs into outputs that it sells to its customers. For example, the final customers buy cars from an automaker, who procures engines from an engine assembly plant, who buys metal castings for the engine block as well as other components from various suppliers. The company that casts the engine block, in turn, buys materials and other inputs from its suppliers, and so on. An automotive supply chain is a vast series of relationships between suppliers and customers. Banks provide checking accounts and other services to its customers, and banks depend on suppliers to provide checks, process transaction, transfer funds electronically, and many other activities. Both auto making and banking illustrate classic supply chain relationships.

Why is higher education different? If the supply chain perspective is applied to higher education, applicants would be the raw material for the university. The parent would be the supplier, and the organization who hires the graduates would "buy" the finished product, graduates, from the university. Not only is this view dehumanizing, it is fundamentally flawed. Applicants with help from their parents make choices about which college or university to attend and what major to study. Once accepted, students have many options. They may decide to change majors, have a double major, transfer to another university, or drop out because higher education is not for them. They can choose to work hard or not, which impacts their grades, the quality of their education, and the jobs for which they may qualify. In addition, students decide for which companies they may work, where they would be willing to live, and the level of compensation they would like. Certainly, the organizations that offer the jobs have something to say about the conditions of employment. This becomes a negotiation with the graduate.

A better way to look at higher education and its relationship with customers is as a matchmaker, who provides applicants with opportunities to learn and prepare for life. The university mediates the relationships between students and their potential employers using a set of experts (tenured faculty) who work together and pool their resources to create the appropriate outcome (graduates who are in demand). A key and sometimes forgotten part is that universities should have a responsibility to ensure that educational pathways lead to good jobs.

It is important to recognize that colleges and universities are professional service organizations (PSOs), which are complex and difficult to manage and rely on the knowledge and expertise of their highly trained and educated "servers" to deliver high-quality outputs.[2] In universities the servers are tenured faculty from a wide variety of disciplines, who must work together to design and deliver programs and curricula, packaged as courses that meet graduation requirements. The implication of this reality is that tenured faculty must have a significant role in directing and governing universities because PSOs rely heavily on these highly educated servers. Examples of other PSOs would be hospitals, law partnerships, and engineering design firms.

In PSOs and even in some manufacturing firms, service-dominant logic (SDL) has emerged as an important way to create value for customers. SDL contends that value is co-created in interactions among customers (students and organizations that hire graduates), employees of the firm (faculty), and even suppliers (textbook publishers) rather than in a traditional supply chain with a long-linked sequence of two-party interactions.[3] The rapid exchange of information among the participants facilitates faster and more effective learning that is tailored to the needs of students and organizations that hire graduates. PSOs and SDL are discussed more fully as the solution is developed. What is important for now is an understanding that relationships with customers are different in higher education.

In addition to a different perspective offered by PSOs and SDL, third parties complicate the "who is the customer" question by paying a large portion of the costs for higher education. Students pay only 11% from their income and savings and student borrowing accounts for another 16%,[4] which may be repaid by parents, other family members, or friends. As a result, universities have a trifurcated customer: students who are the learners, third-party payers, and organizations that hire graduates. These customers have different values and perspectives, which lead to different expectations.

4.2.1 Unclear Messages

When the message from customers is muddled, different parts of the organization step in and use their values to steer it. Tenured faculty and administrators, who often hold faculty rank, are the strongest and most vocal employees in higher education. They tend to believe that the pursuit of knowledge is a noble ambition and that knowledge/learning is a goal unto itself. For them, it is a priceless gift that everyone should appreciate and strive to attain. Many of them would go as far as to claim that learning, not job attainment, is the ultimate goal of higher education. In addition, they want the academic experience to be rigorous and have high standards. Based on these beliefs, tenured faculty members work hard to

1. Expand the knowledge base of humankind through basic and applied research
2. Communicate this newfound knowledge to faculty colleagues and practitioners through academic journals as well as applied, practitioner-focused publications
3. Incorporate these new ideas in their teaching
4. Write textbooks and create other tools to facilitate learning
5. Develop and implement innovative teaching techniques
6. Offer service to the academic community, often called the academy, by forming and managing organizations to share research ideas and teaching techniques, creating and supporting journals to publish research, and reviewing and evaluating research papers before they are published.

This is consistent with the three criteria on which tenured faculty members are evaluated: research and publication, teaching and learning, and service. This is the essence of tenured faculty work life. Quite honestly, it has substantial value for creating new knowledge and ideas, which have led to innovative products such as health testing equipment and smartphones, and better economic performance. This perspective should be retained and enhanced, but universities must also (1) build effective relationships with organizations that hire their graduates and (2) include inputs from these important customers as they engage in research as well as designing and delivering curriculum.

4.2.2 Customers' Values and Perspectives

For universities to deliver the right product at the best price while using its resources effectively and efficiently, they must reconcile the values and perspectives of the trifurcated customer. Following is a discussion of those.

1. Undergraduate students usually want the degree and a job or a path to a graduate degree and then a job. Their interest in research and publications is minimal. Typically, they are not interested in an "ivory tower" vision of learning that makes them better people or improves society. In some cases, students are unwilling to put forth significant effort to understand topics for which they see no immediate value. Their view is the here and now. Learning enhancements that make it easier to grasp concepts that they perceive as relevant are highly important.
2. Third-party payers have a diverse set of needs.
   a. Parents, other family members, and friends want students to earn a degree and have happy lives and successful careers. They see great value in teaching enhancements, educational rigor, high standards, and economic prosperity. They may see more value in research than a typical student but value it much less than universities and tenured faculty do.
   b. Government wants the best education so people can graduate, secure good jobs, and support economic growth and prosperity. This increases societal wealth, which drives down demand for government services and leads to higher tax collection, so their job is easier. It sees value in academic rigor and high standards. Government, especially the federal government, sees value in research that leads to whole new industries, dramatic technical innovations, and new products that greatly increase quality of life.
   c. Scholarship providers are substantial third-party payers, and higher education is the largest scholarship provider. University scholarships in reality are price discounts that cut costs for students

who (1) are members of athletic teams (although not all schools can offer athletic scholarships), (2) have performed well on standardized tests as well as in high school, and (3) have financial needs. Students who are high performers, have financial needs, and fit affirmative action criteria are particularly attractive applicants.
3. Organizations that hire graduates want the best educated and brightest students, so teaching enhancements, academic rigor, and high standards are essential. They want employees who can start work with limited training, are loyal to the company, and can grow and eventually hold leadership positions. Economic prosperity and innovation are key to their success.

An overview of the values and perspectives for each customer is provided in Table 4.2. The row headings list the customers (students, various third-party payers, and organizations that hire graduates), and the column headings are the attributes (values and perspectives) discussed previously. The cells at the intersection of each row and column indicate whether a customer attaches the highest worth to this attribute. Because a cell is blank does not necessarily mean that the customer feels this attribute is unimportant; it only means it is not highly important.

A review of Table 4.2 provides some interesting insights. Only government and universities feel that research is highly important, whereas all customers believe that teaching enhancements are highly important. Only universities believe that service to the academy, which provides support for leading-edge research and innovative teaching, is important. Yet if society wants these outcomes, and they should, then service to the academy must be maintained. Academic rigor and high standards have broad support. Even though students may push back against them while they are in school, when they become job holders and parents, they will see their value. Economic prosperity and creating innovative products are important for the following parties:

1. Parents, other family members, and friends because they have jobs or retirements that depend on a strong economy
2. Government so that tax revenue increases and fewer people need assistance
3. All universities so that demand is strong and public universities see robust government subsidies
4. Organizations so that they have innovative products and stronger earnings

TABLE 4.2

Attributes of Higher Education That Each Customer Believes Are Highly Important[a]

Customers	Basic and Applied Research	Teaching Enhancements	Service to the Academy that Supports Research and Teaching	Earn 4-Year Degree and Get a Job	Earn 4-Year Degree and Pursue Graduate Degree	Academic Rigor and High Standards	Economic Prosperity and New Innovative Products
Students		High importance		High importance	High importance		
Third parties							
Parents, other family members, and friends		High importance		High importance	High importance	High importance	High importance
Government	High importance	High importance		High importance	High importance	High importance	High importance
Higher education	High importance	High importance	High importance	High importance	High importance	High importance	High importance
Organization that hire graduates		High importance		High importance	High importance	High importance	High importance

[a] High importance means that a customer attaches the highest worth to this attribute. Because a cell is blank does not necessarily mean that the customer feels this attribute is unimportant. For example, parents, other family members, and friends may value economic prosperity and new product ideas, but they are not typically thinking of these when they pay tuition or room and board for a student. Some organizations that hire graduates may also seek help from the university to research the performance of a material in a specific application or investigate the best managerial practice to use in certain situation, but that is not the primary reason that most organizations interact with universities.

Using Table 4.2, it is possible to think about and discuss which customers should pay for what attributes or outcomes. An effective solution must allow customers, who have various needs, to have their funds used in ways that support those needs. Thus, when undergraduate students pay to attend universities, their funds should support the educational process. When the federal government supports research, it should set criteria for how these funds are used. It may not always be possible to calculate a precise formula to accomplish this, but efforts must be made to align customers' needs and wants with how much they pay. It is also possible to see cross-currents among the attributes. For example, teaching enhancements and innovative products are supported by advances in basic and applied research.

Without an accurate appreciation of customer's needs and expectations, it is difficult to identify the root causes and to understand how these causes created the underlying problems. Table 4.3 is an organizing mechanism with the row headings being the underlying problems and the column headings being the root causes. The cells at the intersection of the rows and columns indicate how the root cause impacts the underlying problem. Ultimately, the solution must be comprehensive and integrated because there is not a one-to-one relationship among problems, root causes, and the elements of the solution. The following sections explain Table 4.3.

4.3 HOW A LACK OF UNDERSTANDING CUSTOMERS (ROOT CAUSE 1) AFFECTS UNDERLYING PROBLEMS

When there are multiple customers and the needs of these customers are not clearly defined and understood, there is little hope that good decisions will be made about how resources are allocated, which can lead to higher costs, lower quality, more limited access, lower graduation rates, longer completion times, and poorer job placements. Not knowing and understanding the customers may be the most important root cause, as it impacts all the underlying problems.

The vast majority of university cost is salaries and fringe benefits for people,[5] so poor resource allocation typically means hiring the wrong people, for the wrong job, and paying them more than they deserve. The personnel at universities can be classified into two large groups: administration and faculty. *The New York Times* reports that full-time faculty salaries, when adjusted for inflation, are only slightly higher than they were in the 1970s.

TABLE 4.3

Linking Root Causes to the Underlying Problems with Higher Education

	Root Causes								
Problems	**1. Lack of Understanding—Who Is the Customer?**	**2. Declining State Support for Public Universities**	**3. Rise of the Ruling Class—Administrators**	**4. Limited Productivity Improvements for Universities**	**5. Rapidly Growing Costs for Books and Supplies**	**6. Funding Finesse—Mixing Fees and Tuition**	**7. Expanding Student Expectations**	**8. Eroding Standards**	**9. Lack of Student Preparation**
1. Cost	Cost increases	Cost shifts from states to students and others	Cost increases	Cost increases	Cost increases	Cost increases	Cost increases		Cost increases
2. Quality	Quality decreases	Quality decreases	Quality decreases	Quality decreases	Quality decreases	Quality decreases	Quality decreases	Quality decreases	Quality decreases
3. Access[a]	Access decreases	Access decreases	Access decreases	Access decreases	Access decreases	Access decreases	Access decreases		Access decreases
4. Graduation rate[b]	Graduation rate decreases	Graduation rate decreases	Graduation rate decreases	Graduation rate decreases	Graduation rate decreases	Graduation rate decreases	Graduation rate decreases	Graduation rate increases	Graduation rate decreases
5. Completion time[c]	Completion time increases	Completion time increases	Completion time increases	Completion time increases	Completion time increases	Completion time increases	Completion time increases	Completion Time Decreases	Completion Time Increases
6. Job placement	Job placement decreases	Job placement decreases	Job placement decreases	Job placement decreases				Job Placement Decreases	Job Placement Decreases

[a] Any root cause that increases cost also reduces access because high cost is a barrier to potential applicants from low- and moderate-income families.

[b] Any root cause that increases cost also reduces graduation rate because high cost may cause students to work too many hours so they fail courses and "flunk out," or it may discourage students from continuing because they see debt mounting.

[c] Any root cause that increases cost also increases completion time because high cost may force students to take fewer courses per term or leave school for a term to make money.

Plus, the mix of faculty has shifted dramatically toward lower paid, part-time teachers, which means that overall faculty costs are lower. On the other hand, administrator pay increased by 60% from 1993 to 2009, which is 10 times faster than the growth rate of tenured faculty.[6] Other sources report on the ever-shrinking role of tenured university professors.[7–10]

Another report shows that from 2000 to 2010 salaries for top administrators and presidents at public universities grew by 39% and 75%, respectively, while tenured faculty salaries grew by only 19%. The study also showed that the number of administrative positions increased by 369% from 1978 to 2014, while tenured faculty increased by only 23%.[11] For the same period, enrollment in undergraduate degree programs grew by 73%, which is much higher than the rate of growth in tenured faculty and much lower than the growth in administration.[12] Although these data are not absolute proof that universities have made poor decisions about resource allocation with respect to administration, the data would support a hypothesis that administrative spending is excessive.

The following bullet points examine the impact of root cause 1, "Lack of Understanding— Who Is the Customer?," on the underlying problems listed in Table 4.3.

- *Problem 1. Cost increases:* Lack of understanding the customer has led to poor resource allocation, which has increased the cost of higher education.
- *Problem 2. Quality decreases:* It is important to strike the right balance in spending on faculty and administration. Based on the data, it appears that universities are underinvesting in tenured faculty, which may impact the quality of research and teaching. Reducing administration and investing in tenured faculty should improve quality and has the potential to reduce cost.
- *Problem 3. Access decreases:* Actions that increases cost should decrease access because potential students from families with low and moderate incomes may not have the resources to afford higher education, even with financial aid from the institution and support from government.
- *Problem 4. Graduation rate decreases:* Activities that increases cost should decrease graduate rate because higher costs force some students to work longer hours to earn more money, thereby jeopardizing their classroom performance. They leave school, often with substantial debt, and never return. In other cases, students become discouraged as they

work hard to achieve good grades and earn money during the school year and the summer. When this pressure is piled on top of the stress associated with tests and term papers, students may decide to drop out.

- *Problem 5. Completion time increases:* Any activity that increases cost increases completion time. When cost increases, many students take longer than four years to complete a degree because they take fewer courses in a term to save money on tuition and fees. They may leave school for a term or two so they can work full-time, earn money, and pay for school. As mentioned in the previous bullet, some of these students never return. In addition, tenured faculty who set the course requirements may not consider students' needs. Many degree programs take longer than four years to complete because, in part, there are too many courses and credit hours. The logic for adding credit hours is that there is so much to learn that curriculum must expand. This seems to be in conflict with the idea of life-long learning that many universities espouse. There is always more to learn than the time available, plus new knowledge and ideas are being created continuously, so it is impossible to teach everything in four years. Administrators are complicit because higher degree requirements lead to more revenue. Faulty are not concerned about university revenue; they are driven by self-interest. Their status is linked to the subjects they research and teach, so having their course in the requirements list, or at least as an identified elective, is important to them. Some of the hardest fought battles among tenured faculty are about which courses to add to the curriculum. No one is seeking to have his or her course removed. In addition, department budgets are determined, in large part, by the number of student credit hours taught by the department. More student credit hours lead to a larger budget.
- *Problem 6. Job placement decreases:* Many universities do not recognize organizations that hire their graduates as important customers. They often provide a placement service, which is a mechanism so graduates and companies can meet and discuss job opportunities. However, many universities do not have well-identified methods to ensure that the skills and abilities that organizations want in entry-level employees are part of the curriculum. This hampers graduates' ability to find good jobs. Most important, there is little if any effort on the part of universities to ensure that the size of their graduating class in a particular subject area is consistent with the needs of industry. Too many graduates can lead to low wages and low placement rates.

4.4 HOW DECLINING STATE SUPPORT FOR PUBLIC UNIVERSITIES (ROOT CAUSE 2) AFFECTS UNDERLYING PROBLEMS

A common way to examine states' support for public, higher education is to consider their contribution to revenue. One report claims that states paid about two-thirds of the cost of undergraduate education in the early 1980s.[13] Another report claims that the peak share for state and local government was 60.3% in 1975. This report also claims that, with a few exceptions, the state funding for higher education has declined dramatically, down to 25% or less in many states.[14] A report by the Pew Charitable Trusts shows that in 2013 state support for public colleges and university was only 21% of their revenue.[15] These data may be confounded by the fact that undergraduate enrollment grew by 73% from 1978 to 2014 because an increasing portion of the U.S. population pursued advanced degrees.[12]

Another way to look at state funding is per full-time equivalent (FTE) students (five part-time students, each taking one 3-credit hour course in the Fall semester and another in the Spring semester would be one FTE—30 semester hours). Using this data point adjusts for increasing enrollment. The Economic of Higher Education report prepared for President Obama shows that state support per FTE declined from almost 60% of revenue at state public, four-year institution in 1986 to slightly below 40% in 2010.[1] Regardless of which data are considered, it is clear that state support for higher education, as a percent of public university revenue or as subsidy per FTE student, has declined significantly.

It can be argued that this decline in state support is not caused by states spending too little, but by universities spending too much. Because universities overspend on administration and other things, they raise tuition faster than the rate of inflation to compensate for the "perceived state shortfall."[6,16] The point is this: If universities were better managed, their costs would be lower and state support for public higher education would be adequate.

In other words, *state funding as a percent of public universities' revenue would not have declined if these institutions had properly controlled their budgets and costs.* State governments chose to push back on public university spending by holding the line on their funding, but students, parents, other family members, friends, and the federal government have not pushed back, so tuition and fees continue to increase. It is time for states to address this "underfunding" by taking proactive steps to support and require public universities to seek ways to lower costs for tuition, fees, and learning materials dramatically.

The following bullet points examine the impact of root cause 2, "Declining State Support for Public Universities," on the underlying problems listed in Table 4.3.

- *Problem 1. Cost shifts from states to students, parents, other family members, friends, and the federal government:* As states held the line on subsidies, universities raised tuition and fees to keep up with their exploding cost structure. Students and their supporters pay higher tuition and fees, and the federal government provides more grants and loans.[1] The net effects are (1) a selective state tax increase for students and their supporters and (2) a cost transfer from states to the federal government. Practically speaking, it should be possible to reduce administrative costs and charge less for tuition and fees.
- *Problem 2. Quality decreases:* Non-value-added spending limits the funds available to invest in improving student outcomes such as creating new programs and hiring more faculty members.
- *Problem 3. Access decreases:* As tuition and fees increase, access declines.
- *Problem 4. Graduation rate decreases:* As tuition and fees increase, the graduation rate decreases.
- *Problem 5. Completion time increases:* As tuition and fees increase, completion time increases because anything that increases cost means students have to work more and save more.
- *Problem 6. Job placement decreases:* Fewer resources, whether caused by low state funding or excessive spending on administration, limit the amount that can be invested in working with organization so students have better job opportunities.

4.5 HOW THE RISE OF THE RULING CLASS—ADMINISTRATORS (ROOT CAUSE 3)—AFFECTS UNDERLYING PROBLEMS

For centuries the distinctions between administrators and tenured faculty were minimal. Most administrators were tenured faculty who took their turn in administration and gladly returned to the faculty after a few years on the job. This ensured that administrators would do what they thought was best for the institution because they would most likely return to a faculty position at that university for the remainder of their career, facing the consequences, good or bad, of their actions. There was an incentive to treat faculty fairly because the next administrator may be a tenured faculty member whom they treated poorly. In addition, this process naturally created experienced administrators, who could mentor new ones, thereby creating an understanding of and links to the past. This process maintained institution memory, which was valuable when writing new policies and plans. There were not big differences in salaries. Administrators may receive a summer salary if they worked twelve months rather than nine months, which is the length of a typical faculty contract. Plus, they might get a modest stipend. Because administrators were usually senior, tenured faculty members, they had above-average salaries, but there would often be tenured faculty who earned as much as or more than top administrators.

Today, many high-level administrators, from college deans up the ranks to president, are outsiders who are hired through a national search process. Most of these administrators began their careers as tenured faculty but have shifted to administration for various reasons. As part of a cadre of professional academic leaders, they often arrive at a new job looking for the next step up the ladder, seeking a similar position at a better university, a better position at a comparable university, or both a better university and position. They have limited knowledge of the university, so it takes a year to learn the ropes, another year to revise the strategic plan, and soon after they are occupied with looking for their next job. There is very limited institutional memory, so the same ideas and plans are considered and the same mistakes are repeated again and again. Most of these people are honest, hard-working, and fair, but having a professional administrative class and only a few years on the job does not provide consistent, effective leadership. There are high-level administrators who stay longer than a few years, and they have the potential to be very effective. To cope with the administrative change, a new industry has emerged to help universities. These firms specialize in running job searches that include building a large pool of qualified applicants, doing reference checks, and managing the process. These firms often see the same applicants more than once as they move up the ladder to better jobs at better universities.

The allegiance for this new breed of administrative leaders is to the boards of trustees, who hire them and will provide recommendations for their next job. This breaks the bond that once naturally existed between administrators and tenured faculty. In this new environment, it is common for new leaders to blame problems that cannot be easily resolved on "difficult" faculty and tenure. A typical response to fixing a budget deficit is increasing productivity by having faculty teach more sections per term with more students in each section. The effect is to align the administrator and the board against tenured faculty. When administrators take jobs while looking toward their next position, there is a propensity to implement quick-fix solutions to attention-getting problems. For example, they form committees or fund institutes to enhance diversity, or they fund a center for teaching innovation to improve learning. Administrators can point to these successes as they look for their next job. On the other hand, they avoid the conflict and turmoil caused by making radical changes to fix fundamental problems, so important issues that require substantial work and carry great risk are rarely addressed.

It is reasonable to ask: Why does this problem exist when hiring leaders in higher education but not in for-profit business. The answer has two parts. The first is that these businesses often seek leaders from within the organization so they avoid some of the problems of hiring an outsider. Second, for-profit businesses have "bottom lines." When these companies are publicly held, a stock price is reported daily, and it changes in response to important outcomes such as sales, market share, profits, and return on investment. Based on these outcomes, stockholders can pressure boards of directors who, in turn, question the actions of top managers. When outcomes do not meet these bottom-line criteria, changes are made. In for-profit companies, expectations for new leaders and whether they have met those expectations are clear. Leadership teams in for-profit businesses move forward quickly and are willing to take risks to achieve outsized improvements.

It is also important to know that most high-level university administrators are not trained in management or leadership. They may know a great deal about specific topics like nineteenth-century literature, sociology, quantum physics, or geology, but typically know little about leading, planning, organizing, and managing a large and complex organization. What they know about these topics is inherent in their being, learned on the job, or part of a short course offered from groups like American Council of Higher Education (ACE)[17] or Leadership Education for Asian Pacifics (LEAP).[18]

It seems reasonable for universities to tap tenured faculty from business colleges or other fields of study that teach and research in leadership, planning, and management, but this is rare. Business faculty members are substantially underrepresented in leadership positions in higher education. According to ACE, the typical president has a doctorate in education. The most common career path to the presidency is Chief Academic Officer (CAO), sometimes called the provost or vice president for academic affairs. Most presidents have spent their entire life in higher education, and 70% have been tenured faculty at some point. The primary duties of most presidents are fundraising, budgeting, community relations, and strategic planning. Most academic issues such as program development, hiring faculty, and managing the educational and research aspects of universities are overseen by the CAO, who reports directly to the president. The vast majority of CAOs have been tenured faculty members.[19]

The following bullet points examine the impact of root cause 3, "Rise of the Ruling Class—Administration," on the underlying problems listed in Table 4.3.

- *Problem 1. Cost increases:* The evidence is clear that growth in the number of administrative positions and the rate of increase in salaries of administrators have increased the costs of higher education to the point where spending on administration exceeds spending on faculty. From 1978 to 2014, administrative positions have increased by 369%, while tenured faculty positions have increased by only 23%.[11]
- *Problem 2. Quality decreases:* When more money is spent on administration, there are fewer resources to invest in enhancing educational and research quality.
- *Problem 3. Access decreases:* As spending on administration increases, access declines.
- *Problem 4. Graduation rate decreases:* As spending on administration increases, graduation rate decreases.
- *Problem 5. Completion time increases:* As spending on administration increases, completion time increases.
- *Problem 6. Job placement decreases:* With more spending on administration, there are fewer resources to invest in working with organizations so students have better job opportunities.

4.6 HOW LIMITED PRODUCTIVITY IMPROVEMENTS (ROOT CAUSE 4) AFFECT THE UNDERLYING PROBLEMS

The idea of improving productivity is not foremost in the minds of administrators and tenured faculty because they focus on creating new ideas and improving teaching and learning. But increasing productivity and keeping costs low is consistent with these goals. Productivity is the outputs of a company, department, or person divided by the related inputs. So an increase in productivity means generating more outputs with the same or lesser input/resources. Thus, increasing productivity leads to lower costs.

Prior discussion clearly illustrates that the efficiency and productivity of administration have declined substantially as growth in administrators has outpaced enrollment increases. To illustrate this point, recall that the number of administrative positions increased by 369% from 1978 to 2014,[8] while undergraduate enrollment grew by only 73%.[9] This means it takes more administrative time to cope with the needs of one student in 2014 than it did in 1978. There should be little doubt that the growth in administration must be reversed and replaced by a decline. This can be achieved by applying appropriate tools and systems that leverage administrators' time and substantially increase their productivity.

Although it can be effectively argued that the primary drivers of high costs are lack of knowledge about customers and the rise of administration, the faculty is culpable as well. Faculty should not be immune from improving their productivity, that is, (1) increasing the number of students they educate, (2) improving the quality and quantity of what graduates learn, and (3) improving research and service outcomes.

For teaching, the heart of the problem is to make the process easier for faculty so they can teach more students and make learning more effective and enjoyable, while using the same time and effort. All companies attempt to do this. Automakers and software developers provide tools and training so their workers can produce more and better cars and computer systems. It is time to design and implement innovative teaching and learning systems that improve outcomes and reduce costs. There are islands of improvements such as cooperative education and internship programs for engineering and business students, which place students in actual job settings. Here they begin to understand the value of what they are learning and are motivated to learn more. Other ideas are emerging that use computer and information technology to provide access to knowledge as well as to build interactive, individualized learning platforms. Much more effort is needed.

Tenured faculty, who should have substantial research commitments, must have tools to leverage their time, and these tools vary depending on their discipline. Typically, business faculty needs fast and easy online access to books and journals, resources to collect data, and computer technology and software to prepare charts, graphs, and manuscripts. They also need travel funds and online meeting software to discuss ideas with faculty colleagues. Scientists and engineers need these things as well, plus they need sophisticated laboratories and equipment, which are expensive so these investments should be carefully considered. The service commitment is much smaller than the research and teaching commitments. Tenured faculty members need Internet access, computer technology, travel funds, and online meeting tools. Universities are much closer to meeting faculty's needs for research and service than they are with teaching, so teaching should be the point of emphasis.

The following bullet points examine the impact of root cause 4, "Limited Productivity Improvements for Universities," on the underlying problems listed in Table 4.3.

- *Problem 1. Cost increases:* The productivity of administration is very poor, which increases the cost of higher education dramatically. This is often caused by trying to solve problems with people. If there is a retention problem, universities create a vice president or vice provost for retention management. If they want more diversity, they create a diversity taskforce. When students complain about teaching effectiveness, administration responds with an office for teaching excellence. All of these solutions lead to a new administrative unit with more administrators. In addition, all faculty members have a responsibility to improve their productivity; otherwise, costs will continue to increase as faculty wages increase.
- *Problem 2. Quality decreases:* With more and more pressure driving costs higher, efforts to improve instructional quality are more difficult and there are fewer resources for innovative new programs, investing in new learning devices, and rewarding outstanding performance.
- *Problem 3. Access decreases:* As productivity declines and cost increases, access declines.
- *Problem 4. Graduation rate decreases:* As productivity declines and cost increases, graduation rates decrease.

- *Problem 5. Completion time increases:* As productivity declines and cost increases, completion time increases.
- *Problem 6. Job placement decreases:* With fewer resources because of declining productivity, it is more difficult to work with organizations that hire graduates.

4.7 HOW RAPIDLY GROWING COSTS FOR BOOKS AND SUPPLIES (ROOT CAUSE 5) AFFECT THE UNDERLYING PROBLEMS

In the 1960s, a reasonable estimate for books and supplies for one year of full-time study was about $120[20] with textbooks being about $100. The estimate for books and supplies today is more than 10 times that amount.[21] These data seem to conflict with textbook inflation data, which are presented in Chapter 2 and indicate that the cost of textbooks has increased from about $10 per book in the 1960s to $200 per book today and even more in some cases. How can the cost of books and supplies increase by a factor of 10, while the costs of individual books increased by a factor of 20? The answer seems to be free markets and technology.

In the 1960s, most bookstores were owned and operated by universities, and many universities did not release their book lists so other bookstores were unable to acquire and sell textbooks. University bookstores had a monopoly. The Internet and online shopping were decades away. Textbook prices were high for three reasons. University bookstores were not efficient because universities had no special expertise at managing bookstore and no competitors to keep costs in line. Second, university bookstores had three periods when they had nearly all of the sales—a few days around the beginning of Fall, Spring, and Summer semesters, although summer had much lower sales. University bookstores had high fixed costs for infrastructure and managers that were fully used only a few weeks each year. To put it in the vernacular of economics, they had no economies of scale—no way to spread their fixed costs over larger sales volume. Third, university bookstores, for reasons that are unclear, chose to sell new books and did not participate heavily in the used book market.

For a variety of reasons, including lack of expertise, no economies of scale, pressure from various interest groups for lower costs, and a desire for one less problem to deal with, universities began to outsource their bookstore operations to private concerns. These private-sector organizations understood the price sensitivity associated with textbooks—students only bought them because they thought they had to. They did not want them when the term was over. So the bookstores began to aggressively buy back books from students at the end of the semester and sell them at much lower prices than new books to the next wave of students. Over time, the demand for new books waned, but the cost of producing fewer copies of a particular book did not drop proportionately. The costs of acquiring, proofing, editing, and marketing are fixed. If fewer copies are printed, the publisher saves the ink and the paper, but it still has most of the fixed costs for printing presses, typesetting, and the like. Thus, when a textbook publisher sold one fewer copy, it lost all of the revenue from the sale, but its cost savings were only the ink, paper, binding, and royalty to the author, but little else.

With sales volume declining substantially and cost dropping only modestly, the book publishers lost economies of scale and felt they must raise the price for new textbooks. Increasing the price for new textbooks only made more room for people and organizations to buy back more books, resell them, and make even more money. This led to further declines in the demand for new books, which resulted in even higher prices, and this vicious cycle of price increases continued for many years. For a while textbook publishers cut into the used book market by coming out with a new edition, but that only worked for a while. Today, many textbooks are on a three-year refresh cycle, and the cycle is unlikely to be reduced further. The used textbook market is so profitable that people are willing to roam the halls knocking on the doors of faculty asking to buy the complimentary copies they receive from publishers when they are considering a textbook for adoption. In addition, the Internet has expanded competition by providing access to many sellers and offering opportunities to rent the book or buy an e-book.

The following bullet points examine the impact of root cause 5, "Rapidly Growing Costs for Books and Supplies," on the underlying problems listed in Table 4.3.

- *Problem 1. Cost increases:* As the costs for books and supplies increase, the cost of higher education increases as well.
- *Problem 2. Quality decreases:* As the cost of books and supplies increased, students are opting not to buy textbooks, sharing textbooks among two or more people, or purchasing old editions of the book. These actions, especially the first two, can alter the quality of their education.

- *Problem 3. Access decreases:* As the costs for books and supplies increase, access declines.
- *Problem 4. Graduation rate decreases:* As the costs for books and supplies increase, graduation rate decreases. Also, students without good access to textbooks are more likely to fail and drop out.
- *Problem 5. Completion time increases:* As the costs for books and supplies increase, completion time increases.
- *Problem 6. Job placement:* No change.

4.8 HOW THE FUNDING FINESSE—MIXING FEES AND TUITION (ROOT CAUSE 6)—AFFECTS THE UNDERLYING PROBLEMS

Student fees have been a part of academia for decades, but fees and tuition should have different purposes. As described in Chapter 2, fees were intended to cover nonlearning aspects of student life and were often called student activity fees, whereas tuition covered learning activities. The line became blurred as universities used fees to mask tuition increases. As this tactic matured, the purpose of the fees became so broad that funds could be used for anything.[22] In some cases, new fees were instituted and existing fees were increased to finesse state bans or limits on tuition increases.

The following bullet points examine the impact of root cause 6, "Funding Finesse—Mixing Fees and Tuitions," on the underlying problems listed in Table 4.3.

- *Problem 1. Cost increases:* Regardless of the reason, fees have grown faster than tuition and much faster than the rate of inflation, leading to an increase in costs for higher education.
- *Problem 2. Quality decreases:* As fees increase, students are pressured to work more, taking time away from studying.
- *Problem 3. Access decreases:* As fees increase, access declines.
- *Problem 4. Graduation rate decreases:* As fees increase, graduation rate decreases.
- *Problem 5. Completion time increases:* As fees increase, completion time increases.
- *Problem 6. Job placement:* No change.

4.9 HOW EXPANDING STUDENT EXPECTATIONS (ROOT CAUSE 7) AFFECT THE UNDERLYING PROBLEMS

Without concluding whether it is good or bad, part of the reason that higher education costs more today is the high expectations among students, which were caused, in part, by better living standards across the United States. In the 1960s, dormitories tended not to have air conditioning, and women were not allowed in men's dormitories and vice versa. The only phone was the pay phone in the hall that cost a nickel to use; the toilets and showers were down the hall and shared by 30 people; and dining was worse than hospital food and limited to traditional breakfast, lunch, and dinner hours. There was one TV for the entire dorm, and it was located in the basement and usually did not work. The bunk beds were uncomfortable and the furnishing stark. There were no significant recreation facilities save for a couple of tennis courts, two or three pool tables in the student union, and a six-lane bowling alley that was always crowded. This seemed like utopia to a recent high school graduate who shared a room in his or her parent's home with one or two siblings and shared a phone with the entire family. If he or she was lucky, there was an extension in the basement for privacy. A car was out of the question. A trip home meant hitchhiking, a bus or train ride, or a parent coming to get the student. Today, this would not pass muster.

For most students, smartphones, tablet devices or computers, privacy, entertainment, organic and GMO-free foods, and vacations are important. Some part of these expectations is the result of better living standards and smaller families than two or three generations ago. Universities did not create these expectations, but they have responded with enticements to recruit students. Universities are investing in sports teams and their practice and playing facilities, palatial new buildings, elegant dining options and dormitories, fancy student unions, and recreational facilities that rival country clubs.[11] Usually, students pay for part of the sports teams, which are important to alumni and communities, as well as for student unions and recreational facilities through their student activity fee. It is unclear how much value these activities deliver to students. They also pay for dining facilities and dormitories through usage fees.

The following bullet points examine the impact of root cause 7, "Expanding Student Expectations," on the underlying problems listed in Table 4.3.

- *Problem 1. Cost increases:* As student expectations increase and universities respond with more high-cost amenities, students pay more.
- *Problem 2. Quality decreases:* If donor funds could go to academic uses and scholarships for students rather than for sports teams and their facilities or other peripheral uses, educational quality could increase.
- *Problem 3. Access decreases:* As costs rise to support more amenities, the burden on students increases and access declines.
- *Problem 4. Graduation rate decreases:* As fees rise to support more amenities like bigger sports programs or fancy recreation centers, the cost burden for students increases. As costs increase, students feel the pressure to work more, which negatively impacts their grades and may cause them to drop out or flunk out.
- *Problem 5. Completion time increases:* As costs rise to support more amenities, the burden on students increases and completion time increases.
- *Problem 6. Job placement:* No change.

4.10 HOW ERODING STANDARDS (ROOT CAUSE 8) AFFECT THE UNDERLYING PROBLEMS

Most states provide funding to public colleges and universities based on the number of students enrolled, which is usually measured by student credit hours (SCHs)—the sum of all credit hours taken by all students. A subsidy is paid per SCH, and the rate may be different between disciplines such as engineering and business, between freshman-level, general education courses and senior electives, and between undergraduate and graduate courses. To address concerns about high dropout rates, some states have redesigned their subsidy to consider course completion, graduation rates, and degree completion time. This change puts pressure on universities to have more successful students, which sounds like, and is, a good idea, assuming that expectations for student learning are maintained.

Despite the economic recovery that began in 2008, many public universities face tight budgets. This is exacerbated by a lull in the number of high school graduates in the United States. Between 1998 and 2010, the number increased by 27%, but a decline of 2% is expected by 2023,[23] so universities seeking enrollment growth face a difficult market. Their response to state pressure to increase student success and a smaller pool of high school graduates has been to focus on keeping the students they have by creating Offices of Retention Management or Offices for Student Success. These entities study why students leave the university before graduation, and they develop support systems to help students cope with their problems, stay in school, and graduate. Universities benefit from these efforts in two ways: (1) more state subsidy because they meet the state mandates for student success and (2) students stay in school, take more SCH, and generate more revenue for the university.

These ideas are well intended and are designed to help students, but there are two important and potentially serious problems. First, the financial best interest of the university is served by identifying students who are having problems and "advising" them toward fields of study that are, to put it bluntly, easier and require less work. This is not radically different from the approach universities are accused of using for some of their top athletes. To assume that all programs are equally challenging is unrealistic, and to deny that less challenging programs exist is like the ostrich with its head in the sand. This certainly does not mean that counseling students to take advantage of their strengths and pursue a field of study that meets their interest is a bad thing as long as the path leads to a job that pays enough so the graduate can have a financially and intellectually satisfying life. Pushing students into programs that are already overcrowded depresses wages and limits access to good jobs. While this is happening, there are many jobs in the United States with very good starting salaries and career paths that go unfilled.

Second, with part-time jobs, studies, and social activities, students are busy, and many are looking for ways to reduce their academic workload. This manifests itself in a number of ways, including requests to instructors to push back the due date for term papers, smaller reading assignments, fewer topics in the course and on tests, and more in-class review time, which take time away from covering new topics. When this push for less work is combined with subtle and sometimes not so subtle pressure from university administration to meet retention goals, faculty members feel compelled to reduce their coverage and standards. When standards and coverage are reduced and enrollment increases, faculty, departments, and programs are rewarded because higher enrollment leads to more resources.

There is another important factor that exacerbates the tendency to cover fewer topics and require less work in a course: the change in the mix of faculty. For many years, universities have asked students to evaluate the classroom performance of faculty. Although these evaluation instruments can provide useful feedback so faculty can improve, they have a number of flaws. They ask students to assess the value of what they have learned. For most students, especially those who are early in their studies, they have a very limited basis on which to judge the relevance of topics in a course. Most students do not have enough life experience or a good understanding of what they need to know to be successful. Students can assess whether the faculty member was on time, spoke clearly, was organized, and treated them with respect. The instrument, which likely has a dozen or two dozen questions, is often boiled down to a single question that goes something like this: How would you (the student) rate the faculty member on teaching effectiveness? This question is often used to assess a faculty member's teaching performance in annual merit evaluations, promotion and tenure deliberations, and contract extension decisions. Also, the instrument is likely to have an open comment section, so students can share specific insights. Among the most common comments are "This course required too much work" or "This course is too difficult." These comments from students are often triggered by a desire to keep their workload low.

Evaluations have biases. Students who give instructors low ratings are more likely to perform poorly and claim courses are too difficult. In addition, student evaluations are affected by the type of course and its placement in a degree program. Students in PhD programs tend to give faculty very high ratings. Students in master's programs give ratings that are high, but not as high as PhD courses. Graduate students are more mature and often have work experience so they have a better understanding of how to apply the concepts and techniques they are learning. At the undergraduate level, courses that are required but outside the field of study, especially courses in the first two years of school and courses with a quantitative bent, tend to have very low evaluations. These evaluations are much lower than those for junior- and senior-level courses that are within the students' major field of study.

One buffer against the bias in student evaluation is tenure. This is not meant to imply that tenure should shield faculty who are poor teachers. A case can be made to fire tenured faculty for any number of reasons, including poor teaching. Tenure does provide protection for faculty who demand more from students by covering more topics and demanding a higher level of performance. Faculty members who do this are trying to give students more knowledge for each tuition dollar, making higher education a better value. As reported earlier, the problem is that the percent of faculty who have tenure has dropped dramatically and now represents about 30% of all faculty at colleges and universities.[24]

Tenured faculty have been replaced mostly by full-time contractual employees, who can typically be dismissed at the end of a school year and who may or may not have a PhD, and part-time contractual faculty, who are hired for one course at a time and usually do not have a PhD. Sometimes, they are professors of practice with substantial, relevant work experience, but most often they are not. They can be hired to teach specialized courses in the junior or senior year or at the graduate level, but most often they teach general education courses in the first two years of an undergraduate degree. Some examples of these courses are English composition, basic economics, the fundamentals of computer systems, college algebra, and dozens more. Universities embrace contractual faculty because they tend to work cheaply, can be dismissed without cause, and do not make waves. Typical concerns are their level of commitment and their ability to teach effectively. Unfortunately, too often there are few mechanisms to support the development of these faculty and only modest efforts to evaluate their teaching ability prior to their selection and during employment, other than student evaluations.

The primary duty of most nontenured faculty is to teach, so having very good student evaluations is vital for receiving a new contract. Although the teaching criteria for most universities are long and include many items such as course development, innovative teaching techniques, service on curriculum committees, and overseeing internships, the reality is that contracts for these faculty members are based on how students evaluate them. Often the evaluation is based on the single question about teaching effectiveness mentioned earlier. A poor showing means that a new contract may not be forthcoming. This gives students tremendous power over the rigor of the course content in roughly 70% of the undergraduate curricula. Because so many of these faculty members teach required courses in which students have little interest, they are likely to get low evaluations unless they take actions that please the students. From the students' perspective, they do not want to take this course, so they enter with a negative attitude. It seems clear that there is pressure on faculty to soften the standards and cover less material. Those who do not may not get a new contract. This is not intended to blame these faculty members because most people, put in these circumstances, would respond similarly. The blame belongs to universities that created this situation, first, by shifting hiring to less expensive contractual faculty and, second, by providing a mechanism for students to impact course content and academic standards.

A better approach would have course content set by tenured and professional faculty in close cooperation with organizations that hire graduates. For example, business programs would rely on the needs of manufacturing and service firms to set accounting or finance curriculum, engineering programs would meet the requirements of professional engineering examinations and the needs of engineering design firms, and premedicine programs would consider admission standards for medical schools as well as the content of the Medical College Admission Test (MCAT). Student evaluation should be used to assess elements of the classroom experience, including what tools students need to make learning faster and easier. Evaluation of faculty performance should emphasize things that students can assess such as whether faculty members prepared for class and whether they treat students with respect.

The following bullet points examine the impact of root cause 8, "Eroding Standards," on the underlying problems listed in Table 4.3.

- *Problem 1. Cost:* No change.
- *Problem 2. Quality decreases:* As standards decline, the quality of education suffers.
- *Problem 3. Access:* No change.
- *Problem 4. Graduation rate increases:* As standards are reduced, graduation rates may actually increase, which addresses this underlying problem in a way that ultimately harms students and the companies that hire them.
- *Problem 5. Completion time decreases:* As standards are reduced, completion times may actually decrease as students learn less.
- *Problem 6. Job placement decreases:* Graduates with insufficient education may not find or keep good employment. They may find jobs that are outside of their field of study and pay less.

4.11 HOW LACK OF STUDENT PREPARATION (ROOT CAUSE 9) AFFECTS THE UNDERLYING PROBLEMS

Lack of preparation may be the most difficult root cause to address because higher education has as its inputs graduates from primary and secondary schools. This problem is acute in large urban schools and some rural areas, especially where strong family structures are limited and unable to put pressure on schools to offer high-quality programs and motivate and support children to excel in school. As reported by CNN in 2014, the average high school graduation rate for large urban high schools, which serve the most disadvantaged students, was only about 50%.[25] For the 2013–2014 school year, the public high school graduate rate, including these poorly performing schools, hit a record high of 82%.[26] The results for rural schools are mixed, but overall these students are graduating at a rate of about 80%.[27] Iowa and Nebraska, generally considered rural states, had the highest high school graduate rate, both topping 90%. New Mexico, also considered a rural state, was the only state with a rate below 70%. The District of Columbia was also less than 70%.[26] An examination of graduation rates on a county-by-county basis shows that a disproportionate share of the rural counties with above-average dropout rates is in the southern United States.[28] The ultimate point is that these urban and rural dropouts do not have access to colleges and universities unless these problems are resolved.

There is another large group of high school graduates who did not take a college preparatory curriculum in high school, and they may not meet university admission requirements. It seems clear that not everyone will or should attend a two-year or four-year institution, but it is very difficult to know who should take what path as students enter high school. If students do not take a college-prep track, they can pursue vocational education, which may lead to a good career. Opting into or out of a college-prep track should not be irrevocable. If students want to switch from vocational to college preparatory or vice versa as they move through high school, they should be able to fill gaps in their education.

There is yet another group of students who graduated from high school but do not learn what they should have because they were pushed forward and protected. This is a silent conspiracy. The student and parents are happy and have a graduation party; teachers and schools feel good and report a better graduation rate to the state board; and the state looks good as it reports data to the U.S. Department of Education. Success is celebrated and failure is postponed. Everyone is happy, at least in the short run.

To put U.S. high school performance in perspective globally, consider a recent competition among 57 countries. The United States placed 16th in science and 23rd in mathematics.[29] Another study of 64 countries by Pew Research Center has the United States ranked 27th in science and 35th in mathematics.[30] The United States must close the gap and improve its primary and secondary educational system, a topic for another time.

The following bullet points examine the impact of root cause 9, "Lack of Student Preparation," on the underlying problems listed in Table 4.3.

- *Problem 1. Cost increases:* A lack of student preparation can lead to additional coursework, which drives up costs. For example, students seeking an engineering degree, who take only three years of high school mathematics, must take at least one additional math course in college for which they earn no credit toward graduation. Students who fail courses because high schools did not prepare them properly must retake the course, which means they pay tuition a second time.
- *Problem 2. Quality decreases:* When students are not fully prepared, they may pass the course but they do not learn all they should have, so their education and job opportunities may suffer.
- *Problem 3. Access decreases:* High school dropouts have no access. Ill-prepared high school graduates may not choose college because it seems too difficult.
- *Problem 4. Graduation rate decreases:* Poorly prepared high school graduates are more likely to fail courses and drop out.
- *Problem 5. Completion time increases:* When students have to take remedial courses and repeat courses they fail, it takes them longer to graduate.
- *Problem 6. Job placement decreases:* Graduates who have not learned as much as they should have in college because they were poorly prepared in high school may not find employment. If they find jobs, their compensation is likely to be low.

4.12 SUMMARY

A thorough understanding of Table 4.3 implies that a solution must consider (1) the interconnected nature of the underlying problems (rows) and (2) the interconnected nature of the root causes (columns). The following examples illustrate these points.

1. Interrelated underlying problems: When cost is high, access and graduation rate decline, while completion time increases.
2. Interrelated root causes: When there is confusion about customers, poor decisions are made about resources allocation, leading to

excessive spending on administration. And declining state support results in larger tuition increases and more emphasis on fees to generate revenue.

Table 4.3 shows there are no simple one-to-one relationships between a cause and a problem, so it is impossible to make one change and resolve one problem. Every problem has multiple root causes, and every root cause impacts more than one problem. For example, to improve access, it is critical to address all of the root causes that have contributed to higher costs for tuition, fees, and books (root causes 2, 3, 4, 5, and 6), as well as resolve misallocating resources (root cause 1) and expanding student expectations (root cause 7). In addition, improving access means addressing a lack of student preparation (root cause 9), which is a significant problem for many students.

Looking forward, Chapter 5 contains an overview of the solution, and the remainder of the book provides the details for the solution. The proposed solution has multiple elements, and each element impacts more than one root cause. For example, redesigning and streamlining the curriculum can reduce the number of credit hours students must take, which lowers tuition, and changes the requirements for books and learning materials, which also lowers costs. Curriculum redesign can also make faculty more productive and better prepare students for the job market.

These complexities lead to three conclusions about the solution. It must be comprehensive, integrated, and implemented as a whole.

1. *Comprehensive:* The underlying problems and root causes are many so the solution must be based on careful analysis and broadminded thought. It is not enough to address questions about who is the customer, tackle administrative costs, or stabilize and increase eroding standards. The solution should address all of these issues; it must be multidimensional.
2. *Integrated:* Because there are complex relationships among the problems and among the root causes and between problems and root causes, the solution must be coherent and consistent.
3. *Implemented as one package:* Creating a comprehensive and integrated solution to higher education's problems requires change on the part of many participants. In most cases, it also requires sacrifices. Getting people onboard for a solution means that all the parties understand what they are contributing, what others are contributing, and how the system will be better.

REFERENCES

1. United States Department of the Treasury and Department of Education. 2012. *The Economics of Higher Education*, December. https://www.treasury.gov/connect/blog/Documents/20121212_Economics%20of%20Higher%20Ed_vFINAL.pdf (accessed June 23, 2016).
2. Heineke, J. 1995. Strategic operations management decisions and professional performance in US HMOs. *Journal of Operations Management* 13(4): 255–272.
3. Lusch, R., and Vargo, S. 2006. Service dominant logic: Reactions, reflections, and refinements. *Marketing Theory* 6(3): 281–288.
4. SallieMae. 2015. *How America Pays for College*. http://news.salliemae.com/files/doc_library/file/HowAmericaPaysforCollege2015FNL.pdf (accessed June 16, 2016).
5. TopUniversities: Worldwide University Ranking, Guides, and Events. 2012. *University Budgets: Where Your Fees Go*. http://www.topuniversities.com/student-info/student-finance/university-budgets-where-your-fees-go (accessed August 8, 2016).
6. Campos, P. F. 2015. The real reason college tuition costs so much. *New York Times*, April 4. http://www.nytimes.com/2015/04/05/opinion/sunday/the-real-reason-college-tuition-costs-so-much.html?_r=0 (accessed August 8, 2016).
7. June, A. W. 2012. Adjuncts build strength in numbers. *The Chronicle of Higher Education*, November 5. http://chronicle.com/article/Adjuncts-Build-Strength-in/135520/ (accessed June 24, 2016).
8. Jaschik, S. 2009. The disappearing tenure-track job. *Inside Higher Education*, May 12. https://www.insidehighered.com/news/2009/05/12/workforce (accessed June 26, 2016).
9. Wiessmann, J. 2013. The ever-shrinking role of tenured college professors. *The Atlantic*, April 10. http://www.theatlantic.com/business/archive/2013/04/the-ever-shrinking-role-of-tenured-college-professors-in-1-chart/274849/ (accessed June 24, 2016).
10. American Association of University Professors. 2014. *Losing Focus: The Annual Report on the Economic Status of the Profession, 2013–2014*. https://www.aaup.org/reports-publications/2013-14salarysurvey (accessed June 24, 2016).
11. McNutt, M. I. 2014. Why does college cost so much? *US News World Report*, September 22. http://www.usnews.com/news/college-of-tomorrow/articles/2014/09/22/why-college-costs-so-much-overspending-on-faculty-amenities (accessed June 24, 2016).
12. United States Census Bureau. 2016. *College Enrollment of Students 14 Years Old and Over, by Type of College, Attendance Status, Age, and Gender: October 1970 to 2014*. http://www.census.gov/hhes/school/data/cps/historical/index.html (accessed August 8, 2016).
13. Cohen, H. 2003. Who should pay for higher education? *New York Times*. http://www.nytimes.com/ref/college/collegespecial2/coll_aascu_povcohen.html (accessed August 8, 2016).
14. Mortenson, T. G. 2012. State funding: A race to the bottom. *American Council on Education*, Winter. http://www.acenet.edu/the-presidency/columns-and-features/Pages/state-funding-a-race-to-the-bottom.aspx (accessed August 9, 2016).
15. The Pew Charitable Trusts. 2015. *Federal and State Funding of Higher Education: A Changing Landscape*, June 11. http://www.pewtrusts.org/en/research-and-analysis/issue-briefs/2015/06/federal-and-state-funding-of-higher-education (accessed June 16, 2016).

16. Skorup, J. 2013. Five reasons the government shouldn't subsidize higher education. *Michigan Capital Confidential*, February 13. http://www.michigancapitolconfidential.com/18279 (accessed August 9, 2016).
17. American Council on Education. 2016. *ACE Leadership*. http://www.acenet.edu/leadership/Pages/default.aspx (accessed July 25, 2016).
18. Leadership Education for Asian Pacifics, Inc. 2016. *Leadership Development Programs for Higher Education*. http://www.leap.org/develop_ldphe (accessed July 25, 2016).
19. Cook, B. J. 2012. The American College President Study: Key findings and takeaways. *American Council on Education: Leadership and Advocacy, (Spring Supplement)*. http://www.acenet.edu/the-presidency/columns-and-features/Pages/The-American-College-President-Study.aspx (accessed July 26, 2016).
20. The University of Toledo. 1966. *Financing Your Higher Education at the University of Toledo*. Provided by Barbara Floyd, University Archivist on July 18, 2016.
21. College Board. 2016. *Trends in Higher Education: Published Prices—National*. http://trends.collegeboard.org/college-pricing/figures-tables/published-prices-national#Published Charges, 2015–16 (accessed June 20, 2016).
22. Office of the State Auditor, State of Colorado. 2010. *Higher Education Student Fees*, Department of Education: Performance Audit, July. http://www.leg.state.co.us/OSA/coauditor1.nsf/All/BCE425B0727916C18725777D00766A3D/$FILE/2046%20Higher%20Ed%20Fees%20July%202010.pdf (accessed July 8, 2016).
23. Adams, C. 2014. Number of high school graduates to decline by 2022, NCES predicts. *Education Week*, March 4. http://blogs.edweek.org/edweek/college_bound/2014/03/new_estimates_show_number_of_high_school_graduates_declining_by_2022.html (accessed August 16, 2016).
24. National Education Association. 2016. *The Truth about Tenure in Higher Education*. http://www.nea.org/home/33067.htm (accessed June 24, 2016).
25. Guryan, J., and Ludwig, J. 2014. Why half of urban kids drop out. *CNN*. http://www.cnn.com/2014/03/12/opinion/ludwig-guryan-chicago-education/index.html (accessed August 18, 2016).
26. National Center for Education Statistics. 2016. *Public High School Graduate Rates*. http://nces.ed.gov/programs/coe/indicator_coi.asp (accessed August 18, 2016).
27. National Center for Education Statistics. 2013. *The Status of Rural Education*. http://nces.ed.gov/programs/coe/indicator_tla.asp (accessed August 18, 2016).
28. The Daily Yonder. 2012. *Reducing the Rural Dropout Rate*. http://www.dailyyonder.com/preventing-rural/2013/09/30/6827/ (accessed August 18, 2016).
29. Wilde, M. 2015. Global grade: How do U.S. students compare. *GreatSchools.org*, April 2. http://www.greatschools.org/gk/articles/u-s-students-compare/ (accessed August 18, 2016).
30. Desilver, D. 2015. *U.S. Students Improving—Slowly—In Math and Science, but Still Lagging Internationally*. Pew Research Center, February 2. http://www.pewresearch.org/fact-tank/2015/02/02/u-s-students-improving-slowly-in-math-and-science-but-still-lagging-internationally/ (accessed August 18, 2016).

5

A Customer-Focused, Resource Management Perspective

When organizations face a broad set of problems related to product cost, quality, and customer satisfaction, they have fundamental problems that are most likely caused by errors in strategic planning. These firms have misjudged customer expectations and have not put in place the appropriate resources nor allocated them properly. A successful organization, whether it is a for-profit or not-for-profit, must do the following:

1. Identify its customers and markets, including a clear understanding of its customers' wants.
2. Design goods and services to meet those wants.
3. Determine which resources are needed, assemble them, and allocate and manage them in order to design, produce, and deliver products at prices that customers are willing to pay.

Through this process, organizations create value for customers by producing a good or service with benefits that exceed its price.

In higher education, dissatisfaction is triggered by excessive student loan debt, limited access, low graduation rates, long completion times, and poor job placements (not in all fields of study but in some). Strategic planning is difficult because universities face a trifurcated customer—students who pay and learn, third parties who pay, and organizations that hire graduates. (Going forward, these organizations are called employers or potential employers.) As illustrated in Figure 5.1, customers' expectations must drive resource acquisition and management. As part of the process, universities must design products (curriculum) that meet customers' needs.

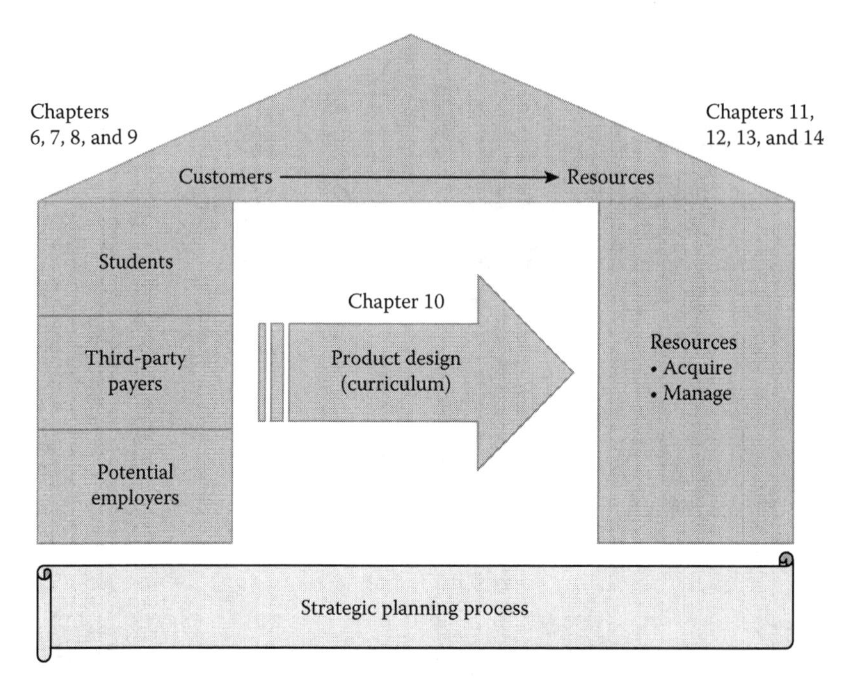

FIGURE 5.1
Relationships among strategic planning, customers, product design, and resources in higher education.

When customers are not properly identified, strategic planning is based on a false premise, and this takes universities in the wrong direction.

As shown in Figure 5.1, the solution proposed here has three key components. They are as follows:

1. *Customers:* As part of the strategic planning process, universities focus on developing a better understanding of the multifaceted, trifurcated customer (Chapters 6, 7, 8, and 9).
2. *Product design:* Once universities understand their customers' needs, they can design effective curricula (Chapter 10).
3. *Resource management:* With knowledge of the customers and an effective product, universities can acquire and manage resources to achieve appropriate outcomes (Chapters 11, 12, 13, and 14).

Customers and product design (curriculum) issues are discussed in Section 5.1, an organizing paradigm is described in Section 5.2, and resource issues are discussed in Sections 5.3 and 5.4.

5.1 CUSTOMER-FOCUSED: WHO ARE THE CUSTOMERS?

The trifurcated customer is discussed in Chapter 1, and a summary of the key points is provided here:

1. *Students:* Pay part of the cost and gain knowledge so they can have good jobs and better lives.
2. *Third-party payers:*
   a. *Parents, other family members, and friends:* The provide financial support and want what is best for students.
   b. *Government:* The federal government offers aid to students who attend public or private colleges and universities. State and local governments subsidize tuition at public colleges and universities.
   c. *Universities, foundations, and other organizations:* Universities are major scholarship providers. Foundations and other organizations provide scholarships directly to students, and this allows them to use these funds at institutions of their choice.
3. *Potential employers:* They want quality employees. Many universities do not recognize this group as a customer, do not understand this group's expectations, and spend little time and effort creating links between students and potential employers.

Based on this discussion, universities have three distinct customer groups: (1) students, parents, other family members, and friends; (2) governments; and (3) potential employers. Students and their supporters can be treated as one customer because their interests are closely aligned. Governments have different reasons to fund higher education than students because they are seeking economic prosperity and job growth, so governments are in a separate group. University scholarships are marketing tools, and in reality, they are price discounts that are used to attract students they want. Universities are not customer of themselves. Scholarships from foundations and the like tend to be given directly to students, so the interest of these scholarship providers and students are aligned. These entities are not customers because students typically control the funds. Although potential employers do not pay universities for their graduates, they are customers because they hire the output from universities, which allows graduates to pay their debts and live comfortable lives. Without employers wanting to hire graduates, few people would attend universities. This clarification of the trifurcated customer is essential to ensure that universities develop effective strategic plans, design relevant curriculum, and acquire and manage resources appropriately.

As the solution unfolds, these three customer groups are examined. Two chapters are devoted to students, parents, other family members, and friends, which is followed by a chapter on potential employer and a chapter describing the role of government. These chapters represent the customer pillar on the left side of Figure 5.1, and they are essential for understanding customers' expectations. These chapters begin to shape Table 5.1, which relates the elements of the solution (column headings) to the root causes (row headings) of the underlying problems. An overview of these chapters follows.

- *Chapter 6:* Changing Attitudes and Expectations of Students, Parents, Family Members, and Friends: Although there are multiple customers, universities would cease to exist without students. As shown in Table 5.1, the attitudes and expectations of students and their supporters impact all root causes. This group must be active in working with states to pressure public universities to improve performance. When this group is not assertive in discussing rising costs, declining standards, and other problems, they lose their clout as customers and costs rise.
- *Chapter 7:* Becoming Student Centered: The Right Way: Decades ago, "student centered" became the buzzword to champion efforts to treat students fairly, which is important. Unfortunately, as universities became more "student centered," they did not carefully examine the needs of potential employers that want graduates with a strong knowledge base. The implication is that learning content and performance standards should be set by these organizations, not by students. Having students set standards would be like a state medical board claiming it is physician centered as it developed its licensure exams. In fact, its role is to protect the public from substandard physicians. Becoming student-centered should mean developing teaching tools and methods that enable students with different learning styles to learn best. When "student centeredness" is applied improperly, universities lose focus on efficiency and low costs, performance standards erode, and the lack of preparation by some students is hidden.
- *Chapter 8:* Building Bridges to Potential Employers: Universities are student centered when they prepare graduates for success, whether that involves finding a good job, gaining admission to graduate school, or

TABLE 5.1

Impact of the Solution on the Root Causes

	Chapters (Solution)							
Root Causes	**Chap. 6: Changing Attitudes and Expectations**	**Chap. 7: Becoming Student Centered**	**Chap. 8: Bridges to Potential Employers**	**Chap. 9: Gov't Role**	**Chap. 10: Redesigning Curriculum and Pedagogy**	**Chap. 11 Reforming Administration and Management**	**Chap.12: Reshaping Faculty's Role**	**Chap. 13: High-Tech Learning Materials**	**Chap. 14: Revamping Relationships**
1. Lack of Understanding—Who Is the Customer?	X	X	X	X	X	X	X		X
2. Declining State Support for Public Universities	X		X	X		X			
3. Rise of the Ruling Class—Administrators	X	X	X	X		X	X		
4. Limited Productivity Improvements for Universities	X	X	X	X	X	X	X	X	
5. Rapidly Growing Costs for Books and Supplies	X	X	X	X	X	X	X	X	
6. Funding Finesse—Mixing Fees and Tuition	X	X		X		X			
7. Expanding Student Expectations	X		X						
8. Eroding Standards	X	X	X	X	X	X	X		X
9. Lack of Student Preparation	X	X	X			X			X

Note: In some cases, chapter titles have been shortened to fit the space.

passing a licensure exam. As shown in Table 5.1, missing a key customer group impacts all root causes. It leads to a poor understanding of the universities' missions, less support for government subsidies, and less pressure to control costs. When employers are involved, standards are maintained and enhanced, students focus on outcomes, and there is support for having high performance standards.

- *Chapter 9:* Government's Role in Higher Education: No entity exists without some government oversight, and higher education is no exception. It is impacted more than usual because the federal government and, in the case of public universities, state and local governments provide substantial funding. Over the past several years, federal subsidies have increased while state and local subsidies have declined as a percent of university revenue. Table 5.1 shows that government impacts nearly all of the root causes. As a customer, the government has a right to expect the efficient and effective use of resources, determine how much support it provides, be concerned about the cost and quality of degree programs, and maintain standards.

5.2 ORGANIZING PARADIGM FOR HIGHER EDUCATION

When organizations, like universities, have multiple customers and offer a knowledge-intensive service, they need a different approach—one that can rapidly adapt to new ideas and meet the needs of all customers. The organizing paradigm is listed here and discussed in the following sections.

1. *Mediator:* Universities mediate relationships between students who want to learn and potential employers who want to hire qualified employees.
2. *Professional service organization (PSO):* Universities are PSOs with highly educated experts who provide assistance to address complex problems; specifically they conduct research and develop high-quality curricula.
3. *Service dominant logic (SDL):* These highly educated experts have frequent interaction with customers and suppliers. This exchange of knowledge continuously improves the value that customers receive. This is sometimes called value co-creation.

5.2.1 Coping with Multiple Customers: Universities as Mediators

Many academic leaders believe that students attend universities to be educated and earn a diploma, but most students, supported by their parents, other family members, and friends, attend because they want opportunities for good jobs and happy lives. The degree is a step in the process. Admittedly, a few students enroll because they like to learn and are not interested in employment, but these students will face the harsh economic realities of adulthood and want a good job—unless they win the lottery or have wealthy parents. Most universities do not understand the needs of employers that want qualified and capable employees, so universities must adjust their focus.

When examined from this perspective, universities are mediators or brokers that match the needs of potential employers and the desires of the students.[1,2] This role is different from companies that buy resources, change them in some way, and sell their outputs. To act as mediators, universities must do the following:

1. Gather information about the knowledge needed for careers, and then design and deliver curricula, thereby ensuring that students have the "right stuff" to work effectively. These efforts set the content in the major field of study. For civil engineering, this would include structural design and other technical skills. This does not mean that education is devoid of topics that create well-rounded citizens, including cultural opportunities, political awareness, and historical context. Curricula must also deliver knowledge in key topics like mathematics, science, and economics.
2. Provide data about current and future jobs so students can chose careers they enjoy in fields where they excel. Universities, possibly working together and using government data, should provide reliable information about current and future job openings and salaries.

When universities are successful mediators, governments are satisfied because students graduate and have financial and societal success, and organizations flourish because they have qualified employees.

Although working with potential employers is relevant for many university degrees, especially professional degree programs such as business, engineering, education, law, and medicine, there are circumstances where the process must be modified.

1. *Licensure:* Some jobs like certified public accountant, mechanical engineer, high school teacher, and many others require licensure and/or profession examinations. The requirements for these certifications, which should be consistent with the needs of employers, must be considered when designing degree programs.
2. *Graduate school:* Many professions, such as physician, lawyer, and university professor, require advanced degrees, so the undergraduate degree programs must build a foundation so interested students can apply and enroll in graduate degree programs. In most cases, this requires performing well on standardized tests such as the Medical College Admission Test (MCAT), Law School Admission Test (LSAT), or the Graduate Record Examination (GRE).
3. *Entrepreneurship:* Some graduates may wish to start their own business, so students who identify with entrepreneurship should be prepared for the job market with appropriate classroom instruction, hands-on work experience, and qualified, practicing mentors.
4. *Nonprofessional degree programs:* For some four-year degree programs, such as art, foreign language, history, or philosophy, the path to a job is not as well defined as it is in professional degree programs. Graduates from these fields may have the knowledge base to teach a foreign language, art, or history in high school, but in most cases they cannot do so without a teaching certificate, which requires additional study. Programs like philosophy are rigorous and demanding, but the path to a job is not well defined, so students working with faculty mentors must spend time planning their future. Examinations of commencement programs at public universities are likely to show that graduates from professional degree programs outnumber graduates from nonprofessional degree programs by three or four or more to one.

There are other parts of the U.S. economy that operate as mediators or brokers such as real estate, where agents negotiate relationships between buyers and sellers, and finance, where experts guide mergers and acquisitions among two or more companies. In fact, Internet websites that sell goods and services, such as eBay or Orbitz, also provide this type of mediating relationship. However, the mediation task faced by universities is more complex because they are also professional service organizations.

5.2.2 Universities Are Professional Service Organizations

A professional service organization (PSO) is a group of highly educated experts who provide assistance to solve problems, improve performance, and take advantage of opportunities. These experts have special education and training that they apply to complex problems, and they often hold professional licenses that are earned through independent testing. Hospitals, law firms, architectural enterprises, accounting firms, consulting companies, and universities are a few examples. PSOs typically have high customer contact and differentiated, if not customized, product offerings.[3,4] Most often, the leadership of PSOs is provided by these professionals who have an in-depth understanding of the strong and close relationship between the professionals and the customers. Universities are PSOs, and tenured and professional faculty members are the highly educated experts who

1. Create new thoughts and ideas
2. Disseminate these ideas through academic and practitioner publications
3. Design, develop, and deliver knowledge through a wide variety of programs that educate future leaders, technical experts, and a competent workforce for a wide variety of jobs
4. Interact closely with students and employers to create a strong curriculum that satisfies the needs of both groups.

Tenured and professional faculty members are the experts who create value through innovative curricula. They develop the curriculum because students, especially in undergraduate programs, are often recent high school graduates and know little about what they need to learn to qualify for a particular job. So faculty experts—working with employers, graduate programs, licensure groups, and others as appropriate—create curricula that lead to four-year degrees. They determine the content of the curriculum and set the learning standards. These efforts in curriculum design are fundamentally important to the success of higher education, so a chapter is devoted to this vital activity, which is represented by an arrow connecting customers and resources in Figure 5.1.

- *Chapter 10:* Redesigning Curriculum and Pedagogy: This redesign must consider the needs of potential employers and students. Curricula content and standards of performance are set by the needs of employers, and pedagogy is adjusted so students can be successful. Table 5.1 indicates that doing so improves the effectiveness and productivity of universities and enhances the quality of learning materials while keeping their costs low.

In addition to tenured and professional faculty's critical role in curriculum design, they are key players in determining research output, institutional quality, marketing strengths, and revenue generation. These roles are summarized in the following list.

1. *Research output:* Tenured faculty sets and executes research agendas. They write most of the externally funded research proposals submitted to industry, foundations, and governments.
2. *Institutional quality:* The quality of universities is determined in large measure by the quality of its research and instruction. Tenured faculty members are leaders in research, whereas tenured and professional faculty members have critical roles in designing and implementing curricula.
3. *Marketing:* Students are often attracted to one university over another because of the reputation of its degree programs, the status of its faculty, or an opportunity to work on research projects with eminent scholars.
4. *Revenue:* Research conducted by tenured faculty and teaching conducted by all types of faculty generate most of the academic-related revenue. (Note: This does not include revenue from ancillary services, which should be self-sustaining, such as sports programs, dormitories, and food service. These entities should not use tuition dollars for support.)

It seems clear from this summary that tenured faculty should have an important, maybe even dominant, role in decisions regarding strategic planning, resource allocation, and university governance. This explains why the bond between tenured faculty and administrators must be both close and strong.

Because universities are PSOs that depend on tenured faculty experts, it is *not* appropriate to think of them as interchangeable and easily replaceable production employees who assemble goods, fill orders for customers, perform basic services such as lawn care or loan applications at branch banks, or even serve as staff economist at the U.S. Department of Commerce. While these employees impact quality, reputation, and revenue at their firms, their impacts are far less significant than the impacts of tenured faculty. Tenured, faculty experts are like MDs in hospitals, lawyers in legal firm, or scientists in biotech companies. They should be at the core of the organization. They must work closely with customers, suppliers, and others professionals, and some of them should become administrators who organize and manage the process. These factors, which are attributes of service dominant logic, are vital for success.

5.2.3 Service Dominant Logic

In addition to being PSOs, universities operate in an environment where value is created by close and careful cooperation among customers, service providers, and suppliers. This is referred to as SDL. Dominant logic is a model of exchange from economics, and it is based on the exchange of "goods" that emphasizes transactions and uses *tangible resources* and *limited information* about customers to *create embedded value.* SDL argues that the logic of exchange should be different because it applies to *intangible resources,* uses *close and continuing working relationships* with customers, and *co-creates value.* Intangible resources, including knowledge and information, and close relationships are used to intensify interactions among the organization (university) providing the goods or services, academic leaders (tenured faculty), customers (students, governments, and potential employers), and key suppliers (providers of learning materials). These interactions lead to an exchange of knowledge and information that continuously improves and fits the value of the good or service to the needs of specific customers; thus, value is co-created through this process.[5] SDL seems particularly useful under the following conditions:

1. *Products have high intellectual content:* Designing and producing goods such as sophisticated computer hardware, surgical equipment, or even today's automobile requires in-depth knowledge of customers' changing expectations and emerging technologies. Creating services such as hospital care or university research projects depends on frequent exchanges of information and continuing efforts to improve outcomes.
2. *Organizations have multiple customers:* It is essential for the experts within the organization to synchronize expectations and mediate relationships among the customer groups through repeated contacts so value is co-created.

5.2.3.1 Higher Education, Service Dominant Logic, and Curricula

Higher education is consistent with SDL because it is intellectually rich, has a highly educated workforce, and faces multiple customers. Figure 5.2 shows the key participants in curricula design and delivery, which are tenured and professional faculty, customers such as students and potential employers, other contractual faculty, graduate teaching assistants, placement specialists, student advisors, and suppliers of learning materials. Governments as customers are not listed in Figure 5.2 because their interests overlap with the interests of students and potential employers.

The eight groups, shown in Figure 5.2, work together to create a learning environment that meets the needs of customers (the "what" for curricula design) and create the pedagogy or method to deliver the content effectively and efficiently (the "how" for curricula delivery). The following points describe the interactions among the participants.

1. *Curricula content:* For each degree program, the needs of the potential employers—along with requirements of licensure, graduate school admission, and becoming entrepreneurs—are combined with the expert knowledge held by tenured and professional faculty to determine the course content, including the depth of coverage for each

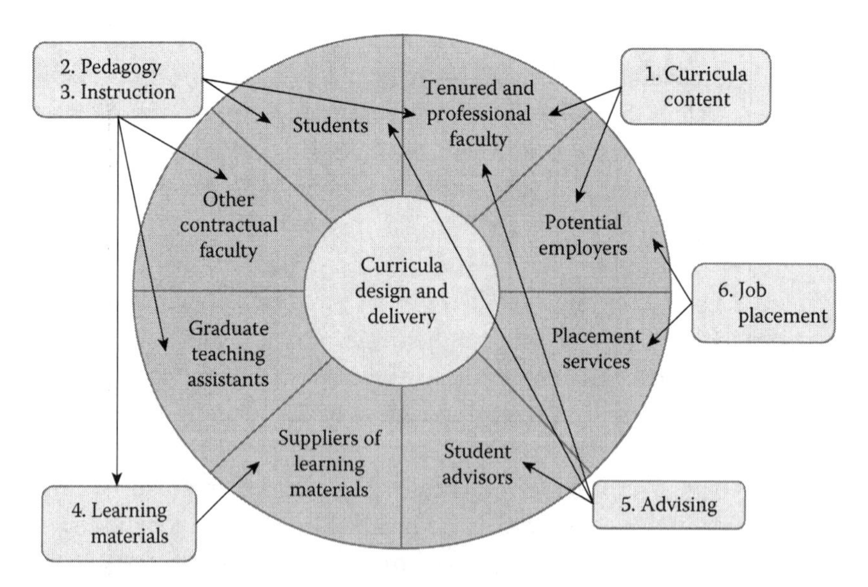

FIGURE 5.2
Service dominant logic perspective on curricula design and delivery.

topic and the standards for assessing performance. See the curricula content callout in Figure 5.2. This is the "what" portion of the curriculum, and it should not be determined by students. These interactions occur continuously to incorporate research that identifies new concepts and techniques that improve the curricula as well as to include the changing needs of organizations, licensing agencies, and so on.

2. *Pedagogy:* All faculty and graduate teaching assistants work with students to investigate the best instructional methods to deliver this knowledge so learning is optimized. This is the "how" for delivering curricula. There should be a close working relationship that unifies course content, pedagogy, and the types of learning materials and how they are used. See the pedagogy, instruction, and learning materials callouts in Figure 5.2. When done properly, students learn more with the same or less effort. It is important to make learning easier, more fun, and more effective.
3. *Instruction:* Using the pedagogy, tenured faculty, contractual faculty, and graduate teaching assistants educate the students. Contractual faculty and graduate teaching assistants often deliver a majority of the instruction for undergraduate degree programs. They provide feedback to tenured faculty about the strengths and weaknesses in the curricula content and pedagogy.
4. *Learning materials:* For many years, textbooks dominated this category, and tenured faculty often authored them. As pedagogy is changing to include methods of instruction other than lecturing, learning materials are shifting from traditional textbooks to more sophisticated instruments that may include online learning tools, videos, and other technologies.
5. *Advising:* Students need guidance so they make on-time progress toward graduation, address scheduling and other problems, and provide faculty feedback on the effectiveness of pedagogy. The use of computer-based tracking systems allows students to assess their progress and to use advisors as problem solvers. See the advising callout in Figure 5.2.
6. *Placement:* As tenured and professional faculty work with organizations that hire graduates to determine curriculum content, it is necessary to complete the circle by having effective placement that links students who are approaching graduation with these organizations. This is more than having signup sheets and providing space so organizations can interview students. See the job placement callout in Figure 5.2.

A SDL perspective on curricula design and delivery offers important insights. First, potential employers drive curricula content, and students' learning abilities drive pedagogy. Second, interaction among the participants is critical in this value creation process, and it should be both ongoing and frequent. Third, this interaction leads to a process where value is enhanced by exchanging ideas, making higher education a value co-creation process.

5.2.3.2 Higher Education, Service Dominant Logic, and Research

A second set of relationships define the process for research and innovation. As shown in Figure 5.3, tenured faculty members create partnerships with entities that fund research. They employ and supervise graduate research assistants who execute the work plan that may require specialized equipment. Academic journals and learned societies become mechanisms to disseminate research outputs. The following points describe the interactions among the participants.

1. *Project proposal:* All research and innovation efforts require funding, but not all receive external funding. External research funding tends to be available in technical fields like basic science, engineering, and medicine. Tenured faculty members seek out requests for proposals from industry and governments, and they write proposals to secure funding. They identify equipment needs and work with

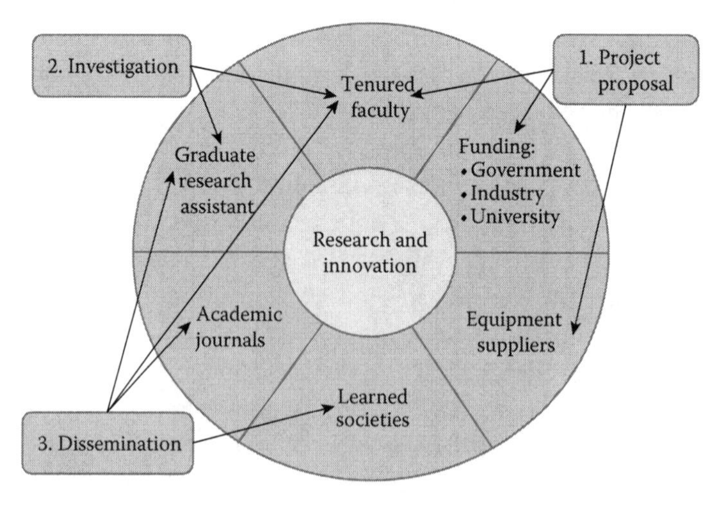

FIGURE 5.3
Service dominant logic perspectives on research and innovation.

suppliers to ensure that necessary equipment is either available or can be acquired as part of the proposal. In many fields such as art, business, humanities, and social science, external funding is limited. In many cases, research in these fields does not require expensive equipment, facilities, or supplies. To support research, universities reduce the workload for tenured faculty so they can devote time to research, and universities may fund travel, computer hardware and software, data acquisition, and other expenses.

2. *Investigation:* Tenured faculty and graduate research assistants execute the plan. In some fields of study, postdoctoral researchers and technical support people may be involved. When external funds are available, graduate research assistants may be supported by government or industry, but in other cases they are funded by the university.
3. *Dissemination:* Tenured faculty and graduate research assistant collaborate in writing up the results and disseminating the research. In some but not all cases when private industry funds research, results are proprietary because the entity does not want to share the outcomes with its competitors. In nearly all cases when governments and universities fund research, results are published in academic journals and discussed with colleagues so ideas are shared, duplication is reduced, and the greater good is enhanced. Academic journals are important avenues for publishing results. Here the results can be examined and critiqued. Learned societies are groups of researchers who meet, share ideas, discuss the meaning of their research, examine synergies among different research projects, and outline future research agendas.

5.3 STRATEGY: VISION, MISSION, VALUES, AND GOALS

An institution of higher learning, like other organizations, has a strategic planning process that identifies a vision for what it wants to become, a mission describing what it wants to achieve, values that clarify acceptable behavior in reaching its vision and accomplishing its mission, and institution-wide goals that drive its actions. Ultimately, these actions determine what resources to acquire, to what programs they should be allocated, and how they are used.

Most institutions, especially four-year colleges and universities, have a tripartite mission that includes research, teaching, and service, although service has morphed into outreach and engagement. Although the intent of research and teaching should be clear, service may not be. Service is faculty providing support for membership organizations and learned societies that focus on research, knowledge creation, and teaching excellence through a wide variety of activities, including forming, managing, and helping these organizations attain their goals. Outreach and engagement expand this notion to include community support such as faculty working with government to design marketing plans for economic development or creating new drug rehabilitation programs. Most universities do not identify a new source of funding to support this expanded role, so funds tend to come from existing sources and typically include faculty's and administrator's time. This implies that tuition dollars are used to support outreach and engagement.

Many people would be surprised to learn that the vision and mission statements for institutions of higher learning do not focus exclusively or even primarily on educating students so they can find jobs and earn livings. As an example of what might be considered a well-reasoned statement for a comprehensive university with bachelor's, master's, doctoral, and specialized programs, consider the following, which is taken from the Ohio State University's (OSU) website.

1. "*Vision:* The Ohio State University will be the world's preeminent public comprehensive university, solving problems of world-wide significance."
2. "*Mission:* We exist to advance the well-being of the people of Ohio and the global community through the creation and dissemination of knowledge."
3. "*Values:* Shared values are the commitments made by the Ohio State community regarding how work will be conducted. Our values at Ohio State include: Commitment to Excellence, Collaboration as One University, Acting with Integrity, Personal Accountability, Diversity in People and Ideas, Change and Innovation, Simplicity in our Supporting Processes, and Openness and Trust."[6]
4. *Core goals:* The institution-wide goals at OSU are research and innovation, teaching and learning, outreach and engagement, and resource stewardship.[6]

Teaching and learning are mentioned indirectly in the mission statement as dissemination of knowledge, which means publishing scholarly research, writing practitioner-oriented articles, and teaching.

Teaching and learning are not mentioned specifically until the core goals. Even so, there is no mention of graduates getting good jobs.

The intent is not to say that OSU or any other comprehensive university has the wrong strategy and core goals. There are good reasons for universities to engage in these activities, which are as follows:

1. Research and innovation lead to groundbreaking new ideas that improve quality of life.
2. Teaching and learning provide graduates with an education that helps them become better citizens.
3. Outreach and engagement leads to economic expansion and societal enhancement.
4. Good stewardship of resources is a basic requirement for any institution, public or private.

When examining these core goals, a number of important questions emerge about the allocation of university resources, the sources of the funding, and the beneficiary.

1. How are the three primary goals of universities—research and innovation, teaching and learning, and outreach and engagement—funded?
2. What portion of undergraduate students' tuition dollars are spent on research and innovation and how much on outreach and engagement?
3. How do the payers, whether they are students, parents, other family members, friends, and governments, benefit from research and innovation and outreach and engagement?
4. Students may receive some benefits from these activities, but are the benefits commensurate with the portion of their tuition spent on these activities?

5.4 RESOURCE MANAGEMENT

These are important questions about the sources and uses of funds, and Figure 5.4 is a simplified version of this for public universities. It excludes funds used for ancillary services, which include athletics, housing, and the like. For simplicity, this is referred to as the "academic budget."

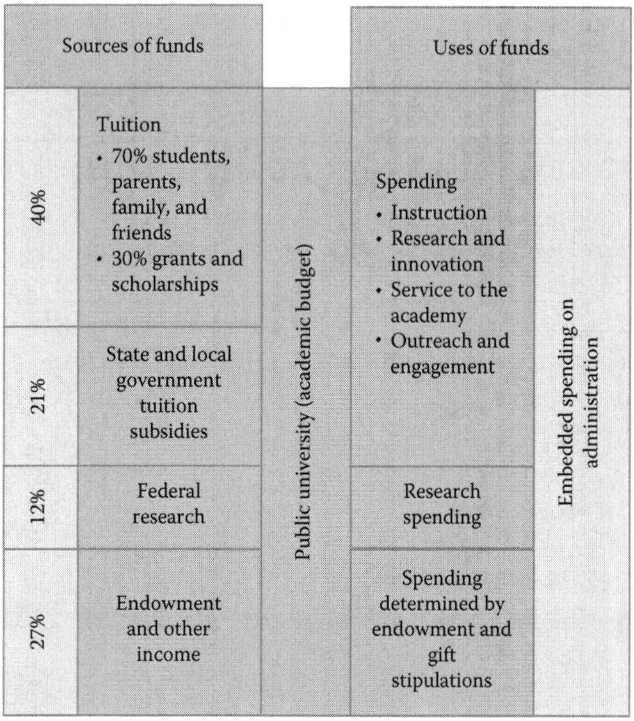

Sources of funds		Public university (academic budget)	Uses of funds	Embedded spending on administration
40%	Tuition • 70% students, parents, family, and friends • 30% grants and scholarships		Spending • Instruction • Research and innovation • Service to the academy • Outreach and engagement	
21%	State and local government tuition subsidies			
12%	Federal research		Research spending	
27%	Endowment and other income		Spending determined by endowment and gift stipulations	

FIGURE 5.4
Sources and uses of fund for public universities academic budgets.

5.4.1 Sources of Funds

The largest source of funds in academic budgets is tuition at about 40%,[7] and a critical point is who pays tuition. To begin, Figure 1.2 from Chapter 1 sheds light on how the typical family pays university expenses. Students pay 27% of their tuition, including student borrowing. Parents contribute the most at 38%, including parent borrowing. Other relatives and friends pay about 5%. The total paid by students and their support group is 70% (27% + 38% + 5%). See Figure 5.4. Students and their support group also pay for room, board, and books, but these items are ancillary services that are not part of the academic budget. Grants from federal and state governments and scholarships account for the remaining 30% of tuition revenue.[8] Grants from federal and state governments[7] are given directly to students. Some tuition scholarships are provided by other entities, but the majority is provided by the universities either as cash awards from endowments or as tuition discounts. In the final analysis, more than 70% of the tuition and fee payments to institutions of higher learning are made by or on behalf of students.

In addition to tuition, Figure 5.4 shows that state and local governments support public higher education by adding 21% to their revenue stream. The primary purpose of this subsidy is to keep tuition at public universities affordable for residents. This can be seen by comparing the in-state tuition at public universities to tuition at private, not-for-profit universities, which is shown in Table 1.1 in Chapter 1. Nearly all of the difference is higher tuition at private, not-for-profit universities.

Figure 5.4 also shows that universities receive approximately 12% of their revenue from the federal government in the form of research grants. These funds are different from the federal grants for tuition described earlier. The balance, approximately 27%, comes from endowments and other income.[8] Research funding, endowments, and gifts are described here.

1. *Research grants and contracts:* Universities pursue grants and contracts, which are funds from governments, foundations, industries, and other organizations for doing specific tasks, including basic research in chemistry or biology, applied research in engineering, investigating new teaching methods, creating new computer technology, and dozens of other topic of interest to the funders. The amounts received vary widely with more funds going to larger and better known universities. There are strict spending guidelines, which universities must follow or they will lose the research grant and put future grants in jeopardy. Most universities have a grants accounting office that monitors these projects to validate that dollars are spent according to the guidelines.
2. *Endowments:* They usually come from individuals, companies, or foundations, and only the earnings from endowments can be spent. Although some of the earnings support scholarship, a significant amount is used to fund research, support faculty development, pay for equipment, and build and operate facilities. Endowment amounts vary widely. A community college or technical school is likely to have a small endowment with a total in the millions or tens of millions of dollars. Regional universities are likely to have endowments measured in the $100s of millions. Nationally and internationally known universities have endowments in the billions of dollars with Harvard University leading the pack at $36.4 billion in 2015.[9] Each year, Harvard University is likely to generate more than a billion

dollars of spendable earnings. Endowments usually have a well-defined purpose that must be followed or the donor can ask to have the funds returned.

3. *Donation/gifts:* Like endowments, these gifts may come from individuals, companies, or foundations; funds can be spent on the same kinds of activities; and they often have identified spending restrictions. The difference is that the entire donation can be spent. Amounts vary widely, with nationally and internationally known institutions receiving the most.

5.4.2 Uses of Funds

The mission and goals of universities identify activities that consume resources: instruction, research and innovation, service to the academy, and outreach and engagement. As illustrated in Figure 5.4, funds received for research (12% from federal sources) and endowments and other gifts (27%) typically have well-defined spending requirements, so universities must spend them as directed. For the small portion of these funds that give universities discretion, the institution is within its rights to spend the money in any way that helps it achieve it mission and goals. One thing is clear, however, this spending, which totals 39% of university revenue, is typically subject to a generous charge for administrative overhead. This includes indirect costs for things like libraries, facilities, and administrative staff, and it can be 30% to 70% of the dollars in a research grant.[10]

The challenge is to know if tuition payments and government tuition subsidies, which total about 61% of the revenue shown in Figure 5.4, are used effectively. Not all of these funds are spent on instruction. Some, probably more than necessary, are consumed by administration in the colleges and the central bureaucracy. In addition, some funds are spent on research and innovation because, as described previously, not all research is externally funded. Professional faculty members spend little time on research, and instructional faculty members spend none, while tenured faculty may spend 40% to 50%, or even more time. This is consistent with the fact that many tenured faculty members teach about half as many student credit hours or even less than full-time instructional faculty. It is unclear whether students, especially undergraduate students, benefit sufficiently from the time that tenured faculty members spend on research. This becomes a less significant concern as the portion of tenured faculty, which is about 30%, continues to decline. Service to the academy, which is a small commitment of tenured faculty time, typically 10% or less, is justified by the value it creates in enhancing teaching and research and participating in university governance. However, when service expands to include outreach and engagement, which serves the external community, more faculty time is consumed, but the benefits to tuition payers are minimal. There is no corresponding revenue stream to support outreach and engagement, so resources are diverted from instruction and research to cover these costs.

As shown in Figure 5.4, regardless of the source of funds or how they are used, all the activities have embedded spending on administration. To illustrate the impact of this, recall that from 1978 to 2014, tenured faculty increased by only 23%, and undergraduate enrollment grew by 73%, yet administrative positions grew by 369%.[11,12]

5.4.3 Resource Allocation

Although this discussion does not provide complete answers to the questions about resource allocation, it does offer insights about how to improve resource management. Universities should strive to make resource allocation consistent with the needs and wants of the customers paying the bill. Based on the discussion, administration and management must be carefully examined, restructured, and streamlined, so they are more effective, more efficient, and costs much less. The roles and responsibilities of faculty, who are also a major cost component, must be adjusted so students get what they need and the research mission of the university is enhanced. To make learning more effective and efficient, different learning tools are needed to communicate concepts and techniques to students. To ensure that applicants are better prepared, universities should improve their relationships with community and technical colleges and high schools. These elements of the solution are discussed in the following chapters. An overview of the relationships between the elements of the solution and the root causes is given in Table 5.1.

- *Chapter 11:* Reforming Administration and Management: These reforms impact not only the cost and productivity of administrators, but they provide an avenue for lowering faculty costs, improving instructional materials while keeping their costs low, and better utilizing student fees. Administration, working with faculty, is critical for keeping standards high and ensuring that applicants are well prepared. If public universities make a sincere effort to reduce costs, the states may provide additional funding as an incentive when universities succeed.

- *Chapter 12:* Reshaping Faculty's Role: Tenured faculty should have an active role in university governance as well as provide more leadership in designing and implementing curricula, including leading and working closely with potential employers and professional faculty. If this is accomplished, the costs should be reduced and standards should be maintained.
- *Chapter 13:* Creating High-Tech Learning Materials: There are new technologies that can be implemented to improve the learning process. These efforts will cost less than current textbooks, enhance learning, and improve the productivity of faculty.
- *Chapter 14:* Revamping Relationships among High Schools, Community and Technical Colleges, and Universities: Building stronger relationships among these learning institutions is essential. There are too many high school graduates who are unprepared and cannot gain admission to colleges and universities. Too many students are admitted who need remedial course work, and they pressure faculty either directly or indirectly to reduce standards.

5.5 THE SOLUTION

The solution must be comprehensive because there are multiple problems and the problems are complex and systemic. Table 5.1 shows that there are no one-to-one relationships between the elements of the solution and the root causes, so each element impacts more than one root cause, and no root cause is addressed by a single element. In addition, the root causes and the elements of the solution are interconnected. Following are some examples.

1. *Root causes (rows in Table 5.1) are interconnected:* When universities misunderstand customer expectations, they make poor decisions about resource allocation, and they may ignore the lack of productivity by administrators and faculty. Excessive spending on

administration makes it more challenging for universities to cope with poorly prepared students.

2. *Elements of the solution (columns in Table 5.1) are interconnected:* Redesigning curricula requires reshaping faculty's role. Building bridges to potential employers may require additional administrative staff while, overall, administrative expenses should be reduced.

The elements of the solution, which are described in detail in Chapters 6 through 14, address the root causes of the underlying problems. A summary of the recommendations for each element is given at the end of each chapter, and a compilation of the recommendations is provided in Appendix A.

REFERENCES

1. Thompson, J. D. 2003. *Organizations in Action: Social Science Bases of Administrative Theory* (Originally published in 1967, with a new preface by Zald, M. N. and a new introduction by Scott, W. R. ed.). New Brunswick, NJ: Transaction Publishers.
2. Thompson, J. D. 1967. *Technology Typology*. ProvenModels.com. http://www.provenmodels.com/40/technology-typology/james-david-thompson (accessed September 27, 2016).
3. Dobrzykowski, D. D., McFadden, K. L., and Vonderembse, M. A. 2016. Examining pathways to safety and financial performance in hospitals: A study of lean in professional service organizations. *Journal of Operations Management* 42–43: 39–51.
4. Heineke, J. 1995. Strategic operations management decisions and professional performance in US HMOs. *Journal of Operations Management* 13(4): 255–272.
5. Vargo, S. L., and Lusch, R. F. 2004. Evolving to a new dominant logic for marketing. *Journal of Marketing* 68: 1–17.
6. The Ohio State University. 2016. *Ohio State Vision, Mission, Values, and Goals*. https://oaa.osu.edu/vision-mission-values-goals.html (accessed June 22, 2016).
7. United States Department of the Treasury and Department of Education. 2012. *The Economics of Higher Education*, December. https://www.treasury.gov/connect/blog/Documents/20121212_Economics%20of%20Higher%20Ed_vFINAL.pdf (accessed June 23, 2016).
8. SallieMae 2015. *How America Pays for College 2015*. http://news.salliemae.com/files/doc_library/file/HowAmericaPaysforCollege2015FNL.pdf (accessed June 16, 2016).
9. Wikipedia. 2016. *List of Colleges and Universities in the United States by Endowment*. https://en.wikipedia.org/wiki/List_of_colleges_and_universities_in_the_United_States_by_endowment (accessed June 23, 2016).
10. Callier, V. 2015. Overspending on overhead. *The Scientist*, February 1. http://www.the-scientist.com/?articles.view/articleNo/41962/title/Overspending-on-Overhead/ (accessed May 2, 2017).

11. McNutt, M. I. 2014. Why does college cost so much? *US News World Report*, September 22. http://www.usnews.com/news/college-of-tomorrow/articles/2014/09/22/why-college-costs-so-much-overspending-on-faculty-amenities (accessed June 24, 2016).
12. United States Census Bureau. 2016. *College Enrollment of Students 14 Years Old and Over, by Type of College, Attendance Status, Age, and Gender: October 1970 to 2014.* http://www.census.gov/hhes/school/data/cps/historical/index.html (accessed August 8, 2016).

6

Changing Attitudes and Expectations of Students, Parents, Family Members, and Friends

At public universities, students, parents, other family members, and friends pay about 70% of the cost of a four-year degree,[1] and they have the right to seek, even demand, something of commensurate value for their investment. For too long, many people have subscribed to the notion of the "infallible and benevolent university," an institution that puts the needs of others first and does what is best for students, third-party payers, potential employers, and humankind. Although universities may be more committed to do "the right thing" than other entities that sell goods and services, they tend to do what is best for the institutions and their employees. Universities pay market wages, seek long-term survival, and emphasize activities such as outreach and engagement that have limited direct benefit to students. Students and their support groups must change the way they think about universities, how they interact, and what they should expect.

Attitude is a way of thinking about something that is ultimately reflected in a person's behavior. When students and their support group believe that universities are looking out for their best interests, they do not hold universities responsible for high costs, restricted access, and other problems. When pushback is muted, the changes required to address the underlying problems are deflected and replaced with claims that state funding is insufficient and declining or that tenured faculty are resisting change and straining university budgets. It is imperative that students and their support group treat decisions to pursue a university degree like purchasing new cars, homes, or other products. They must seek the best value and outcome. After all, investing in a university degree is the biggest and most important purchase that applicants have made at this point in their young lives, and looking forward, it is one of the most important decisions they will ever make. Students and their support groups have the right and responsibility to hold universities accountable for meeting their expectations.

An expectation is thinking that something should or may happen. For example, if people work hard and contribute to their organization's success, they expect to be well compensated. If people drive recklessly, they may have a fatal accident. When students apply to a university, they should have in mind a set of outcomes/expectations that take place after four years of study and $100,000 or more in expenses. Although students may have some things in mind as they prepare for their university education, such as starting a new adventure and enjoying more personal freedom, they should expect other things by the time they graduate, including (1) to be in debt, (2) to have learned enough to be employable, and (3) to find an interesting job that allows them to earn enough money to pay their debt and lead a comfortable life.

6.1 CHANGING ATTITUDES

Students and their support groups are key players in transforming the behavior of universities. To do so, they must change their attitude toward universities from benevolent knowledge dispensers to providers of important services. They must hold universities accountable for high costs, limited access, and other concerns, and they must make their feelings known to universities, governments, and other oversight groups. They must shop around, pursue discounts (scholarships), and pick their university base on finding the best value (a combination of the right price and appropriate benefits). They should consider and evaluate ways to earn and save more money as well as keep educational costs low, so borrowing is greatly reduced or eliminated. Long-term financial planning is a vehicle to identify appropriate levels of earning and saving as well as to spend funds wisely.

6.1.1 Holding Universities Accountable

Three elements of cost have risen much faster than inflation: tuition, fees, and learning materials. There are also activities that are not mandated for universities, such as athletic programs and outreach and engagement, which consume resources that should be spent on research and teaching.

Students and their supporters must push back by making it clear to universities that prices are too high and tuition must be spent on activities related to education. With strong feedback from this group, states may be encouraged to offer financial incentives to universities who achieve lower costs and better outcomes.

State legislators, boards of regents, and higher education commissions as well as university boards of trustees are groups that must hear this message. A good approach is to prepare thoughtful letters and emails that describe the issues. At the state level, contacting the governor, leaders of the state senate and state house of representatives, and the director of the board of regents is important. At the university, the president and the chair of the board of trustee are the best contacts. It is important for these groups to hear from as many people as possible. Although these efforts may have a larger impact on public universities, private universities are not immune from this pressure.

6.1.1.1 Tuition, Fees, and Learning Materials

Public universities and private, not-for-profit universities set the price for tuition and fees to cover the cost of providing an education, whereas private, for-profit universities also have a profit margin. The price of textbooks and other materials are set by publishers, but universities are complicit as faculty and administrators typically choose these items without considering the price that students pay. So the decision about what to purchase is made by one group (faculty and administrators), and another group (students) pays the bill. Splitting the choice of what to purchase from payment responsibility allows unchallenged price increases. Thus, students are in a difficult position; they must either buy the expensive items or not have the tools to take full advantage of their education. One solution is to require universities to cover the cost of all textbooks and learning materials. Universities have the bargaining power to deal with publishers that students and their support groups do not, plus universities would be more careful about what learning materials students need to be successful if they covered the cost. Universities would decide to work closely with publishers to create less expensive ways to deliver knowledge.

6.1.1.2 Athletic Programs

A hidden cost factor is athletics. Only 23 of 228 National Collegiate Athletic Association (NCAA) Division I athletic departments generated enough revenue from sports activities to cover their costs in 2012. (The percentage for other divisions is most likely even lower.) Division I is a combination of the Football Bowl Subdivision (FBS) and Football Championship Subdivision (FCS). All 23 were members of the Power Five Conferences, which typically compete in the FBS championship playoff. Of the 23 "self-sufficient programs," 16 received some type of subsidy "relying on institutional and government subsidies as well as student fees to make ends meet."[2] Athletic department spending by the 48 universities that were members of the Power Five Conferences increased from $2.6 billion in 2004 to $4.4 billion in 2014, a jump of nearly 70%. Many Power Five schools need student fees and school money to pay their bills.[3] *USA Today* reported that universities depend on student fees to support athletics as well as subsidies from general funds.[4] The terms "institutional subsidies," "school money," and "general fund" are typically nice ways of saying that universities use student fees and tuition dollars to fund sports programs. This tactic can and has been used to subsidize other money-losing activities.

6.1.1.3 Outreach and Engagement

A third factor, which is even further below the surface, is mission creep—from an emphasis on research, teaching, and service to a push for research, teaching, and outreach and engagement. Initially, service involved supporting the academy to improve research and teaching, which are primary elements of a university's mission. Outreach and engagement expanded service to include supporting the external community by working to enhance economic development and social services. It is a partnership between universities and communities. The problem as illustrated in Figure 5.4 in Chapter 5 is that universities are not routinely funded for outreach and engagement. Governments do not usually allocate resources to universities to lead or even participate in outreach and engagement, and students and their support groups do not pay tuition for it. Typically, universities do not receive a meaningful amount of donated money for outreach and engagement, so the support for these efforts comes from faculty and administrators who should be working to improve research and instruction. In short, tuition dollars are spent. There is no pushback from state and local governments because part of their job is to improve the economy and quality of life. To get the needed change, students and their support groups must clearly state that universities should not use tuition dollars for outreach and engagement.

6.1.1.4 Putting Pressure on Universities and Government

Students and their support groups must reinforce their feedback with commitments to seek value for their education dollar, which includes "shopping around" and finding a high-quality education at a low price. If universities feel the same pressure from customers that other organizations such as airlines, automakers, and consulting firms feel, universities will respond by offering better values.

Some people may wonder whether pressure on government can make a difference. State governments do have the power to regulate tuition and fees at public universities. In some states such as California, many public universities charge the same tuition.[5] In other states such as Ohio, the state oversees tuition costs, but public universities can and do set different prices. Tuition at Youngstown State University was $7,847 in 2015–2016, which is among the lowest in the state, whereas Miami University charged $11,673, which was near the highest, so Miami's costs were about 50% higher.[6] In either case, comments and actions from customers/voters will have an impact.

It is time for universities to take actions that lower costs and improve performance. A key question is: How can universities respond to pressure from customers and governments and accomplish this? To address the problems, Chapters 10 through 14 offers solutions involving the curriculum, administration, faculty, learning materials, and relationships with high schools and community and technical colleges.

6.1.2 Seek a University with the Best Value Rather Than the Best University

There is often intense competition among high school students to be accepted to the best universities—in essence, bragging rights when they are admitted to an Ivy League school, Massachusetts Institute of Technology, Stanford University, University of Chicago, or other top-level private and public universities. For the best and brightest students, being accepted to and attending a top university separates them from their colleagues. It is similar to a high school football player who is recruited to play in the Big Ten or Southeastern Conferences. One problem is that tuition and fees at elite universities can be three, four, or more times the costs of a public university education. See Table 6.1. Using these data, students at elite universities may spend about $150,000 more for tuition and fees over four years

TABLE 6.1

Comparing Full-Time, Undergraduate Tuition and Fees for One Year (2015–2016)

University	Tuition and Fees
Harvard University	$45,278[7]
Massachusetts Institute of Technology	$46,400[8]
Stanford University	$46,320[9]
University of Chicago	$49,026[10]
Average Four-Year, Public University	$9,410[11]

Note: The average premium to attend these elite universities is about $150,000 over four years of study. [($45,278 + $46,400 + $46,320 + $49,026) divide by 4 to get the average for the elite schools, then subtract the average for public universities $9,410, then multiply by 4 to get the cost over four years.]

compared to the average public university. (Calculate the average annual cost of tuition and fees at the four elite schools, subtract the average cost at public universities, and multiply by four years of study.)

Top universities offer scholarships to the "brightest of the bright" and to good students with strong financial needs, but so do public universities. Typically, excellent students, who are a notch below the brightest in grade point average or standardize test scores, have a substantially better chance of getting scholarships from very good public universities than from elite, private schools.

Why can elite schools charge so much for a university education? The reason, at least in part, is the same reason people buy expensive Rolls-Royce, Ferrari, or Lamborghini automobiles; there is exclusivity, a perception of high status, and better outcomes such as performance and comfort. With elite universities, there is a strong, inverse correlation between the price charged for tuition and fees and the acceptance rate. When universities have a reputation for high quality, they receive a large number of applications and can be very selective about who they admit. For example, Harvard University receives about 35,000 applications each year and accepts only about 6%.[12] Because elite schools have large applicant pools, they can charge much higher tuition and still admit a full complement of students.

Although competing to be accepted to the best universities should be encouraged, the important questions for applicants to consider are as follows: Can they afford it? Do students who attend an elite university earn a fair return on this extra investment? Affordability is far less important for applicants who receive substantial tuition discounts (scholarships) and for the few applicants who have parents, families, members and friends with the resources to pay the additional $150,000 without straining their budgets. The remaining students, which represent a substantial majority, are required to find other funding sources to cover the extra costs, and this is often met, in large part, by additional borrowing.

The second question is more interesting because it considers whether the benefits of a degree from an elite university exceed the cost. Paying $150,000 extra means that graduates have $150,000 less to save and invest. Investing $150,000 and earning an annual return of 6% for 40 years would cause this amount to grow about 10 times and become about $1,500,000. So, students attending an elite university must earn $1,500,000 more over 40 years of working than students attending an average public university, just to break even. (Actually, the $1,500,000 would be wages that are saved plus investment returns on those savings.) What advantages do elite universities offer? Many people claim that these graduates receive a better education and have better networking opportunities and status. By extension, these advantages lead to greater income and happier lives. The following statements examine these claims.

1. *A better university provides a better education:* Proving that one university provides a better education than another is difficult, especially if the assessment involves how much knowledge is gained during the process. Universities that admit only the best high school graduates should have the best educated graduates. When ability and knowledge are better to begin with, the expected outcome for that person should be higher. Considering an example from sports, average athletes may run the 40-yard dash in 5.0 seconds. They hire trainers and cut the time to 4.7 seconds. Elite athletes may run the 40-yard dash in 4.4 seconds. They hire elite trainers and cut the time to 4.32 seconds. The elite athlete is still faster, but the average athlete showed more improvement. These facts do not prove that one trainer is better than the other. In academics, the ACT, which is a standardized test used by many universities to judge the quality of applicants, is like the 40-yard dash for athletes. To provide some perspective, the national average for the ACT is between 20 and 21, and a perfect score is 36. Accepted applicants at Ivy League schools typically score between 30 and 35.[13] It would not be shocking if Ivy League graduates who scored 33 on the ACTs know more and are better prepared for work than

graduates from open-enrollment, public universities who scored 19 on the ACT. The information, which is difficult to attain, is whether applicants with 19 on the ACT would gain more knowledge at an elite school than they would at a public university.

2. *Salaries as outcome measures:* Some prefer to use the salaries of graduates to measure the quality of education, but this approach does not resolve the fundamental advantage that elite schools have because they accept top students. Besides, surrogates like salary are impacted by other factors, including cost of living and the quality of university alumni networks, which is discussed in the next numbered point. There are parts of the United States along the East and West Coasts where the cost of living is very high such as financial districts and technology corridors. A $75,000 salary goes much farther in Fort Wayne, Indiana, than in New Brunswick, New Jersey. Serious efforts to measure the educational quality should assess what was learned, which means pretesting as students begin their university education and posttesting at graduation.
3. *Better networking and status:* This may be the real advantage of a degree from an elite school. A degree from the University of Pennsylvania opens doors at financial institutions and on Wall Street, and it provides a network that is willing to consider fellow alumni for employment. A degree from Stanford University may do that for graduates who seek jobs in Silicon Valley. Measuring the long-term impact of this advantage on job satisfaction and income is challenging.

6.1.3 University Rankings

For more than 30 years, *US News and World Report* has ranked universities in the United States. There are now dozens of rankings that consider a wide variety of criteria, have very different schemes to weight the criteria, and use subjective judgments to compile their lists from best to worst. In all of these rankings, the elite universities tend to be at the top, followed by a jumble of institutions without much rhyme or reason. Some of these systems use objective criteria like the average ACT scores of incoming students or the percent of applicants admitted, so a university with an average ACT of 33 that admits only 6% of its applicants has a natural advantage. A university that is open enrollment may have an average ACT below 20 and a 100% acceptance rate. This university may do an excellent job at fulfilling its mission, but it will never rank high in this poll. There are many universities between these two extremes, and it is a challenge to know which one is better. Assuming that institutions have rigorous content and high performance standards, the most important factor in determining how much students learn is the amount of effort they put into it, not the name of the institution.[14]

6.1.4 Creating an Educational Database

Applicants need a fast and easy way to get relevant and reliable information about various institutions of higher learning so they can start their search for the best value. This can be accomplished if they have access to data about price, graduation rates, completion time, passing licensure and certification exams, and job placement. In fact, these data should be available for all institutions of higher learning that receive government support. A database of Higher Education Pricing and Outcomes (HEPO) would be built and maintained by government using verified data from accreditation bodies and regulatory agencies. HEPO would provide applicants with enough information to narrow down their list of options for a more detailed investigation, including campus visits. Government could use HEPO to determine if the educational products being offered meet reasonable performance outcomes, given the institution's admissions policy and criteria.

6.1.5 Earning and Saving More While Keeping Costs Low

Parents, other family members, and friends should understand how much universities cost and begin saving when the potential student is very young. There is enough time to increase earnings and reduce spending, so more money can be saved. The report about How America Pays for College shows that 22% of parents who are planning to help their children with university expenses work more and 45% reduce spending.[1] When done early enough, this has a major impact on parental savings. Each dollar saved when the child is born is worth $2.85 when the applicant is 18 years old, assuming a 6% compounded annual return on investment. The report also shows that 70% of students work while earning a degree.[1]

No matter how hard some families try, they simply do not have the income to save. The federal government offers Pell Grants, subsidized student loans, and work study jobs, and universities and other entities offer need-based scholarship. It is possible that more should be done for promising students from low-income families, but that topic alone commands an entire book.

Earning more income and saving more of it is one side of the equation; finding ways to spend less for a high-quality bachelor's degree is also important. Following are things students and their families can do to cut their spending for university degrees. These are important for everyone but most important for low- and moderate-income families.

1. *In-state, public universities:* As shown in the prior section, choosing a public university reduces cost substantially. About 69% of applicants for bachelor's degrees make this choice. Many public universities provide strong curricula and a high-quality education. Well-qualified applicants have a better chance to earn scholarships at public universities than at elite schools.[1]
2. *Reduce housing costs:* About 48% of students live at home. For universities, this number is less because the 48% includes students attending community and technical colleges. Nevertheless, it is an option to cut expenses by about 40%. Students who are unwilling or unable to live at home can choose apartment living to save money, and 35% add a roommate to save even more.[1]
3. *Personal spending:* About 60% of students take steps to reduce spending on things like mobile phones, entertainment, and transportation.[1]
4. *Community and technical colleges:* As described in Table 1.1 in Chapter 1, tuition and fees at these institutions cost substantially less ($3,435) than at in-state, public universities ($9,410). If students live at home, they can earn an associate degree, which may count toward the first two years of their bachelor's degree. The total cost of a year would be about $9,000 or $18,000 for two years of study. The $9,000 includes tuition, fees, books, supplies, transportation, and miscellaneous living expenses. This sounds like a great idea, but there are pitfalls to avoid.
   a. *Useful transfer:* Applicants should take time to work with the community and technical college and the university to ensure that all courses taken at the two-year college transfer *and fulfill requirements in the bachelor's degree they are seeking.* Most states require public universities to accept all coursework taken at two-year colleges, but they do not and should not force public universities to count these courses toward a particular bachelor's degree.

Useful transfer means that courses count toward the bachelor's degree in which a student is interested. For example, a course in basic management taken at a two-year college has no place in an electrical engineering degree. Business schools at universities may have an accreditation rule that precludes accepting too many business courses taken at a two-year college.

b. *Curriculum match:* Even though a course title at a two-year college is the same or similar to a course title at a university, the contents may not match. The two institutions may even use the same textbook. For example, two courses may be labeled inferential statistics, but the depth of coverage for the two-year college course may be quite different, making it unsuitable for the bachelor's degree. It transfers as a free elective, which, most likely, does not count toward the bachelor's degree.

6.2 CHANGING EXPECTATIONS

Too many students and their parents expect to borrow money to pay for a university degree. Over time, the resistance to borrowing has declined and the amounts borrowed have increased substantially, placing many students in a difficult financial position.[15] It is important for students and their supporters to set a goal/expectation to graduate and be debt-free. To accomplish this, they should develop and implement plans to save more and spend less. Although seeking freedom from debt, they should demand a rigorous education so they receive the best value for their educational dollar. Better preparation leads to better jobs, higher pay, and more satisfaction.

6.2.1 Becoming Debt-Free

The scope of student loan debt is enormous. In 2016, the outstanding student load debt was $1.35 trillion with a default rate of nearly 12%. The average debt per borrower at four-year, public universities was nearly $27,000, whereas the comparable amount at four-year private universities was nearly $32,000. The average graduate student had a debt of $57,600.[16–18] The borrowing at two-year, community and technical colleges tended to be much less—about $2,000 per year.[1] In 1993, fewer than half of the graduates with bachelor's degrees borrowed money, but in 2015, it was 68%.[19] Student loan debt is the only form of consumer debt that has grown since the debt crisis in 2008. It has surpassed car loan and credit card debt, placing it second only to mortgage debt. Almost 30% of borrowers delayed getting married and moved back with their parents, over 40% delayed starting a family, over 60% delayed buying a car, over 70% delayed saving for retirement, and about 75% delayed buying a house.[19] The impact of student loan debt is substantial for the U.S. economy.

To most people, purchasing goods or services, even a $500 flat screen television, without debt seems out of kilter. Debt is the "American way," so there is a natural bias to use debt to pay for a university degree. Children see their parents and others use credit cards repeatedly to buy things, but the children rarely see the consequences of repaying debt. They only see how easy it is to buy things. With the rising costs of higher education and this cavalier attitude toward debt, it has become an important and accepted way to attain university degrees. Consider the following.

1. *Debt replaces planning:* Families often ignore or postpone financial planning for retirement, university costs, and other major purchases because it is a daunting task to identify future needs and deny current and sometimes impulsive consumption. For many people, the here and now is real and pressing, while intermediate and long-term needs are amorphous and uncertain. Instant gratification is satisfying, so the short-term path of least resistance is to spend more, work longer to build retirement, and borrow to pay for higher education. But, in fact, planning works to reduce the costs of higher education. The average borrowing by students in families with financial plans was 40% less than borrowing by students in families without plans. In addition, students in families that borrowed were less likely to live at home, only 40%, and incurred higher costs compared to nonborrowing families where 53% lived at home.[1]
2. *Borrowing begets borrowing:* Once parents and students accept borrowing as an important, even necessary, part of the solution, it is easier to borrow more, so students can work less and live more comfortably. Students do not have to compromise, just borrow.
3. *Borrowing is the contingency plan:* Borrowing is the way to deal with change and uncertainty. As problems arise, students are very comfortable with borrowing more to pay for things like repeating failed courses, taking extra courses because they changed their major, or

pursuing a double major. When borrowing is easy, students are more likely to accept these outcomes.

4. *Universities encourage borrowing:* "Everyone is doing it," so borrowing is becoming normal behavior, at least in the minds of many parents and students. Universities encourage and benefit from this viewpoint. They are quick to suggest that students, who are concerned about cost, borrow more. Universities use loans as a way to deflect criticism about the high cost of education, which is rising much more rapidly than the rate of inflation.

Families should have a financial plan that includes a budget for daily, weekly, and monthly operating expenses as well as for longer term expenditures such as automobiles, retirement, and higher education. Specifically, a budgeting for higher education should include the following:

1. *Cost estimation:* It begins with descriptions of what is required to attain a bachelor's degree: tuition, fees, learning materials, room and board, transportation, and miscellaneous expenses. These are discussed and presented in Chapter 1, Table 1.1 for the different types of institutions.
2. *Spend less on higher education:* These ideas are discussed earlier in this chapter.
3. *Spend less on other purchases:* Because higher education is only one part of the household budget, there are opportunities to spend less on other aspects of the operating and capital budgets. Cutting back on things like leisure, entertainment, clothing, and household expenses can over time generate substantial savings. Refinancing a house to lower the interest rate and mortgage payment, making cars last longer, and avoiding luxuries like hot tubs and power boats are a few of many ways to reduce capital expenses.
4. *Earn more:* Find a better job or secure part-time work to generate more income.
5. *Start early:* Financial consultants strongly suggest that planning begins as soon as possible. It is easier to pay for major purchases without borrowing, including higher education, when there are 15 or 20 years to save and invest.

Budgeting, planning, earning more, and spending less are all useful tools in becoming debt-free, but there are other important tips that can help students graduate without student loan debt. Many of these ideas require a long-term focus.

1. Taking advanced placement (AP) or international baccalaureate (IB) courses while in high school. Many high schools offer these courses, and there is no tuition or fees. High school students who complete these courses earn university credit.
2. Attending a university while in high school. In some states this is possible and students can attend tuition-free. More on this topic in Chapter 14 on revamping relationships with high schools and community and technical colleges.
3. Using employer benefits to pay for courses.
4. Working while in high school and saving money.
5. Having a parent work at the university. Universities often offer a discount or even free tuition for dependents of employees.
6. Using military benefits to pay for a university degree.
7. Taking 15 or 16 credit hours each term rather than 12. Students who take 12 credits each term require an extra year or maybe even two to complete their degree, which means another year or more of tuition, fees, room and board, and so on. Plus, the cost of tuition and fees for 12 credit hours and 16 credit hours is often the same. In addition, taking an extra year or two to complete the degree takes time away from career employment and good pay.
8. Attending online classes. Even if tuition is the same, students may not have to pay activity fees and they can live at home and take classes. Just make sure the courses are rigorous.[20]
9. Working in public service. There are some public service jobs that merit loan forgiveness under the College Cost Reduction and Access Act of 2007.[21]

6.2.2 Demanding a Rigorous Curriculum

Students, parents, other family members, and friends should demand a curriculum that has rich content and high performance standards. Such a curriculum has the following characteristics:

1. It is practical and linked to the needs of employers so graduates have the knowledge and skills that make them attractive employees.

2. It is theoretically and conceptually powerful so graduates understand the reasons for doing things a certain way and can adjust their knowledge, skills, and actions to meet changing circumstances.
3. It is useful for explaining the relationship between practice and theory.

The risk-averse nature of many students and the desire to graduate and find a good job causes some of them to want to learn less and follow a safer and easier path to these outcomes. When this attitude is held by a small portion of the student body, it can be dealt with by pressure from other students who want to learn more. However, as this portion of the student body increases, the problem becomes more acute. When it reaches a tipping point, this attitude causes standards to decline, which means all of the students learn less and the graduates are not as well prepared. As learning standards decline, graduates have fewer job opportunities and those jobs pay less, so students wanting to learn more and seeking better jobs select other universities. In fact, many organizations have preferred lists of universities where they recruit employees.

Rigorous has two dimensions: one related to content and the other related to standards. First, students should expect, in fact demand, that they learn as much as possible—learning more makes higher education a better value. Students get more for their money, and isn't that what shoppers want? It is difficult to understand why some students want to do less and learn less when they are paying thousands of dollars for each course and about $100,000 for a four-year degree at a public university. In fact, students should expect faculty to find ways for them to learn more and to do so in the same time and with the same effort. Although some may view this as a pipe dream, a plan so fanciful that it is very unlikely to be realized, advances in information technology, interactive video, and the Internet present learning opportunities that are uninvestigated and difficult to imagine. Faculty must consider new and innovative teaching methods, textbook publishers must develop better learning tools, and students must provide feedback on what helps them learn more, which is a powerful motivator for faculty.

Second, in an ideal world, students would demand high performance standards, but there are factors inhibiting this, including the desire for good grades and the good job that goes along with those grades. In addition, the traditional 18- to 22-year-old college students has limited if any knowledge about the performance standards for an accountant, engineer, pharmacist, or other professional. For these reasons, students should not have a role in setting learning standards. If a university's role is to prepare graduates for employment, then standards must be set by the needs of potential employers working with tenured and professional faculty. This approach would tend to set standards that are similar across different universities, one that does not fluctuate with students' abilities and expectations. As a result, the standards at an elite university and a regional university would not be radically different. This approach also helps to balance the curriculum content because potential employers tend to focus on the practical nature of higher education and faculty members tend to focus on theory and concepts.

6.2.3 Securing a Good Job

Graduates have every right to expect good jobs in their field of study, and universities have an important role in working with students to secure such a job. But universities do not create jobs in physical therapy, automotive design, urban planning, or other fields. Universities must provide applicants, students, and graduates with information about job availability, starting salaries, and career paths. Universities can help students network with leaders and key managers of organizations and create mechanisms to bring graduates and potential employers together. A discussion of how universities facilitate the job search process for graduates is offered in Chapter 8.

Students also have responsibilities to help themselves find good jobs. Generally speaking, students must consider the available information about job descriptions, wages, and career opportunities; try to assess what they would like to do in their working careers; consider trade-offs among various jobs; and select their field of study. In some cases, the choice is difficult. In one scenario, an applicant really wants to be a zoologist, but job growth is forecasted to be slow. Also, growth is uncertain because it depends in large measure on government funding, which is subject to budget cuts.[22] The second choice is registered nurse, which actually pays better, and nursing jobs are expected to grow at four times the rate of jobs for zoologists.[23] Should the student stick with his or her first choice or move to the second choice, which provides a better chance of employment and higher wages? Is the student willing to live with the possibility that a zoologist position is not available?

Many applicants come to universities with hopes and dreams, and they should pursue them with a full understanding of the risks they take. The student athlete who majors in recreational therapy, but really wants to make it in the National Basketball Association (NBA), may have to be satisfied with much lower pay and very different working arrangements if the NBA is unattainable. Starting salary for a recreational therapist in 2015 was about $30,000.[24] A political science major, who wants to run for public office, may end up in a staff position in a government office. Students who pursued the noble profession of social worker faced a median annual salary of $45,900 in 2015. The bottom 10% earned less than $28,530, while the top 10% earned more than $76,820.[25] Starting salaries with a bachelor's degree are "up to" $30,000.[26] There are jobs available. But can graduates live and repay their student loans on $30,000 or less? These are the difficult trade-offs that applicants must consider.

Data about job growth and salaries are available from the Bureau of Labor Statistics, which is part of the U.S. Department of Labor. (For access, go to http://www.bls.gov/ooh/) Consider the data in Table 6.2,[23,24,27] which is for three jobs in healthcare that have strong job growth and substantial patient contact: recreational therapist, registered nurse, and respiratory therapist. Recreational therapists typically require a bachelor's degree. Registered nurses usually have a bachelor of science in nursing (BSN), a three-year diploma, or an associate degree, although the trend is moving toward a BSN. Respiratory therapists typically have associate degrees, but they may have bachelor's degrees. Anyone who wants to be a recreational therapist

TABLE 6.2

Salary Data and Job Prospect for Recreational Therapist, Registered Nurse, and Respiratory Therapist

Job Title	10% Earned Less than	Median Salary	10% Earned More than	Projected Growth Rate from 2014 to 2024
Recreational therapist	$28,020	$45,890	$71,790	12%
Registered nurse	$46,360	$67,490	$101,630	16%
Respiratory therapist	$41,970	$57,790	$80,440	12%

Sources: Recreational Therapist, *Occupational Outlook Handbook*, 2015. http://www.bls.gov/ooh/healthcare/recreational-therapists.htm#tab-1; Registered Nurse, *Occupational Outlook Handbook*, 2015. http://www.bls.gov/ooh/Healthcare/Registered-nurses.htm#tab-1; Respiratory Therapist, *Occupational Outlook Handbook*, 2015. http://www.bls.gov/ooh/Healthcare/Respiratory-therapists.htm#tab-1

may want to consider the other two jobs because the median salary for registered nurses is about 50% higher and for respiratory therapists it is about 25% higher. Starting salaries for these professions are likely to be close to the amount listed under the "10% Earned Less Than" heading.

6.3 DRIVING FORCES FOR CHANGE

Students and their supporters can plan better and make better decisions about saving and spending. They also must take the lead and demand changes by universities by selecting universities that have kept costs low and maintained high quality. They must also work through governors, state legislatures, state boards of regents, state departments of education, university boards of trustees, and even the federal government as appropriate. High cost, limited access, and other problems with higher education have been bubbling to the surface for several decades. The time to take action is now.

6.4 IMPACT OF CHANGING ATTITUDES AND EXPECTATIONS ON HIGHER EDUCATION OUTCOMES

The first and probably the most important element of the comprehensive and integrated solution is changing customers' attitudes and expectations. Students, parents, other family members, and friends pay about 70% of the cost,[1] so it is critical that universities as well as state and local government hear loudly and clearly from them about the underlying problems, which are identified in Chapters 2 and 3. Changing attitudes and expectations (1) forces universities to learn more about customers, examine key cost drivers, and improve student services while keeping costs low and (2) it requires governments to examine how and to what extent they support higher education. Changing attitudes and expectations offers a way for students and their supporters to change the services they seek from universities so costs decline yet quality is maintained or even enhanced. It suggests that students come to the university with better preparation, and it encourages students to seek higher performance standards so they are better prepared.

The following list examines how this element of the solution impacts the root causes, which are discussed in Chapter 4 :

1. *Lack of understanding—Who is the customer? (root cause 1):* When students, parents, other family members, and friends shift their view from universities as "infallible and benevolent" to a provider of services, they will let universities know what they think of their product and what they expect for their educational dollar. Universities will be forced to understand what customers want and employ resources to do that more effectively and efficiently.
2. *Declining state support for public universities (root cause 2):* When students and their support groups let governors, state legislatures, and others know how they feel about high tuition costs, there may be opportunities for states to pressure universities to reduce costs. This could be coupled with additional state funding for universities that are successful.
3. *Rise of the ruling class: Administration (root cause 3):* Demanding a better education at a lower price requires universities to examine their cost structure, including the rapid increase in administrative cost over the past three plus decades.
4. *Limited productivity improvements for universities (root cause 4):* Continuing pressure on costs from students and their supporters would force administrators and faculty to consider ways to improve their efficiency, which means doing more or the same work with less effort and fewer resources.
5. *Rapidly growing costs for books and supplies (root cause 5):* Students and their supporters would have little direct impact on textbook publishers but can pressure universities to work more closely with publishers to reduce costs and improve the quality of learning. Making universities responsible for the cost of learning materials and including this cost in tuition would ensure a strong effort by universities to lower cost and enhance quality.
6. *Funding finesse—Mixing fees and tuition (root cause 6):* Fees should be for nonacademic activities. It seems reasonable to reduce or eliminate some fees and make others optional.
7. *Expanding student expectations (root cause 7):* Students control this directly by making choices to attend universities that have invested less heavily in expensive infrastructure such as lavish student housing and large sports programs.

8. *Eroding standards (root cause 8):* Students, their parents, other family members, and friends should demand to have more learning and higher performance standards, which would benefit students in their life after graduation.
9. *Lack of student preparation (root cause 9):* When parents understand what is expected from their children by universities, they are more likely to help their grade school and high school students understand the value of being well prepared to succeed in college.

6.5 SUMMARY OF RECOMMENDATIONS

Following is a list of the key recommendations that comprise this element of the solution.

1. Students, parent, other family members, and friends should change their attitude toward universities from benevolent dispensers of knowledge to providers of a key service. They must:
   a. Press universities for improvements in effectiveness and efficiency.
   b. Hold universities accountable for high costs, limited access, and the other problems facing higher education. This is relevant for sports programs, which can consume tuition dollars.
   c. Universities should not participate in outreach and engagement using tuition dollars. Government or other sources must provide special funding if universities are to participate.
   d. Make their feelings known to government and other oversight groups, so additional pressure is brought to bear.
   e. Shop around, pursue discounts, and pick their university based on finding the best value.
   f. Consider and evaluate ways to earn and save more money as well as keep educational costs low, so borrowing is greatly reduced or eliminated.
2. Government would create a database of HEPO that offers information about costs, graduation rates, completion time, passing rates for licensure and certification exams, and job placement. This should help applicants make informed choices.

3. Universities should be responsible to pay for textbooks and learning materials as part of the tuition payment. Universities have more leverage with companies who provide this material and can negotiate better prices.
4. Students and their supporters should change their expectation so they graduate debt-free. Long-term financial planning is a vehicle to identify appropriate levels of earning and saving as well as spending funds wisely and making good investments.
   a. Prepare and follow a budget for a university education so spending is targeted on essential items. Those who did spent 40% less.
   b. Students and their support group can earn more, save more, and borrow less. The key is to start early.
5. Students should demand a rigorous curriculum so they have a more valuable education.
6. Students should pick their major based on both interest in the work and the opportunity to secure a job that pays well. Too often students pick majors with limited job opportunities.

REFERENCES

1. SallieMae 2015. *How America Pays for College 2015*. http://news.salliemae.com/files/doc_library/file/HowAmericaPaysforCollege2015FNL.pdf (accessed June 16, 2016).
2. Berkowitz, S., Upton, J., and Brady, E. 2013. Most NCCA Division I athletic departments take subsidies. *USA Today*, July 1. http://www.usatoday.com/story/sports/college/2013/05/07/ncaa-finances-subsidies/2142443/ (accessed November 1, 2016).
3. Hobson, W., and Stevens, R. 2015. Playing in the red. *The Washington Post*, November 23. http://www.washingtonpost.com/sf/sports/wp/2015/11/23/running-up-the-bills/ (accessed November 1, 2016).
4. Peale, C. 2013. Athletics cost colleges, students millions. *USA Today*, September 15. http://www.usatoday.com/story/news/nation/2013/09/15/athletics-cost-colleges-students-millions/2814455/ (accessed November 1, 2016).
5. CollegeCalc. 2016. *Cheapest Colleges in California by State Tuition*. http://www.collegecalc.org/lists/california/most-affordable-in-state-tuition/?view=all (accessed October 29, 2016).
6. CollegeCalc. 2016. *Cheapest Colleges in Ohio by State Tuition*. http://www.collegecalc.org/lists/ohio/most-affordable-in-state-tuition/?view=all (accessed October 31, 2016).
7. Harvard University. 2016. *Cost of Attendance*. https://college.harvard.edu/financial-aid/how-aid-works/cost-attendance (accessed October 31, 2016).
8. Massachusetts Institute of Technology. 2016. *MIT Facts*. http://web.mit.edu/facts/tuition.html (accessed October 31, 2016).
9. Stanford University. 2016. *Tuition Costs and Other Expenses*. http://www.collegetuitioncompare.com/colleges/CA/Stanford/Stanford-University.html (accessed October 31, 2016).

10. The University of Chicago. 2016. *College Tuition Rates*. https://bursar.uchicago.edu/page/college-2015-16-tuition-rates (accessed October 31, 2016).
11. College Board. 2016. *Trends in Higher Education: Published Prices—National*. http://trends.collegeboard.org/college-pricing/figures-tables/published-prices-national#Published Charges, 2015–16 (accessed June 20, 2016).
12. Harvard University. 2016. *Acceptance Rate*. http://www.acceptancerate.com/schools/harvard-university (accessed October 31, 2016).
13. University Language Services. 2013. *Ivy League Average ACT Scores*, May 20. https://www.universitylanguage.com/blog/28/ivy-league-act-scores/ (accessed November 1, 2016).
14. Bruni, F. 2016. How to make sense of college rankings. *New York Times*, October 29. http://www.nytimes.com/2016/10/30/opinion/sunday/how-to-make-sense-of-college-rankings.html (accessed November 4, 2016).
15. United States Department of the Treasury and Department of Education. 2012. *The Economics of Higher Education*, December. https://www.treasury.gov/connect/blog/Documents/20121212_Economics%20of%20Higher%20Ed_vFINAL.pdf (accessed June 23, 2016).
16. Rathmanner, D. 2016. Student Loan Debt Statistics 2016. *Lendedu*, July 1. https://lendedu.com/blog/student-loan-debt-statistics (accessed October 29, 2016).
17. Harvey, J. T. 2014. Student load debt crisis? *Forbes*, April 28. http://www.forbes.com/sites/johntharvey/2014/04/28/student-loan-debt-crisis/#41b5c0c7614d (accessed October 29, 2016).
18. Federal Reserve Bank of New York. 2013. *Student Loan Debt*. https://www.newyorkfed.org/studentloandebt/index.html (accessed October 29, 2016).
19. Lobosco, K. 2016. Students are graduating with $30,000 in loans. *CNN Money*, October 18. http://money.cnn.com/2016/10/18/pf/college/average-student-loan-debt/index.html (accessed October 29, 2016).
20. Batai, M. 2016. 17 ways to pay for and afford college without student loan debt. *Money Crashers*. http://www.moneycrashers.com/ways-pay-for-afford-college/ (accessed November 4, 2016).
21. United States Government Publishing Office. 2007. *College Cost Reduction and Access Act*, September 27. https://www.gpo.gov/fdsys/pkg/PLAW-110publ84/pdf/PLAW-110publ84.pdf (accessed November 4, 2016).
22. Zoological and Wildlife Biologist. 2015. *Occupational Outlook Handbook*. http://www.bls.gov/ooh/life-physical-and-social-science/zoologists-and-wildlife-biologists.htm#tab-1 (accessed November 20, 2016).
23. Registered Nurse. 2015. *Occupational Outlook Handbook*. http://www.bls.gov/ooh/Healthcare/Registered-nurses.htm#tab-1 (accessed November 7, 2016).
24. Recreational Therapist. 2015. *Occupational Outlook Handbook*. http://www.bls.gov/ooh/healthcare/recreational-therapists.htm#tab-1 (accessed November 7, 2016).
25. Social Workers. 2015. *Occupational Outlook Handbook*. http://www.bls.gov/ooh/Community-and-Social-Service/Social-workers.htm#tab-1 (accessed November 7, 2016).
26. National Association of Social Workers. 2016. *Social Work Salaries*. http://careers.socialworkers.org/findajob/salarysurvey.asp (accessed November 7, 2016).
27. Respiratory Therapist. 2015. *Occupational Outlook Handbook*. http://www.bls.gov/ooh/Healthcare/Respiratory-therapists.htm#tab-1 (accessed November 7, 2016).

7

Becoming Student-Centered: The Right Way

Five decades ago, universities had not embraced the notion of being student friendly. Dormitories were best described as basic and cramped, food service was poor, registering for classes was an 8-hour ordeal, recreation centers were not available, and student services were inadequate and often unfriendly. Newly admitted students knew, or at least thought they knew, that universities had flunkout courses, which would separate the wheat from the chaff. The following story went around college campuses at the time, although there is no evidence that it actually happened. A university president began his (at the time nearly all university presidents were men) opening remarks at first-year student orientation. He said, "Look at the person to your immediate left and the person to your immediate right. Only one of you will graduate." Universities were not welcoming places.

As enrollment continued to grow for reasons discussed in Chapter 1, there seemed to be an endless supply of applicants. But, in the first half of the 1980s, the number of high school graduates began to decline as the last of the baby boomers graduated and children from the leading edge of the baby boomers, or the boomers' echo, were in elementary and middle school. As a result, universities faced a shortage in their primary feedstock: fresh-faced high school graduates. After decades of growth, which covered up overspending and poor management, many universities had to figure out how to attract more students, cut cost, or do both. Elite universities only had to reach a bit deeper into their applicant pool to maintain enrollment, but universities with less stature faced declines.

In response, universities adopted student-centered learning, which is the use of varying pedagogies, modified assignments, and different academic support strategies to address the distinct learning needs, interests, and cultural backgrounds of individual students. In essence, this is customized learning and is consistent with service dominant logic as discussed is Chapter 5. Student-centered learning, which dates back to the 1930s, is a substantial departure from teacher-centered learning where the instructor asserts control over the material and determines the pedagogy.[1] With teacher-centered learning, all students receive the same learning package. As the notion of student-centeredness was adopted to address enrollment concerns, it morphed into a student-first mentality across all aspects of student life, because it was not clear how to deliver customized education to thousands of students without busting the budget.

As a result, student-centered learning, the most important aspect of being student centered, was lost. In addition, becoming student centered caused universities to misjudge the needs of potential employers, who want highly capable graduates with up-to-date knowledge. When an intense focus on pleasing students and limited attention to potential employers are combined with an emphasis on retaining students, performance standards gradually eroded. Faculty members feel the pressure to lessen standards from students, who are pressed for time, and from administrators, who want higher retention rates. These tendencies are not counterbalanced by pressure from potential employers to maintain or increase standards. These factors also cover up a lack of preparation by many students.

Becoming student centered should be a positive experience because students get more respect, better treatment, and courteous, responsive, effective, and efficient services. Student services such as online registration and online financial aid make students' lives easier and may actually lower costs. Better facilities, such as dormitories and dining halls, and more amenities, such as student activities and legal services, have improved quality of life, but they have increased room and board costs as well as student activity fees. One irony is that some universities, which built these expensive dormitories, have vacant rooms, and they are requiring students who are unable to commute to live in campus housing. Being student centered seems to be in conflict with this requirement.

These points are related to becoming student centered and are discussed in the following sections.

1. *Cost impacts:* With respect to facilities and amenities: Has the pendulum swung too far? Are universities investing too much? Can student services be improved further while the cost of providing those services is reduced?

2. *Plans of study:* Being student centered means that students must have plans of study to identify what courses to take and when to take them in order to complete their degree on time and without paying for unneeded courses.
3. *Student-centered learning:* It is time to circle back and address this notion, which is designed to cope with the different ways students acquire knowledge. If learning can be tailored to match the needs of individual students, they can learn more in less time and use fewer resources, making education more efficient, thereby reducing costs.
4. *Student evaluations of teaching:* Being student centered has increased the incidence of student evaluations and given credence to their use in assessing faculty for contract renewal, promotion, and tenure. It seems reasonable and logical for students to have a role in evaluating faculty teaching, but it must be done so that academic standards are maintained.

7.1 UNDERSTANDING THE COST IMPACTS OF BEING STUDENT-CENTERED

Construction on university campuses boomed, as the growth in demand for higher education combined with efforts to become student centered. Students who stepped on campuses in the late 1940s, the 1950s, the 1960s, and even the 1970s would find today's campuses unrecognizable. Although it is difficult to know whether spending on facilities and amenities has gone too far, there are prominent people who believe that it has. Robert Reich, former U.S. Secretary of Labor and Professor of Public Policy at the University of California at Berkeley, claims that universities are spending on unnecessary programs and campus perks often at the expense of hiring faculty. These facilities and amenities are very expensive, contribute to escalating costs, and have little to do with educating students. Some universities are showcasing their value through impressive dining halls, palatial new buildings, and fancy student unions, which have little to do with the quality of education.[2] Some administrators defend the practice by claiming that facilities are often funded by major gifts from donors and do not consume tuition dollars or other operating funds.[2] There are two rebuttals. Each new building must be heated, cleaned, and maintained, which adds to operating expenses. Second, it is possible, maybe even likely, that donors would be willing to contribute to scholarships, which helps students and universities, or to other worthy projects rather than to new buildings.

The first step toward a solution is to ask: Does the university need more new buildings? The answer may be no for several reasons.

1. Even if enrollment continues to grow, the trend toward distance learning, where students do not attend classes on campus, will continue. Fewer students on campus mean fewer dormitories, eating establishments, parking structures, and classrooms.
2. Some have asked whether universities should outsource student housing to private companies. These companies could manage existing dormitories and likely build new ones more cheaply than universities. Let these organizations invest the capital and take the risk of offering student housing, and allow universities to focus on education.
3. If universities are really student centered, they would not require students who are not within a reasonable commuting distance to live on campus.
4. If universities change pedagogy to achieve student-centered learning, the new methods may require less classroom time and more time on the Internet, which means fewer classrooms, more capable computer networks, and high-speed data delivery across multiple platforms.
5. Administration has grown rapidly, and it has placed a huge cost burden on universities.[2] If and when this is addressed, there should be less demand for office space and parking garages.

The second step is to ask: If the university needs more buildings, how can they be designed and built to be functional, attractive, and cost less. At public universities, future construction must come under careful scrutiny by the university, state government, and the general public. This cannot be left to universities alone because senior leaders, especially presidents, like to point toward striking new buildings as major accomplishments that are part of their lasting legacy and a key factor in securing their next job. Not building or building only modestly is not a point of pride that attracts praise.

Amenities, like sports programs, student newspapers, clubs, and recreation centers, are paid for by student activity fees, which do not, at least in theory, support learning. Chapter 4 describes problems with the notification, collection, and use of fees. The following changes should be made.

1. Universities should adopt policies that student fees cannot, under any circumstances, be used for academic programs or academic-related administrative purposes, including building or refurbishing classroom facilities, faculty offices, and administrative spaces.
2. Students should have the right to decide whether they pay student fees or not. If fees do not support learning, why must students pay them? If they do not pay the fees, they do not get the services. Students can make the decision to opt out for many reasons. Students may not have interest in sports, clubs, and recreation; they may prefer spending money on other forms of entertainment and exercise; or they may live at home and commute. Some students are married with children, work full-time, and are part-time students, and other students have jobs, study hard, and attend classes. Neither group has time to participate in these activities. Other students may enroll in distance learning classes and never or rarely step foot on campus.
3. Tuition dollars must be spent for academic purposes and for administration that is directly related to academics. This precludes universities from increasing tuition to cover nonacademic amenities like sports programs and recreation centers.
4. All costs for learning, such as day-to-day student access to computers or library expenses, must be paid by tuition. When there are academic expenses for particular courses that compel an additional charge, such as laboratory courses requiring expensive equipment and supplies or design courses needing extraordinary computer access, these must be clearly designated as "tuition surcharges." These exceptions should be rare and well documented by the institution.

Part of becoming student-centered is offering better services such as online registration and automated systems so students can easily monitor progress toward graduation. As universities seek to make these improvements, and they should, it is essential to use technology, lean thinking, and value stream mapping to design innovative systems that eliminate waste and use resources more efficiently. Too often, universities simply automate the current manual process, capturing the error and redundancies and not taking advantage of capabilities inherent in the technology.

For more information on this, there are a few books that describe the application of lean thinking to universities, including W. K. Balzer (2010), *Lean Higher Education: Increasing the Value and Performance of University Processes* (Boca Raton, FL: CRC Press/Taylor & Francis Group).[3]

7.2 PREPARING A PLAN OF STUDY

A plan of study is a list of courses that students must complete as well as a timetable for completion, so students graduate in the shortest possible time and avoid paying for courses that are not needed for graduation. For a bachelor's degree, the plan is an eight-semester schedule that students should follow. For students without prior coursework, this means finishing the degree in four years, so graduates can begin their careers as soon as possible. For transfer students, it is the shortest path to graduation.

In effect, plans of study are contracts between students and the institution that place demands on the institution to offer courses in sufficient quantities and at the proper times so students are not "closed" out of classes and forced to wait for graduation. Plan of study software must have the ability to track progress toward graduation. Students must have fast and easy access so they can check and verify their progress as often as they like. This software would be linked to registration software and would warn students and their advisor, when students are (1) registering for a courses that is not in the plan of study, (2) not registering for a course that is in the plan of study, and (3) registering for a course now that should be taken later. This provides students and advisors with sufficient time to discuss the schedule for the semester and to keep students on track for graduation. There are other circumstances that may require a change to the plan, such as illness that causes students not to complete courses. No matter the cause, a new plan of study is created with the intent of enabling students to complete the degree in as short a time as possible. All changes must be agreed to by the students.

7.3 IMPLEMENTING STUDENT-CENTERED LEARNING

The heart of student-centeredness is creating pedagogies that are customized to meet the different learning strengths of individuals. A first reaction might be that customized learning is too expensive because faculty and students would have to work closely in one-on-one sessions or in small groups, much smaller than typical class sizes used at public universities today with 30, 40, 50, or 300 or 400 students. Using traditional pedagogies, such as lecture and discussion or case analysis, in small groups, even in groups as small as 10 or 15, would drive instructional costs at public universities "through the roof."[1] The plan is to use advanced technology to develop customized learning so costs are low.

Experts in the field have identified the following seven learning styles. Understanding these styles may provide useful information about appropriate careers. For example, engineers often learn visually, logically, and physically, whereas psychologists may learn best verbally and socially.

1. *Verbal (Linguistic):* These learners like to read, write, and communicate verbally, and they learn best by saying, hearing, and seeing words.
2. *Visual (Spatial):* They are very good at working with colors and pictures and using the "mind's eye" to understand and resolve complex problems. They learn best when words are replaced with pictures and when colors are used to highlight important points.
3. *Logical (Mathematical):* These are analytical problem solvers who learn best by categorizing, classifying, and working with abstract patterns and relationships. A systems perspective and thinking help them understand the big picture.
4. *Aural (Auditory-Musical):* They use sound, rhythm, and music to learn. They often learn best when reading or studying with music in the background.
5. *Physical (Kinesthetic):* Hands-on learning using physical objects suit these learners. They may also create and use drawings and diagrams to learn and explain ideas.
6. *Social (Interpersonal):* They prefer to learn in groups and with other people. They enjoy role playing and tackling group assignments.
7. *Solitary (Intrapersonal):* They prefer working alone. They are independent, pursue their own interests, and have a deep understanding of themselves. They do best in self-paced instruction and individualized projects.[4,5]

A review of these learning styles indicates that the distinctions among the seven types are not razor sharp. For example, both visual and physical learners prefer drawings and diagrams as learning tools, whereas social and physical learners benefit from role playing. Further, there is not a one-person to one-learning style relationship. People often learn well in more than one way, and they may use different learning styles when facing different topics and circumstances. Some people may find it easier to learn statistics using the logical learning style because it suits the topic better, but they may grasp philosophical concepts more effectively using the social learning style. It is important for students to experiment and understand what works best for them. Universities should provide a set of learning tools for each course that delivers knowledge using different methods, although it is possible that one tool could incorporate more than one learning style. Having several learning tools allows students to choose the ones that work best for them.

The following example illustrates how this might work for a basic course in statistics. This should be considered a first pass at designing a course to cope with different learning styles.

1. *Lecture:* It may be possible to offer this course without face-to-face lecture and discussion.
2. *Reading materials:* Electronic reading materials or e-books are available that have text, diagrams, and charts, as well as example questions and problems, which students can read and follow. Collectively, universities are in a position to negotiate better prices with textbook publishers than students, especially for e-books. They can use their leverage to gain more content and features at a lower price.
3. *Electronic sample test questions:* Computer-based, conceptual questions are provided that students can respond to. The computer identifies correct and incorrect answers, and takes students to the point in the e-book where information about the question is found.
4. *Electronic sample test questions:* Computer-generated problems are provided for students to solve, and they know immediately whether the answer is right or wrong as well as get hints about the errors that were made. Students may work these problems repeatedly because the computer can generate new data. (E-books with these questions and problems capabilities are being developed by textbook providers.)
5. *Videos:* Video vignettes explain key concepts and work problems in a step-by-step manner, so students understand why they are doing

something, how to do it, and what it means when they are done. The videos would be short, maybe 10 to 15 minutes, and focus on a topic. They could replace traditional lectures, and students could access them repeatedly.

6. *Written assignments:* Even courses like statistics should require some written communication. So assignments would include describing statistical concepts and application in written form as well as discussing and interpreting the numerical answers to problems. These assignments could be completed on a computer network, and students would receive immediate feedback.
7. *Instructors' duties:* Hold voluntary, weekly help sessions where students can raise question and get answers. Instructors are also available online to answer questions and chat with students.
8. *Working groups:* Groups of five or six students may be established so they can share knowledge and work together on concepts and problems. There would be opportunities for the group to query the instructor for help.

There are three important outcomes to pursue when designing instructional packages.

1. *Enhance learning:* Students learn more in less time and with less effort, thus freeing time so they can take addition courses in a semester, work more hours, or participate in other activities.
2. *Reduce costs:* If the instructional packages are creative and thoughtful, universities can deliver a student-centered learning course at a lower cost than one offered in a traditional lecture mode. With this new approach, less tenured and professional faculty time is needed and much of the face-to-face as well as the Internet interactions can be done by instructors and lecturers, who earn substantially less.
3. *Effective design and implementation:* Tenured and professional faculty members design the learning materials. They also create and grade tests, taking this duty away from instructors and lecturers. Financial incentives could be given to instructors and lecturers based the number of students who meet all the learning objectives for the course, as determined by the final examination. Incentives can be given because the design of course content, test construction, and grading are not part of their responsibility, but good teaching and learning are.

One final point is that universities would have to make a more substantial investment in course development than they do currently. Now, faculty members spend time designing the curricula, picking a textbook and cases, and creating or selecting lecture materials such as PowerPoint slides and homework assignments. With videos, interactive learning systems, and other tools, someone has to take the time and invest in their development. This upfront cost should be recovered through instructional savings. This approach is consistent with the concept of economies of scale, which means investing in fixed cost so the variable cost of operating is reduced, thereby reducing total cost. Designing course materials to address different learning styles interacts with Chapter 10 on Redesigning Curriculum and Pedagogy, Chapter 12 on Reshaping Faculty's Role, and Chapter 13 on Creating High-Tech Learning Materials.

7.4 CHANGING THE WAY STUDENTS EVALUATE FACULTY

Chapter 4 describes the problem created when students evaluate faculty, especially instructional faculty. In summary, instructional faculty members are not protected by tenure and are evaluated for contract renewal based on teaching performance as assessed by students. As a result, they are susceptible to comments from students that a course is too difficult and/or covers too much material. Therefore, instructional faculty members are under pressure to cover less and reduce standards to appease students. Professional faculty members are far less susceptible to this pressure because they have decades of experience, which helps them understand what students should know and hold the line against this pressure.

The solution to the problem has three parts, and the first part is discussed in the prior section.

1. *Take instructional faculty out of the line of fire:* When instructors and lecturers have no control over course content and do not write or grade the test, they receive less pressure and fewer negative comments from students. Content and performance standards for courses are set by potential employers working with tenured and professional faculty.

2. *Measure teaching effectiveness by student performance:* Assessing the teaching effectiveness of instructional faculty is no longer done with student evaluations. Rather, it is accomplished by pretesting and posttesting each student. A subject matter pretest is given during the first class to determine the students' level of competence. The final examination measures what students know at the end, and the difference between the two is what the students have learned. Both the final exam, which is an absolute learning standard, and the difference between the two tests, which is a relative standard, are used to assess the teaching performance of instructional faculty. This approach is useful for tenured and professional faculty as well.
3. *Gather different student input:* Student evaluations are still used, but they no longer ask questions such as: How much have students learned? Was the faculty member a good teacher? Did the students like the faculty member? Asking most 18- to 22-year-old students about these issues presupposes that they have some idea of what they should learn, when in fact they have limited knowledge about what they need to know to compete for good jobs at graduation. The revised student evaluation gathers feedback on the following:
   a. Student experiences, including what learning tools would help them learn faster and easier. This relates to student-centered learning and the seven learning styles, so the evaluation might ask if and how they used specific tools and were these effective.
   b. Faculty performance, which should emphasize things students can readily and reliably assess. Were students treated courteously and respectfully? Did the instructor provide clear and prompt feedback on performance? Did the instructor arrive on time? Was the instructor well prepared? Students can provide meaningful feedback about treatment and process, and their answers can be part of the instructors' evaluation.

7.5 DRIVING FORCES FOR CHANGE

Some of the changes are within the control of universities, so government, students, parents, other family members, and friends should be providing the pressure. If universities want to attract more students, they must embrace all aspects of being student centered, including student-centered learning. Faculty members are key players in this change, so they must buy into and lead these efforts. Although this entails upfront investment, university leader who understand the value and potential costs savings will choose to move forward. Public universities, under pressure from government, students, and students' support groups, should work hard to improve student services and lower administrative costs. This creates better value for students, which leads to lower tuition costs and higher enrollment. University administrators and tenured faculty must work together to change how faculty are evaluated so instructional faculty feel less pressure to reduce course content and decrease learning standards.

Two parts of the solution require government to take the lead. Universities are likely to resist any attempt to make student fees optional. They may go along with the ideas that student fees can only be spent for nonacademic purposes and that funds cannot be comingled, but even these ideas are likely to meet resistance. Second, state governments provide funds to expand infrastructure and should press public universities to thoroughly examine their plans for new buildings to prevent overinvestment. As a last resort, states can decide to provide capital funds only for maintaining existing buildings.

7.6 IMPACT OF BECOMING STUDENT-CENTERED ON HIGHER EDUCATION OUTCOMES

Universities have been working to become student-centered for many years, and they have improved in some areas such as treating students with more respect and providing better services. But they have not reached the top of the mountain, which is finding ways to customize their pedagogies to cope with different learning styles and focusing on what may be the single biggest problem with higher education: rapidly rising costs. The following list examines how this element of the solution impacts the root causes, which are discussed in Chapter 4.

1. *Lack of understanding—Who is the customer? (root cause 1):* The essence of being student centered is to understand the needs of students, but it goes further to recognize that students are best served

when universities create strong links with another of its customers, potential employers. Finding employment is a critical outcome that students want.

2. *Rise of the ruling class: Administration (root cause 3):* Becoming student centered also means providing students with the best value, so cutting administrative cost is important because it improves the value proposition.
3. *Limited productivity improvements for universities (root cause 4):* Changing the pedagogy to create an environment for student-centered learning offers a way to improve the productivity of faculty and lower instructional costs.
4. *Rapidly growing costs for books and supplies (root cause 5):* Student-centered universities must work with textbook publishers to create new and innovative ways to learn while cutting costs. Universities are in a better position to negotiate prices with publishers than students.
5. *Funding finesse—Mixing fees and tuition (root cause 6):* Student-centered learning means that students determine whether they pay fees or not.
6. *Eroding standards (root cause 8):* Student-centered learning requires universities to do what is best for students. To do this, universities must maintain standards so students are qualified for good jobs with organizations that hirer their graduates.
7. *Lack of student preparation (root cause 9):* An intense focus on satisfying students and declining enrollment creates an environment that covers up the lack of preparation. It is important to expose this problem and create a solution.

7.7 SUMMARY OF RECOMMENDATIONS

Following is a list of the key recommendations that comprise this element of the solution.

1. Being student centered means that students get more respect, better treatment, and services that are courteous, responsive, effective, and efficient.

2. Building new dormitories must be carefully examined given the trend toward distance learning, and outsourcing the ownership, construction, and operation of dormitories must be considered.
3. Universities that make students a priority should not require them to live on campus.
4. Universities must examine future trends in higher education to determine how changes in the pedagogy, size of administration, and other factors impact the need to build new facilities.
5. After this careful examination, if universities need more buildings, they must find ways to design and build them to be functional, attractive, and cost less.
6. Student fees must be spent for nonacademic purposes and paying fees is at the option of the students. Funds for academic purposes and nonacademic purposes must not be comingled.
7. Students deserve fast and easy access to services. It is important to use technology, lean thinking, and value stream mapping to design and implement new and innovative processes.
8. Every student must have a plan of study that identifies which courses to take and when they should take them to graduate in the shortest possible time.
9. Universities must diversify their pedagogy to cope with the various learning styles of students. Efforts to do so should enhance learning, reduce costs, and change the roles and responsibilities of faculty. Universities must invest in the upfront cost to create this new pedagogy.
10. The process for students to evaluate faculty must change so instructional faculty are under less pressure to reduce course content and lower learning standards.
    a. Take instructional faculty out of the line of fire by making tenured and professional faculty responsible for course content, test creation, and grading.
    b. Assess teaching effectiveness of contractual faculty and tenured faculty by evaluating them based on what students learned in their courses, using pretesting and posttesting.
    c. Student evaluations assess the (1) availability and use of learning tools to help students learn faster and easier and (2) performance of faculty, which emphasize how students were treated.

REFERENCES

1. The Glossary of Education Reform. 2014. *Student-Centered Learning.* http://edglossary.org/student-centered-learning/ (accessed November 8, 2016).
2. McNutt, M. I. 2014. Why does college cost so much? *US News World Report*, September 22. http://www.usnews.com/news/college-of-tomorrow/articles/2014/09/22/why-college-costs-so-much-overspending-on-faculty-amenities (accessed June 24, 2016).
3. Balzer, W. K. 2010, *Lean Higher Education: Increasing the Value and Performance of University Processes.* Boca Raton, FL: CRC Press/Taylor & Francis.
4. Gardner, H. 2011. *Frames of Mind: The Theory of Multiple Intelligences.* Philadelphia, PA: Basic Books.
5. Lepi, K. 2012. The 7 styles of learning: Which works for you? *Edudemic: Connecting Education and Technology*, November 27. http://www.edudemic.com/styles-of-learning/ (accessed January 24, 2017).

8

Building Bridges to Potential Employers

Some faculty and administrators may push back on the notion that most students attend college to get better jobs and earn more money. But logic supports these motives, and there are data to back this up. A national survey of first-year college students reports the top-five reasons for attending college. The number next to the reason is the percent of respondents who rated it very important. Three of the top-five objectives are about jobs and money.

1. Get a better job—85%
2. Learn about things that interest me—83%
3. Train for a specific career—78%
4. Gain a general education and appreciation of ideas—72%
5. Make more money—71%

The same survey listed the number-one life priority as "Being well off financially" with 77% considering it to be essential or very important.[1] It seems reasonable to speculate that if these questions were given to parents that the percentages for good jobs and money would be even higher.

It seems clear that job opportunities and earnings are important to students and their parents. Elite universities with deep pockets and lots of applicants may be able to ignore these priorities and maintain enrollment and revenue, although one of their big advantages is networking, which is very useful in securing good jobs. Public universities, especially those with a regional reach, have an opportunity to separate themselves from their competitors by building strong links to potential employers. When junior high and high school students and their parents see high school graduates succeeding at a university and getting good jobs, they are inclined to consider this university seriously. Even without this incentive, asking students to spend $100,000 and four or more years of their lives to earn university degrees requires a substantial payoff. Good careers and incomes are important parts of that payoff.

8.1 CONTEXT FOR REACHING OUT TO POTENTIAL EMPLOYERS

A key premise of this book is that universities face a trifurcated customer: students who seek learning, third parties who typically pay a substantial part of the bill, and potential employers. Universities, operating as professional service organizations, should mediate the relationship between students and potential employers by (1) gathering information about the needs of employers, (2) designing the curricula to satisfy those needs, and (3) delivering the curricula to students. In the process, universities engage in service dominant logic, which is close cooperation among tenured and professional faculty, students, potential employers, and suppliers of learning materials. The intent is to continuously improve and individualize the service/education to meet the needs of specific customers[2]—the essence of student-centered learning. In the process, value is co-created, which means all participant groups contribute in a meaningful way.

1. *Tenured and professional faculty:* They are mediators who understand and pull together students' expectations and employers' needs for qualified workers. They also have the technical expertise and know-how to create curricula that can be effectively delivered to meet the various learning styles of students. They work with suppliers of textbooks and other learning materials to develop a set of tools to satisfy these different learning styles. This is a dynamic process that improves continuously as it learns how to do things better, faster, and cheaper. The process must also adjust to different student capabilities, new knowledge requirements, and technical innovations in teaching and learning.
2. *Students:* They should make efforts to understand how they learn best and what tools and techniques are best suited to their learning style. Tenured and professional faculty members mediate interactions between students and potential employers. This interaction provides an understanding of what students need to learn to have

successful careers, thereby creating a dynamic learning process that links students and employers.

3. *Potential employers:* They have opportunities to participate at the beginning, in the middle, and the end of the learning process. In curricula design, they work with tenured and professional faculty to offer information about the capabilities and knowledge their future employees must have. During the instruction phase, they can offer internship and cooperative education opportunities so students have hands-on experiences. They can meet with student groups to discuss working in this business or that industry as well as offer projects and programs where students and student groups compete. At graduation, potential employers work closely with university placement services to find the "right" employees—matches that are good for both.
4. *Suppliers of learning materials:* They contribute knowledge and experience in designing high-technology, innovative methods for delivering knowledge across multiple formats. They are key players in providing a diversified portfolio of learning tools.

Figure 8.1 illustrates these relationships. Tenured and professional faculty is the hub of the network, interacting directly with all participants, including suppliers of learning materials. Moving from left to right in Figure 8.1, applicants, who have expectations about job opportunities and earnings, become students and follow the curricula designed by tenured

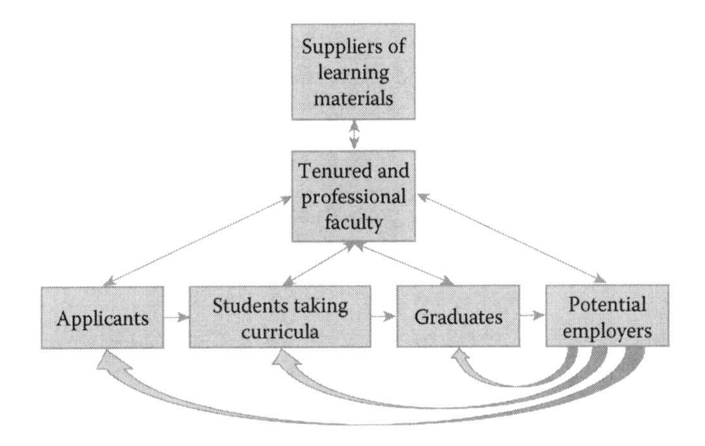

FIGURE 8.1
Reaching out to potential employers and bringing them into the learning process.

and professional faculty with inputs from potential employers. Ultimately, students become graduates seeking jobs. Potential employers interact with (1) applicants through their expectations, (2) students by offering advice as well as opportunities for hands-on education, and (3) graduates at the recruiting and hiring stage. This three-stage approach effectively links applicants, students, and graduates to potential employers.

It is important to clarify that potential employers are not limited to private-sector, for-profit firms. In fact, there are many good job opportunities in government, foundations, and other not-for-profit organizations. Also, many applicants-students-graduates seek admission to graduate schools, which have roles that are similar to the roles of potential employers because they identify what students must learn to secure admission. In addition, some professions such as engineering and nursing have certification processes and licensure exams, and the criteria for these must be incorporated in the curricula.

Creating meaningful relationships with potential employers, graduate schools, and entities that oversee certification and licensure requirements demands (1) a commitment from universities that this is important for educating students properly and (2) a structure that is capable of exchanging ideas and using this to improve learning outcomes. The following activities represent a good start. References to potential employers are meant to include graduate schools and entities for certification and licensure as appropriate.

1. *Establish program advisory boards:* Advisory boards bring potential employers into the process. The time commitments by universities and employers as well as a willingness by universities to share curricula design duties provide compelling evidence of the importance of this activity.
2. *Link admissions to degree programs to job placement:* Applicants, students, and graduates see benefits from interacting with employers. At the same time, potential employers see how they benefit by having opportunities to recruit better prepared graduates. At each stage, the following are needed to make this work.
    a. *Access to job opportunity and wage data:* Applicants should have current, four to six years, and long-term data about jobs and wages, so they can select a program of study.
    b. *Build relationships between students and potential employers:* These relationships help students understand the value of what

they are learning, see how they might apply it, and study harder and learn more so they are better prepared.

c. *Create better mechanisms to link graduates and employers:* Universities should develop mechanisms so students and employers can become better acquainted and gain insights about each other so job placements are enhanced for both groups.

8.2 CREATING PROGRAM ADVISORY BOARDS

Program advisory boards (PABs) are vehicles for reaching out to potential employers, graduate schools, and licensure and certification agencies. The primary purposes of PABs are to determine curricula and set performance standards so graduates are well prepared; that is, they are able to work in entry-level positions without substantial supplemental training and education. PABs enable tenured faculty to understand the hands-on aspects of work and give potential employers an appreciation of concepts and theories. It is this blending process that (1) increases common ground between faculty and employers and (2) enhances the quality of curricula. PABs should allow employers to get to know students and provide faculty with "real-world" support as they seek approval for new curricula through a laborious and convoluted university review process.

PABs should be built at the program/major level rather than at the college or university level. This is essential because having separate PABs in mechanical engineering, chemical engineering, finance, social work, and nursing enable relationships with different employers so content and standards are appropriate for the subject matter and employment opportunities. In departments with only one program/major, it is clear that only one PAB is needed. Other departments may have more than one program, and they require one PAB for each program. A few interdisciplinary programs are supported by faculty in more than one discipline or department, so only one advisory board is needed, even though two or more departments support the program.

Membership in PABs usually includes leadership from the university, which may be a department chair or program director, as well as tenured and professional faculty from the program and well-placed industry executives. These executives should be working in the field of study around which the PAB is organized. Thus, a PAB for a civil engineering degree might include a civil engineer who is the head of design services for a construction company but not someone from human resources who assists in the hiring process. A PAB for social work might include a lead social worker who supervises case workers at the county's Children Services unit. Choosing practicing professionals provides better insights about the knowledge and skills needed by entry-level employees. PAB leadership can be shared between university and employer members through an executive board that has a mix of both groups and possibly a student member or two, who can provide their perspective. Many degree programs have student clubs or associations, and a leader from one of these entities could be an ideal member.

There are some important operational points to consider. Well-placed executives, the people who can contribute effectively to PABs, are busy, so it is essential to use their time wisely. Meetings involving the entire group should be no more than quarterly, and semi-annually is better. The real work is done by the executive committee and small subcommittees with a few members and a specific charge.

8.3 LINK ADMISSIONS TO DEGREE PROGRAMS TO JOB PLACEMENT

As PABs are established, it is important to understand the touch points among tenured and professional faculty, potential employers, and applicants who become students and eventually graduate. Applicants should be interested in jobs, starting salaries, and career advancements, and they need data and career advice to make these decisions. As students, they want to learn many things, including relevant theory and concepts, best practices, written and verbal communication, and presenting themselves well, so they can compete for the best jobs. Prior to graduation, they must be connected to potential employers that are interested in their talents.

8.3.1 Providing Placement and Job Data

Some applicants know their field of study and graduate without changing their major. However, many do not, so they begin in a general education curriculum. Others who think they know what they want begin in one field of study and change their major after being disappointed by the content of the courses and/or having a fuller understanding of what the career involves. These events usually increase completion time and costs. They are difficult to eliminate completely, but it is possible to minimize these delays and extra costs by providing as much placement and job data as possible. It is worth the time to investigate and make better decisions because enrolling in even one course that does not count toward graduation can cost a few thousand dollars extra.

Universities should be required to offer placement and job data for their graduates and alumni. Data from recent graduates are relatively easy to collect as students apply for and are cleared for graduation. They may chose not to respond, but most will, and nonrespondents can be counted and reported as such. However, it is more difficult to collect data for alumni who graduated several years ago. The good news is that universities invest considerable effort and spend large amounts of money to track alumni for the purpose of fundraising. The same system can be used to collect placement and job data for alumni. Once again, some may chose not to respond, but that can be addressed. These data provide applicant, students, and graduates with useful information about jobs, salaries, and careers. It is also true that these data are likely to contain biases and errors, but the intent is to show big differences in outcomes that may cause a student to select a different field of study.

Job information and placement data are also available in the Occupational Outlook Handbook (https://www.bls.gov/ooh/), which is published by the U.S. Bureau of Labor Statistics. It is a rich source of information on hundreds of jobs, and it provides a national perspective on current and future job markets, but it is not broken down by university. The information in the handbook is summarized here and is a useful complement to the university data.

1. *Pay:* The median salary as well as the salary floor (the "lowest 10% earned less than" amount or the 10th percentile) and the salary ceiling (the "highest 10% earned more than" amount or the 90th percentile) are available.
2. *Job outlook:* Discusses the job market broadly and breaks it down by occupational title. This includes short-term job prospect as well as 10 years in the future. It provides the estimated percent change in employment (job growth rate) as well as employment by industry.
3. *What holders of the job do:* Describes the duties and responsibilities of the job.

4. *Work environment:* Lists the industries that employ these workers, discusses the settings where they work, and describes work schedules and conditions.
5. *How to become one:* Explains the educational requirements, licenses, and certification that are necessary, as well as other important qualifications.
6. *State and area data:* Occupational employment projections are provided by labor market or individual states.
7. *Similar occupations:* Basic information is available for jobs with similar duties and responsibilities, and links to those jobs are provided.[3]

The responsibilities for universities are clear. They must make a concerted effort to provide access to both university data and handbook data for applicants, students, and graduates. Applicants must be encouraged to examine this information and have the Internet addresses for these websites. As applicants visit universities, presentations and discussion should refer to these data and show applicants how to access them. When advisers and counselors discuss fields of study with students, they must use this information. Each plan of study, which is a description of the course requirements for a specific major, must include a brief description as well as links to these data. Departments and programs should display salary and job availability data from these websites.

8.3.2 Building Relationships between Students and Potential Employers

PABs play a key role in making students more aware of the world of work, the importance of professional behavior, and the value of building closer linkages between students and potential employers. This can take many forms, including cooperative education and internships, where students work in "career-like" jobs, as well as mentorships that allow potential employers to counsel students.

8.3.2.1 Cooperative Education and Internships

In professions like pharmacy, engineering, finance, education, medicine, and others, there is substantial value in hands-on learning, which is identified as one of the learning styles discussed in Chapter 7. Hands-on learning is widely used in training physicians and teachers with residency programs and student teaching. It is also used in engineering, pharmacy, and business. PABs can be the foundation for creating strong and effective cooperative education and internship experiences, which put students to work in jobs that are career related.

1. *Internship experiences:* An internship is career-related employment that can take place during the Fall, Spring, or Summer semesters. Students may be compensated, and they earn credit toward their university degree, so they are required to pay tuition for the internship. The work is often part-time, and students may take traditional classes simultaneously. Internships are usually nearby because students are taking other classes. Colleges of Education have used student teaching, which is an internship, for decades as a way to prepare students. They earn credit but are usually not compensated. Many Colleges of Business allow students to work at career-related jobs, receive a salary, and earn credit toward graduation. Some internships require full-time employment and are offered during the summer months with students assigned to project teams and given responsibility for specific tasks.
2. *Cooperative education (COOP):* Although this option has similar intent to internships, that is, providing hands-on learning, its structure is different. COOPs are full-time work experiences that are compensated. A COOP session usually lasts for one semester, and students take more than one. Students do not take courses simultaneously, and the job does not have to be close by. Students typically do not earn university credit, so no tuition is paid.

There are a number of advantages associated with COOPs and internships for both students and employers. Students (1) gain a measure of professionalism as they understand what it takes to arrive on time, be responsible for doing a job, and work with others to accomplish goals, (2) see the application of theories and concepts that they are learning in school, and (3) become motivated to prepare, study, and learn because they see the value of their education. Without making a substantial commitment, employers can evaluate the talents of students and make better decisions about whom to hire.

8.3.2.2 Working Directly with Students

PABs are also useful to create mentorships between employers and students. Employers can offer advice about career options, answer questions about certificates and licensure, and facilitate students as they create their professional networks. Students can gain experience with social media, such as LinkedIn, to build their networks. Employers on the PAB can meet with small groups of students to (1) offer their perspective on interviewing and creating attractive resumes, (2) give advice and answer questions related to students' professional development, and (3) make presentation to clubs and student groups that explain important ideas and practices students may use in their jobs. PABs also help students prepare for the recruiting process.

8.3.3 Creating the Mechanism for Recruiting

As students approach graduation, universities must build robust processes that support recruiting. This begins when applicants gain insights about salaries, job responsibilities, educational requirements, and other information about careers. This continues with COOPs, internships, and other interactions with PABs. The next step is developing mechanisms for recruiting. Most universities have an office called placement services or something similar, but it is often nothing more than a list of organizations that are coming to campus to conduct interviews, a set of signup sheets so students can get interviews, and a bank of rooms and a lounge with coffee for the interviewers and the interviewees.

In developing a recruiting mechanism, an essential parameter is decentralizing the design and operation of the system, so it effectively meets the needs of potential employers and students. The processes for hiring high school teachers, geographers, social workers, supply chain managers, and botanists are different. In some disciplines such as premedicine, nearly all graduates pursue admission to graduate school, so the placement model is very different. Expertise regarding the needs of students and expectations of potential employers is held by faculty and administrators who operate at the program level or possibly the college level but not at the university level. There may be some basic resources, including information systems and interview facilities, that could be shared, but how these resources are used should be determined by program or college leaders and their faculty.

Preparation for the job search should begin no later than the sophomore year of study. Most people will work for 40 plus years after graduating with a bachelor's degree. They are likely to work 40 plus hours each week out of a total of 168 hours. After sleeping, work is the biggest time commitment for many adults. It only seems reasonable to expend significant effort to make the best choice possible.

1. *Sophomore year:* In addition to COOP and internship opportunities as well as meeting with PAB members, starting a formal process for professional development is appropriate. A short course on professional development in the sophomore year would discuss the jobs available in different fields as well as writing resumes, preparing for interviews, and being and acting in a professional manner. This is discussed in Chapter 10 on Redesigning Curriculum and Pedagogy. Some faculty and administrators may object to making this course a requirement for graduation, but if universities do not do so, most sophomores will simply not attend.
2. *Junior year:* COOPs, internships, and other activities with the PAB continue. Students are invited to interact with potential employers, which could be in many forms. A job fair is a common one. Potential employers are invited to campus to meet with juniors and seniors. Juniors are invited in order to become acquainted with the kinds of jobs that are available. They must prepare a resume and present it to potential employers. Juniors are not necessarily asking for a job or seeking an interview, but they gain experience and prepare for their senior year.
3. *Senior year:* For seniors, the job fair, which should be held in the Fall semester, kicks off the recruiting season. Program directors and college leaders must be proactive and seek potential employers to participate in job fairs and come to campus for interviews. Students should not rely solely on these efforts. There are many jobsites on the Internet that allow students and others to post their resume. Students who have developed a network of contacts can use the network to find job opportunities.

The response from universities is likely to be: "Where are the funds to support these efforts? It will cost too much." The fast and easy answer is that having employed graduates should be a vital part of a university's mission, and they need to find the resources. The more careful, deliberate, and accurate answer is that resources are already being consumed. Faculty must design effective curricula, so they need to reach out to potential employers. With potential employers providing input, it is possible that curricula development may take less time because there is an independent arbiter, a potential employer, who can help to resolve issues quickly and as a result lead to less bickering among faculty. COOP programs can be funded by a small fee charged to students for securing these jobs. COOP jobs often pay thousands of dollars for working during a 16-week semester. Internships are usually for-credit courses, so students are required to pay tuition; therefore, funding is available for this activity. Universities already spend money on placement, and these funds could be transferred to and spent by programs and colleges. A modest amount of additional funding may be needed, but it would be money well spent.

8.4 DRIVING FORCES FOR CHANGE

Universities through their strategic planning process should carefully evaluate the needs of students and potential employers and recognize both as customers with mutually beneficial relationships. This becomes clear when universities examine the reasons why applicants want to attend a particular university and the students' parents, other family members, and friends are willing to pay a big part of the cost. Jobs are at the top of the list. Applicants and their support groups must make it clear to universities that they expect graduates to have good jobs. Applicants and their support groups must hold universities accountable for deficiencies in this important outcome area. Also applicants must hold themselves accountable for making their best effort to perform well in the classroom and do all they can to take advantage of the services offered.

8.5 IMPACT OF BUILDING BRIDGES TO POTENTIAL EMPLOYERS ON HIGHER EDUCATION OUTCOMES

Considering potential employers as customers is a fundamental step to improve higher education, and it requires universities to focus on their role as a mediator of the relationship between students and employers. The following list examines how this element of the solution impacts the root causes, which are discussed in Chapter 4:

1. *Lack of understanding—Who is the customer? (root cause 1):* As potential employers are recognized as customers and included in the process of transforming applicants into graduates, universities make better choices about customers' needs and desired outcomes.

2. *Declining state support for public universities (root cause 2):* When potential employers, graduates, and the graduates' support group see better outcomes, they are more likely to favor an increase in state support for public universities.
3. *Rise of the ruling class: Administration (root cause 3):* As universities focus on the trifurcated customer and their role as mediator, they are more likely to reexamine costs. Administrative costs, which have shown substantial increases, should be an area of focus.
4. *Limited productivity improvements for universities (root cause 4):* When working closely with potential employers to maintain curricular standards, improve pedagogy, and enhance outcomes, faculty will see opportunities to improve their productivity.
5. *Rapidly growing costs for books and supplies (root cause 5)*: As curricula and pedagogy are refined, textbooks and other learning materials can be redesigned substantially to reduce cost.
6. *Expanding student expectations (root cause 7):* When potential employers interact with students, students are more focused on outcome, and they see new opportunities, so their expectations for themselves and the university change.
7. *Eroding standards (root cause 8):* When potential employers are involved, learning content and performance standards are maintained or increased. As this happens, educational outcomes improve and students are better prepared for the workforce.
8. *Lack of student preparation (root cause 9):* As learning content and performance standards are maintained or increase, the problem of poorly prepared students is exposed and can be resolved with higher admission standards or remedial work.

8.6 SUMMARY OF RECOMMENDATIONS

Following is a list of the key recommendations that comprise this element of the solution.

1. Universities should create PABs for each area of study by reaching out to potential employers, graduate schools, and certification and licensure agencies. PABs are vehicles that tenured and professional faculty can use to determine curricula and set performance

standards so graduates are well prepared. PABs also provide a point of contact between students and employers.

2. Universities should provide placement and job data for applicants to evaluate. Universities currently invest considerable effort and large amounts of money to track alumni for the purpose of fundraising. This mechanism can be used to collect placement and job data.
3. Universities should provide students with easy access to the *Occupational Outlook Handbook* prepared by the U.S. Bureau of Labor Statistics, which provides employment information about hundreds of jobs.
4. Universities help to build strong relationships between students and employers.
   a. Cooperative education and internship programs are ways for students to achieve appropriate professional behaviors, learn how to apply theory and techniques to real problems, and become more interested and motivated to learn. In return, employer can evaluate the talents of students
   b. Potential employers can work directly with students as mentors or in small groups to offer advice and counsel about various aspects of professional life.
5. As students move toward graduation, programs and colleges within the university must provide better mechanisms for placing students in good jobs. In addition to traditional placement services, programs and colleges should be proactive in finding potential employers and bringing them to campus for job fairs and other interactions with students, including job interviews.

REFERENCES

1. Top Test Prep. 2016. *Why Students Go to College and What Are Their Life Priorities?* http://toptestprep.com/why-students-go-to-college-and-what-are-their-life-priorities/ (accessed November 16, 2016).
2. Vargo, S. L., and Lusch, R. F. 2004. Evolving to a new dominant logic for marketing. *Journal of Marketing*, 68: 1–17.
3. Bureau of Labor Statistics. 2016. *Occupational Outlook Handbook*. http://www.bls.gov/ooh/ (accessed November 17, 2016).

9

Government's Role in Higher Education

When people think of the role of government in higher education, they focus on money—the amount of the subsidy provided—to the exclusion of other factors like regulations and quality assurance. There are diverse perspectives: those who want free tuition at public, two-year colleges and four-year universities, and those who believe that government funding should be eliminated or at least dramatically reduced. With free tuition, students would be responsible for paying for fees, textbooks and other learning materials, room, board, and miscellaneous expenses. Free tuition implies a nearly 40% discount for students who attend a public university and live on campus and an 80% discount for those who live at home and commute. For students at public community and technical colleges, the discount is about 20% if they live on campus and 70% if they live at home.[1] (See the data in Table 1.1 in Chapter 1.)

Governments have divergent patterns in funding higher education. As described in Chapter 4, federal funding for higher education has increased substantially since President Johnson signed the Higher Education Act 50 years ago,[2] while state support per full-time equivalent (FTE) student has declined significantly during the same period.[3] There are a variety of federal programs with difference purposes and different funding formulas. Federal Pell Grants are given to students with financial needs, and veteran benefits are assigned to members of the military for service to the country. Both of these benefits are portable, so students can take them to any university. On the other hand, state general-purpose appropriations and local appropriations are allocated to universities as tuition subsidies, so there is no financial test or service credit required to earn the discount.

Local government support has declined as well because city and county budgets became tighter. Local subsidies represent only about

5% of government support for higher education, and they usually fund operating expenses at community colleges.[4] State budgets are also under continuous pressure. Elementary and secondary education plus Medicaid payments, which are the top-two line items in state budgets, consume more than half of state funds, whereas higher education consumers less than 10%, barely edging out prisons.[4] State and local governments usually have balanced budget constraints, so they cannot engage in deficit spending to support higher education, whereas the federal government can.

Although federal, state, and local governments fund higher education, these political entities also drive up costs. Regulation and compliance are pervasive and expensive problems that cover a wide range of issues from affirmative action for admitting students and hiring faculty and administrators, to complying with financial aid requirements to satisfying spending guidelines established by state and local governments.[5–7] On top of that, sports programs bring the burden of NCAA rules and reporting requirements. It is critical to identify all regulations, assess their value, and eliminate regulations that increase the cost of higher education while having little if any impact on improving quality. Doing this could reduce tuition costs significantly. The NCAA and sports are discussed in Chapter 11.

A key to changing the regulatory environment is shifting the focus from rules and requirements that mandate how things are done, which is process, to assessing outcomes, which is more important for economic progress and personal enhancement. As major funders of higher education, governments have the right to expect positive outcomes, and outcome data are readily available for many things. As an example, graduation rates and time to completion data, which are reported in Chapter 4, indicate problems in higher education, and the problems are particularly acute with for-profit, private universities. It is time to shift the focus to outcomes and consider questions such as:

1. What are the four- and six-year graduation rates?
2. Why does it often take six years to complete a four-year degree, and three years to complete a two-year degree?
3. What percentages of graduates have jobs at graduation and within six months of graduation?
4. How do starting salaries for graduates from one university compare with regional and national averages?

To address these and other questions, the following sections discuss:

1. *Government funding for higher education:* Should federal, state, and local governments fund higher education? If funding is appropriate, how much and in what form?
2. *Regulation and accreditation:* Substantial reductions in government regulations and unneeded accreditation rules provide administrators with opportunities to cut costs and reduce overhead.
3. *Focusing on outcome measures:* Regulation and accreditation should focus less on inputs and processes and more on key outcomes that are consistent with the mission of the university.

9.1 MAKING PUBLIC COLLEGES AND UNIVERSITIES TUITION-FREE

The primary arguments for free tuition are listed in Table 9.1. The more forceful and clear reasons are that (1) today's high-tech, knowledge-based economy requires more education and (2) higher education is too expensive for the average family. Two other reasons are advanced but are less compelling. Some public colleges and universities had free tuition; and, second, grade school and high school are free, so higher education should be free.[8,9] The points and their counterpoints are discussed in Table 9.1.

The point about a knowledge economy is difficult to refute; the United States and every country in the world must have brainpower. Higher education is a key part of this effort, but the United States also needs a highly skilled workforce, including welders, mechanics, electricians, manufacturing engineers, and others, who can produce high-tech goods and services. Accepting the importance of higher education is not the same as agreeing with the assertion that tuition at public institutions must be free. Graduates receive benefits from their education, and it seems reasonable that they should pay some part of the tuition. After all, only 33% of 25- to 29-year-olds held a bachelor's degree in 2015. When two-year degrees are added, the number approaches 40%.[10,11] It seems unfair to provide a valuable asset, a higher education degree, to a small, select group of people with no cost for tuition.

Figure 9.1 illustrates the attrition that takes place in education. Over the past few years, about 20% of students in the United States did not graduate

TABLE 9.1

Discussing Why Public Colleges and Universities Should Have Zero Tuition

Stated Reason	Supporting Logic	Counterpoint
1. Knowledge economy	It is clear that knowledge, education, training, and skills are keys to success for individuals and the country. Designing, creating, building, planning, managing, and organizing are critical activities that can be learned in higher education.	About 20% of people in the United States do not graduate from high school, and many who do are not qualified for or interested in higher education. Thus, a large portion of people would not benefit directly from free tuition.
2. Universities are too expensive	There is no doubt that the cost of a university education has risen much faster than the rate of inflation. About four decades ago, students could work full-time in the summer and pay for a university degree.	Some, may be even much, of the cost increase is caused by overspending and waste. It seems likely that costs could be cut. Do state subsidies make universities complacent about seeking cost reductions?
3. Many universities had free tuition	This was true because states had the economic growth and their budgets had the flexibility to support public colleges and universities.	Pressure on state budgets increased while the costs of higher education accelerated. State legislatures were unwilling to raise taxes to cover tuition costs fully.
4. Primary and secondary education are free	Higher education is a right like primary and secondary school, so the cost of tuition should be zero.	The skills in grade school and high school provide basic knowledge in reading, writing, and math as well as other capabilities needed for day-to-day living. Everyone needs these skills. Higher education has value to the individual, and the individual should bear some of the costs.

from high school.[12] See the leftmost column of Figure 9.1. Many of those who did graduate were unprepared and/or uninterested in higher education. In 2014, about 68% of high school completers (graduates and General Educational Development [GED] recipients) enrolled in two-year colleges or four-year universities the following Fall semester. This is illustrated

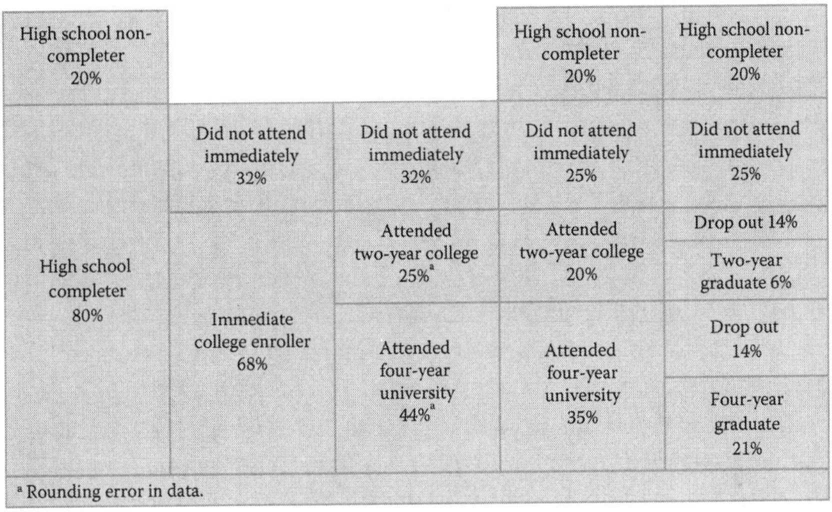

High school non-completer 20%			High school non-completer 20%	High school non-completer 20%
High school completer 80%	Did not attend immediately 32%	Did not attend immediately 32%	Did not attend immediately 25%	Did not attend immediately 25%
	Immediate college enroller 68%	Attended two-year college 25%[a]	Attended two-year college 20%	Drop out 14%
				Two-year graduate 6%
		Attended four-year university 44%[a]	Attended four-year university 35%	Drop out 14%
				Four-year graduate 21%

[a] Rounding error in data.

FIGURE 9.1
Tracing high school students to college enrollers to higher education graduates. (Note: The numbers in the second and third columns are based on high school completers, so the percentages are adjusted accordingly. For the fourth and fifth columns, the numbers are adjusted to include the non-completers. This is done to get an estimate of the percent of high school students who graduate with a higher education degree.)

in the second column of Figure 9.1. This is called the immediate college enrollment rate. The third column of Figure 9.1 shows that about 25% of the completers attended two-year colleges and 44% attended four-year universities.[13] (These two numbers add up to 69%, not to 68%, indicating a rounding error.) The fourth column of Figure 9.1 restates the college and university attendance as a percent of high school students, which includes completers and noncompleters. Only about 20% and 35% of high school completers and noncompleters attended two-year colleges and four-year universities, respectively, in the Fall semester of what should have been their high school graduation year.

The last column of Figure 9.1 shows the percent of high school students who graduated from two-year colleges in three years or less and from four-year universities in six years or less. For two-year students, only 29.3% graduated within three years,[14] leading to a graduation rate of about 6% (29.3% multiplied by 20%). So, for all high school students, including completers and noncompleters, only 6% received a two-year degree within three years of graduating from high school. For four-year students, only 59.4% graduated within six years,[14] leading to a graduation rate of only 21% (59.4% multiplied by 35%). So, for all high school students, including completers and noncompleters, only 21% received a four-year degree within six years of graduating from high school.

There are two caveats to these data. First, the attendance figures for two-year and four-year institutions are based on immediate enrollment. There are certainly some students who seek a degree in higher education at some later point. It is not clear how many or whether their success rate will be higher, lower, or the same as immediate enrollers. Second, the three-year and six-year graduation rates do not count students who take longer to earn a degree or who transfer to another school to complete their degree. This likely understates the percent of graduates from both two- and four-year institutions. Educational attainment in the United States in 2015 indicated that about 33% of adults age 25 to 29 held bachelor's degrees.[10,11] Therefore, it appears that about 12% (33% minus 21%) eventually earn their four-year degree. Even with this higher number, it seems clear that the primary and secondary education systems are not preparing enough students for higher education and that higher education is not very efficient at transforming high school graduates into advanced degree holders.

The second point in Table 9.1 is that tuition is too expensive, and the evidence presented in Chapter 2 confirms this. However, that information does not justify making two-year colleges and four-year universities tuition-free. "Free" tuition confirms the validity of current practices at a time when universities should be better stewards of their funds, using resources more effectively and efficiently to improve outcomes. Besides, designating institutions as tuition-free does not make it so; taxpayers would pay the bill, including wasteful spending. If homes or cars are too expensive, the solution is not to make them free. The solution begins by finding ways to cut costs. It should be the same in higher education. Efforts must be made to understand what is driving costs and determine how costs can be reduced.

If public, higher education has no tuition for associate and bachelor's degrees, it is likely to attract applicants who are not well suited for higher education as well as those who are unsure of what they want to do. If free tuition attracts students who are not well prepared, graduation rates are likely to sink even lower. For students who are unsure about their future, attending college is socially acceptable behavior that provides time to figure out what to do. Also, if tuition is free, does this mean that more students will major in fields of study with relatively few jobs and low salaries?[15,16] It seems clear that encouraging these types of behavior is not appropriate. If a two- or four-year degree has value, it only seems fair that the people who benefit from it should pay part of the tuition.

The third point in Table 9.1 is as follows: A while ago, tuition was free at many but not all public colleges and universities. It hardly seems convincing to argue that things "use to be" this or that way, so they should be that way again. Circumstances change. There are many actions and practices that were at one point common and accepted behavior. For decades Irish, Italian, Hispanics, and others faced discrimination based on ethnicity or religion; young woman were require to wear dresses or skirts to high school; and consumers could buy a full-size candy bar for a nickel. Today, these are illegal, unacceptable, or infeasible. The problems with higher education are that tuition has risen much faster than the rate of inflation, and the growth in state budgets tends to be in line with economic growth. Plus, other parts of the state budget, specifically Medicaid, have grown faster than inflation. Even if states can find ways to allocate the same percent of their budgets to higher education each year, they cannot keep pace with the extraordinary rise in tuition. It is time for universities to shoulder the responsibility for high costs.

The fourth point in Table 9.1 is as follows: Elementary and secondary schools are tuition-free so public colleges and universities should be tuition-free. A primary difference is the legal requirement for students who are 6 to 18 years old to attend school. State mandates for providing free primary and secondary education usually begin at age 5 and end when students turns 23.[17] The primary purpose of this education is to provide basic knowledge that people need to live in society no matter their job. Seeking a two-year or four-year degree is a choice, so there is no compelling reason for government to pay for it. Those who do not graduate from high school are not able to pursue an advanced degree, and not everyone who graduates from high school is interested in such a degree. These points do not stop government from passing laws to make public colleges and university tuition-free, but doing so hardly seems fair to those who cannot or choose not to attend.

9.2 ELIMINATING OR DRAMATICALLY REDUCING SUBSIDIES

Some argue that government should not subsidize higher education, and the reasons are summarized in Table 9.2. The most compelling argument is that increasing subsidies leads to wasteful spending because they reduce pressure to keep costs low. Grove City College and Hillsdale College, which

TABLE 9.2

Discussing Why Public Colleges and Universities Should Have Tuition Subsidies Eliminated or Dramatically Reduced

Stated Reason	Supporting Logic	Counter-Point
1. More subsidies means more wasteful spending	Providing subsidies takes the pressure off administrators and faculty to seek out and implement less costly, higher quality, and more effective, ways to educate students.	Subsidies help low- and moderate-income families afford higher education.
2. Link between higher education subsidies and economic growth is tenuous at best	Data seem to indicate that the correlation between spending on higher education and economic growth is low.	The limited correlation may be affected by the law of diminishing returns and wasteful spending in higher education.
3. Earning advantage of university graduates is overstated	Evidence shows that university graduates do earn more than high school graduates. These data are available in Table 4.1 in Chapter 4. The point of the detractors is that the advantage for college graduates does not consider the cost of earning the degree or four years of lost wages while attending.	Section 2.7 in Chapter 2 considers whether a university degree is a good investment. The analysis shows that, on the average, it has a favorable return on investment, even though the return is lower when tuition costs and lost wages are included.

offer bachelor's degrees and accept no government funding, are substantially cheaper than the average cost of private colleges and universities.[16,18] The attitude surrounding higher education has been to "spend, spend, spend," and generally speaking, society encourages borrowing to acquire more goods and services. These attitudes and actions create a system where high school graduates and their parents believe they must borrow to afford an advanced degree.[19]

A study by the New York Federal Reserve claims that subsides are "enabling college institutions to aggressively raise tuitions."[20] For every dollar of loan that students or parents incur to pay tuition, 65 cents is consumed without increasing service or quality. Considering that the increases in tenured faculty have lagged behind enrollment growth, the assumption must be that administration, bureaucracy, and spending on luxuries are consuming the 65 cents.[20] In addition, federal programs are rife with waste, fraud, and abuse. In 2014, leaders at a Florida College were indicted for receiving $6.5 million from fraudulent student loans and Pell Grants, and in 2015, an Ohio couple went to prison for defrauding the government of $2.3 million for student aid at their fly-by-night college.[21]

The second point in Table 9.2 is that the link between subsidies for higher education and economic growth is tenuous at best. Although the link between educational investment and economic prosperity may seem intuitive, the relationship has many anomalies and outliers.[22] An academic study of this issue by Harvard University found some support for the hypothesis that investments in four-year institutions led to increased economic growth for all states, but no such relationship was found for two-year institutions. Their conclusion was that "despite the enormous interest in the relationships between education and growth, the evidence is fragile at best."[23] Another report indicates that educational attainment might account for only 10% of U.S. growth in GDP.[24] It appears that the impact of government spending on economic output does not show up robustly in the data.

Argument can be constructed to support the link between education and economic growth. Although it would not show cause and effect, a scatter plot of educational attainment and GDP would show that underdeveloped countries with low GDP per capita have low educational attainment. Also, there is logic to support the relationship. At an extreme, it is difficult to believe that a country where no one can read, write, or do arithmetic could become an economic powerhouse. Exchanging ideas and communicating basic information would be difficult, making all aspects of commerce challenging. At the other extreme, if everyone had a PhD, who would be available to make plans, create products, and do the work? It seems clear that the sweet spot for economic growth is somewhere between these extremes, so each unit of education must have a value or propensity to stimulate economic growth. It is also likely that the value or propensity of a unit of education depends on the circumstances. For example, in the industrial era, where products were simpler and there was limited variety, education was important for the "work planners," but not for the "work doers" who toiled on the factory floor. When the industrial era began more than 100 years ago, the United States emerged as the economic leader, and many of its "work doers" were immigrants who could not read or write English. The need for education changed in the postindustrial era where complexity and high product variety required more flexible production systems and university degrees for "work planners" and high school degrees or more for "work doers." This argument suggests that increasing economic success depends on more education.

Consider two reasons why this may not show up in the data: wasteful spending and a mismatch in degrees and available jobs. Waste impacts the relationship between spending and economic growth. If the cost of a university degree should be $80,000 and excessive spending drives the price to $100,000, then spending increases, but knowledge gained by students has not changed. If the assumption is made that knowledge gained is the factor that creates economic value, then the extra $20,000 provides no benefit to the economy. As a result, the impact of higher education spending on economic growth is diluted. Second, graduates from some degree programs are unable to find jobs, or are forced to take jobs that do not require an advanced degree, or find a job in their field that has low pay because there are too many graduates seeking too few jobs. Once again, spending in higher education increases and the economic benefit from the learning is minimal.

Point 3 in Table 9.2 is that the lifetime compensation advantage of university graduates is overstated because studies do not consider the cost of the advance degree or the four years or more of wages they lose while learning. The analysis in Section 2.7 in Chapter 2 shows that, on average, there is a favorable return on investment for university graduates even when these costs are considered. The analysis does not mean that each individual university graduates gets a good return on his or her investments or that every university graduate earn more than any high school graduate. One of the best known and wealthiest dropouts from higher education is Bill Gates, a cofounder of Microsoft.

9.3 GOVERNMENT'S ROLE IN FUNDING HIGHER EDUCATION

Given the discussion so far, it seems reasonable for government to provide some funding for higher education, if for no other reason than creating access for students from low- and moderate-income families. Table 1.1 in Chapter 1 shows that in 2015–2016 the average public university cost $24,061 per year for in-state students and the average not-for-profit, private university cost $47,831 per year, which is a difference of $23,770. The difference was caused almost entirely by the difference in tuition, which was

$22,995 per year.[1] Middle- and low-income families, even families in the lower reaches of the upper-income group, would find it anywhere from impossible to challenging to pay almost $200,000 for a four-year degree from a not-for-profit, private university. According to the U.S. Census Bureau, the median household income in 2015 was $55,775.[25] Thus, a family in the middle of the middle class would pay nearly all of its income for four years so one of its children could graduate from a not-for-profit, private university. The cost to attend a public university would be about half that, which is still too much. Funds from state and local government help to keep tuition low at public universities, and federal funds enable students to pay part of the cost regardless of whether they select a public or private university.

The data in Table 9.3 provide a summary of government funding for 2013–2014. The following sections discuss this two-pronged approach, describe the different types of government funding, and make recommendations for how the allocations might be improved.

9.3.1 State and Local Funding

Public universities, which are subsidized by state and local tax dollars, are an alternative to private universities and are important competitors that serve about 60% of the full-time and part-time students seeking bachelor's degrees.[3] In 2013, state and local funding totaled $81.9 billion, and $62.2 billion or about 76% were general appropriations that are used to subsidize tuition for the average student. All of the local funding, $9.2 billion, was general appropriation dollars. As shown in Table 9.3, the other two parts were state financial aid grants totaling $9.6 billion, which are scholarships and other funds given to state residents, and $10.1 billion in specific appropriations for research, agriculture, and medical education. State funding per FTE student varied widely from $3,465 in New Hampshire to $19,575 in Alaska. Local funding varies widely from zero in some states to a few thousand dollars per FTE students in others.[4] The following sections discuss each of these options and make recommendations.

9.3.1.1 State and Local General-Purpose Appropriations

This is the largest part of the subsidy, and it has been declining, not in absolute dollars but as an amount provided per FTE student and as a percent of university revenue.[3] The bottom line is that state and local

TABLE 9.3

Summary of Government Funding for 2013–2014 Academic Year (billions of dollars)

Federal Funding	Amount	Comments
Pell grants	$31.3	Allocated to students based on financial need
Other financial aid grants	$1.6	Other need-based grants
Research grants	$24.6	Research support such as the National Science Foundation
Veteran education benefits	$12.2	Benefit to men and women of the armed services
Other grant programs	$2.2	Funds to help disadvantaged students prepare for success—provided to minority serving institutions
General-purpose appropriations	$3.8	Expenses to selected institutions such as military schools, historically black colleges, and land grant universities
Total federal support[a]	**$75.6**	
State Funding	**Amount**	**Comments**
Financial aid grants	$9.6	Primarily need-based and merit-based grants
Research, agriculture, and medical appropriations	$10.1	Support for research facilities, agricultural experiment stations, cooperative extension services, public healthcare, and medical schools
General-purpose appropriations	$53.0	Tuition subsidy that are based on enrollment and go directly to public colleges and universities
Total state support	**$72.7**	
Local Funding	**Amount**	**Comments**
General-purpose appropriation	$9.2	Typically given to subsidies tuition

Source: The Pew Charitable Trusts, *Federal and State Funding of Higher Education: A Changing Landscape*, 2015. http://www.pewtrusts.org/en/research-and-analysis/issue-briefs/2015/06/federal-and-state-funding-of-higher-education

[a] Difference in total compared to individual amounts caused by rounding error.

governments should decide the level of support that is best for their constituents without the federal government mandating zero tuition or some other amount. It is clear that public colleges and universities as well as students would like to see state and local funding increase, but that, for reasons already discussed, is unlikely to fix the underlying cost problems. Further reductions in state and local appropriations may not be the right response because public colleges and universities educate a large portion of the students and provide a lower cost, high-quality alternative to private universities.

There is an opportunity for state and local governments to use their funding as a mechanism to pressure public colleges and universities to lower costs and improve performance. Analysis of the cost factors for higher education, which is contained in Chapter 2, indicates that tuition, fees, and textbooks have risen much faster than the rate of inflation. Following are actions that state and local governments could take to lower costs.

1. *Tuition:* A key factor that is driving cost increase is administrative spending. Public colleges and universities would be required to prepare a five-year rolling plan to reduce administrative expenses by a substantial amount. The cuts must be large because administrative positions increased by 369% from 1978 to 2014, while tenured faculty increased by only 23%.[26] For the same period, enrollment in undergraduate degree programs grew by 73%.[27] By the numbers, administrators grew five times faster than student enrollment. A specific recommendation on administrative cuts is given in Chapter 11, which discusses administration and management.
2. *Student fees:* State and local governments should require public colleges and universities to change these fees as described in Chapter 7. Fees cannot be used for academic purposes and are paid at the option of students. Routine, learning-related activities such as day-to-day computer services must be paid by tuition dollars, not by student fees.
3. *Textbooks and other learning materials:* In line with the second point in this list, these items are learning related and should be covered by tuition. This is not simply a cost transfer from one place to another on students' budgets for higher education. As discussed in Chapter 7 on becoming student centered and Chapter 13 on high-tech learning materials, this is a different approach where institutions work with publishers to create better learning tools and negotiate better prices. As third-party payers, state and local government are positioned to require public colleges and universities to make this happen.

In addition, as discussed in Chapter 3, there are problems with graduation rates, time to completion, and job placements. State and local governments can condition a portion of their appropriation to public colleges and universities on setting and meeting goals that are consistent with their mission. The goals may be different for the flagship university in the state compared to an open enrollment university that accepts anyone with a high school diploma or equivalent. State and local governments are third-party payers who have the right and responsibility to make these requests, and inputs from students, parents, other family members, and friends should reinforce their resolve.

9.3.1.2 State Financial Aid Grants

Almost every state education agency has at least one grant or scholarship program for residents, and many have a long list.[28] They tend to be a hodgepodge of politically motivated offerings. For example, California lists 12 programs on its website, including the California Dream Act, California Middle Class Scholarship, and Law Enforcement Personnel Dependent Grants Program.[29] Texas lists 14 programs, although 3 of them are federal programs. Texas has the Fifth Year Accounting Student Scholarship, Marine Corp Foundation Scholarship, and the Texas Equalization Grant Program.[30]

Without extensive investigation into each program across 50 states, it is difficult to make meaningful recommendations. The examples seem to confirm that there is no overall plan or compelling logic that determines who receives the funds and for what purpose. Why should dependents of law enforcement have access to special funds that dependents of firefighters or elementary school teachers do not? What is especially important about fifth-year accounting students? There are two options that state legislators might consider. The first would be to shift these funds to general appropriation. This would be fairer to the population as a whole. If there is a reason to identify groups of people that deserve funding, they could be put into three broad categories: those with (1) financial need; (2) excellent performance; and (3) both attributes.

9.3.1.3 State Research, Agriculture, and Medical Education Appropriations

These fund total $10.1 billion across the states, which is an average of about $200 million per state. It is clear that larger states with more income and population are likely to have more funds than smaller ones. Certainly, food and medical care are two important requirements for living, so there may be value in targeting these areas. A special allocation for research may have some value as well, but this spending needs careful oversight by the state legislatures. Once again, these decisions are likely to be different from one state to the next, so it is difficult to make specific recommendations. What are the returns on this research investment? How will an investment lead to economic growth and jobs? Having well-defined expectations for these programs and holding people accountable are essential.

9.3.1.4 Lack of Funding for Outreach and Engagement

Whereas the other subsections under the heading "State and Local Funding" discuss one or another aspect of support for public colleges and universities, it is important to note that no funds are identified to pay for outreach and engagement. Chapter 5 discusses how service to the academy morphed into outreach and engagement, where institutions of higher learning work in the community to improve the economy and human conditions by tackling important projects. The problem is that states and local governments do not provide funding to support these activities. Money collected from students and others to pay tuition, fees, room, and board are not intended to pay for outreach and engagements. It is safe to say that students, parents, and other third-party payers would be unhappy to know that the money they provided for tuition was spent for other purposes. Research dollars also have a defined purpose and should not be spent on outreach and engagement. Unless governments are willing to provide funds to support these efforts, universities should disengage. If they do not, it is like a tax on students, parents, and other third parties that pays for education and research.

9.3.2 Federal Funding

Unlike state and local funding that for the most part goes directly to public colleges and universities, most federal funding, including (1) grants, which do not require repayment, (2) student loans, which require repayment with interest, and (3) work-study jobs, which provide employment for students with financial needs, is assigned directly to students. Students can use these funds at public or private universities. Following is a description of each program and actions that should be considered.

9.3.2.1 Pell Grants and Other Grant Programs

As shown in Table 9.3, the federal government provided $35.1 billion in grants for 2013–2014 (not including research grants), with Pell Grants being the largest component at $31.3 billion.[31] Having need-based grants for higher education is appropriate, and they have strong support for continuation. However, the ultimate goal, although it may not be reachable, should be for need-based grants to disappear as the following occurs:

1. The economy improves and more good jobs are created.
2. Families implement financial plans that help them reduce day-to-day expenses and big-ticket purchases, improve earnings, and save more.
3. Universities find ways to cut costs.

9.3.2.2 Student Loans

There are two broad categories of loans, federal and private, and there are several different types of federal loans—some are subsidies, whereas others are not.[32] Annual borrowing is more than $100 billion,[33] and total student loan debt has reached a staggering $1.35 trillion.[34] This has allowed colleges and universities to continue to increase tuition and fees substantially. Actions must be taken to rein in borrowing on the demand side so students want and need to borrow less because they find ways to spend less on their education. These actions are described in Chapter 6.

It is important to help students understand their obligation to repay loans and how repayment may impact their living standard. To do this, students must prepare a student borrowing and repayment plan (SBRP) that specifies how much they plan to borrow, the precise use of these funds, and what they will forego after graduation to make loan payments. The lender is required to review the SBRP with students and their families. This is a logical extension of the family budget, which is discussed here and in Chapter 6. It requires students and their families to think clearly about how much they are borrowing and the consequences of repayment. Are students willing to postpone buying new cars and taking vacations until their loans are repaid? This process may provide incentives to spend less and borrow less.

9.3.2.3 Work-Study Jobs

This program provides part-time jobs for students who have financial needs. The program encourages community service work and work related to the student's course of study.[35] More than 3,400 institutions of higher learning participate in this program, and about 7% of all undergraduate students receive an average of $2,400 a year. In 2009, more than $1.4 billion was spent on this program, including matching funds from states and institutions. The federal government can pay up to 100% of the wages, but the typical federal share is about 75%. Most jobs pay the federal minimum wage.[36,37]

Unfortunately, these jobs are often make-work jobs that put money in students' pockets. Often, little of value is accomplished, and if something is learned, it is because students are told they can study during this time. Work study is another example of a federal program that sounds like a good idea, putting students with financial needs to work to help them finance their education. It puts money in the pockets of students, but it is unclear if anything is learned or if there is benefit from the work. Plus there is a bureaucracy at both the federal and institutional levels that consumes significant resources. One of two things should be done: (1) require institutions to provide evidence that students are learning and that the work they are doing has value or (2) close the program and roll the funds into the Pell Grant program. If students have skills that are valuable, they will find work.

9.3.2.4 Research Grants

As shown in Table 9.3, the federal government provided $24.6 billion in research grants that were awarded on a competitive basis to institutions of higher learning. These funds are used for many purposes such as basic and applied research for the National Science Foundation and the National Institutes of Health. Research grants are offered by the U.S. Department of Defense and Department of Transportation among other parts of government. These grants typically have limited direct impact on undergraduate education. Quite often these research grants ask for and receive funding for graduate students, so these grants can be drivers of graduate educations. These grants are also used to buy out faculty time, so they teach less. In theory, the buyout funds are used to hire additional faculty to teach courses that would have been taught by the faculty researchers. Universities have been known to charge a portion of the research faculty member's salary and fringe benefits, which can be considerable, and replace him or her with part-time faculty or graduate assistants who earn a small fraction of this amount. Although there are other "tricks of the trade" that could be discussed with respect to research grants, these issues are outside the scope of the book.

9.3.2.5 Veteran Education Benefits and General-Purpose Appropriations

As shown in Table 9.3, the remaining two parts of federal government support are for veterans and a special allocation for military schools, historical black colleges, and land grant universities. Veterans' educational benefits are an important part of defense spending. Allocations to military schools are also defense related as they help to prepare future leaders. Special funding for minority and historically black colleges should continue. Special funding for land grant universities no longer seems necessary.

9.3.2.6 Problems with Private, For-Profit Universities

For-profit universities receive funds from the federal government but not from states and local governments. These institutions have major problems. Table 3.1 in Chapter 3 shows that private, for-profit universities have by far the worst four-year and six-year graduation rates at 22.5% and 31.5%, respectively. The same rates for public universities are 33.5% and 57.7%.[14] Looking at the six-year rate, public universities are 26.2 points higher (57.7% minus 31.5%), which yields 83% more graduates.

Other problems have been reported. *The Atlantic* claims that private, for-profit institutions have made headlines for poor performance, high prices, and exploiting vulnerable, low-income students as well as veterans who often bring with them a rich financial aid package.[38] *The New York Times* reports that the Obama administration has decided to bar ITT Educational Services from using federal financial aid to enroll new students. ITT received an estimated $580 million in federal funding for higher education in 2015.[39–41] In addition, the U.S. Department of Education has moved to close the largest accreditor of for-profit colleges, which oversaw failing institutions like Corinthian Colleges and ITT Technical Institute.[42–45] One advantage for state and local governments is that their funds are not available to private, for-profit universities.

These instances do not mean that all private, for-profit universities have similar problems, but buyers should beware. The best way to improve conditions is for consumers to investigate alternatives and chose the best one. This is facilitated by creating a HEPO database, which is described in Chapter 6. It should include reliable information about price, graduation rates, completion time, passing certification and licensure exams, and job placement.

9.4 REGULATIONS AND ACCREDITATION

Regulation by government and accreditation by independent agencies are mechanisms to monitor and control the actions and ultimately the outcomes of institutions of higher learning. Figure 9.2 illustrates how governments shown at the top of Figure 9.2, accreditation agencies shown at the bottom, and potential employers on the right side can work together to ensure that these institutions create high-quality outputs (i.e., graduates and research). As shown in Figure 9.2, these outputs are determined by the process, which includes acts of teaching and advising students as well as creating and executing research programs. The effectiveness of the process is determined at least in part by the quality of the inputs, which are faculty, administrators, facilities, and curricula. Figure 9.2 captures the input, process, and output dimensions in the box labeled Colleges and Universities. The role of potential employers is discussed in Chapter 8, and the roles of government and accreditation agencies are discussed in this chapter.

9.4.1 Governments: Regulation, Resources, and Outcomes

Regulations are well-intended actions to protect government, taxpayers, students, and the public from institutions that are providing

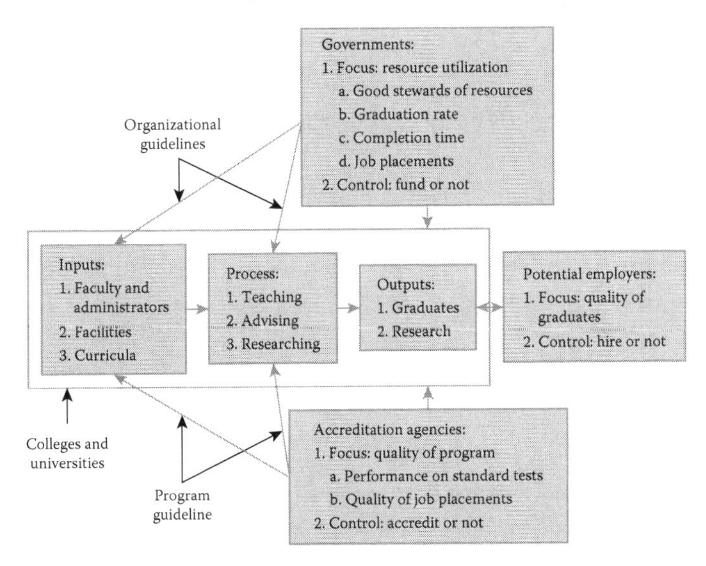

FIGURE 9.2
Government, accreditation agencies, and potential employers combine to determine the performance of higher education.

substandard services. But regulations are costly for governments and the institutions that must follow them. Government hires staff to write, assess, and enforce regulations. Universities hire staff to comply with them and report on a wide variety of input, process, and output variables. Taxpayers, which include students and their supporters, pay the governments' costs, and students and all third-party payers cover the universities' costs. Therefore, ultimately everyone pays the bill. It seems clear that a balance should be struck between the cost of regulations and their perceived benefits. Legislators, who usually approve regulations, tend to see only the perceived benefits, so it is easy for them to support regulations for the "greater good." The term *perceived* is used because proponents of regulations can claim that things would be much worse if these regulations did not exist.

It is important to put a mechanism in place to assess government regulations and determine if they are working as intended and doing so at a reasonable cost. This is challenging because there are many regulations coming from three different levels of government, and some may be duplicative, even contradictory. To address what appears to be overregulation, each state should assemble a Higher Education Committee (HEC) using existing agencies. Representatives from federal and local governments as well as from public colleges and universities in the state would be included. The HEC would have the authority to recommend elimination of the most expensive and least beneficial regulations. The HEC would do the following:

1. Categorize regulations by type such as tuition and fees, housing, and facility utilization.
2. Identify and eliminate or consolidate regulations that are redundant.
3. Assess the cost of compliance.
4. Estimate the potential benefits that are achieved.
5. Compare the cost and benefits from a regulation and determine its overall value.
6. Recommend elimination of regulations that are not achieving a reasonable benefit given the cost.

HECs would share information about regulatory ideas and planned changes with HECs from other states. Changes that would impact federal and local regulations would require approval of these governments.

As shown in Figure 9.2, governments' focus would be on resource utilization, specifically on ensuring that colleges and universities are good stewards of government funds as well as the tuition and fees paid by students and third-party payers. The focus would be on outcomes that are linked to the effective use of resources, including graduation rates, completion times, and job placements rates. Governments can use funding as a means to control institutional behavior and achieve the outputs that it feels are important. Government would spend much less effort on regulating the inputs and processes that institutions use to achieve their outcomes. Guidelines and suggested behavior would be the preferred way to affect inputs and processes, so universities could diverge from standard practice when it made sense without fear of reprisal. Substandard outputs would trigger actions by government to request additional information and would require institutions to find the root cause of the problem and fix it.

9.4.2 Accreditation Agencies and Potential Employers: Enhancing Quality

Accreditation is a useful tool to ensure that universities are high performers. As shown in Figure 9.2, accreditation should focus on the quality of outputs and offer guidelines about how to build inputs and processes to achieve those outcomes. Outcome assessment should take into account the mission of the institution, which includes its strategies, goals, and key policies. Beyond graduation rate and completion time, output measures should include improving knowledge creation through research, performance of graduates on standardized tests, and the quality of job placements. Accreditation agencies get compliance from university programs because they decide to accredit or not. As a way to control behavior, they put programs on continuing review, giving them an opportunity to address deficiencies.

A focus on job placement includes potential employers. As shown in Figure 9.2, this is the third part of the scheme to ensure quality outputs. Recall that potential employers work with tenured and professional faculty to determine curricular content and academic rigor. When done properly, inputs from employers are fed back into universities. This is symbolized by the two-headed arrow between potential employers and outputs. Ultimately, the potential employer choses to hire or not to hire based on the quality of the graduates. This should incentivize students to work harder and institutions to enhance quality. These three factors—government, accreditation agencies, and potential employers—help students receive a high-quality education while keeping regulatory costs low.

9.5 FOCUSING ON OUTCOMES IN THE CONTEXT OF INSTITUTIONAL MISSION

The key is to focus on outcome measures that are mission appropriate and provide guidelines with respect to the inputs and processes that might be helpful to achieve these outcomes. This focus allows government regulatory bureaus and accreditation agencies to understand the goals of the institution, recognize problems, and seek additional information in order to resolve them. It is critical that the outcomes are consistent with the institution's strategic plan because not every institution is striving for the same results in research and instruction. For example, community and technical colleges have research interests that are applied, whereas universities with graduate programs tend to have larger and more diverse missions that are a mixture of basic and applied research. Some public universities have high admission standard, whereas others in the same state may accept anyone with a high school diploma.

9.6 DRIVING FORCES FOR CHANGE

Federal, state, and local governments with support, comment, and feedback from students and their support group have the right, responsibility, and authority to change subsidy polices and amounts. Altering subsidies can be used as leverage to encourage institutions to reduce administrative cost, lower tuition, make fees optional, and include textbooks and other learning materials as part of tuition. This tactic can also be used to incentivize universities to find ways to reduce time to complete a degree and increase the graduation rate. Preparing a five-year plan would be an important tool to set universities on course for better educational outcomes and lower costs. Accreditation agencies and potential employers also have a role in achieving better outcomes.

9.7 IMPACT OF CHANGING THE GOVERNMENT'S ROLE ON HIGHER EDUCATION OUTCOMES

As a third-party payer, governments have the right to expect better performance from institutions of higher learning. Governments have control over a substantial portion of the revenue and can use it as leverage to expect better outcomes. The following list examines how this element of the solution impacts the root causes, which are discussed in Chapter 4:

1. *Lack of understanding—Who is the customer? (root cause 1):* Governments should present themselves to institutions of higher learning as customers and demand that they get better value for their investment.
2. *Declining state support for public universities (root cause 2):* Governments can change their level of subsidies in response to the actions and performance of institutions.
3. *Rise of the ruling class: Administration (root cause 3):* Administrative costs may be the single biggest reason why higher education costs have increases. Governments can respond by modifying subsidies to gain the changes in staffing that they deem appropriate.
4. *Limited productivity improvements for universities (root cause 4):* Productivity of administrators and faculty is relevant. Governments should encourage investments in technology to enhance productivity and reduce administrative and instructional costs.
5. *Rapidly growing costs for books and supplies (root cause 5):* Universities can help publishers design more effective and less expensive learning materials. Governments provide the incentive.
6. *Funding finesse—Mixing fees and tuition (root cause 6):* Governments can require public colleges and universities to use student fees for nonacademic purposes only, make fees optional for students, and prohibit comingling of tuition dollars and fees.
7. *Eroding standards (root cause 8):* Governments, potential employers, and accreditation agencies want to maintain learning content and performance standards so graduates are better prepared and have more successful careers.

9.8 SUMMARY OF RECOMMENDATIONS

Following is a list of the key recommendations that comprise this element of the solution.

1. Governments' role in higher education should be somewhere in the middle between the extreme positions of making high education

tuition free and eliminating or dramatically reducing government support. The status quo is an appropriate place to begin.

2. State and local governments should use their funding as a mechanism to pressure public colleges and universities to lower costs and improve outcomes. Public colleges and universities would be required to do the following:
   a. Prepare a five-year rolling plan to reduce administrative expenses.
   b. Use fees for nonacademic expenses, make fees payable at the students' option, and require learning-related activities to be paid by tuition dollars.
   c. Take financial responsibility for providing books and other learning materials.
3. State and local governments can condition their funding for higher education on meeting mission-appropriate goals for graduation rates, time to completion, and job placements.
4. States have a hodgepodge of financial aid grants that seem to be politically motivated. Unless there are compelling reasons, state funds that support these grants should become part of the state's general appropriation.
5. States also make appropriations for research as well as agriculture and medical education. These appropriations must have careful oversight with specific outcomes identified.
6. Universities should disengage from outreach and engagement until and unless there is a specific funding source to support it. States provide no funding. Funds for tuition, fees, research, room, and board are intended for these activities and not for outreach and engagement.
7. Federal Pell Grants and other grants should be maintained, but hopefully demand for them declines as the economy improves, saving for education increases, and universities find ways to reduce costs.
8. Student loans must be reduced substantially by reining in demand so students want and need to borrow less. Students need to understand their repayment obligation, so they must prepare a SBRP that specifies how much they will borrow, the use of these funds, and what they are willing to forego to make payments.
9. Work-study jobs often do little more than put money in students' pockets. Universities must provide evidence that students are learning something and/or doing work that has value or close the program and roll the funds into the Pell Grant program.

10. Federal funds are used to support private, for-profit universities that have very poor performance outcomes. The poor performers must be disqualified from receiving federal aid.
11. Higher Education Committees (HECs) should be established to examine the cost and benefits of government regulations and eliminate regulations that have gone too far.
12. Government regulations and actions by accreditation agencies should focus on outputs to reduce the amount of regulation and make it easier to spot and resolve problems.
13. When performance is below expectations, governments, accreditation agencies, and employers that hire graduates have the power to cut funding, deny accreditation, and not hire graduates, respectively.

REFERENCES

1. College Board. 2016. *Trends in Higher Education: Published Prices—National.* http://trends.collegeboard.org/college-pricing/figures-tables/published-prices-national#Published Charges, 2015–16 (accessed June 20, 2016).
2. Selingo, J. J. 2015. Baby boomers and the end of higher education. *The Washington Post*, November 12. https://www.washingtonpost.com/news/grade-point/wp/2015/11/12/baby-boomers-and-the-end-of-higher-education/ (accessed June 14, 2016).
3. United States Department of the Treasury and Department of Education. 2012. *The Economics of Higher Education*, December. https://www.treasury.gov/connect/blog/Documents/20121212_Economics%20of%20Higher%20Ed_vFINAL.pdf (accessed June 23, 2016).
4. The Pew Charitable Trusts. 2015. Federal and state funding of higher education: A changing landscape, June 11. http://www.pewtrusts.org/en/research-and-analysis/issue-briefs/2015/06/federal-and-state-funding-of-higher-education (accessed June 16, 2016).
5. Higher Learning Commissions. 2016. *Accreditation.* https://hlcommission.org/ (accessed June 21, 2016).
6. The Higher Education Compliance Alliance. 2015. *Compliance Matrix*, last update December. http://www.higheredcompliance.org/matrix/ (accessed June 24, 2016).
7. Zack-Decker, K. 2012. *Compliance at Hartwick College: A Special Report to the President of the College*, December. http://www.naicu.edu/docLib/20130315_Compliance-HartwickColl-12-12.pdf (accessed June 24, 2016).
8. Sanders, B. 2015. *Make College Free for All*, October 22. https://www.washington-post.com/opinions/bernie-sanders-america-needs-free-college-now/2015/10/22/a3d05512-7685-11e5-bc80-9091021aeb69_story.html?utm_term=.e584a3d72d01 (accessed November 27, 2016).
9. Wittner, L. S. 2015. *Why Tuition-Free College Makes Sense*, November 1. http://www.truth-out.org/opinion/item/33473-why-tuition-free-college-makes-sense (accessed November 27, 2016).

10. U.S. Census Bureau. 2016. *Educational Attainment in the United States: 2015*, March. https://www.census.gov/content/dam/Census/library/publications/2016/demo/p20-578.pdf (accessed June 23, 2016).
11. U.S. Department of Education. 2012. *New State-by-State College Attainment Numbers Shows Progress Toward 2020 Goal*, July 12. http://www.ed.gov/news/press-releases/new-state-state-college-attainment-numbers-show-progress-toward-2020-goal (accessed December 18, 2016).
12. National Center for Education Statistics. 2016. *Public High School Graduate Rates*. http://nces.ed.gov/programs/coe/indicator_coi.asp (accessed August 18, 2016).
13. National Center for Education Statistics. 2016. *Immediate Transition to College*. https://nces.ed.gov/fastfacts/display.asp?id=51 (accessed November 28, 2016).
14. National Center for Education Statistics. 2015. *Graduation Rates*. https://nces.ed.gov/fastfacts/display.asp?id=40 (accessed July 5, 2016).
15. Luebke, B. 2016. *Civitas Institute. Why Free College Tuition is a Bad Idea*, February 6. https://www.nccivitas.org/2016/16909/ (accessed November 27, 2016).
16. Chen, D. W. 2017. New York's Free-Tuition Program will help traditional, but not typical, students. *New York Times*, April 2017. https://www.nytimes.com/2017/04/11/nyregion/new-yorks-free-tuition-program-will-help-traditional-but-not-typical-students.html?_r=0 (accessed May 5, 2017).
17. National Center for Education Statistics. 2016. *Compulsory School Attendance Laws*. https://nces.ed.gov/programs/statereform/tab5_1.asp (accessed November 30, 2016).
18. Skorup, J. 2013. Five reasons the government shouldn't subsidize higher education. *Michigan Capital Confidential*, February 13. http://www.michigancapitolconfidential.com/18279 (accessed November 27, 2016).
19. The American Spectator. 2014. *Student Loads, Student Loan Debt, and Subsidies to Universities Should Be Eliminated*, May 22. https://spectator.org/59306_student-loans-student-debt-and-subsidies-universities-should-be-eliminated/ (accessed November 30, 2016).
20. Worstall, T. 2015. Increased tuition subsidies increase the price of college tuition. *Forbes*, August 3. http://www.forbes.com/sites/timworstall/2015/08/03/increased-tuition-subsidies-increase-the-price-of-college-tuition/#7bfbc38b2b88 (accessed November 30, 2016).
21. Edwards, C., and McCluskey, N. 2015. *Higher Education Subsidies. Downsizing the Federal Government*, November 1. https://www.downsizinggovernment.org/education/higher-education-subsidies (accessed November 30, 2016).
22. Aghion, P., Boustan, L., Hoxby, C., and VandenBussche, J. 2009. *The Causal Impact of Education on Economic Growth: Evidence from the U.S. Harvard University*, March 9. http://scholar.harvard.edu/files/aghion/files/causal_impact_of_education.pdf (accessed November 30, 2016).
23. Fox, E. 2011. The correlation between education and the economy. *Investopedia*, September 7. http://www.investopedia.com/financial-edge/0911/the-correlation-between-education-and-the-economy.aspx (accessed November 30, 2016).
24. Kenny, C. 2014. Why education spending doesn't lead to economic growth. *Bloomberg*. http://www.bloomberg.com/news/articles/2014-04-07/why-education-spending-doesnt-lead-to-economic-growth (accessed December 1, 2016).
25. United States Census Bureau. 2015. *US Household Income*. https://www.census.gov/content/dam/Census/library/publications/2016/demo/acsbr15-02.pdf (accessed December 1, 2016).

26. McNutt, M. I. 2014. Why does college cost so much? *US News World Report*, September 22. http://www.usnews.com/news/college-of-tomorrow/articles/2014/09/22/why-college-costs-so-much-overspending-on-faculty-amenities (accessed June 24, 2016).
27. United States Census Bureau. 2016. *College Enrollment of Students 14 Years Old and Over, by Type of College, Attendance Status, Age, and Gender: October 1970 to 2014.* http://www.census.gov/hhes/school/data/cps/historical/index.html (accessed August 8, 2016).
28. National Association of Student Financial Aid Administrators. 2016. *State Financial Aid Programs.* http://www.nasfaa.org/State_Financial_Aid_Programs (accessed December 2, 2016).
29. California Student Aid Commission. 2016. *Financial Aid Programs.* http://www.csac.ca.gov/doc.asp?id=33 (accessed December 2, 2016).
30. College for All Texans. 2016. *Types of Financial Aid.* http://www.collegeforalltexans.com/apps/financialaid/tofa.cfm?Kind=GS (accessed December 2, 2016).
31. Federal Student Aid. 2016. *Grants and Scholarships.* https://studentaid.ed.gov/sa/types/grants-scholarships (accessed December 2, 2016).
32. Federal Student Aid. 2016. *Loans.* https://studentaid.ed.gov/sa/types/loans (accessed December 2, 2016).
33. Rathmanner, D. 2016. Student Loan Debt Statistics 2016. *Lendedu*, July 1. https://lendedu.com/blog/student-loan-debt-statistics (accessed October 29, 2016).
34. Cauchon, D. 2011. Student loans outstanding will exceed $1 trillion this year. *USA Today*, October 25. http://usatoday30.usatoday.com/money/perfi/college/story/2011-10-19/student-loan-debt/50818676/1 (accessed December 4, 2016).
35. Federal Student Aid. 2016. *Work Study Jobs.* https://studentaid.ed.gov/sa/types/work-study (accessed December 2, 2016).
36. U.S. Department of Education. 2016. *Federal Work-Study Programs.* http://www2.ed.gov/programs/fws/index.html (accessed December 4, 2016).
37. Barksdale, M. 2010. *How Work-Study Programs Work. How Stuff Works: Money.* http://money.howstuffworks.com/personal-finance/college-planning/financial-aid/work-study-program.htm/printable (accessed December 4, 2016).
38. Wong, A. 2015. The downfall of for-profit colleges. *The Atlantic*, February 23. http://www.theatlantic.com/education/archive/2015/02/the-downfall-of-for-profit-colleges/385810/ (accessed December 2, 2016).
39. Cohen, P. 2016. Crackdown on for-profit colleges may free students and trap taxpayers. *New York Times*, August 28. http://www.nytimes.com/2016/08/29/business/crackdown-on-for-profit-colleges-may-free-students-and-trap-taxpayers.html (accessed December 2, 2016).
40. Binkley, C. 2016. ITT Tech banned from taking new students with federal aid. *US News*, August 25. https://www.usnews.com/news/business/articles/2016-08-25/itt-tech-banned-from-taking-new-students-with-federal-aid (accessed May 11, 2017).
41. Associated Press. 2016. *US Department of Education Bans Federal Aid for New Students at ITT Educational Services*, August 26. http://www.turnto23.com/news/local-news/us-department-of-education-bans-federal-aid-for-new-students-at-itt-educational-services (accessed May 11, 2017).
42. Cohen, P. 2016. Government moves to close watchdog of for-profit colleges. *New York Times*, September 22. http://www.nytimes.com/2016/09/23/business/government-moves-to-close-a-watchdog-of-for-profit-colleges.html (accessed December 2, 2016).
43. ITT Technical Institute. 2017. *Home Webpage.* http://itt-tech.info/ (accessed May 11, 2017).

44. Yan, S. 2015. *Corinthian Colleges to Close All Remaining Campuses*, April 27. http://money.cnn.com/2015/04/26/news/corinthian-colleges-close/index.html (accessed May 11, 2017).
45. Halprin, D. 2017. Court win for students over predatory for-profit colleges. *Huffington Post*, February 24. http://www.huffingtonpost.com/entry/breaking-judge-rejects-for-profit-college-accreditor_us_58acc0cae4b0d818c4f0a322 (accessed May 11, 2017).

10

Redesigning Curriculum and Pedagogy

Curriculum and pedagogy are the instructional elements of education. Curriculum is determining learning content, the substance of the degree, and pedagogy is designing the method for teaching and delivering content. When curriculum and pedagogy are combined with assessing performance, which is discussed in Chapters 4 and 7, an instructional and learning paradigm is established. As shown in Figure 10.1, curriculum content should determine pedagogy with success or failure being measured by assessment. The results of assessment drive changes in content and pedagogy, and the cycle repeats.

Although the focus of this discussion is undergraduate education, many of the points apply to certificate programs, two-year degrees, and graduate education. Certificates are typically short programs that concentrate on specific subjects such as health information systems or supply chain management. They may require as few as three to five courses but could be much longer, and they are often taken by individuals who already have a degree in higher education and wish to gain knowledge in a specific field to advance their careers. Associate degrees can provide the first two years of a bachelor's degree or specific skills that lead to employment. Graduate education is more challenging, tends to have a tighter topical focus, and has smaller class sizes, especially doctoral courses where five or six is a common size. In 2014, graduate enrollment was about 15% of the enrollment in higher education.[1,2]

Curriculum is packaged in courses that are usually three-credit hours, although others sizes are used. A three-credit course typically meets three hours per week for 14 or 15 weeks. To graduate in four years, students must complete 15 credit hours each semester, or 30 credit hours per year (excluding summers) for a total of 120. A small percent of colleges and universities use the quarter system, which contains three 10-week terms, for a total of 180 credit hours in four years. Semester-hour and quarter-hours are mathematically

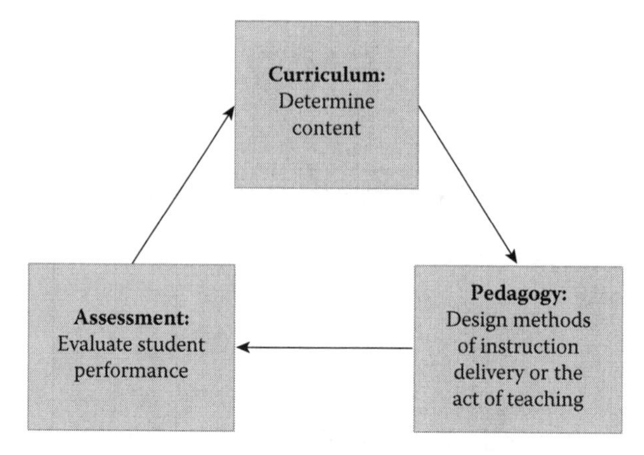

FIGURE 10.1
Paradigm for instruction: curriculum, pedagogy, and assessment.

related with each quarter-hour equaling two-thirds of a semester-hour. The discussion focuses on the semester system because it is far more common.

Pedagogy is the method or practice of teaching, so it defines how knowledge is transferred to individuals. The traditional pedagogical approach, which is commonly used in undergraduate courses, is lecture-discussion, where (1) faculty members explain concepts, models, processes, and techniques and (2) students ask questions, respond to inquiries from faculty, and offer opinions on the topic. As described in Chapter 7, changes in pedagogy that provide different methods of learning for different learning styles should improve the quality of education and lower the cost of instruction.

The goals of redesigning curriculum and pedagogy are as follows:

1. To graduate a higher percentage of students in four years
2. To prepare students better so employers are more satisfied and job placement rates increase
3. To educate students at a lower cost so their debt is substantially reduced or eliminated and their access to higher education improves

10.1 CURRICULUM

It is not feasible to discuss specific curriculum content for all degree programs offered because there are hundreds of them. Plus, no one person or even modest-sized group of people understands the nuances of these programs and has sufficient knowledge to examine content and recommend specific changes. In spite of this, there are still important things to consider.

1. *Curriculum structure:* Although the curriculum contents from engineering to business to education to political science are different, the structure of curriculum is similar. Knowledge is packed into individual courses taught by different faculty members who typically work alone.
2. *Length of a bachelor's degree:* Data show that less than 40% of students graduate with their bachelor's degree in four years.[3] Part of the reason is that many degrees require more than 120 credit hours.[4,5] Having more credit hours raises cost and extends completion time. An important question is: Why should a degree program require more credit hours than can reasonably fit into four years or eight semesters of education?
3. *Unblock path to graduate in four years:* In some popular disciplines, students are unable to enroll in classes because they are "closed," meaning they have reached their enrollment limit. When students follow their plans of study, which they prepare with help from their university advisor, students must be allowed to enroll in these classes so graduation is not delayed.
4. *Incorporate ideas from potential employers and others:* Inputs from potential employers, graduate school admission requirements, and performance on licensure and certification exams must guide universities as they revise curriculum and set performance standards. These ideas are explored in Chapter 8, and no further discussion in necessary.
5. *Career development:* Traditional students, who are straight from high school, may have the intellectual abilities to graduate and work effectively at a job, but they may not understand the job market and how to present themselves to secure the best employment.

10.1.1 Curriculum Structure

Curricula content for various undergraduate degrees are different, but the structure is likely to be similar to the following.[6,7]

1. *General education:* These courses are taken by all students attending the university, regardless of their field of study. This element prepares students to value, participate, and contribute in a changing

and diverse world, and it encourages and facilitates lifelong learning. It provides critical thinking skills and perspectives that help students with decision making. The contents usually include English composition, communication, mathematics, economic, humanities, fine arts, social science, natural science, and cross-cultural studies. Many times, students are given a list of courses in each area of study and must select one or more. General education requires about two full-time semesters of coursework, and it is typically completed in the first two years.

2. *Disciplinary core:* This is a set of courses that are foundational and/or complementary to the field of study selected by students and are typically taken during the first three years of a four-year degree. The following examples illustrate this point.
   a. *Business administration degree:* Requires basic course work in accounting, statistics, information technology, management, marketing, finance, operations and supply chain management, and international business.
   b. *Education degree:* Requires knowledge in applied psychology for teaching, instructional methods, technology and multimedia, and assessment and remediation.
   c. *Engineering degree:* Often requires knowledge in computer-aided design, materials science, technical writing, engineering statics, and mechanic of materials.
   d. *Social work degree:* There is supporting course work in psychology, anthropology, and human behavior that complements a major in social work.
   e. *Geography and planning degree:* Students seeking this degree may take courses in closely related fields such as sociology, economic, and anthropology.
3. *Major field of study:* This segment of the curriculum defines the specialty area where students study and plan to gain entry-level employment. The major is usually completed during the last two years of study. Business students may major in accounting, finance, supply chain management, and a dozen or so additional fields. Engineers may build expertise in several fields, including civil, electrical, and mechanical engineering. Educators may specialize in elementary, secondary, or other educational choices. Social worker, geographers, biologists, geologists, and others build depth in their fields of study.

4. *Minor field of study and/or free electives:* Some programs have a minor that complements the major. For example, a psychology major may find value in a philosophy minor. Free electives are satisfied by any course, so they help transfer students because courses completed for their first degree but that are not needed in the new program can be counted as free electives. For example, if a student completed a material science course and decided to transfer from engineering to business, this course may count as a free elective because there is no similar course in business.

10.1.2 Length of a Bachelor's Degree

The nominal length of a bachelor's degree is 120 semester credit hours, which can be completed in four years when taking 15 hours per semester. However, Complete College America, a national nonprofit organization, estimates that nearly half of all undergraduate degree programs require more than 120 credit hours for a bachelor's degree. Some examples are listed in Table 10.1.[5] Even when students take 15 credit hours each term, these degree programs may require 4.5 or 5 years of study, possibly more, so too many students take longer than four years to earn a bachelor's degree. As shown by the first column of data in Table 10.1, all degrees have at least one option that offers the program in 120 credit hours. Professional degree programs tend to have a higher median number and a higher maximum number of student credit hours than the nonprofessional programs.[5]

The financial impact of another year on campus at a public university was $24,061 in 2015–2016. The amount was half as much when only one semester was needed. For these data, see Table 1.1 in Chapter 1. There may be ways to reduce this extra cost. Students can move home, take courses at a local, public university, and transfer the credits back so they can graduate. Whether students move home or not, they lose nearly four months of wages for each semester they are unable to work at their new career. Lost wages mount up quickly and are not recoverable.

The arguments against a bachelor's degree requiring more than 120 semester credit hours are as follows: it (1) prolongs graduation; (2) increases costs for tuition, fees, textbooks, and so on; and (3) prevents graduates from earning career-level wages during this time. The argument in favor of setting the graduation requirement higher than 120 credit hours is that there is simply too much for students to learn so they can (1) succeed in their jobs and careers, (2) pass certification and licensure

TABLE 10.1

Credit Hours Required for Various Bachelor's Degrees

Degree	Minimum Number of Semester Credit Hours[a]	Median Number of Semester Credit Hours[b]	Maximum Number of Semester Credit Hours[c]
Professional Degrees			
Computer science	120	123	137
Education	120	124	172
Engineering	120	128	143
Nursing (4-year)	120	124	149
Social work	120	120	150
NonProfessional Degrees			
Communications	120	120	128
Foreign language	120	120	128
History	120	120	141
Philosophy	120	120	130
Political science	120	120	128
Woman's studies	120	120	128

Source: Complete College America, *Program Requirements for Associate's and Bachelor's Degrees: A National Survey*, 2012. http://www.completecollege.org/docs/Program%20Requirements%20-%20A%20National%20Survey.pdf

[a] The lowest number of credit hours among all universities responding to the survey.

[b] The midpoint of the data, such that half the data points are higher and half are lower among all universities responding to the survey.

[c] The highest number of credit hours among all universities responding to the survey.

exams, or (3) gain admission to graduate school. Certification and licensure exams are part of the reason why professional degrees tend to have more student credit hours. For example, accounting is moving toward a five-year program that requires 150 credit hours. Although applicants can take the CPA exam with fewer hours, many states now require 150 semester hours of education, in addition to passing the CPA exam, to obtain a CPA license.[8] Upward pressure on the number of credit hours is easy for universities and faculty to support because it increases demand for their services and generates more revenue.

When the "explosion of knowledge" argument is used to justify more credit hours, the question is: When does it stop? The argument goes, knowledge has expanded greatly over the past 50 years, so more credit hours are justified. But it is likely that the next 50 years will generate even more new ideas. Should another semester or year of study be added to a bachelor's degree? Should it take at least five years for students to graduate, with many taking up to seven years? Hopefully the answer is no. The better approach is to (1) make learning more efficient so students learn more in less time, the essence of student-centered learning from Chapter 7 and (2) rely on graduates to become lifelong learners.

Universities are proponents of lifelong learning, implying that graduates do not know all they need to know for a happy and productive life. Plus, graduates from 50 years ago learned many things that are not remotely relevant todays such as (1) using punched cards as input to computers, (2) programming with the Formula Translation language, more commonly known as FORTRAN, and (3) making design drawings with a T-square and triangles. Graduates could prepare a much longer list of things they learned, which they have never or rarely used because they worked in a different field or new ideas and techniques have replaced old ones. There is even a longer list of things they had to learn along the way to keep pace with the growth in knowledge. For these reasons, universities are correct in claiming that people must become lifelong learners, and because they are correct about this, they are not correct when they expand curricula because existing knowledge will become obsolete and new knowledge will be created. Following are some recommendations to consider:

1. *120 credit hour mandate:* State government should require undergraduate programs at public universities to have no more than 120 credit hours.
2. *Potential employer needs:* Content is determined by interactions between potential employers and tenured and professional faculty. These groups must work together to determine what is best learned in the classroom and what can be learned on the job, so programs like engineering, accounting, and social work can meet the 120 credit hour requirement.
3. *Cooperative (co-op) education and internships:* These programs blend classroom education with work experience in ways that accentuate learning. Internship programs, including student teaching, can be accomplished within 120 credit hours. Completing a co-op program in four years may take a little more thought and careful planning, but it can be accomplished.
4. *Healthcare-related degree:* Many healthcare professionals such as nurses and therapist earn a four-year degree. In fact, the Bachelor of Science in Nursing (BSN) is becoming the preferred degree for

registered nurse (RN). Although some may hesitate to recommend a cap on credit hours because these professionals deal with human life, there does not appear to be a good reason to exceed a 120 credit hour limit. Prior to the BSN, and even today, students can earn nursing diplomas after three years of study. They can also become nurses by earning an associate degree. Regardless of which degree they earn, nurses become RNs after passing the appropriate National Council Licensure Examination (NCLEX-RN), which insures a certain level of knowledge. In addition, knowledge changes quickly and healthcare professionals require continuing education. Who wants a healthcare professional with 40-year-old knowledge?

5. *Licensure and certification:* Other professionals require certification and licensure and some degree programs are accredited. Educational leaders must work with licensing bodies and accrediting agencies to ensure that bachelor's degrees require no more than 120 credit hours.

10.1.3 Unblock Path to Graduate in Four Years

As mentioned in Chapter 7, plans of study are contracts with students, and institutions must honor them by providing enough seats in courses so students can complete their degree on time, which is four years for full-time students. This means that students who are following their plans of study do not face closed classes when their plans specify that a course is to be taken in a particular semester. In some cases, the enrollment limit is real–equipment, lab space, and other items are required for each student–so only a specific number of seats are available. There are other reasons why seats are limited, such as courses are writing intensive or require verbal presentations by students. Even in traditional lecture-discussion courses, the assigned rooms have a specific numbers of seats, although these courses could be reassigned to larger classrooms. In some cases, class limits are arbitrary and quite meaningless and can be easily changed. Regardless of the reason for the limit, universities must find seats for students who have a course identified in their plan of study. The only other option for universities is to provide a new plan of study that allows students to graduate on time and to which the students agree.

Some administrators argue that ensuring available classes for all students with plans of study is too difficult, but it is not. Universities should proactively plan to address trends in demand. For example, when the U.S.

Bureau of Labor Statistics project an increase in demand for nurses, universities may respond by putting more resources in that program and taking resources from programs that have declining demand. Often the response is that this is not possible because universities have tenured faculty who cannot be terminated. Recall from Table 1.3 in Chapter 1 that only 30% or so of faculty members are tenured. This provides substantial flexibility for decreasing or increasing teaching capacity through contractual faculty and graduate teaching assistants. If universities feel uncomfortable about expanding capacity, they should admit the number of students that they can educate rather than taking all who apply and are qualified. This type of long-term planning yields a meaningful and useful faculty hiring plan.

On an operating basis, universities can do the following. As they prepare for each semester, which should take place several months prior to any semester, they can load plans of study for all students onto their tentative class schedule to determine where they have surpluses and shortages of courses. Universities can use this approach to plan for a year or even more, and they can adjust capacity in the short term by hiring additional contractual faculty to meet demand or releasing contractual faculty when they have excess capacity. If they have an effective long-term planning process and have created a faculty hiring plan, as described in the prior paragraph, this operational plan should allow universities to fine-tune course offerings, ensuring that students are not closed out of classes.

10.1.4 Career Development

Students who come directly from high school often lack the knowledge and experience to pick the right major, search for jobs, and create professional relationships. These students often do not get the job they want or deserve because they lack skills in these areas. Short courses on professional development that are two credit hours in total would help students:

1. Perform self-assessment to understand their strengths, weaknesses, and interests.
2. Explore career options with help from faculty, who can explain the various majors, and industry executives, who can describe job opportunities and the work environment.
3. Understand the value of improving communication, listening, and organizational skills.
4. Develop a resume and cover letter.

5. Enhance job search skills and networking.
6. Prepare for interviews, have practice interviews, and know how to dress professionally.

A one-hour course in the sophomore year could address the first three points, and a second one-hour course in the junior year would prepare students for the job search process in their senior year. Program advisory boards (PABs), which are discussed in Chapter 8, are useful resources for this endeavor.

10.2 PEDAGOGY

A critical change in pedagogy is switching from teacher-centered to student-centered learning, meaning that the method of instruction is customized to match how students learn. Another element is online learning, which has the potential to fundamentally change how knowledge is delivered by greatly reducing or possibly eliminating face-to-face interactions, traditional printed textbooks, student activities fees, and dormitories. These two changes should be viewed together because online learning presents opportunities for faculty to redesign how knowledge is delivered in both traditional courses and 100% online courses. These important points are discussed in detail in the following sections.

10.2.1 Student-Centered Learning

Chapter 7 discusses student-centered learning, describes different learning styles, and offers an example of how this might be accomplished for a course in basic statistics. The following discussion takes a step back and describes how the different types of courses—general education, disciplinary core, major field of study, and minor field of study—impact what and how students are expected to learn. For this discussion, major and minor fields are combined because a minor field of study is often a subset of courses in a major. For example, students who decide to minor in psychology would take fewer psychology courses than students who are taking a major.

Figure 10.2 shows that the learning environment changes as students transition from general education courses to their major and minor fields. Course content becomes more challenging and learning more focused. As students

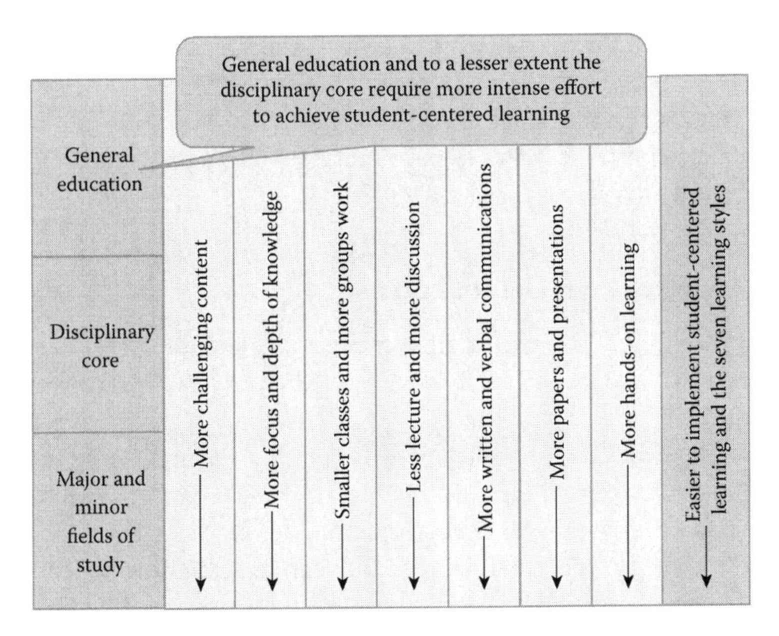

FIGURE 10.2
Curriculum structure, the learning environment, and student-centered learning.

transition from their general education to their disciplinary core and then to their major courses within the discipline, their depth of knowledge increases substantially. This is the essence of the phrase "sharp, deep, and narrow." Students strive to gain expertise, so they have the knowledge to secure an entry-level position. As they mature and learn on the job, they gain more knowledge and expertise, which makes them more valuable. They begin to see the "big picture" and advance up the organizational ladder to jobs that require greater vision, hold more responsibility, and demand leadership.

The transition from general education to the major and minor fields of study typically means that students are in smaller classes where there is more group work and group projects, and the learning process changes so there is less lecturing and more interacting. (See Figure 10.2.) During this transition, there are opportunities to use different learning styles. There is more written and verbal communications and more student papers and presentations that require students to integrate ideas and solve problems. There are also opportunities for hands-on learning such as studio courses that require performing; cooperative education and internships programs that are often part of professional degree programs; and mentorship programs that link students with experts in the workforce. Because of these opportunities, it is easier to use the seven learning styles in major and minor courses than in general education courses, so faculty must become especially creative in general education courses. The example of the statistics course in Chapter 7 illustrates that it is possible even in a quantitative course. It is the responsibility of faculty to achieve student-centered learning across the curriculum.

10.2.2 Online Programs and Courses

Online learning is the twenty-first century's version of correspondence courses, which have been offered by universities for nearly 200 years. The University of London was the first to offer distance learning degrees in 1828. In the United States, only one-third of the population lived in cities with 100,000 or more people in 1920, so the correspondence technique became an effective way to reach the rural population.[9] Obviously, computer technology and Internet communication, including video, have transformed the way distance learning is conducted. Most public universities offer online courses and some offer online degree programs. Some private, not-for-profit universities, like Southern New Hampshire University and Western Governors University, and many private, for-profit universities, like the University of Phoenix and Strayer University, have substantial online offerings.

10.2.2.1 Online Learning Concerns

Part of the problem with online learning is that people tend to view new technology from their current circumstance. Some administrators see online learning as a budget bonanza. There are no physical classrooms, so facility costs are much lower; and there are no space limitations, so class size can be very large—literally thousands of students could be taught by one instructor. Even with these savings, they are willing to charge the same tuition for online and classroom classes. Preparing an online course is thought to be easy because it is only necessary to scan a copy of the textbook to make an e-book (early on copyrights were ignored); put the PowerPoint slides and homework problems online; and have a way to answer students' questions such as e-mail, group chats, and texts/instance messaging. Students would submit assignments electronically using e-mail or other technology. The approach simply "electrifies" the old way without taking advantage of the unique capability of the technology.

Many faculty members are concerned about the quality of online education, wondering how much and what students are learning. Do students gain knowledge and conceptual insights or do online courses encourage memorization of terms and facts? In some cases, faculty compensation for online courses is based on the number of students enrolled, so reducing content and setting lower standards for student performance might encourage enrollment. The latter point is easily addressed if course content, test preparation, and determination of final grade are separated from instruction. When online learning has no face-to-face meetings, there are concerns that students cannot have meaningful interactions with faculty, so they do not have the same learning opportunities. There is little chance to network with other students, and it is more difficult to build study groups and learn from each other.

Security is important with online learning. Even with face-to-face classes there are concerns about whether students prepare their homework assignments, write their term papers, and construct PowerPoint slide decks for their presentations. Or does someone else do the work? But in face-to-face classes, it is clear who shows up to take tests. Even in very large face-to-face classes, picture IDs can be checked to verify that the right person takes the exam. That explains why most face-to-face courses rely heavily on in-classroom midterm and final exams to determine final course grades. Online courses typically use electronic rather than face-to-face testing, which makes it easier for someone else to take the test.

10.2.2.2 Moving Forward with Online Learning

Having online capabilities is also advantageous for face-to-face classes. Passing course syllabi, homework assignments, reading materials, and other items electronically is so much easier, consumes less paper, and prevents the excuse that students do not have course materials because they missed class. Plus, interactive, e-learning tools, video capture of lectures, electronic collection of homework assignments, and other capabilities make face-to-face classes better. This approach, which is called blended learning, is used in many courses because it captures the best features of traditional and online methods.

There are great opportunities for online courses and programs that have no face-to-face meetings and all interactions are electronic because costs can be less and student assess can be easier. Plus, the reach of top faculty and the best universities is greatly enhanced, so students have access to the best education.[10] The balance of the e-learning discussion considers 100% online courses.

Proponents argue that online learning will eventually eliminate traditional education methods whether applied to K-12 or higher education. They further suggest that massive open online courses (MOOC) will revolutionize how knowledge is presented. MOOCs are available to anyone with Internet access and are often free of charge. The Khan Academy is the most commonly known entity that provides these courses,[11] but institutions including Stanford University and the University of Michigan have some offerings.[12] The claim is that online learning will drive down the cost of education by eliminating waste, bloated administration, and overpaid, underworked tenured faculty.[13]

There is little doubt that higher education will move along the continuum from where it is currently toward the point where all courses and programs are 100% online, closing dormitories and classrooms. What is unclear is whether it goes all the way and how long will it take. New technology, especially technology that incites radical change, goes through a series of stages.

1. *Ignored:* At first, people do not see its potential and how it might be used. Those who have some understanding of how the technology might be used to lower costs and improve outcomes have a vested interest in the status quo so they ignore the opportunity and may even resist change. This was the case with electronic health records, where the advantages were clear and the technology was feasible for decades before it was actually implemented.
2. *Overhyped:* The rise and fall: At a later point, people begin to see the advantages of the new way of doing things, and there are wild projections about how quickly and how much change will take place. The online surge in the late 1990s, which was about 20 years ago, led to the tech-bubble in the stock market. At the time, online retail was supposed to "lay waste to" brick-and-mortar retail. To provide a picture of the rise and fall of online retail, follow Amazon's stock price. In 1997, its stock price was less than $2 per share, but in 1999, during the growing tech-bubble, it rose to more than $110. In 2001, after the bubble burst, it dropped to about $5.[14] During the bubble, many, many technology companies went out of business. Online retail may never entirely replace brick-and-mortar stores, but it will continue to grow and take market share from them. It seems reasonable to think of online learning in the same manner.

3. *Real and sustainable growth:* After the plunge, many people were skeptical of online commerce or e-commerce, but there was real value, and over the next few years it slowly recovered and ultimately gained steam and grew rapidly. Amazon's stock price reflects this recovery, topping $800 per share in late 2016.[14]

Online learning is no longer ignored as it has emerged as an important tool for higher education. Online learning has grown rapidly, especially in private, for-profit universities that find this technology easier to implement, less costly, and more useful for their customers. As evidence of this growth, consider that from 1997 until 2010, the number of private, for-profit institutions has grown from about 600 to nearly 1,200, while the number of public and private, not-for-profit institutions is virtually unchanged.[15] Growth of for-profit universities has been fueled, in part, by demand for online learning, but as described in Chapter 9, these universities have performed poorly with low graduation rates and long completion times. The perception of many is that their overall quality must improve.[16]

Online learning must be more than a sprinkling or even an inundation of MOOCs or other online courses. Up to now, public universities as well as private, not-for-profit universities offer some online courses and may have a few programs that are 100% online. But they do not appear to have an overarching plan for implementing online learning to improve quality, enhance student access, and lower costs. They select courses for online delivery because a certain faculty member is interested in developing the course. The outcome is an online course here and an online course there, rather than an entire online degree program. To illustrate the haphazard nature of online learning and the attitude of students, it is not uncommon for students who are living on campus to enroll in online courses for reasons that have nothing to do with easier access.

10.2.2.3 Implementing Online Learning

For online learning to succeed, universities must offer well-designed degree programs with exceptional quality, high performance standards, and impeccable security. The programs should be easy to access and cost less. Private, for-profit universities have dropped the ball with respect to online learning, opening a window of opportunity for public and private, not-for-profit institutions to develop strategies and plans that include well-constructed online offerings. These efforts must include the following:

1. *High quality:* The most important element is ensuring that online programs and individual courses have the same high quality as their face-to-face counterparts. Universities have standing and these offering must maintain, even enhance, their reputations. On-line offerings must be designed so students can interact with faculty and other students to create networking opportunities and mechanisms to exchange ideas and create study groups.
2. *Invest in technology and program content:* It is not enough to use electronic copies of existing books, put power point slides online, and use video capture to allow students to view previous lectures. Quality depends on universities investing in the technology to deliver online content reliably and quickly, but more importantly, investing in high-quality productions that deliver outstanding content. This means working with publisher to create good e-learning tools and with firms that can provide high-quality instructional videos. This new approach is very different from the way courses are currently developed where individual faculty is responsible for designing and preparing a course. The new approach requires a substantial investment in course development, which universities have not done and do not seem to understand.
3. *Security:* There must be effective ways to ensure that the person who enrolls in the course is actually doing the work. When students live close, it is possible to have them come to campus for exams. If they live too far from campus or live close by but are unable to come to campus, there must be a way to verify who is taking the exam. It is possible to use libraries or other entities that are close to the students, so their identification can be checked. This can be a logistics nightmare when all or most students in a large class need this service. It is even more challenging when students are outside of the United States. Therefore, having a sophisticated electronic identification method to ensure security is essential.
4. *Getting started:* It makes sense to begin the process with high-enrollment courses, where it is possible to enjoy the economies of

scale and more easily recoup the investment in course development. These tend to be general education courses or disciplinary core courses.

5. *Complete programs:* Once universities understand the pitfalls and problems in developing online courses and see the advantages of their efforts, they should quickly move to offering entire programs online rather than a hodgepodge of courses that spark the interest of administrators and faculty. Students should see an online path to their degree. Graduate and certificate programs are good initial candidates because they are short, and graduate students and individuals who pursue certificates tend to be mature and motivated to follow through.
6. *Sharing online offerings:* States tend to have more than one public university in order to serve different regions. Having multiple public universities in the state offering the same online programs should not be necessary. It seems to make sense for two or more state universities, possibly all of them, to work together in order to share infrastructure, development costs, program delivery, and revenue from online programs.
7. *Student fees:* Online students should not pay activity fees because they are not on campus to enjoy the benefits.

10.2.2.4 Productivity and Online Learning

Many faculty members believe that teaching online actually takes more time and effort than teaching a face-to-face class. They argue that online courses require faculty to answer the same question multiple times, whereas in a face-to-face class, the question is raised, answered, and the issue is resolved. Answering complex questions online can be more challenging because there is less opportunity for dialogue that enriches the discussion. It might take a few hours to a few days for the dialogue to take place using email or some form of instant messaging. Courses that require showing and demonstrating such as statistics, mathematics, and physics are more challenging in the online mode.

Although there may be elements of truth in these statements, these problems can be resolved when course designers think about these issues from a new perspective, a perspective that understands the capabilities of the new technology. For example, demonstration can actually be better with high-quality, short videos that show students how to calculate standard deviation or perform physics experiments. With careful design, the instructor can anticipate questions and build in answers, and students can view it over and over to catch the nuances. Plus, they can view it in small groups and help one another.

In healthcare and education, increasing productivity is often viewed negatively by professionals because these "enhancements" often involved simple-minded ideas, like cut the number of nurses in a hospital wing or increase the number of students in a class. The pushback was that administrators do not want quality care/instruction. Plus, this "load-on-the-work" mentality implies that nurses and faculty were slackers who should be working harder. A better approach is the application of technology that actually makes the work faster and easier. This approach implies an understanding that the work is challenging and resources are needed to make the job faster and easier. In medicine, the clearest examples are advancements in technology that have substantially increased the productivity of surgeons whether they are ophthalmologists or orthopedists. In higher education, the productivity of secretaries and clerical staff has been increased by information technology, which has virtually eliminated dictation, dramatically reduced typing duties, and simplified bookkeeping entries and other routine actions. The application of technology to teaching, which is discussed in Chapter 12, can improve productivity and may be able to improve it dramatically. The productivity of administrators is discussed in Chapter 11.

10.3 DRIVING FORCES FOR CHANGE

Tenured faculty members and universities are key players in changing curriculum and pedagogy, but they need persuasion. For public universities, federal, state, and to a lesser extent, local governments can require changes that reduce curriculum length as well as improve pedagogy. Governments should be supported by students, parents, other family members, and friends, who want a high-quality education, lower cost, better graduation rates, completion in four years, and good job opportunities. Private universities only receive money from the federal government, so there is less opportunity for government pressure to drive changes, but if public universities are successful at improving outcomes, many private universities will take notice.

10.4 IMPACT OF REDESIGNING CURRICULUM AND PEDAGOGY ON HIGHER EDUCATION OUTCOMES

The heart of higher education is curriculum content and pedagogy. Improving these and making the process more efficient should drive costs lower and improve quality. The following list examines how this element of the solution impacts the root causes, which are discussed in Chapter 4:

1. *Lack of understanding—Who is the customer? (root cause 1):* Redesigning curriculum and pedagogy forces universities to consider the needs of customers, including students, governments, and other third-party payers.
2. *Limited productivity improvements for universities (root cause 4):* Efforts to reduce curriculum length to 120 credit hours, implement student-centered learning, and increase the use of online learning should improve productivity and reduce costs.
3. *Rapidly growing costs for books and supplies (root cause 5):* Changing how students learn should be done in ways that lower the cost of textbooks and other learning materials.
4. *Eroding standards (root cause 8):* Focusing on curriculum as well as involving potential employers and accreditation agencies helps to maintain robust curriculum content and rigorous performance standards.

10.5 SUMMARY OF RECOMMENDATIONS

Following is a list of the key recommendations that comprise this element of the solution.

1. Bachelor's degrees should be limited to 120 credit hours to lower tuition costs and enable students to graduate in four years.
2. Universities should engage in effective long-term and short-term planning to ensure that students do not face closed classes that prohibit them from graduating in four years.
3. Potential employers work with tenured and professional faculty to set curriculum content and performance standards so graduates learn more and are prepared for the job market.

4. Students should have short courses in professional development to prepare for their job search.
5. Student-centered learning, which is customized to meet individual learning needs, should make it easier and faster to learn. This may be more challenging in general education courses, but it can be accomplished using technology.
6. Online programs and courses can become a low-cost way to deliver a quality education and make it more accessible. Universities should do the following:
   a. Make the upfront investments to develop high-quality programs and courses.
   b. Invest in technology to deliver program content effectively.
   c. Start with high-enrollment courses, where it is possible to enjoy economies of scale.
   d. Offer complete programs so online students can graduate without setting foot on campus.
   e. Create educational programs that are secure so the person who received the grade is the person actually doing the work.
   f. Share online offerings with other universities to spread the fixed costs of course development.
   g. Have no activity fees for students enrolling in online learning.

REFERENCES

1. National Center for Education Statistics. 2015. *Undergraduate Enrollment*. http://nces.ed.gov/programs/coe/indicator_cha.asp (accessed December 13, 2016).
2. National Center for Education Statistics. 2015. *Postbaccalaureate Enrollment*. http://nces.ed.gov/programs/coe/indicator_chb.asp (accessed December 13, 2016).
3. National Center for Education Statistics. 2015. *Graduation Rates*. https://nces.ed.gov/fastfacts/display.asp?id=40 (accessed July 5, 2016).
4. eHow.com. 2016. *Credit Hours Needed for a Bachelor's Degree*. http://www.ehow.com/facts_4779696_credit-hours-needed-bachelor-degree.html (accessed December 11, 2016).
5. Complete College America. 2012. *Program Requirements for Associate's and Bachelor's Degrees: A National Survey*. http://www.completecollege.org/docs/Program%20Requirements%20-%20A%20National%20Survey.pdf (accessed December 11, 2016).
6. The University of Pennsylvania. 2016. *College Curriculum: Structure and Requirements*. https://www.college.upenn.edu/curriculum-structure (accessed December 7, 2016).
7. The University of Toledo. 2016. *University Core Curriculum*. https://www.utoledo.edu/catalog/pdf/University_Core_2009_2010.pdf (accessed December 7, 2016).

8. American Institute of CPAs. 2016. *150 Hour Requirement for Obtaining a CPA License.* http://www.aicpa.org/BecomeACPA/Licensure/Requirements/Pages/default.aspx (accessed December 12, 2016).
9. Wikipedia. 2016. *Distance Education.* https://en.wikipedia.org/wiki/Distance_education (accessed December 15, 2016).
10. Tabarrok, A. 2012. Why online education works. *CATO Unbound: A Journal of Debate,* November 12. https://www.cato-unbound.org/2012/11/12/alex-tabarrok/why-online-education-works (accessed December 19, 2016).
11. Khan Academy. 2016. *Course Offerings.* https://www.khanacademy.org/ (accessed December 15, 2016).
12. MOOC-List.com. 2016. *MOOC-List.* https://www.mooc-list.com/ (accessed December 15, 2016).
13. Sandefer, J. 2016. *The Death of Higher Education in America and the Rise of the 21st Century Entrepreneur.* http://popecenter.org/acrobat/JeffSandefer.pdf (accessed December 15, 2016).
14. TD Ameritrade. 2016. *Amazon Stock Price: Past 20 Years.* https://invest.ameritrade.com/grid/p/site#r=jPage/https://research.ameritrade.com/grid/wwws/research/stocks/charts?symbol=AMZN&c_name=invest_VENDOR (accessed December 15, 2016).
15. United States Department of the Treasury and Department of Education. 2012. *The Economics of Higher Education.* December. https://www.treasury.gov/connect/blog/Documents/20121212_Economics%20of%20Higher%20Ed_vFINAL.pdf (accessed June 23, 2016).
16. Wong, A. 2015. The downfall of for-profit colleges. *The Atlantic,* February 23. http://www.theatlantic.com/education/archive/2015/02/the-downfall-of-for-profit-colleges/385810/ (accessed December 2, 2016).

11

Reforming Administration and Management

The evidence is overwhelming. A primary reason for the rising costs in higher education is a rapid increase in spending on administration and management. *Inflation-adjusted* tuition at public universities tripled from 1980 to 2000. This was much faster than the rate of increase in health-care costs. In the U.S. economy, only cigarettes and other tobacco products increased faster. Universities have not used the additional funds for instruction/faculty because student-faculty ratios have not changed since 1975.[1] Instead, universities choose to increase spending on administration and staff. At the same time, they began to replace tenured faculty who held key administrative positions with professional managers. When tenured faculty held these posts, administrators and faculty tended to work cooperatively, but as these jobs transitioned to professional managers, administrators could act independently and faculty inputs were marginalized.[1] Efforts by universities to shift hiring from tenured faculty to contractual faculty, who serve at the pleasure of administrators, further divided administration and faculty.

Growth in administrations combined with less faculty involvement creates a blame game that pits administrators against faculty, wastes valuable resources, and stymies innovation. When administrators are asked what are the most difficult issues facing public universities, the two primary answers are (1) declining state support and (2) difficult and uncooperative faculty. At the same time, faculty members describe their university as being highly centralized and bloated with too many administrators earning exorbitant salaries and having leadership that is balancing the budget on the backs of faculty.

The Huffington Post claims that administrative growth has outpaced enrollment and faculty growth, and this disparate increase has continued unabated for many years.[2] The National Center for Policy Analysis states that tuition has grown much faster than the rate of inflation, yet the increase is not going to instruction; rather, it is going to administrators who do no teaching and conduct no research.[3]

The New York Times argues that the large increase in administrative spending is highly correlated with the tremendous increase in tuition. State support for higher education has increased substantially, but per capita subsidies are lower because enrollment has increased significantly over the past three or four decades. On the federal side, Pell Grants are three times larger than they were in 2000. When adjusted for inflation, full-time faculty salaries are only slightly higher than they were in 1970. When the trend towards part-time faculty, who make substantially less money, is included, instructional costs are actually lower today. In contrast, the administrative positions and spending have grown rapidly.[4]

In Chapter 4, as well as other places in the book, the following data have been cited, and these data are consistent with the comments in the preceding discussion. From 1978 to 2014, the number of administrative positions increased by 369%, whereas tenured faculty increased by only 23%.[5] For the same period, enrollment in undergraduate degree programs grew by 73%, which is much higher than the rate of growth in tenured faculty and much smaller than the growth in administration.[6] In addition to the rapid growth in the number of administrators, wages for top- and mid-level administrators are growing much faster than faculty wages or the rate of inflation.[1] These data along with other information cited earlier indicate that universities have made poor decisions about allocating resources to administration. The key questions are as follows: How did universities get to this point? How can this be resolved?

11.1 ADMINISTRATIVE STRUCTURE

Before diving into these questions, it is helpful to understand a university's structure. Figure 11.1 is a simplified version of an organizational chart. A university tends to have a governing body, which is often called the board of trustees. At public universities, the board is appointed by state government. The board approves strategies, plans, budgets, personnel, and

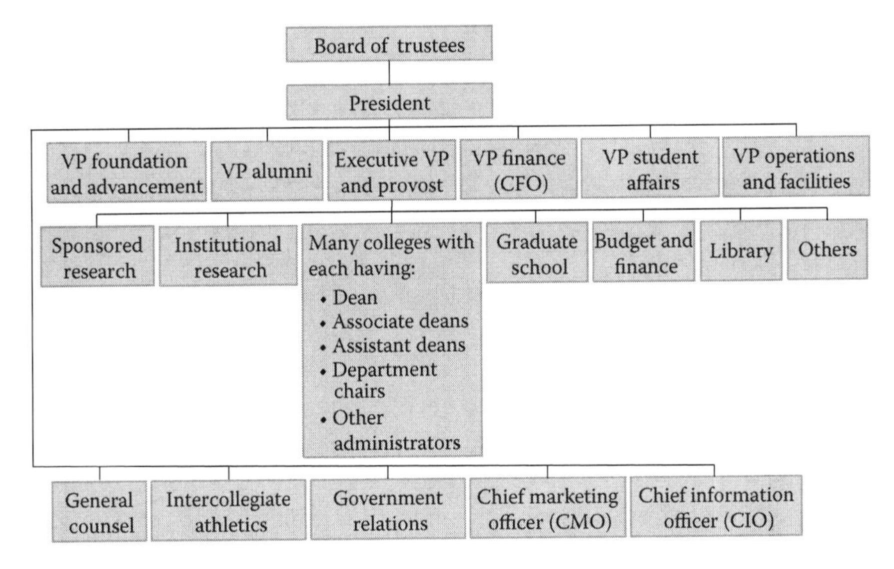

FIGURE 11.1
Simplified organizational chart for public universities.

other key decisions. The president is the chief executive officer and has a large executive team. In some cases, universities own and operate hospitals as part of their mission to educate physicians, nurses, and other medical professionals. This is not shown in Figure 11.1. It is vital to realize that the boxes in Figure 11.1 do not even show the "tip of the iceberg" because there are many deputies, associates, and assistants who work with the board, president, vice presidents (VPs), and other top managers. In turn, the deputies, associates, and assistants have directors, managers, specialists, supervisors, and staff who are part of the administration. The size and complexity of the structure are staggering. Brief descriptions of the president's direct reports are provided here.

1. *VP foundation and advancement:* This is the fundraising arm that seeks money from alumni and other donors. The foundation, which holds the funds, is often a separate legal entity with its own board so it has fiscal autonomy and does not have to abide by spending restriction that states impose, such as a prohibition on purchasing alcohol.
2. *VP alumni:* This entity tracks alumni, gathers information about their success, and keeps them up to date on what is happening at the university. This is useful for fundraising.

3. *Executive VP and provost:* This is often the most powerful person at a university after the chairperson of the board and the president. The provost is responsible for all aspects of academics. Figure 11.1 shows some of the elements within the purview of the provost.
   a. *Sponsored research:* This function supports the pursuit, budgeting, and compliance of research grants from federal, state, and other sources.
   b. *Institutional research:* Information about students, resources consumed, and outputs achieved are collected and analyzed by this group.
   c. *Colleges:* Each college has a dean who reports to the provost, and each dean is supported by associate and assistant deans as well as other administrators. Faculty report through their academic department chairs to the dean and to the provost.
   d. *Graduate school:* This is the management home for graduate programs. It usually supports admissions, provides and controls the budget for graduate assistantships, and creates and monitors compliance with university guidelines and state rules regarding graduate education.
   e. *Budget and finance:* Ensures that colleges and other entities do not overspend, and what they do spend is in accordance with university and state policy.
   f. *Library:* Universities may have multiple libraries that support learning and research.
4. *VP finance:* Responsible for budget preparations, accounts receivable, accounts payable, payroll, and other functions
5. *VP student affairs:* This is a very large bureaucracy as it deals with all aspects related to students such as housing, student activities, food services, book stores, campus security, parking service, student healthcare, and more. At some universities, this function reports to the provost.
6. *VP of operations and facilities:* Deals with day-to-day support for facilities, including comfort and cleaning as well as sustainability of buildings and equipment, renovations and new construction, and requirements driven by government regulation.
7. *More Presidential Direct Reports:* The president has a legal staff to deal with various issues. Intercollegiate athletics, by itself, is a major undertaking. Government relations, marketing the institution, and ensuring high-quality, reliable, and safe information systems are critical.

11.2 CREATING AN EXTERNAL RULING CLASS

It is a challenge to know when and how the separation between administration and faculty began, but it most likely started after World War II when the GI Bill and other factors stoked demand and an era of unprecedented enrollment growth began. During this period, the oversight boards for public universities were perfunctory—filled with alumni of the university, supporters of the governor, and other political and community leaders. These boards rarely said no. In responding to unprecedented growth, errors were made, especially in allocating resources as universities built facilities to serve what appeared to be unending demand and hired administrators to solve problems. Little attention was paid to rising costs.

As enrollment grew and problems that accompany growth continued, states began to take board appointments more seriously. Wealthy alumni, who were appointed to the board and made their money in business, engineering, medicine, or other endeavors, began to exercise authority. They wanted more responsiveness and accountability from top administrators. Thus, a process began to centralize decision making and move away from faculty administrators to professional managers who were hired through a national search process. Professional managers owed allegiance to the board and depended on its chairperson for recommendations for their next job. The idea of national searches and hiring external candidates expanded beyond the presidency to include VPs, provosts, deans, and others. Many, even most, of the people hired to fill these positions, including the president, held faculty rank, but make no mistake, these hires represent the "ruling class" with allegiance to the board, not the faculty. These professional tended to view management as an end in itself. They did not want to return to the faculty.

In addition to this change in leadership, public universities became large, complex entities that are difficult to manage. Universities are not command and control organizations with top-down decision making and a singular bottom-line metric. They are PSOs that depend on the expertise and creativity of faculty to mediate relationships between students and potential employers. Faculty members co-create value by working closely with students, potential employers, and suppliers of learning materials to develop and deliver educational programs. They also work closely with government agencies, private companies, and other entities to develop and execute research projects that benefit society. Education and research, not football, are the two primary outputs of universities.

Many organizations are PSOs, so it is wise to ask: How do other PSOs cope with tendencies to hire more administrators? The simple answer is this: These tendencies are counterbalanced by a desire to be profitable. For example, when partners in a law firm hire an assistant, they must judge whether the assistant allows the firm to be more productive; that is, to generate more work and make more money.

The lack of an identifiable and measurable "bottom line," which does not have to be profit, causes universities to lose focus. Boards of trustees and leadership are trying to hit multiple targets that change over time. One day a university is pushing a research agenda in this field or that field. Another day it is developing a student-centered help program so students make better choices about what courses to take, get assistance with their financial aid, or gain access to courses they need for graduation. All of these and many others sound like good ideas, so universities move forward. Yet questions arise: Where does one proposal rank among others? Who benefits from this investment and by how much? How does this impact the bottom line? These questions are neither asked nor answered. Consequently, decisions are made that are defensible and sound reasonable when looked at in isolation, but when examined in total are inconsistent, increase costs, and often do not achieve the benefits described in the proposal. For decades, universities simply increased tuition to pay for these programs. In the last decade or so, customers, including students, parents, other family members, friends, and governments, have pushed back and want to know why costs have risen so rapidly.

The unfocused approach, which expanded programs, services, and facilities, as well as the natural tendency for administrators to beget administrators caused universities to hire an army of highly paid functionaries including executive VPs, VPs, associate VPs, assistant VPs, provosts, deputy provosts, associate provosts, executive vice provosts, assistant vice provost, deans, executive associate deans, senior associate deans, and so on.[1] These people have subordinates, specialists, and clerical staffs, which further expands the network of administrators. Hiring administrators becomes learned and insidious behavior. The results are illustrated in Figure 11.2 as administrators and support staffs have grown at an alarming rate in both central/university-level administrations and college administration.

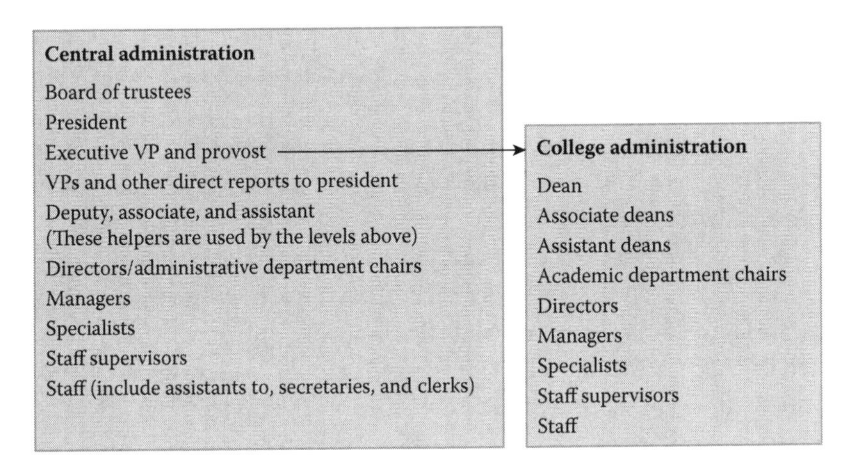

FIGURE 11.2
The scope of central and college administration in public universities.

In the current circumstances, when the institution proposes to hire administrators to fix a problem or perform a task, there may be no effort to determine (1) how the problem or task could be done differently and better, (2) if there is an information technology solution that would allow existing staff to do the work, or (3) if these tasks should be done at all. This type of hiring is often a reaction to a specific problem such as the university's accounting firm finds that accounts payable is vulnerable to fraud or a survey shows that students are unhappy with this or that service. New assistant VPs or directors are hired to fix the problems, and they, in turn, hire staff to help them.

Eliminating administrators is rarely contemplated because their status and power are derived from the size of their domain. More subordinates mean more people to whom work can be delegated and more opportunities to distribute blame when things go wrong. When administrative cuts are proposed and taken, these are most often tokens that are limited to low-level managers, clerical workers, student advisors, and the like. It is rare to eliminate a VP, assistant VP, or associate provost position.

It is important to state that administrators are not careless, bungling, selfish people. The vast majority work hard, attempt to make positive contributions, want the university to flourish, and are concerned about student success. It is the system in which they operate that must change. Goals are not clearly articulated and effectively disseminated to guide decisions and influence behaviors. There are no clear and consistent directives that unify actions and stimulate employees to make positive change. Without well-defined goals and effective management, employees do not receive useful feedback. They do not know if they are performing well, do not know what actions to take to improve the processes and achieve better outcomes, and are unaware of their accomplishments. In the current system, administrators move forward, almost mechanically, doing what they have done previously without thinking about what they do, why they do it, or how to do it better. This is learned behavior because if they recognize problems and develop new methods that improve outcomes, the system in which they operate is not receptive to change and the ideas eventually die. As this happens, others are discouraged from making similar efforts, so the innovative spirit is lost and the status quo becomes entrenched.

11.3 CONFIGURING A SOLUTION

A good solution must deal with excessive administrative cost and poor relations between administrators and faculty. Resolving these problems means addressing their causes, which are tied up in the strategic plan and manifest when acknowledging that universities are PSOs with a trifurcated customer. Issues regarding universities at PSOs and the trifurcated customer are discussed in Chapters 5, 6, 7, and 8 and are not repeated. The discussion continues with a focus on key cultural, managerial, and structural issues that should emerge from the strategic planning process.

1. *Organizational culture change:* To design and implement radical changes that can dramatically improve performance, it is necessary to change goals, reduce costs, and enhance quality. These, in turn, require a change in the attitudes and values of administrators, staff, and faculty. The board and executive leadership must drive this new culture.
2. *Management change:* As attitudes and values change, a number of important management practices must change to increase productivity and reduce administrative and instructional costs. Instructional/faculty productivity is discussed in Chapter 12.
3. *Structural change:* Some organizational changes should be considered to streamline administration and improve performance.

11.4 CHANGING ORGANIZATIONAL CULTURE

Organizational culture is a set of shared values and beliefs that guide employees toward acceptable and rewarding behavior. It includes the experiences, expectations, and philosophies that create the social and psychological environment of organizations. It determines how power and information flow through the organization, the level of freedom in decision making, and how organizations treat their employees and customers. These factors collectively define how organizations perform, including new product ideas, productivity gains, and quality improvements. Organizational culture is difficult to change.[7]

In many cases, the need for culture change becomes evident only when organizations underperform and are headed toward failure. As General Motors (GM) emerged from bankruptcy in July of 2009, its CEO Fritz Henderson recognized that GM needed to change its culture and focus on accountability, customers, and products to be successful.[8] As Mary Barra took the helm in early 2014, she faced the ignition safety switch crisis that was linked to 32 or more deaths, and she continued efforts to change the culture at GM.[9] After more than four years of effort (July 2009 to January 2014), the change was not complete. But the real story is that GM faced these problems for more than five decades before attempting to address the underlying culture. The most telling statistic is that GM's market share in the United States was more the 50% in the 1950s and today sits at less than 18%. It has been a long and slow decline, and customers have voted with their pocketbooks.[10,11]

Universities in the United States are still riding high. Although they face problems, as noted earlier in the book, enrollments continue to grow. To put universities in a "GM perspective," it is the 1950s with serious problems on the horizon but no perceptible change in outcomes. The question for universities is: What forces can disrupt success? There are at least three possibilities. Some public universities may grasp these problems and change how they operate so costs decline and quality increases, thereby capturing demand and running other institutions out of business.

Second, private, for-profit universities may eventually understand why they are failing and make the changes needed to improve graduation rates, lower completion times, enhance quality, lower cost, and increase job placements. That is a lot to do, but smart and resourceful academicians working with capable business leaders can achieve the right blend of academic rigor, connectivity to potential employers, and productivity improvements from administrators and faculty that drive costs lower.

Third, universities from outside the United States could offer degree programs, either online or face to face, that are high in quality and low in cost. Before readers disparage this possibility, consider the attitudes of executives at GM in the 1950s when Toyota made an initial attempt to penetrate the U.S. market. Its car had significant quality problems, was not well suited to U.S. roads, and was withdrawn from the market in 1960 after poor sales and big losses.[12] At that point, U.S. auto executives would have rolled in the aisle with laughter at a statement that Japanese cars would someday be a dominant force in the U.S. market. In the late 1950s and early 1960s, German cars, specifically Volkswagen's Beetle and Microbus, were purchased by a few "oddballs and hippies," and by the end of the 1960s Japanese cars began to penetrate the market. Through the next three decades, GM continued the same behavior, and its market share continued to drop. GM executives went from laughing to proclaiming unfair practices by the Japanese to serious concern. It may not be a good idea to align oneself with GM executives of that era by jumping to the conclusion that the status quo will continue for higher education.

11.4.1 Process for Changing Organizational Culture

Changing culture is difficult and takes time. To make it happen, it is essential for executive leadership to be aligned with customers and their wants and to drive changes throughout the organization. In one way, this may be easier for public universities than for GM because state government, which is one of the customers, has legislative authority. The federal government could have a role here as well because it provides funding, but it is probably best for states to take the lead. State government supported by students, parents, other family members, and friends as well as potential employers must work through the board at each state institution to hire a president who understands these problems, is willing to work toward meeting the needs of the trifurcated customers, and accept this as a long-term, difficult task. The president must be willing to sign on for five years, preferably more, to have a realistic opportunity to make the changes described in this book.

Once the president is onboard, the next step is to hire a provost, who agrees with these changes and is willing to make a long-term commitment to change culture and redeploy resources to meet the needs of customers.

The board, president, and provost would interview and evaluate the college deans to determine their willingness and ability to operate in the new environment, replacing quickly those who are judged to be unable to do so. These efforts, which include a willingness to decentralize decision making and give faculty a larger role in governance, are likely to be well received by college faculty, even though there are aspects of the change that faculty may not like, For example, faculty may not embrace efforts to increase their productivity and redefine their work as described in Chapter 12, but they should see, on balance, a better way to educate students and conduct research.

Although this is going on, the president, provost, and college deans are evaluating and working with their VPs, deputies, associates, and assistants to ensure they are onboard with the new ideas, gauge how the organization will respond, and determine the best way to move forward with these new priorities. This process is likely to take at least two years, but if this is successful, key decision makers should be onboard and the change process should be underway. The board, president, provost, and deans must be steadfast in their commitment to change. Any wavering on the part of these leaders would embolden the heart of the administration, which could be called middle managers, to rise up and defeat change. The keys to implementing radical change are executive leaders who are

1. Committed to the task; that is, they stay with it and push change
2. Supportive of the task and provide adequate resources to make change
3. Involved in the design, implementation, and communication of these efforts.

11.4.2 Summary of the Key Cultural Changes

There are a number of important attitudes and values, which are described in Chapters 6 through 14, that must be altered if universities are to take actions to address the root causes and underlying problems described in this book. Table 11.1 provides a summary of the most important changes.

Universities must accept the idea that they face a trifurcated customer, including governments and potential employers, and that the primary goal of students and their support group is typically not the pursuit of knowledge for its intrinsic value but rather securing good jobs and careers and leading happy lives. Going forward, the United States and other

TABLE 11.1

Comparing Existing and New Culture

Dimension	Existing Attitudes and Values	New Attitudes and Values
Customers	Students are the primary customer	Trifurcated customer: (1) students, their parents, other family members, and friends; (2) government; and (3) potential employers
Students' and their support group's goal	Students seek knowledge for its intrinsic value	Students seek knowledge to qualify for jobs and careers and to lead happy lives
Cost	Cost is secondary in the pursuit of knowledge	Increasing productivity and lowering costs are essential to improve value and educate an increasing number of people
Books and learning materials	The university selects books and learning materials and students pay	Tuition should cover all routine aspects of learning—books and learning materials included
Organizational structure	Command and control, which includes centralized decision making and top-down management, is vital for university success	Universities are PSOs that depend heavily on the expertise of faculty to bring together key players and co-create value—this is service dominant logic
Relationship between administration and faculty	Combative: The best interests of administration and faculty are in conflict with each other	Cooperative: Administrators and faculty must become allies, identifying and pursuing common goals
Administration	Administrators make unreasonable requests of faculty	Administrators must be willing to share leadership responsibility with faculty and look inwardly to examine and improve their productivity and their role in universities
Faculty	Faculty resist change and are uncooperative	Faculty should have a role in managing the institution, and they must seek ways to improve their productivity
State funding	Cuts in state funding are to blame for financial problems in public universities	Universities must look inwardly to determine why the costs for tuition and fees have risen much faster than the rate of inflation

developed and developing countries must educate an ever-larger portion of their populations to compete in the knowledge economy, so universities must recognize that cost can no longer be a secondary or tertiary consideration. The productivity of university administrators and faculty must become a critical concern. In addition, universities must accept that they can no longer select books and learning materials without regard to their costs. Tuition should cover all routine learning expenses, including books, allowing universities to use their collective purchasing power to reduce the cost and improve the quality of these learning tools.

With respect to organizational structure, universities should realize that they must move away from command and control, which emphasizes top-down management and centralizes decision making. Universities must think of themselves as PSOs that use faculty experts to engage in service dominant logic to meet the needs of their customers. This means that the attitudes of administrators and faculty must change from combative to cooperative. Administrators and faculty must be willing to share leadership responsibilities, while engaging in activities that enhance their productivity.

Last but certainly not least, universities must get over the notion that declines in state funding have created their problems. They *must* take responsibility for their actions and lower their cost.

11.5 CHANGING MANAGEMENT PRACTICES

The attitudes and values listed in Table 11.1 are associated with important managerial changes involving customers, decision making, faculty involvement, funding, and cost. The following list identifies and describes the management changes that support this new culture.

1. *Working with a trifurcated customer:* Universities must establish processes to work closely with potential employers, master's and doctoral degree programs that accept their graduates, and agencies that offer certification and licensure. These ideas are discussed in Chapter 8. Nearly all universities receive revenue from government with public universities receiving more. As discussed in Chapter 9, these institutions must build a close and cooperative working relationship with governments to improve quality and reduce costs simultaneously. These discussions about customers are not repeated here.

2. *Decentralizing decision making:* The primary operating units in a university are its colleges such as arts and letters, business, education, and engineering. These colleges and their faculty generate most of the universities' revenue through instruction and funded research. Colleges often have limited autonomy and discretionary funding, but they should have the freedom to be more entrepreneurial and pursue opportunities to generate revenue by offering innovative services that are consistent with the mission of the institution.
3. *Involving faculty:* Consistency with the prior point and a need to create buy-in means tenured faculty must be involved. Faculty should be encouraged to apply for administrative positions and have a real chance to be selected. Faculty should participate in planning and budgeting.
4. *Increasing productivity:* Substantial and meaningful effort must be made to improve the productivity of administrators and faculty, so universities can accomplish more and spend less. Doing more with less is the essence of productivity and has allowed developed countries to improve living standards and increase leisure time for their residents.
5. *Addressing skyrocketing administrative salaries:* In addition to growth in the number of administrators, which has outpaced enrollment growth, administrative salaries have increased at a much faster pace than faculty salaries and inflation.

11.5.1 Decentralizing Decision Making

As higher education grew after World War II, there was an unceasing and increasing drum beat to centralize decision making. This has transformed college deans into budget cutters, who plead their cases for another faculty position or student advisor, and academic department chairs into clerks, who monitor faculty performance and ensure that it meets workload standards set by central administration. Although budgets, hiring, and workload are legitimate issues, they should not be imposed. Deans and academic department chairs tend to be very bright people who should be involved in planning and managing the university. These professionals can improve the quality of instruction and research, lower costs, and increase job placement rates if they have the discretion and resources to pursue innovations.

In addition, deans and department chairs often have little or no control over how revenue that their college or department generates is used. They cannot use it to hire additional faculty, reward high performers, expand programs, advertise to attract more students, and other actions that leaders should be able to do. It is quite common for some colleges and departments to generate revenue that is far in excess of their costs, even when university overhead is added. Excess revenue from these cash cows subsidizes colleges and departments that have substantial losses. How well would a for-profit company function if one division is very profitable, but it cannot invest in new technology and skilled people to expand its operations because it is forced to subsidize another unprofitable division? Colleges and departments need autonomy, access to resources, and permission to become entrepreneurial, so they can package and sell instructional programs or research services that add value and generate revenue.

One college or department subsidizing another might be acceptable if a new college or department is being created and the subsidy is necessary for a year or two until sufficient revenue is generated. The problem with universities is that these subsidies occur year after year. The cash cows, who have to fight to replace faculty who retire or take a different job, spend countless hours preparing proposals to justify the replacement and arguing with central administration about the importance of this position to its mission and revenue stream. Their time would be better spent on finding ways to do the following:

1. Generate additional revenue by improving and expanding existing programs
2. Reduce costs by investing in training and technology to improve productivity
3. Increase revenue by identifying new programs or new platforms for existing programs.

11.5.2 Involving Faculty in Planning and Managing the University

Part of the process to decentralize decision making is creating ways for faculty to participate in planning and managing universities at the highest level, including strategic planning. This begins by encouraging and supporting tenured faculty to apply for high-level administrative positions. Outside candidates are appealing because they put their "best foot forward," and search committees rarely see their weaknesses, whereas the weaknesses of internal candidates are readily apparent.

It may not be possible to go back to the days when faculty would rotate through the presidency or the VP of finance. The presidency has become far more complex, and it needs someone with substantial administrative skills and experience who understands academia. A president is not the primary academic leader; that is the provost's job. Presidents are fundraisers, politicians, and relationship builders, among other things. The president could be a faculty member who has worked his or her way up the ladder and is prepared for the job, but it may not be possible to find that person through an internal search. VPs of finance have become more than budgeting officers who ensure that spending does not exceed revenue. They are experts in capital formation, investing, and risk management. Universities can no longer afford to have a history or biology professor who knows little about finance in this important position.

Having said this, it is time to hire tenured faculty, *who are currently at the university*, for leadership positions, including provosts, VPs, deans, and other high-level jobs where academic credentials and experiences are vital. They understand the environment, know the people, and, most important, have an incentive to make good decisions because they must live with their choices when they return to the faculty. They provide a sense of continuity and history that is lacking with professional managers hired from the outside. When universities fill these key positions time after time with external hires, they lose these benefits, break the bond between administration and the faculty, and send a strong message that "insider faculty" are second-class citizens—unqualified and unacceptable.

Next, a faculty resource council (FRC) should be created to give faculty direct and unfettered access to the board, president, and leadership team. In addition to providing knowledge and awareness for top management, it would represent faculty in strategic planning, resource allocation, and budgeting. It would have the ability to discuss the impact of budget decisions on successfully engaging in research and effectively designing and delivering educational programs. The chair of the FRC would be a member of the president's leadership team and represent faculty at board meetings. The FRC would be a small group with representation from each college, and membership would be determined by faculty votes. Administrators who are academic department chairs or higher such as associate dean, deans, and assistant vice provosts would not be eligible. The reason for the exclusion should be clear: people holding these positions have a strong allegiance to administration. The FRC should not be an arm of the faculty senate, which is often viewed negatively by administration and may not be representative of the faculty. Faculty senate and elements of the administration are often combatants with extreme and divergent views that would be difficult to overcome. The FRC would be an independent entity that provides an important perspective that is currently missing.

11.5.3 Increasing Administrative Productivity

Administrator is a broad term that can include a wide variety of jobs from executives such as president and provost to low-level managers and support staff. There are big differences among administrators in responsibilities and wages as well as how to improve productivity. To consider productivity enhancements, administrators are divided into three groups, which is consistent with the topology used by the College and University Professional Association for Human Resources (CUPA-HR).[13]

1. *Executive-level administrators:* This includes the president, provost, VP, and others shown in Figure 11.1. Also included are the academic deans and their associate and assistant deans; institutional administrators such as deputy, associate, and assistant provosts; and heads of administrative divisions, departments, and centers. At research universities, the median salary for presidents in 2015 was $450,000 per year with some making more than $1 million. Provosts topped $330,000. Of the nearly 200 different job categories reported, only 23 had median salaries less than $100,000 and only one was below $80,000.[14]
2. *Professional managers and specialists:* This level includes academic affairs, student affairs, institutional affairs, fiscal affairs, external affairs, facilities, information technology, research professionals, athletics, extension programs, technology transfer, environmental sustainability, health sciences, and exempt personnel including office and maintenance workers.[15] Exempt staff members are not entitled to overtime pay, whereas nonexempt staff must be compensated for working more than 40 hours per week.[16] At research universities in 2015, the compensation tended to be in the high five figures with a few salaries reaching the low six figures. The primary exception was athletics, where head coaches and some assistant coaches earned much more. Only 33 of the 300 job categories had a median salary of less than $50,000.[15]

3. *Nonexempt support staff:* Jobs in this category are office and clerical, technical and paraprofessional, skilled craft, and service and maintenance staff. At research universities in 2015, only 7 of 150 job categories had a median salary that exceeded $50,000, and those were primarily skilled trades such as electricians and plumbers.[17]

To put the size of administration in perspective, the number of executives (190,000) and professional managers and specialists (566,405) was about 756,000 in 2015. In the same year, there were about 675,000 full-time or full-time-equivalent faculty members.[1] Thus, it took about 1.12 administrators to oversee and manage the work of one full-time faculty. This seems wasteful to the nth degree. The ratio is probably higher than this because the number for administrators does not include academic department chairs who are counted as faculty because their workload involves a significant teaching commitment. Moving on to nonexempt support staff, a rough estimate of size is likely to top 1,000,000. This is based on the number of nonexempt staff (176,123) reported by the institutions (781) that responded to the CUPA-HR survey compared to the total number of institutions in the United States (4,500).[18,19] (The calculation is 176,123 divided by 781 and multiplied by 4,500.) This is not a precise estimate but an approximation that gives a sense of the problem. Thus, the ratio of full-time administrators—executives (190,000), professionals (566,405), and support staff (1,000,000)—to full-time faculty (675,000) was 2.6 to 1 and is likely higher today. Staggering?

11.5.3.1 Improving Productivity for Executive-Level Administrators

When economists discuss productivity, they are usually describing labor productivity, which is output divided by labor used. To increase productivity, an organization can have the same output using fewer employee-hours, more output with the same number of employee-hours, or a blend of more output and fewer hours. In the case of universities, outputs may be measured as the number of students taught or graduates produced. The sheer magnitude of the increase in full-time administrative position, 369% from 1978 to 2014,[5] indicates that more is needed than a small change here and a little tweak there.[20]

Table 11.2 lists possible job titles and duties for an office of the provost at public universities. It is an expansion of the "Executive VP & Provost" box in the organization chart in Figure 11.1. This list does not include secretarial or clerical staff within the provost's office. Excluding the executive assistant and the senior vice provost, each member in the list has deputies,

TABLE 11.2

Example of Job Title for an Office of the Provost at a Public University

Job Title	Job Responsibility
Provost and Executive VP for Academic Affairs	Oversee all academic programs—instructional and research
Executive Assistant	Plans and organizes Provost's schedule
Senior Vice Provost	Works closely with the provost to set academic policy, oversees academic activities, and serves as a stand-in for the Provost
Associate Provost for Undergraduate Education	Oversees undergraduate programs
Associate Provost for Graduate Education	Oversees graduate programs
Associate Provost for Research	Responsible for all research activities, including grants and contracts
Vice Provost of Outreach and Engagement	Responsible for programs that support and work with the community
Vice Provost for Diversity and Inclusion	Monitors and reports on the status of diversity and inclusions and develops programs to enhance these conditions
Vice Provost for Capital Planning and Budgeting	Interfaces with VP of Finance to determine the capital plan for academic buildings and programs, construct the budget, and ensure that the academic side of the university spends according to the budget
Vice Provost for Student Life	Responsible for all things related to students, including housing and resident life, student discipline, student union, counseling for students, and many others
Associate Vice Provost for Academic Programs and Continuing Education	Responsible for off-campus educational programs, including those internationally
Associate Vice Provost for Academic Policy and Faculty Resources	Responsible for setting policy that guides behavior of faculty and administrators and oversee hiring, promotion, and tenure
Associate Vice Provost for Strategic Enrollment Management	Responsible for recruiting and enrolling students
Assistant Vice Provost for Information Systems	Interfaces with the Chief Information Officer to ensure that information systems serve students and faculty
Assistant Vice Provost for Global Studies & International Affairs	Responsible for working with international students, ensuring that international faculty and administrators have the proper work visa and monitor international programs
Deans of Colleges (multiple)	College Deans, which also have a significant administrative contingent, report to the office of the provost

associates, directors, managers, specialists, and/or staff members who assist them. Some elements of provost's office are very large, such as the vice provost for student life, and others, such as the vice provost for diversity and inclusion, are relatively small.

Dramatically reducing the size of executive leadership is difficult because they are the power brokers who prepare budgets and allocate resources. Fortunately, making these cuts is consistent with decentralizing decision making. For public universities, it requires (1) state government, supported by students, parents, other family members, friends, and potential employer, (2) boards of trustee, and (3) presidents to make substantial and meaningful reductions in executive leadership. The power of these three entities must drive this change. Hiring faculty from inside the institution into positions of power and creating and using the FRC to advise the board and president would facilitate this change.

These reductions must be both symbolic and real. As a symbol, significant cuts in executive leadership make it much easier to reduce the number of directors, professional managers, specialists, and staff members. Executive leadership cuts can be real. At a research university, the provost and a dozen direct reports are likely to cost $2.5 million in wages, not counting support staff.[14] Cutting one direct report in the provost office without making any other changes would save enough to hire two tenure-track assistant professors who can spend time on teaching and research.

It seems reasonable to phase in these reductions. There are many ways to do this, but consider a five by five plan, which means a 5% reduction in executive-level headcount and salary each year for five years. After five years, executive leadership costs would be down about 22% (not 25% because each year after the first year the base is smaller, so a 5% reduction for the second year is only 4.75% of the initial budget). As the fifth year approaches, government, the boards, and the president would reevaluate to determine if more reductions could be attained. The magnitude of the increase in executive leadership since the late 1970s would indicate that even a bigger reduction may be possible.

Skeptics may argue that this is simply increasing the workload on the remaining executives by an average of 22%, assuming that no new work is created. They are missing at least five key points.

1. *Decentralizing decision making reduces administrative work:* Executive leadership and administration have increased because universities have implemented centralized decision making and a

command and control management system. This requires an army of executives, middle managers, and support staff to microman-age colleges and other entities within the university. When decision making is decentralized, the size of central administration, including the provost's office, can be reduced. Although some but not all of this work must now be done by college administrators and faculty, they are not spending time writing endless and not very useful reports and creating detailed proposals for why colleges should be able to replace a faculty member who has left the university. There is less organizational friction and productivity is likely to increase as col-lege administrators and faculty see new benefits from their efforts.

2. *Existing executives may not be fully engaged:* Some executives have slack in their workweek.
3. *There are synergies when work is combined:* If work is divided among two or more employees, time and resources are needed to communicate and coordinate goals, activities, outcomes, and next steps. When responsi-bilities are consolidated, some of this work goes away. For example, the associate vice provost for academic programs and continuing education listed in Table 11.2 must work closely with undergraduate and graduate programs. If this position is eliminated and the work is allocated to the associate vice provosts for undergraduate and graduate education, that is one less executive and staff to coordinate with.
4. *Not all work is value added:* Some work is not needed and can be elimi-nated. For example, this book suggests that universities eliminate out-reach and engagement initiatives, so the corresponding vice provost position identified in Table 11.2 and his or her staff could be eliminated.
5. *Management tools, training, and information technology (IT) can increase productivity:* Using better management tools and offer-ing more training in areas such as team learning, quality manage-ment, and system thinking should enable administrators to be more effective and productive. In addition, there have been tremendous advances in the use of IT to do work more efficiently—meaning more productively. This is more than email and text. It involves developing decision support systems to gather, organize, and consolidate data and information to make better and faster decisions. It is also easier to prepare reports required by the board, state and federal govern-ments, and accreditation agencies. Higher education is far behind private-sector companies in the use of IT to create an effective and productive organization.

11.5.3.2 *Improving Productivity for Professional Managers and Specialist—Middle Management*

Making improvements here depends on success at the executive level. First, eliminating an executive reduces the need for managers, specialists, and staff who support this person. Second, middle managers are more willing to participate in innovation and change if their bosses are doing their part. At this level, there are opportunities to identify and eliminate unnecessary work, but efforts must be more systemic because the people who hold these positions are part of processes that supports faculty, who are teaching and researching, and students, who are learning. The processes include things like registration, financial aid, IT support, scheduling, and dozens of others that can be improve but not eliminated.

As mentioned earlier, the problem is not the people; it is unreliable, inefficient, and costly processes that take too long. Processes must be redesigned to improve performance, and this requires the following:

1. Understanding how an existing process works, including its strengths and weaknesses
2. Setting stretch goals to signify that a drastic increase in outcomes is expected
3. Designing and implementing a new process that meets these goals
4. Working to continuously improve performance.

It is the right combination of radical change as identified in steps 1 through 3, which leads to dramatic improvements, and continuous change, step 4, which drives uninterrupted, incremental improvements.

Making these changes is a mindset/cultural shift that requires considerable time and effort. Providing details on how to do this cannot be accomplished in one chapter or even an entire book. Following is an overview of the steps including references to books that are likely to be helpful.

1. *Lean thinking:* It is essential to change how legislators, board members, and presidents think about universities. In most cases, their thoughts are of important research, innovative ideas, and graduation. These things are necessary and desirable outcomes, but it is also important to think about the processes for achieving these outcomes: whether universities use resources effectively, have low dropout rates, and have graduates who complete their degrees in four years,

get good jobs, and have little or no student debt. These are resource issues. Did the university spend its resource effectively or was there a lot of waste? Did universities place unnecessary requirements on students and faculty that caused them to spend time on nonproductive activities? Simply stated, these efforts are about the elimination of waste. These ideas can be traced back to Henry Ford, more than 100 years ago, and were expanded and modernized as the Toyota Production System and just in time. The concept of lean thinking is built on this foundation. There are many books on lean, but the best known is by Womack and Jones.[21] The application of lean thinking to universities is a more recent phenomenon. The book by Balzer[22] describes lean higher education and provides important and useful insights.

2. *Quality:* Quality and lean go hand in hand because poor quality is wasteful. Any meaningful discussion of lean must include quality. The book by Voehl et al.[23] on six-sigma quality describes its application: Two books on quality in higher education are suggested. The first one by Frazier[24] does not focus directly on higher education, but it should be useful in formulating a plan to improve quality. The second by Brennan and Shah[25] provides a more academic perspective on managing quality in higher education.
3. *Value stream mapping:* It is a technique to document, analyze, and improve the flow of information and materials to produce a good or provide a service. It allows managers to layout existing processes, identify actions that are wasteful as well as those that add value, and create more productive processes. There are many books on value stream mapping, and the book by Keyte and Locher[26] provides a useful overview.
4. *Implementing process redesign:* Once value stream mapping describes a better way to do registration and financial aid, it must be implemented. This involves the commitment, support, and involvement of the executive level and middle management. Without their strong push, inertia will not be overcome, and radical change will die. The book by Hammer and Champy[27] is a good book on business process redesign and implementation.
5. *Continuous improvement:* No process is perfect, and even if it was, change occurs and the process must be updated. Continuous improvement is a commonly used technique that allows organizations to make incremental process improvements. Once again, there are many books on continuous improvement. One of the books is by Imai.[28]

11.5.3.3 Improving Productivity for Nonexempt Support Staff

Nonexempt support staffers, like secretaries, paralegals, and lab assistants, may work inside a process that supports students and faculty, but they are not responsible for one. They need training, tools, and technologies to help them do their jobs better, faster, and cheaper. These needs should be identified through value stream mapping, process redesign, and continuous improvements efforts. In fact, support staff should be involved in these efforts because they can provide useful information about the current process and may have valuable insights about how to make it better.

11.5.4 Addressing Skyrocketing Administrative Salaries

Although administrative headcount has increased dramatically, their salaries have also increased faster than the salaries of tenured faculty and faster than the rate of inflation. When *adjusted for inflation*, salaries of presidents at public universities increased by 75% between 1979 and 2014, salaries of provosts increased by more than 50%, and salaries for tenured professors increased by about 23%. At private institutions, the percentages were even higher at 171%, 110%, and 45%, respectively.[20]

Benchmarking has put upward pressure on administrative salaries. When hiring new administrators or responding to a request to boost the salary of an "underpaid" administrator, data from other universities are examined. These data are readily available from entities like the CUPA-HR.[13] The tendency is to pay a new hire an above-average salary, which raises the average for the next hire and so on and so on. Also, if a university hires a business college dean, the annual salary in 2014–2015 would have been $334,130, while the provost only made slightly more.[14] Even if the provost does not appeal, the board may feel the need to boost the provost's salary. Plus, the deans in engineering and education who were making $286,989 and $210,636,[14] respectively, may request additional compensation.

Because setting salary is a judgment call, making boards of trustees aware of the problems with benchmarking may be helpful, but the better action is to increase competition. This means stopping the current practice of hiring from the limited pool of professional managers that other universities are pursuing. Whether the search is for president, provost, or dean, universities tend to hire a search firm to help with the process. These firms have lists of the same people, so the pool is still limited. Universities must work together to create a richer pool of qualified candidates by being willing to promote from within. This includes hiring tenured faculty for responsible administrative positions where they can grow and learn and return to the faculty. This creates a deeper pool of viable candidates for all universities.

11.6 CHANGING STRUCTURE

There are changes that universities may consider to lower administrative costs and achieve economies of scale: executing mergers, eliminating branch campuses, and outsourcing nonstrategic services.

11.6.1 Executing Mergers

Universities merge to lower facility and operating costs as well as to slash bureaucracy. Care should be taken because mergers are always risky. There are some cases where public universities are proximate, making this option reasonable, but mergers make more sense for smaller, proximate, private, not-for-profit institutions of which there are many. Enrollment at these institutions is often less than 3,000 students with a significant number under 2,000. In some cases, enrollment is declining so many of these institutions have to rethink how they do business, including cutbacks, mergers, and closures.[29]

Here are two examples of mergers between well-known, private universities. In 1967, Carnegie Institute of Technology and Mellon Institute of Industrial Research, both located in Pittsburgh, merged to form Carnegie Mellon University.[30] Also in 1967, Case Institute of Technology and Western Reserve University, both in Cleveland, merged to form Case Western Reserve University (CWRU).[31] At the time, these institutions were complex with many programs and egos, yet the mergers were very successful. The most difficult part of the CWRU merger may have been the football programs, which did not combine until 1970.[32] After the merger, the president of CWRU was reported to have commented that the most difficult part of the job was watching two football teams lose on the same weekend.

11.6.2 Eliminating Branch Campuses

Some public universities have branch campus where they offer a subset of the courses and programs that are available on main campus. Most branch campuses were established decades ago and seem to have outlived their usefulness. In many cases, they are like community colleges where students can take general education courses, completing part of their degree before moving to the main campus. With online learning opportunities, phasing out branch campuses may make sense. This would eliminate facility costs and reduce administrative overhead.

11.6.3 Outsourcing Nonstrategic Services

This may be the most important and pervasive structural change. Universities know little about organizing and managing on-campus housing, food services, parking services, and other activities, which universities need but are not directly related to their mission. Outsourcing these activities should reduce administrative and operating costs and provide students with better services. Table 11.3 has a list of candidates, which are discussed in the following sections.

11.6.3.1 Outsourcing Athletic Programs

The first item in Table 11.3, athletics, is very controversial. Even though athletics are not required, alumni, donors, presidents, students, and others love athletics. But athletics must not consume tuition dollars or other funds that support instruction, research, learning materials, housing, or other services. Tuition should pay for an education. It seems grossly unfair to students, who are struggling to learn, working part-time to earn money, and taking on student loans, to balance the athletic budget on their backs. For public universities, state government could take legislative action to make this happen. The federal government seems to have every right to mandate that institutions that enroll students who receive federal funds offer clear evidence that tuition and other funds are not diverted to athletics.

Athletics has a separate and identifiable revenue stream. It has no direct impact on the mission of universities, but it may have an impact of fundraising. Outsourcing provides a firewall between athletics and the university, and it requires athletics to live within its means. Athletics would build and maintain facilities, pay it coaches, buy uniforms, and cover all expenses. If athletics wants to offer scholarships, it must provide the university with funds to cover tuition, fees, room, and board. If athletics loses money, it would have to finance those loses, restructure, and repay

TABLE 11.3

Candidates for Outsourcing

Activities	Revenue Generating	Essential to Primary Mission	Funding	Outsourcing Candidate
1. Athletic programs	Yes, fully	No direct link to research and teaching; may help fundraising	Separate revenue stream	Yes: Challenging and no one has done it
2. On-campus housing	Yes, fully	No direct link	Separate revenue stream	Yes: Could lease campus buildings to private company
3. Food services	Yes, fully	No direct link	Separate revenue stream	Yes: Done frequently
4. Bookstores	Yes, fully	No direct link	Separate revenue stream	Yes: Done very frequently
5. Parking services	Yes, fully	No direct link	Separate revenue stream	Yes: Should be relatively easy to do
6. Hospitals and clinics	Yes, fully	Yes, when institution has medical and nursing schools	Separate revenue stream	Yes: External company can manage hospitals and clinics
7. Student healthcare	Partial, students must have insurance	No direct link	May require some tuition funding	Yes: Should be possible when a hospital is proximate
8. Janitorial services	No	No direct link	Fund by tuition	Yes: Basic service that could be easily outsourced
9. Campus security	No	No direct link	Fund by tuition	Yes: Could be contracted to a private company or local police
10. Intracampus bus service	No	No direct link	Fund by tuition	Yes: could be contracted to a private carrier or local public transport company

the loans. Public universities would be prohibited from covering these losses or cosigning loans. Universities often use football and basketball facilities for concerts and graduation. Concerts have revenue, so an appropriate fee can be charged to the promoter. If the university wants to use these facilities for graduation, arrangements can be made.

Proponents may argue that athletics is an essential part of an undergraduate education, but that is not true. To outsource athletics does not argue that athletics has no value and universities should drop their programs. It simply states that athletics must be self-supporting.

11.6.3.2 Outsourcing Ancillary Services with Separate Revenue Streams

Outsourcing services is an effective way to reduce costs, upgrade quality, gain access to specialized expertise, and increase customer satisfaction.[33] Ancillary services, items 2 through 5 in Table 11.3, are activities that are needed by universities but are not critical to their mission, and other organization can provide these services as well as or better than the university. In addition, there are separate revenue streams for housing, food services, book stores, and parking. Hospitals and clinics, item 6, are ancillary services when universities have medical schools. In this case, these facilities are essential to their mission, but they have separate revenue streams. University executives know little about any of these activities, so they are highly attractive candidates for outsourcing. For most of these activities, it should be relatively easy to find private companies to manage them and compensate the university in some manner for the opportunity. There may be other activities that should be outsourced such as university-provided childcare and computer services.[33] Some universities have golf courses and airports located on campus and are considering outsourcing.[34]

For decades, universities have been outsourcing housing, but only by accident. After one or two years of living in dormitories or other university housing, students often seek off-campus apartments or condos because they can live there more cheaply and have more freedom. Outsourcing housing allows universities to reduce administrative staff and place the management of housing with experts who can do the job better and more cheaply.[33] Food services and bookstores have been outsourced successfully at many universities. In some cases, universities have made space available in the student union for private restaurants. Housing, parking facilities, and hospitals and clinics are less commonly outsourced, but interest is growing.[34] In many cases, universities own assets involved in these activities, so arrangement must be made to sell or lease them to private companies. Today, private companies are investing money and building assets on campus.[35]

11.6.3.3 Outsourcing Services with No Independent Funding Stream

The last four items in Table 11.3 are activities to consider outsourcing, but they do not have an independent revenue stream, so it is necessary to pay for these services. Providing students with basic and emergency healthcare is an essential service. All students should have health insurance, and many of them do through their parents' insurance. This provides some compensation, but there still may be costs that universities must cover. For universities with hospitals or large medical clinics close by, these services may be outsourced. For janitorial services, campus security, and the on-campus bus network, there is no revenue, but outsourcing is likely to lead to lower cost and better service.[31]

11.7 DRIVING FORCES FOR CHANGE

Governments hold the leverage, especially for public universities, which receive significant funding from both state and federal sources. Students, parents, other family members, and friends must demand that governments take action to lower the cost of higher education by making important and fundamental changes. This is not about increasing government support, but about spending less. Governments must work through the board of trustees and president to drive these administrative and management changes.

11.8 IMPACT OF REFORMING ADMINISTRATION AND MANAGEMENT ON HIGHER EDUCATION OUTCOMES

Reforming administration and management has major impacts on strategic planning, goal setting, and identifying who are the customers of universities, which broadly impacts the solution. The following list examines how this element of the solution impacts the root causes, which are discussed in Chapter 4:

1. *Lack of understanding—Who is the customer? (root cause 1):* A fresh look at goals and expectations forces universities to recognize that students are primarily interested in securing a job and that government and potential employers are important customers.
2. *Declining state support for public universities (root cause 2):* States control public universities and can use this to drive changes in culture and structure.
3. *Rise of the ruling class: Administration (root cause 3):* As governments encourage universities to increase productivity, the size and cost of administration should be reduced.
4. *Limited productivity improvements for universities (root cause 4):* Efforts to eliminate waste and increase efficiency of administration should increase productivity.
5. *Rapidly growing costs for books and supplies (root cause 5):* As the attitude of administration changes toward students, universities should work to reduce the costs of learning materials.
6. *Funding finesse—Mixing fees and tuition (root cause 6):* As the attitude of administration changes toward students, fees become optional.
7. *Eroding standards (root cause 8):* Considering potential employers as customers and involving them in curriculum should ensure that standards are strong.
8. *Lack of student preparation (root cause 9):* Involving potential employers in setting standards should cause universities to admit students who are well prepared.

11.9 SUMMARY OF RECOMMENDATIONS

Following is a list of the key recommendations that comprise this element of the solution.

1. Universities must reconfigure the strategic plan and the strategic planning process. This means the following:
   a. Recognizing there are multiple customers and goals—students want good jobs and less debt; governments and potential employers want lower costs and better quality graduates.

   b. Increasing faculty involvement in managing universities and the strategic planning process.
2. Universities should change their culture in regard to customers, books and learning materials, organizational structure, relationships between administration and faculty, and state funding.
3. To make change, students, parents, other family members, and friends must support state government as it convinces boards and presidents, who must, in turn influence top and middle management at universities.
4. As culture changes, management practices must change.
   a. Decentralize decision making, so colleges have more freedom to pursue innovative and entrepreneurial activities.
   b. Hire more faculty members for administrative posts and create a faculty resource committee (FRC) to participate in strategic planning and university-level budgeting.
5. Executive leadership must achieve higher productivity by identifying work that is unnecessary, setting targets for reducing administration that can be met over several years, and providing management tools and training as well as information technology that improves productivity.
6. Professional managers and specialists must increase productivity by focusing on systems thinking and process improvements. This involves lean thinking, quality improvement efforts, value stream mapping, seeking process redesign, and implementing continuous improvement efforts.
7. The productivity of nonexempt support staff should improve as processes are redesigned and specific IT projects are implemented.
8. Increases in administrative salaries can be moderated by eliminating benchmarking in salary determination and creating more competition for high-level administrative jobs.
9. Change organizational structure, lower costs, and enhance quality through mergers, closing branch campuses, and, most important, by outsourcing activities.

REFERENCES

1. Ginsberg, B. 2011. Administrators ate my tuition. *Washington Monthly*, September/October. http://washingtonmonthly.com/magazine/septoct-2011/administrators-ate-my-tuition/ (accessed December 27, 2016).

2. Marcus, J. 2014. New analysis shows problematic boom in higher ed administrators. *The Huffington Post*, February 6. http://www.huffingtonpost.com/2014/02/06/higher-ed-administrators-growth_n_4738584.html (accessed December 27, 2016).
3. National Center for Policy Analysis. 2015. *Higher Education Administrative Costs Are Skyrocketing*, January 19. http://www.ncpa.org/sub/dpd/index.php?Article_ID=25264 (accessed December 27, 2016).
4. Campos, P. F. 2015. The real reason college tuition costs so much. *The New York Times*, April 4. http://www.nytimes.com/2015/04/05/opinion/sunday/the-real-reason-college-tuition-costs-so-much.html?_r=0 (accessed December 27, 2016).
5. McNutt, M. I. 2014. Why does college cost so much? *US News World Report*, September 22. http://www.usnews.com/news/college-of-tomorrow/articles/2014/09/22/why-college-costs-so-much-overspending-on-faculty-amenities (accessed June 24, 2016).
6. United States Census Bureau. 2016. *College Enrollment of Students 14 Years Old and Over, by Type of College, Attendance Status, Age, and Gender: October 1970 to 2014*. http://www.census.gov/hhes/school/data/cps/historical/index.html (accessed August 8, 2016).
7. Business Dictionary. 2017. *Organizational Culture*. http://www.businessdictionary.com/definition/organizational-culture.html (accessed January 3, 2017).
8. Smerd, J. 2009. Can a new corporate culture save General Motors? *Crains Detroit Business*, November 9. http://www.crainsdetroit.com/article/20091109/EMAIL01/911099979/can-a-new-corporate-culture-save-general-motors (accessed January 3, 2017).
9. Jusko, J. 2014. CEO Mary is driving culture change at General Motors. *Industry Week*, November 14. http://www.industryweek.com/quality/ceo-mary-barra-driving-culture-change-general-motors (accessed January 3, 2017).
10. Klayman, B., and Ingrassia, P. 2014. 'New GM Has Old Problem': Stagnant U.S. market share. *Reuters: Business News*, January 13. http://www.reuters.com/article/us-autoshow-gm-marketshare-idUSBREA0D03J20140114 (accessed January 3, 2017).
11. Flint, J. 2007. Pumping on the brakes. *Forbes*, January 2. http://www.forbes.com/2007/01/01/gm-market-share-oped-cz_jf_0102flint.html (accessed January 3, 2017).
12. Wikipedia. 2017. *Toyota Crown*. https://en.wikipedia.org/wiki/Toyota_Crown (accessed January 4, 2017).
13. College and University Professional Association for Human Resources. 2015. *Salary Surveys*. http://www.cupahr.org/surveys/results.aspx (accessed January 6, 2017).
14. College and University Professional Association for Human Resources. 2015. *Unweighted Median Salary by Carnegie Classification: Administrators in Higher Education Salary Survey*. http://www.cupahr.org/surveys/ahe-surveydata-2015.aspx (accessed January 6, 2017).
15. College and University Professional Association for Human Resources. 2015. *Unweighted Median Salary by Carnegie Classification: Professionals in Higher Education Salary Survey*. http://www.cupahr.org/surveys/phe-surveydata-2015.aspx (accessed January 6, 2017).
16. Purdue University. 2017. *Non-Exempt and Exempt: What Do These Terms Mean and Why Does it Matter*. http://www.purdue.edu/hr/LeadingEdition/LEdi_704_exempt_nonexempt.html (accessed January 7, 2017).
17. College and University Professional Association for Human Resources. 2015. *Unweighted Median Salary by Carnegie Classification: Non-Exempt Staff Salary Survey*. http://www.cupahr.org/surveys/non-exempt-surveydata-2015.aspx (accessed January 7, 2017).

18. College and University Professional Association for Human Resources. 2015. *2014–15 Non-Exempt Staff in Higher Education Salary Survey: FACT SHEET.* http://www.cupahr.org/surveys/files/salary2015/Non-Exempt-2015-Fact-Sheet.pdf (accessed January 7, 2016).
19. United States Department of the Treasury and Department of Education. 2012. *The Economics of Higher Education*, December. https://www.treasury.gov/connect/blog/Documents/20121212_Economics%20of%20Higher%20Ed_vFINAL.pdf (accessed June 23, 2016).
20. Curtis, J. W., and Thornton, S. 2014. Losing focus: The annual report of the economic status of the profession, 2013–14. *American Association of University Professor*, March–April. https://www.aaup.org/sites/default/files/files/2014%20salary%20report/zreport_0.pdf (accessed January 5, 2017).
21. Womack, J. P., and Jones, D. T. 1996. *Lean Thinking: Banish Waste and Create Wealth in Your Corporation*. New York: Free Press/Simon & Schuster.
22. Balzer, W. K. 2010, *Lean Higher Education: Increasing the Value and Performance of University Processes*. Boca Raton, FL: CRC Press/Taylor & Francis.
23. Voehl, F., Harrington, H. J., Mignosa, C., and Charron, R. 2013. *The Lean Six Sigma Black Belt Handbook: Tools and Methods for Process Acceleration*. Boca Raton, FL: CRC Press/Taylor & Francis.
24. Frazier, A. 1997. *Roadmap for Quality Transformation in Education: A Guide for Local Education Reform Leaders*. Boca Raton, FL: CRC Press/Taylor & Francis.
25. Brennan, J., and Shah, T. 2000. *Managing Quality in Higher Education: An International Perspective on Institutional Assessment and Change*. Philadelphia, PA: Organisation for Economic Co-operations and Development, The Society for Research into Higher Education & Open University Press.
26. Keyte, B., and Locher, D. A. 2015. *The Complete Lean Enterprise: Value Stream Mapping for Office and Services*. Boca Raton, FL: CRC Press/Taylor & Francis.
27. Hammer, M., and Champy, J. 2006. *Reengineering the Corporation: A Manifesto for Business Revolution*. New York, NY: Harper Collins Publisher.
28. Imai, M. 2012. *Gemba Kaizen: A Commonsense Approach to a Continuous Improvement Strategy*. New York: McGraw Hill.
29. Breuder, R. L. 2014. Private colleges face enrollment challenges. *Huffington Post*, February 24. http://www.huffingtonpost.com/dr-robert-l-breuder/private-colleges-face-enr_b_4833794.html (accessed January 15, 2017).
30. Wikipedia. 2017. *Carnegie Mellon University*. https://en.wikipedia.org/wiki/Carnegie_Mellon_University (accessed January 9, 2017).
31. Wikipedia. 2017. *Case Western Reserve University*. https://en.wikipedia.org/wiki/Case_Western_Reserve_University (accessed January 9, 2017).
32. Wikipedia. 2017. *Case Western Reserve Spartan Football*. https://en.wikipedia.org/wiki/Case_Western_Reserve_Spartans_football (accessed January 15, 2017).
33. ERIC Clearinghouse on Higher Education. 2000. *Outsourcing in Higher Education*. http://www.ericdigests.org/2001-3/outsourcing.htm (accessed January 9, 2017).
34. Eichler, A. 2012. Public colleges outsourcing services to private companies as states cut budgets. *Huffington Post*, April 2. http://www.huffingtonpost.com/2012/04/02/public-colleges-outsourcing-private-companies-budget-cuts_n_1398087.html (accessed January 9, 2017).
35. Cirino, A. M. 2003. *Outsourcing Student Housing*. National Association of College and University Business Officers, June. file:///C:/Users/MarkVonderembse/Downloads/2003_06_student_housing%20(1).pdf (accessed January 9, 2017).

12

Reshaping Faculty's Role

Faculty should not be immune from change that improves the quality of higher education and lowers its costs. The faculty is the intellectual heart of the university and provides leadership to improve research and instructional performance, while administrators facilitate these efforts. The focus here is on instruction because it is the primary determinant of a successful bachelor's degree, which is the goal of most students. Research is more interrelated with and supportive of graduate studies, and graduate programs are a small part of higher education (only about 15% in 2014).[1,2]

Success of the instructional mission is determined by three closely related activities.

1. *Determining curriculum content:* Tenured and professional faculty members work closely with potential employers and others to design rigorous content and standards.
2. *Creating and executing pedagogy:* Faculty members work together to design methods of instruction and deliver knowledge in ways that fit the needs of individual learners.
3. *Assessing student performance:* Measuring how much knowledge students gain is essential to demonstrate effectiveness. Pre- and posttests may be used to assess the effectiveness of courses and programs.

The question is: How well are faculty members prepared for these activities? PhD and masters programs focus almost exclusively on content knowledge with minimal exposure to pedagogy and assessment.

The faculty has a responsibility and a role in reducing the cost of higher education. This is the case, even though (1) administration is a primary driver of higher costs and (2) there has been a large shift in the mix of faculty from full-time, tenured faculty to full- and part-time contractual faculty, who earn much less.[3] Further cost reductions mean improving faculty productivity, so *more students gain more knowledge with less effort by faculty and students*, leading to lower tuition. This is not simply increasing class size or asking faculty to teach more classes; rather, it is changing how knowledge is delivered.

To begin, consider the different types of faculty—tenured, professional, and instructional plus graduate teaching assistants—and match their skills with the different levels of curricula from general education to PhD course. The approach is to pair the skills of faculty with needs of the courses so learning is both effective/high quality and efficient/productive. Increasing productivity requires faculty to rethink long-held values about education and technology. For example, why should a three-credit-hour course have three hours of face-to-face instruction each week for 15 weeks? Can multiple faculty members teach a course in ways that take advantage of their different skills? There are a variety of learning styles and supporting technologies that allow faculty to teach more students while expending the same or less effort. This is the essence of productivity improvement and cost reduction.

As universities wrestle with faculty's role, it is important to note that faculty unions are on the rise. Most people would be surprised to learn that about 386,000 college faculty members in the United States are covered by union contracts and a little more than half of these are at two-year institutions.[4,5] This number includes part-time faculty, so it is headcount and not full-time equivalent faculty. Why is the number so large? In general, history shows that unionization is a reaction to poor treatment by owners, and the primary goals are to protect the interests of workers, including higher wages and better working conditions.[6] Faculty chose unionization because of their eroding power and dwindling influence, which has led to slower wage growth, higher workloads, and diminished stature. The natural reaction from disenfranchised faculty is to regain some measure of control, and unionization is one-way. The difficulty is that unions often create an adversarial relationship between administration and faculty, and they inhibit the kind of communication needed to make innovative changes in instructional methods.

12.1 TEACHING TEACHERS HOW TO TEACH

In a knowledge-intensive world, it is essential to have efficient, productive, and high-quality methods to deliver the best ideas, techniques, critical thinking skills, problem-solving abilities, and other knowhow. The methods must include the elements described earlier: curriculum content, pedagogy, and assessment. PhD programs deliver content effectively, but the time spent on pedagogy and assessment is typically minimal to none. Contractual faculty and graduate teaching assistants are usually deficient in pedagogy and assessment unless they have teaching experience.

The following sections describe a process for training full-time faculty, who may be tenured, contractual faculty who may be full- or part-time, and graduate teaching assistants. Before moving to these sections, there are at four points that are common for all types of faculty.

1. *Evaluations:* Faculty members should be subject to evaluation by students as described in Chapter 7. When problems are identified in this or any other way, they would be confirmed by master teachers who work with the faculty to prepare an improvement plan. A master teacher is a senior faculty member who has been recognized for high-quality teaching.
2. *Center for teaching:* Universities must have such institutes that work with faculty and support continuous instructional improvement.
3. *Teaching seminars:* Newly hired faculty with limited teaching experience must participate in seminars led by master teachers who describe teaching expectations and practices. Existing faculty, who are identified as having difficulty teaching, would use these services as well.
4. *Teaching improvement funds:* To improve teaching, faculty should have access to funds to attend seminars, acquire technologies, and learn new instructional methods.

12.1.1 Supporting Full-Time, Tenured Faculty to Become Better Teachers

Efforts to help tenure-track faculty improve their teaching should begin in PhD programs and continue until the end of their careers. There are three primary components: basic education and skills, apprenticeship, and continuous improvement.

1. *Basic education and skills:* The process begins with the PhD program and applies to all students who are pursuing tenured faculty positions.
    a. *Language assessment:* Many students in PhD programs, especially science, technology, engineering, mathematics, and quantitative areas in business, are born and educated outside of the United States, so English is not their primary language. For these students, admission to graduate schools requires reaching a certain score on the test of English as a foreign language (TOEFL). This test measures students' ability to listen, read, speak, and write English at the university level.[7] Many people believe that the TOEFL does not effectively assess the ability to communicate verbally with undergraduate students. A process to assess and improve this ability should be developed and applied before PhD teaching assistants are assigned to teach stand-alone courses, problem sessions, or labs.
    b. *Teaching assessment:* Pedagogy and assessment skills are evaluated, and all PhD students lacking these skills are required to take appropriate courses and seminars before teaching.
    c. *Mentor:* PhD students are assigned teaching mentors, who can advise and counsel them, including sending them to master teachers or centers for teaching.
    d. *Teaching assignments:* All PhD students seeking tenured faculty positions are assigned to teach stand-alone courses. Their performance is monitored and feedback is provided.
2. *Apprenticeship:* Borrowing a term from the skilled trades, this takes place when a newly minted PhD is hired for a tenure-track faculty position and ends when tenure is awarded.
    a. *Initial assessment:* During the hiring process, faculty candidates are required to make an instructional presentation that could be delivered in an undergraduate course as well as the usual research presentation. These presentations are key factors in the hiring decision.
    b. *Master teacher:* Master teachers assess strengths and weaknesses of newly hired faculty and develop a plan to improve their teaching abilities.

   c. *Evaluation:* Each year prior to tenure, there is a detailed teaching assessment directed by a master teacher. These evaluations are considered in making the tenure decision.
3. *Continuous improvement:* Effective teaching requires an ongoing effort to improve.
   a. *Faculty initiatives:* Once tenure is granted, faculty act independently in choosing how to improve. They make annual improvement plans that are reviewed by department chairs.
   b. *Routine assessment:* Regular evaluations ensure that problems are identified. Poor performance triggers an investigation that leads to a detailed improvement plan. Tenured faculty members, who are unwilling to follow the plan and improve, are subject to dismissal.

12.1.2 Supporting Full-Time, Contractual Faculty to Become Better Teachers

At the time of hiring, preparation of full-time, professional and instructional faculty is likely to be uneven with some new hires having extensive teaching experience while others have very little. Faculty with little or no experience would follow a process that is similar to the one identified for tenured faculty.

1. *Basic education and skills:* Typically, contractual faculty members have worked in the United States for many years, so they know English and are good communicators. Universities should describe the presentation, pedagogy, and assessment skills that contractual faculty need, so individuals who might be interested could address their deficiencies before they apply.
2. *Apprenticeship:* Contractual faculty would follow a similar process to the one outlined for tenured faculty. During the hiring process, they would make a teaching presentation, which would help to define gaps in their teaching skill set. Master teachers would evaluate their presentation, pedagogy, and assessment skills and prepare a plan and support system to help them attain these skills. Once they begin to teach, they would receive annual evaluations that guide improvement efforts for a significant period of time, say five years.
3. *Continuing improvement:* After five years of full-time teaching, they would shift to continuous improvement mode and follow the process for tenured faculty described earlier, which includes faculty initiatives on improving teaching and routine assessments of performance.

On the other hand, if newly hired, contractual faculty members have the education and experience in pedagogy and assessment, they would move directly to the continuous improvement phase. For those with knowledge that is between none and substantial, they would be involved in the same three-step process as those with no education and experience. The support system and plan would be adjusted accordingly, filling in the gaps and avoiding duplication.

12.1.3 Coping with Part-Time Contractual Faculty

In theory, part-time, contractual faculty would be subject to the same rigorous standards for teaching and follow the continuous improvement phase as full-time faculty. Part-time, tenured faculty positions are uncommon and those that exist are usually held by senior faculty with substantial teaching experience. Many contractual faculty members, probably most by headcount, are part-time faculty. It may be relatively easy to convince full-time contractual faculty, who are inexperienced at teaching, to participate in the teaching improvement process. But it is very challenging to convince part-time, inexperienced, contractual faculty to participate in this extra work for the $3,000 or so they earn for each course.[8,9] The university has two options: stop hiring part-time faculty with limited teaching experience or pay them more for teaching the first two or three times to compensate them for the training.

12.1.4 Supporting Graduate Assistants to Become Better Teachers

Typically, graduate students who teach classes "on their own" are in PhD programs, although some master's degree students have this responsibility. In either case, they would use the following process, which is described more fully under the section on supporting full-time, tenured faculty.

1. *Communication assessment:* Before teaching, an assessment is made to determine if graduate students can communicate effectively in written and spoken English.
2. *Teaching assessment:* Evaluate pedagogy and assessment skills and prepare improvement plans.
3. *Mentor:* Provide each graduate student with a faculty teaching mentor who can direct the student to resources to improve their skills.
4. *Teaching assignments:* Teaching performance is monitored and feedback provided.

12.2 MATCHING FACULTY CAPABILITIES AND INSTRUCTIONAL REQUIREMENTS

Chapter 1 describes the different types of teaching faculty: (1) tenured, which include faculty who have tenure and those who are on tenure track; (2) contractual, which include professional and instructional faculty who can be full- or part-time; and (3) graduate teaching assistants, who usually have free tuition and a stipend in exchange for their work. These faculty types define the rows in Table 12.1. Chapter 10 on curriculum and pedagogy describes the learning environment for different elements of the undergraduate curriculum, which are general education, disciplinary core, and major and minor fields of study. These elements are combined with master's and PhD programs to represent the columns in Table 12.1. When the course types are examined from general education to PhD, they tend to become more challenging, requiring more interaction and idea exchange between students and faculty. Thus, class size is highest in general education courses and declines dramatically until it reaches very small numbers, likely middle to high single digits for doctoral seminars. This idea is consistent with what is shown in Figure 10.2 and Figure 13.1 in Chapter 13 on creating high-tech learning materials. With a redesigned delivery mode, setting precise limits for class size should be less important. The focus should be on creating tools and processes that offer different ways to learn.

A key to improving faculty productivity is to align the capabilities of the various faculty types with the learning requirements of the different courses. The cells in Table 12.1, which are at the intersection of the rows (faculty type) and columns (course type), identify how faculty resources should be applied to the different course types across the following four dimensions of teaching and learning.

1. *Curriculum design:* Tenured faculty members have the knowledge and training to lead efforts to define curriculum content and set performance standards across the spectrum of course types. Professional faculty members have the experience and contacts to ensure that content and standards at the undergraduate level and master's level are practical and relevant for potential employers. Instructional faculty and graduate teaching assistants may provide inputs to the process but do not have meaningful roles.

TABLE 12.1

Role of Different Faculty Types by Course Types

	Course Type				
Faculty Type	**General Education**	**Disciplinary Core**	**Major and Minor Fields**	**Masters**	**PhD**
Tenured	Curriculum Design Instructional Design Assessment	Curriculum Design Instructional Design Delivery (limited) Assessment	Curriculum Design Instructional Design Delivery Assessment	Curriculum Design Instructional Design Delivery Assessment	Curriculum Design Instructional Design Delivery Assessment
Professional	Curriculum Design Instructional Design Assessment	Curriculum Design Instructional Design Delivery Assessment	Curriculum Design Instructional Design Delivery Assessment	Curriculum Design Instructional Design Delivery Assessment	Minimal: In certain cases, especially applied disciplines, these faculty may have valuable research ideas
Instructional	Instructional Design Delivery Assessment (consultative only)	Instructional Design Delivery Assessment (consultative only)	None	None	None
Graduate Teaching Assistant	Instructional Design Delivery Assessment (consultative only)	Instructional Design Delivery Assessment (consultative only)	None	None	None

Note: Curriculum Design: Defining curriculum content and performance standards. Instructional Design (Pedagogy): Determining pedagogy, which specifies how knowledge is delivered. Delivery: Executing the pedagogy to deliver content in the most effective manner. Assessment: Designing and executing ways to measure performance and determine grades.

2. *Instructional design (pedagogy):* Similar to curriculum design, tenured and professional faculty have key roles in determining how knowledge is delivered. Instructional faculty and graduate teaching assistants should have an important role in setting pedagogy for general education and disciplinary core courses because they have taught these courses and can provide useful insights about what has and has not worked.
3. *Delivery:* Tenured faculty should be capable of teaching at all levels, but they should teach primarily in the major and minor fields of study as well as masters- and PhD-level courses. Besides, instructional faculty and graduate teaching assistants can teach general education and disciplinary core courses very effectively. Professional faculty could teach all course types with the exception of the PhD. Because their level of knowledge, experience, and compensation tends to be higher than instructional faculty, it makes sense to exclude them from delivering general education courses.
4. *Assessment:* Tenured and professional faculty should design and execute mechanisms to measure student performance and determine grades. This goes back to the idea that instructional faculty, either full- or part-time, should not define curriculum content, design tests, or determine results because students can pressure them to lower standards and inflate grades. This same notion applies to graduate teaching assistants. Thus, these two faculty types should have a consultative role in assessment for general education and disciplinary core courses. Professional faculty members are fully involved in assessment because they were senior leaders in their profession and have firsthand knowledge as to why standards must be maintained.

These ideas are guidelines, not rigid rules. Are their instructional faculty members who can and do stand their ground when it comes to maintaining standards and setting grades? Are their tenured faculty members who do not? The answer to both questions is most likely yes, but the proposed ideas attempt to create a system that has a reasonable chance of coming to the "right" outcome. When instructional faculty do not determine curriculum content, construct tests, or make decisions about grades, their teaching lives are easier. When content and performance standards are set with substantial inputs from potential employers, graduate schools, and agencies that conduct licensure and certification exams, rigor is not only defensible but can be described as being in the best interest of students.

There are some who may argue that these ideas "sell short" the abilities of exceptional instructional faculty. The best option for these high performers may be to earn a PhD and the advancement, satisfaction, and compensation that it brings. If that is not possible, there is no legal requirement that prohibits universities from making an exception and letting them do more. Also, there may be good reasons for professional faculty members to teach PhD seminars or an instructional faculty member to teach courses in the major and minor fields of study. As long as these are well-conceived exceptions and not wholesale deviations for convenience sake, then by all means move forward. But the idea is still the same: use resources so that universities take advantage of the skills, knowledge, and characteristics of the faculty and give students the best education possible—even when they may prefer to learn less.

12.3 ECONOMICS OF HIGHER EDUCATION

Before describing ways to increase faculty productivity, it is useful to understand the impact of faculty on revenue and costs. The economics of higher education are similar to those of many businesses—some products are more profitable than others. At universities, some courses and programs have large "surpluses," the differences between their revenues and costs, while others lose money. Universities often generate "surpluses" from general education courses because enrollment and therefore revenue is high and cost measured by faculty compensation is low. The economics are simple yet powerful.

Table 12.2 shows the magnitude of revenue and faculty costs for courses offered in general education, disciplinary core, and major and minor fields of studies when these are taught by tenured, instructional, and part-time faculty. It is difficult to find good estimates for the salaries of professional faculty members, so they are not included in the analysis. They tend to be paid much more than instructional faculty, but less than tenured faculty. The costs in Table 12.2 include only faculty salaries and fringe benefits, and do not include costs for items such as facilities, equipment, supplies, and overhead from departments, colleges, and central administration. The analysis illustrates the rather small cost impact of faculty compensation, and it also helps to explain why universities are moving away from tenured faculty toward full- and part-time instructional faculty.

TABLE 12.2

Surpluses for a Three-Credit-Hour Course at a Public University (Course Revenue Minus Faculty Members Salary and Fringe Benefits)

	General Education	Disciplinary Core	Major and Minor Fields of Study
Enrollment estimate[a]	50	35	25
Revenue from tuition, fees, and state subsidy (per course)	$1,150	$1,150	$1,150
Revenue/course	$57,500	$40,250	$28,750
Tenured faculty cost per course including fringe benefits	$11,400	$11,400	$11,400
Surplus for tenured faculty[†]*(Surplus: As percent of revenue)*	*$46,100 (80%)*	*$28,850 (72%)*	*$17,350 (60%)*
Instructional faculty cost per course including fringe benefits	$7,700	$7,700	$7,700
Surplus for instructional faculty[b]*(Surplus: As percent of revenue)*	*$49,800 (87%)*	*$32,550 (81%)*	*$21,050 (73%)*
Part-time faculty cost per course including fringe benefits	$3,700	$3,700	$3,700
Surplus for part-time faculty[b] *(Surplus: As percent of revenue)*	*$53,800 (94%)*	*$36,550 (91%)*	*$25,050 (87%)*

[a] These estimates are based on data from the following report from the Ohio Board of Regents, which provides overall average for undergraduate class size (33 students/class) as well as the percent of classes smaller than 20 (12%) and percent of classes of 50 or larger (36%).[10]

[b] Only faculty salaries and fringe benefits are deducted from revenue to determine surpluses. Other costs for items such as facilities, supplies, and administrative overhead are not included.

Enrollment estimates in Table 12.2 are for three undergraduate course types at public universities.[10] Liberal arts colleges have smaller classes and lower faculty salaries. Readers are encouraged to try other enrollment levels, tuition costs, and salaries. Average tuition and fees in 2015–2016, which is $9,410,[11] is divided by 30 credit hours, which full-time students take each year. The result is multiplied by three to determine the revenue for a three-credit-hour course. For simplicity, the analysis uses $950 rather than $941. State subsidy varies widely, and the amount selected, $200 per course, is conservative.[12] Thus, revenue per student, $1,150, is multiplied by the number of students to determine revenue per course.

The salary plus fringe benefits for tenured faculty is determined by averaging the compensation for assistant, associate, and full professors at public universities ($114,100).[13] Tenured faculty members have multiple duties—research, teaching, and service to the academy—so only 60% of their compensation is allocated to teaching. It is assumed that tenured faculty members teach six, three-credit-hour courses per year, so $114,100 is multiplied by 0.60 and divided by six to yield about $11,400 per course. Some tenured faculty members teach more while others teach less. Instructional faculty salary plus fringe benefits is determined by averaging the compensation for instructors and lecturer. The result is $69,100.[13] Their teaching load is usually 8 to 10 courses per year, so 9 is selected as the divisor to get about $7,700 per course. The salary per course for part-time faculty is estimated to be $3,200.[14] The typical faculty fringe benefit rate is about 30%,[13] but part-time faculty usually do not receive healthcare and other benefits. They earn Medicare credit and in some states they receive retirement credit, so 15% is used for fringe benefits, making the cost per course about $3,700. By examining surpluses in Table 12.2 and the percent of revenue that these surpluses represent, five things are clear.

1. *Substantial operating margins:* Public universities have tremendous operating margins at the undergraduate level. This is typical of most universities regardless of type. In the worst case, the margin is 60% when tenured faculty members teach courses in the major or minor, which means that 60% of revenue is available to cover administrative and other nonteaching costs. At the other extreme, part-time faculty teaching a general education course produces a 94% surplus.
2. *Enrollment drives surpluses:* As enrollment increases, surpluses surge significantly because virtually all the costs for a course that is already scheduled, including faculty salaries, are fixed.
3. *Explains the shift away from tenured faculty:* Using part-time faculty in general education, disciplinary core, and major and minor courses yields operating margins of 94%, 91%, ad 87%, respectively. The same numbers for tenured faculty are significantly lower but still robust at 80%, 72%, and 60%, respectively. Administrators, eager to balance their budgets, move away from tenured faculty to full- and part-time instructional faculty.
4. *Administrative excesses:* The data points in Table 12.2 are yet another confirmation that administrative costs are excessive, even out of control.
5. *Intrauniversity subsidies:* The data show that, regardless of faculty type, general education courses generate larger surpluses than

disciplinary core courses, which in turn generate larger surpluses than major and minor courses. The subsidization of higher level undergraduate courses may be justified by considering that students who graduate eventually take all three types of courses. Even though dropouts never receive this advantage, they could have. This subsidy provides community and technical colleges an opportunity to attract students because they have low tuition for general education and disciplinary core courses, which can transfer to universities. What cannot be shown as clearly but can be inferred from the data is that undergraduate programs provide meaningful subsidies for graduate programs. Should they?

12.4 RECONCILING UNDERGRADUATE AND GRADUATE STUDIES

Masters and PhD courses usually enroll fewer students than undergraduate courses, typically half as many or less.[15] Even though graduate programs tend to have higher tuition and fees than undergraduate programs, the additional revenue usually does not cover the higher costs. For example, in-state tuition at UCLA was $11,220 in 2016–2017, while the tuition and fees for in-state graduate programs was $16,325.[16,17] Comparable numbers at the University of Iowa were $8,974 and $10,579, respectively. Graduate tuition often varies by program, and the amount used for Iowa is from engineering.[18,19]

1. *Higher faculty costs:* In graduate programs, instructional costs are much higher because most faculty members who teach are tenured. Professional faculty members often teach in graduate programs that train engineers, businesspersons, and other professionals, and they are usually paid much more than instructional faculty who rarely teach graduate courses. Graduate programs rely heavily on research so they must fund these efforts by tenured faculty. This is part of the 40% reduction used to calculate faculty cost for teaching undergraduate courses.
2. *Small classes:* Master's courses tend to have enrollments in the teens or lower, and PhD courses are even smaller, usually in single digits.[15] So in addition to higher faculty costs, average revenue for

graduate courses is substantially lower, even though students pay higher tuition.

3. *Graduate assistantships:* In many master's programs, a significant percentage of students are enticed to enroll with the offer of a graduate assistantship that can provide "up to" free tuition and a full stipend to cover living expenses. Most students in PhD programs receive free tuition and a stipend that vary substantially from as little as $10,000 annually to more than $30,000.[20] Master's stipends are usually much smaller. In some cases, the costs of tuition and the stipend are paid by research grants, but often universities bear them, making graduate programs even more expensive.

Table 12.2 and this discussion offer credible evidence that some parts of undergraduate education subsidize other parts of undergraduate studies as well as graduate education. It seems reasonable to argue that doing so is unfair. Taking this a step further: Why should students attending public universities pay twice as much for general education courses in algebra and economics as students pay at a two-year college?[11] There should be ways for universities to offer these courses at the same price.

State government, working with public universities, should address these subsidizes and determine if differential tuition is a reasonable option. As proposed in Chapter 9, states should create HECs to examine these and other issues and share ideas and progress, but each state would arrive at its own decision. The HEC would make recommendations on the following.

1. To what extent are public universities using general education courses to subsidize other undergraduate courses and programs?
2. Should public universities have differential tuition for undergraduate courses in general education, disciplinary core, and major and minor fields of study? Should the state provide larger subsidies for more expensive courses and programs? Some states already do so.
3. What is the cost of a graduate degree? To what extent does undergraduate education subsidize graduate education? Is it fair for undergraduate education to provide this subsidy? Should universities increase graduate tuition substantially and/or should states provide larger subsidies?

These discussions must occur in a context where universities work hard to cut costs, especially administrative costs. If costs can be lowered significantly, these issues become easier to address.

12.5 IMPROVING FACULTY PRODUCTIVITY

When the surpluses in Table 12.2 are considered, some may question the need to increase faculty productivity because faculty costs are small compared to revenue. But teaching methods have changed little for many decades, and there appears to be opportunities to improve the quality of teaching while lowering costs. Faculty has a responsibility to take leadership so this can happen.

Generally speaking, the essence of productivity improvement throughout the millennia has been the (1) application of automation to mechanize farming, (2) cheap and available power plus automation that drove the Industrial Revolution, and (3) the application of computer and communication technologies that simplified product design, enhanced access to information, and created the postindustrial society. For higher education and education more generally, the ability to prepare, transmit, manipulate, and communicate digitized text, pictures, graphs, diagrams, and videos should revolutionize teaching and learning. The United States is at the beginning of this journey.

Increasing productivity in the classroom requires three actions that are out of character for universities and their faculty.

1. *Capital investment:* Universities typically think of investments as new buildings, including the latest "gee-whiz" classrooms and computer technology. Presidents, donors, alumni, and others love new buildings, but there is a scenario where the need for buildings declines as online learning takes an increasing share of the higher education market. The hoopla over buildings overcomes the need for universities to invest in activities that drive teaching excellence as well as efficiency/productivity. Universities must invest in sophisticated, top-quality, educational methods for communicating knowledge across a wide variety of formats as described a bit later in this section. This requires taking advantage of economies of scale—spreading this investment across a large number of students—to actually reduce the cost of higher education.

2. *Up-front design:* If universities invest, then faculty must be willing to take the time to create a multifaceted pedagogy that accommodates different learning styles. Universities must support these efforts, keeping in mind that the goals are twofold: improve learning and reduce costs.
3. *Three-credit hours does not mean three hours of face time:* Universities and faculty must understand the circumstances under which students learn best and work hard to create those circumstances, rather than churning out three hours of face-to-face lectures each week. The solution must be more than substituting lower paid instructional faculty for tenured faculty.

Some readers may brush aside these recommendations as an attempt to industrialize higher education, and there is truth in their claim. Creating standardization and taking advantage of economies of scale can improve learning and cut costs. But industrialization only makes sense when knowledge changes slowly over time, so the learning infrastructure that supports education can be created once and adjusted as needed—the essence of continuous improvement. So industrialization is most appropriate in general education courses and should be nonexistent in PhD courses. Consider the following subjects, which are part of general education or disciplinary core: introduction to statistics, college algebra, introduction to sociology, and English composition. It makes sense to invest time and money to create a sophisticated set of learning tools because the contents of these courses change slowly, in spite of what book publishers and some faculty may claim. PhD seminars, which focus on cutting-edge knowledge, still require doctoral students to read the latest research papers with a critical eye and ultimately to assimilate the best of these ideas into undergraduate and graduate education.

Administrators and faculty may argue that students taking general education or disciplinary core courses, taught using this industrial approach, miss the opportunity to learn from scholars who are at the leading edge of knowledge. They believe that these scholars can bring great insight to introductory courses that instructional faculty cannot. They attempt to achieve this in one of two ways:

1. *Assign the best scholars:* In a semester, the best scholar is assigned to teach one or two of the many sections offered for a particular general education course with the balance being taught by instructional faculty and graduate teaching assistants. Depending on the

course, there may be six, seven, a dozen, or even more sections. This approach is a token effort, the impact is limited to a small group, and there is no assurance that the impact is positive.

2. *Mass teaching:* A top scholar is assigned to teach a mass lecture with 200, 300, or 400 students. The students spend part of their time in smaller problem and discussion sections, which are staffed by instructional faculty and graduate teaching assistants. There is no real chance for questions in the lecture, and there is rampant speculation that learning is not very effective.

In addition, many top scholars find it difficult to relate to the average 18- to 20-year-old undergraduate student because the scholars (1) have seven or eight more years of higher education than the students, (2) have taught for several years so they know the subject very well, and (3) were among the best students when they attended the university, so their expectations are very high. They may have trouble comprehending how little students know. These experts may not have the patience to deal with young students who are not as dedicated to learning as the faculty member would like.

Besides, having senior scholars teach first- and second-year students is a misallocation of resources unless universities only employ this type of faculty. Senior scholars are educated to teach upper-level undergraduate, masters, and PhD courses. Introductory courses require less depth of knowledge, change slowly, and have little debate as to what is important. The knowledge and skills of instructional faculty and graduate teaching assistants fit general education and disciplinary core courses well.

Given these circumstances, it seems reasonable to improve productivity by "industrializing" aspects of higher education, especially at the general education and disciplinary core levels, through the use of high-tech learning materials. The following proposal has many points in common with student-centered learning (Chapter 7) and online learning (Chapter 10). The first point describes replacing traditional textbooks with high-tech reading materials. Points 2 through 5 discuss how traditional face-to-face lecture can be replaced using technology. Points 1 through 5 are described more fully in Chapter 13.

1. *Reading materials:* E-books with sophisticated, interactive learning tools as well as books-on-tape/on-CD/online that can be used on the go are important.

2. *Video lecture:* There is a need for tenured and professional faculty experts to provide insights and commentary on topic in the courses. When there are multiple sections with large enrollments, it is sensible to invest in a series of high-quality videos by top scholars that can be downloaded and watched repeatedly. These videos would offer a systemic view of the course.
3. *Video vignettes:* For some courses, especially those with problems requiring calculation, math models, and complex procedures, a short video explaining these, anticipating and answering questions, and describing their application would be available for students to view repeatedly.
4. *Problem and discussion sessions:* For many courses, it may be useful to meet face to face to discuss ideas and solve problems, among other things. These sessions, which are commonly used today, could last an hour and would be taught by full- and part-time instructional faculty and graduate teaching assistants.
5. *Group chat with faculty:* There should be times when students have the opportunity to have an online chat with faculty regarding course content.
6. *Note taking:* Some students learn as they take notes. Electronic media should be available with all learning materials so students can make useful notations as they learn.
7. *Group work:* Some students learn best in group settings. There should be opportunities for projects, homework assignments, problem solving, and other activities that can be done in a group. Electronic communications and information technologies facilitate these interactions.
8. *Individual work:* Some students prefer to work alone and should have opportunities to do so. But some disciplines such as business, engineering, and medicine require intense information exchange among experts with different skills, so group interaction may be required.
9. *Hands-on learning:* Cooperative education and internships provide opportunities for hands-on learning, but there are also ways to do this within a course, including projects that involve interacting with experts who are practicing the profession.
10. *Verbal learning:* Some students learn more effectively in role playing and when preparing and making presentations. The audience may benefit from this as well. These can be viewed by faculty, and the best ones can be made available to students for online observation.

11. *Visual learning:* The videos, e-books, discussion sessions, and other activities should use pictures, charts, and diagrams that use colors to explain ideas and techniques.

This list of ideas is intended as a starting point to improve learning and lower the cost of instruction. As faculty investigate courses in order to improve productivity, they are likely to find many more ways.

12.6 UNIVERSITIES AND FACULTY UNIONS

Universities have unions that represent their employees, such as clerks, campus security, custodians, graduate assistants, and other groups, including faculty. Although a broad discussion of unionization may be insightful, the focus is on faculty unions, which have grown significantly in recent years.[21] In 2011, about 21% of all universities had faculty unions with unionization at public universities being 35%.[22] Two-year institutions are about twice as likely to have faculty unions as institutions offering bachelor's degrees.[23]

People believe that unions are formed to increase pay and improve working conditions, but research shows that unionization of full-time faculty in public higher education has at best a modest impact on the level of compensation. The impact tends to be on how salary increases are distributed[24] with unions favoring across-the-board increases to cope with inflation versus merit-based increases. In truth, faculty unions are a reaction to a widening gap between administration and faculty. Unions are often blamed for creating the problems in higher education, but unionization is symptomatic for the following reasons:

1. *Assumption of power:* University boards and administrators have assumed power and limited faculty participation in key management processes, such as strategic planning, and they have restricted faculty input and authority with respect to resource allocation.
2. *Accelerating administrative costs:* As described in prior chapters, the number of administrators has grown much faster than faculty positions and student enrollment. At the same time, administrative salaries have grown much faster than faculty wages and inflation.

Unionization of graduate assistants, part-time faculty, and full-time instructional faculty presents a workable set of issues that center on increasing compensation, setting limits on class size, and improving working conditions. Union contracts and the negotiation process can impede efforts to launch innovative teaching techniques that improve productivity because unions anticipate job losses and are unwilling to take the risk that the new techniques will not be effective. These issues are manageable.

Unionization of professional and tenured faculty presents a different and more complex set of problems because they have a critical role in defining and executing the university's missions. In a professional service organization, when fundamental differences exist among administrators and subject matter experts, unions tend to crystalize differences and polarize adversaries, so disputes are institutionalized. Faculty experts believe strongly that their role is not only important but central to the mission and success of the institution. They hold strong values and beliefs about their role, and they react when their role is diminished. Relationships between faculty and university leaders, especially universities with significant graduate programs and strong research missions, are comparable to those between doctors and hospitals, scientists and bio-tech firms, and engineers and design companies. The key to addressing unions is not "union busting"; rather, it is rebuilding close working relationships between tenured and professional faculty and university leaders.

12.7 DRIVING FORCES FOR CHANGE

States should take the lead in establishing HECs to investigate the cost and tuition charges for different levels of instruction. The HEC would work with universities to determine if tuition should be different for general education and interdisciplinary courses, undergraduate major and minor courses, and graduate courses. Boards of trustees and senior leaders must initiate the process to reconcile relationships between them and tenured and professional faculty. This may require intervention from federal, state, and local governments who provide funding. Faculty must be willing to put aside long-held and negative beliefs about the potential for simultaneously lowering costs and improving the quality of learning.

12.8 IMPACT OF RESHAPING FACULTY'S ROLE ON HIGHER EDUCATION OUTCOMES

Reshaping the faculty's role focuses on improving learning outcomes while lowering the cost of instruction. It requires universities to rethink their investment plans and faculty to adjust teaching methods and assessment practices. The following list examines how this element of the solution impacts the root causes, which are discussed in Chapter 4:

1. *Lack of understanding—Who is the customer? (root cause 1):* Faculty must reach out to potential employers, graduate programs that accept their students, and certification and licensure agencies to ensure that curriculum meets their needs.
2. *Rise of the ruling class: Administration (root cause 3)*: The board, senior leadership, and tenured and professional faculty must work together to make the university more innovative, more responsive, and less expensive.
3. *Limited productivity improvements for universities (root cause 4):* Changing the role of faculty should improve their productivity and reduce operating costs.
4. *Rapidly growing costs for books and supplies (root cause 5):* As the delivery of curriculum changes, the learning materials should change and become less expensive. The costs for these materials should be included in tuition payments.
5. *Eroding standards (root cause 8):* As faculty reach out to potential employers and others, standards should be set at appropriate levels. As the roles of different faculty types are clarified, the erosion of standards should be reversed.

12.9 SUMMARY OF RECOMMENDATIONS

Following is a list of the key recommendations that comprise this element of the solution.

1. To have better, faster, and more efficient education, it is essential to prepare faculty so they are knowledgeable in content, pedagogy, and assessment of learning.
   a. All types of faculty should be subject to evaluation by students as described in Chapter 7, be supported by centers for teaching, participate in teaching seminars as part of their work requirements, and have access to teaching improvement funds.
   b. Full-time, tenured faculty must have the education and skills to teach effectively and this begins in the PhD program. In addition, the teaching performance of all faculty candidates is assessed during the hiring process, and newly hired faculty members are assigned to master teachers and together they create a continuous improvement plan.
   c. Full-time, contractual faculty would follow a similar process, but adjustments would be made for faculty who have not earned a PhD and have little if any teaching experience.
   d. Part-time contractual faculty, especially those with limited teaching experience and a full-time job that takes priority, may be reluctant to participate in teaching improvement efforts. There are two options, stop hiring part-time faculty with limited teaching experience or pay them more for the first two or three times they teach to cover start-up costs.
   e. Graduate teaching assistants would participate in an assessment of their communication skills, including language; have regular teaching evaluations; and work with mentors. They would be carefully supervised as they teach.
2. It is important to identify the capabilities of different faculty types, know the instructional needs for courses, and match these to get the best outcomes, meaning both high quality and low cost. This is summarized in Table 12.1.
3. General education and interdisciplinary core courses tend to generate substantial surpluses, which are used to subsidize other undergraduate courses as well as courses in masters and PhD programs. State governments should create a HEC to examine these issues.
4. It is vital to improve faculty productivity by investing in sophisticated, top-quality methods for communicating knowledge and supporting faculty so they create innovative and efficient ways to disseminate knowledge to students. Universities and faculty must move

away from the notion that a three-credit-hour course requires three hours of face time.

5. Faculty unions have not caused the problems that universities face, but they are the result of poor relationships between university leaders and tenured and professional faculty. State government, boards of trustees, and top management must mend these relationships.

REFERENCES

1. National Center for Education Statistics. 2015. *Undergraduate Enrollment*. http://nces.ed.gov/programs/coe/indicator_cha.asp (accessed December 13, 2016).
2. National Center for Education Statistics. 2015. *Postbaccalaureate Enrollment*. http://nces.ed.gov/programs/coe/indicator_chb.asp (accessed December 13, 2016).
3. McNutt, M. I. 2014. Why does college cost so much? *US News World Report*, September 22. http://www.usnews.com/news/college-of-tomorrow/articles/2014/09/22/why-college-costs-so-much-overspending-on-faculty-amenities (accessed June 24, 2016).
4. National Education Association. 2013. *Frequently Asked Questions: Collective Bargaining in Higher Education*. http://www.nea.org/home/62147.htm (accessed January 20, 2017).
5. Cain, T. 2013. *The Research on Faculty Unions*. International Program for Research in the Humanities, February 9. https://iprh.wordpress.com/2013/02/09/the-research-on-faculty-unions/ (accessed January 20, 2017).
6. History.com. 2009. *Labor Movement*. http://www.history.com/topics/labor (accessed January 16, 2017).
7. Educational Testing Service. 2017. *The Test of English as a Foreign Language*. http://www.ets.org/toefl/ (accessed January 21, 2017).
8. Wiessmann, J. 2013. The ever-shrinking role of tenured college professors. *The Atlantic*, April 10. http://www.theatlantic.com/business/archive/2013/04/the-ever-shrinking-role-of-tenured-college-professors-in-1-chart/274849/ (accessed June 24, 2016).
9. American Association of University Professors. 2014. *Losing Focus: The Annual Report on the Economic Status of the Profession, 2013–2014*. https://www.aaup.org/reports-publications/2013-14salarysurvey (accessed June 24, 2016).
10. Ohio Board of Regents. 2002. *Typical Class Size for Undergraduate Students at Ohio's Public Campuses*. https://view.officeapps.live.com/op/view.aspx?src=http%3A%2F%2Fregents.ohio.gov%2Fperfrpt%2F2002%2FChapter_08_PR_2002_cp.doc (accessed March 20, 2017).
11. College Board. 2016. *Trends in Higher Education: Published Prices—National*. http://trends.collegeboard.org/college-pricing/figures-tables/published-prices-national#Published Charges, 2015–16 (accessed June 20, 2016).
12. The Pew Charitable Trusts. 2015. Federal and state funding of higher education: A changing landscape. June 11. http://www.pewtrusts.org/en/research-and-analysis/issue-briefs/2015/06/federal-and-state-funding-of-higher-education (accessed June 16, 2016).

13. American Association of University Professors. 2014. *Losing Focus: The Annual Report on the Economic Status of the Profession, 2013–2014*. https://www.aaup.org/reports-publications/2013-14salarysurvey (accessed June 24, 2016).
14. Wiessmann, J. 2013. The ever-shrinking role of tenured college professors. *The Atlantic*, April 10. http://www.theatlantic.com/business/archive/2013/04/the-ever-shrinking-role-of-tenured-college-professors-in-1-chart/274849/ (accessed June 24, 2016).
15. University of Nevada, Las Vegas. 2015. *Class Size Summary*. http://ir.unlv.edu/IAP/Reports/Content/ClassSizeSummary.aspx (accessed March 20, 2017).
16. Registrar Office, UCLA. 2016. *Undergraduate Degree Fees*. http://www.registrar.ucla.edu/Fees-Residence/Annual-Fees/Undergraduate-Degree-Fees (accessed March 21, 2017).
17. Graduate School, UCLA. 2016. *Tuition and Student Fees*. https://grad.ucla.edu/funding/tuition/ (accessed March 21, 2017).
18. Graduate Admissions, University of Iowa. 2017. *Engineering, Estimated Costs*. https://grad.admissions.uiowa.edu/engineering-estimated-costs (accessed March 21, 2017).
19. Undergraduate Admissions, University of Iowa. 2017. *Estimated Cost of Attendance*. https://admissions.uiowa.edu/finances/estimated-costs-attendance (accessed March 21, 2017).
20. PhD Stipends. 2017. *PhD Stipend Survey Results*. http://www.phdstipends.com/results (accessed March 20, 2017).
21. Herbert, W. A. 2016. The winds of change shift: An analysis of recent growth in bargaining units and representation efforts in higher education. *Journal of Collective Bargaining in the Academy*, December 8. http://thekeep.eiu.edu/cgi/viewcontent.cgi?article=1647&context=jcba (accessed February 10, 2017).
22. HigherEdJobs.com. 2016. *What Does the History of Faculty Unions Teach Us About the Future?* https://www.higheredjobs.com/HigherEdCareers/interviews.cfm?ID=315 (accessed February 10, 2017).
23. Euben, D. R., and Hustoles, T. P. 2001. *Collective Bargaining Revised and Revisited (2001)*. American Association of University Professor. https://www.aaup.org/issues/collective-bargaining/collective-bargaining-revised-and-revisited-2001 (accessed March 20, 2017).
24. Davis, L. J. 2011. Forum: The future of faculty unions. *The Chronicle of Higher Education*, July 24. http://www.chronicle.com/article/Forum-The-Future-of-Faculty/128305/ (accessed February 10, 2017).

13

Creating High-Technology Learning Materials

For thousands of years, the primary vehicle for disseminating knowledge was the spoken word. Small groups of students gathered around scholars who discussed their thoughts and ideas. Over many years, two factors changed this. New means of transport and expanding trade enabled interaction among communities and countries that were previously isolated. Second, economic growth depended on communicating information and disseminating knowledge to more people. These changes shifted higher education from dependency on spoken words to reliance on written words. Although there were many advances in printing, the creation of the printing press with replaceable type by Johannes Gutenberg in the middle of the fifteenth century made printing easier and cheaper.[1,2] Books, periodicals, and other documents became readily available and have been the learning platform for education.

Higher education and education more generally is ever so slowing moving away from printed books and periodicals because these are expensive and bulky. Technology allows printed works to be easily and inexpensively digitized and therefore more portable and accessible and less expensive. It is an opportunity that cannot be ignored. The new technology has been used for decades to digitize and replicate physical objects in three dimensions (3D) so they can be examined, manipulated, and designed to meet specific requirements. These applications are known as computer-aided design (CAD), computer-aided engineering (CAE), and computer-aided manufacturing (CAM).

1. *CAD:* Computer software used by engineers, architects, artists, and others to create precise 2D and 3D drawings, technical illustrations, and models.[3]

2. *CAE:* The use of software to assist engineers in analyzing components and designing them for safety, endurance, and reliability. Among other things, CAE can perform stress analysis, consider thermal and fluid flows, and simulate processes for forging and casting parts.[4]
3. *CAM:* The use of software to control machine tools that can produce component parts. CAM is usually linked to CAD/CAE systems so the component's designs can be seamlessly and digitally passed to the machine tools that make the parts.[5]

CAD/CAE/CAM systems have their roots in the 1960s,[5] and they have been used extensively to design and produce manufactured parts for more than three decades. More recently, computer-based medical simulation is allowing physician to create 3D replicas of the heart, even the entire body, which can be used to train physicians and other healthcare professionals. It can also be used to diagnose problems, consider treatment alternatives, and assist in creating treatment plans.[6,7]

Readers may be thinking what do CAD/CAE/CAM and 3D medical simulation have to do with higher education? The answer is not much. But it illustrates the fact that higher education is woefully behind other organizations and industries in applying computer and information technologies. If society can design and implement ways for computers to model component parts from design all the way though manufacturing and to replicate the human body in 3D, why has higher education been so slow at digitizing its learning tools?

Manufacturers are forced to respond because they operate in highly competitive global markets, so they must invest in the latest technologies to enhance product performance, improve quality, and keep costs as low as possible. If they do not, competitors take their business. Healthcare has pursued and adopted new technologies that have direct and positive impacts on healing. Higher education has not adopted technology to improve quality and lower costs for the following reasons:

1. Higher education in the United States is generally regarded as the best in the world. This creates complacency, which stifles innovation.
2. Demand for higher education has grown substantially so most universities, especially larger ones, have enjoyed significant growth.
3. State and local governments subsidize tuition for public two- and four-year institutions, which represent about 70% of total enrollment in the

United States. See Table 1.2 in Chapter 1. This creates state-wide rather than nation-wide markets for much of higher education.
4. Universities hire leaders from the same pool of people who have similar attitudes, values, and beliefs, and they hire the same consultants who are typically former administrators that pass along the same advice. Thus, universities are convinced that the status quo is appropriate.

13.1 APPLYING TECHNOLOGY TO LEARNING MATERIALS

All courses can benefit from applying technology to manage routine activities such as distributing course materials and collecting homework assignments. To improve learning and reduce costs, technology must be applied to the learning process, and the amount of technology that can be used effectively depends on the course. As shown in Figure 13.1, class size declines dramatically from general education courses such as basic mathematics and economics in which hundreds of students enroll each semester to PhD courses that are offered once a year with single-digit enrollment. Large courses have powerful economies of scale, so universities and faculty can justify investing substantial resources in creating effective, high-quality, technology-based teaching tools. Publishers and others can afford to invest in sophisticated reading materials, self-study

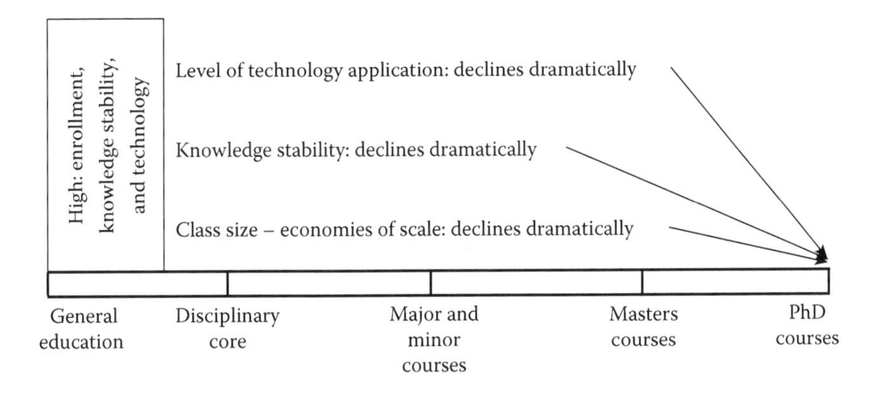

FIGURE 13.1
Relationship between the level of education and the application of technology: class size and knowledge stability.

tests, and problem-solving tools because there is sufficient volume to justify the investment. In addition, the knowledge content in a general education course is stable, so learning materials require only periodic, small adjustments to keep pace with changing knowledge. On the other hand, PhD courses change substantially from one year to the next. The combination of large class size and stable content makes general education courses highly desirable targets for technology, while small class size and rapidly changing content make PhD courses much less desirable. Between these extremes are many good candidates for high-technology learning materials.

Creating high-tech reading materials and high-tech lectures is at the heart of developing sophisticated learning systems.

1. *High-tech reading materials:* These are more than creating an e-book by digitizing traditional textbooks. They are interactive devices that assess what students know and provide mechanisms to address knowledge gaps. This approach may include books, study guides, annotated PowerPoint slides, instructor's manuals, and other aids that are *electronic* and *interactive.*
2. *High-tech lectures:* Face-to-face lectures are replaced in whole or in part by videos that provide context and theory, video vignettes that explain specific ideas and solve problems, discussion sessions that answer questions, and electronic tools that aid communication with faculty.

13.2 CREATING HIGH-TECH READING MATERIALS: THE ECONOMICS

The improvements in quality and access, which can be achieved by transforming traditional textbooks into dynamic, technology-based learning tools, are relatively easy to envision. In fact, all books, periodicals, and reference materials should be available online, and students should be able to view these items on a variety of devices. As a result, they can use time, which was formerly wasted waiting in a doctor's office or standing in a fast-food line, to watch a short video or review PowerPoint slides. This generation of students does not need to be seated in a quiet library with both feet planted on the floor to learn from a printed book. What may be less clear to many people is that these new high-tech tools should cost substantially less than traditional textbooks.

The reasons why a high-tech approach cost less is easier to see when Table 13.1 is examined. Publishing traditional textbooks and creating high-tech reading materials have fixed and variable costs. For printed books, authors engage in idea generation, and they write and create the text and supporting materials, such as instructor's manuals and study guides. Textbooks are professionally edited, and suggested changes are reviewed by authors. Page proofs, which put the book into the proper format, are prepared by the publisher and reviewed by authors. Once this is done, the book is ready for printing. High-tech reading materials have a similar set of actions that represent the fixed costs of their creation.

Over the past three decades, publishers have incorporated technology into their printed textbooks by offering electronic study guides, test banks, and other tools to reduce costs and improve learning. These online efforts require software development as shown in Table 13.1. As publishers move to interactive high-tech reading materials, software investment is likely to increase to create more sophisticated tools. However, there are economies of scale in software development if reading materials for different subjects use the same platform. People can debate whether the fixed costs of publishing a traditional textbook are higher or lower than creating high-tech reading materials, but it is likely that the difference between the two is small. The real advantage for high-tech reading materials is lower variable costs.

Production and delivery costs are much lower for high-tech reading material because each copy of a traditional textbook must be printed and bound, which consumes truckloads of materials and requires large factories full of printing equipment. Next, Table 13.1 lists 10 material handling and transport steps until students walk out of the bookstore with the textbook. Even if textbooks are sold online, many of these steps are required, plus there is packing and shipping from the online retailer to the student. For the unsold books, six steps are needed to return them to the publisher. On the other hand, high-tech reading materials are uploaded to the website so faculty and students can download them as needed. It seems clear that this costs less than all the printing, handling, and storing required for traditional books. Besides, most traditional textbooks have electronic support materials that must be loaded to a website and distributed to faculty and students, so publishers are already incurring many of these expenses.

TABLE 13.1

Publishing Traditional Textbooks and Creating High-Tech Reading Materials: A Comparison

	Publishing a Traditional Textbook		High-Tech Reading Materials	
Action	**Fixed Cost**	**Variable Cost per Book**	**Fixed Cost**	**Variable Cost per Unit**
Idea generation	Yes		Yes	
Writing/creating	Yes		Yes	
Editing	Yes		Yes	
Page proofs/formatting	Yes		Yes	
Software development	Yes: Basic		Yes: Advanced	
Printing		Yes		
Binding		Yes		
Pack for shipping		Yes		
Put in storage at printer		Yes		
Remove from storage		Yes		
Load truck		Yes		
Transport to bookstore		Yes		
Unload truck		Yes		
Put in storage at bookstore		Yes		
Remove from storage		Yes		
Stock shelves at bookstore		Yes		
Checkout and pay		Sold copies only		
Return unsold copies to storage		Unsold copies only		
Pack for return shipping		Unsold copies only		
Load truck		Unsold copies only		
Transport to publisher		Unsold copies only		
Unload truck		Unsold copies only		
Return to storage		Unsold copies only		
Upload electronic learning materials	May have e-supplements		Yes	
Distribute electronically		May have e-supplements		Yes

There are other advantages with the high-tech approach as designers and authors create new ways to present ideas and interactive tools, which enable students to learn better. In addition, they can create a variety of modules, which enables faculty to select the ones that are appropriate for their course. With hardcopies, faculty members are limited to what is in the printed textbook, which cannot be changed until the next edition is published in three to five years. Their only option is to eliminate topics by asking students not to read this or that part of the book. With this in mind, authors tend to put everything, including the kitchen sink, into textbooks to ensure that anything faculty may want is available. This causes books to have 1,000 pages or more, driving up printing, transport, handling, and storage costs.

Another advantage of high-tech reading materials is that errors can be fixed quickly, easily, and cheaply, whereas errors in traditional textbooks cannot be fixed until the next edition, unless the textbooks are recalled, reprinted, and replaced. This rarely happens because the process would be chaotic and very expensive. The second best alternative, which is highly ineffective, is to send errata sheets to all faculty adopters that explain the errors and hope they are given to students. Revising high-tech reading materials to cope with changing ideas is also simpler and cheaper because the electronic text and images can be altered quickly. Adding new ideas to later editions of a traditional textbook requires repetition of the process described in Table 13.1.

As proposed earlier, these high-tech reading materials would be purchased by universities and provided to students as part of their tuition. This is more than a cost shift from students to universities with universities simply adding the cost to their current tuition. It represents a lower overall cost for reading materials. There are several advantages for students, universities, and publisher such as:

1. *Lower costs for students:* Beside the fact that high-tech reading materials should be cheaper than traditional textbooks, universities can negotiate price with publishers more effectively than individual students. Now, universities do not consider the price of textbooks—they make the choice and students pay the price.
2. *Better content for universities and students:* Because the process for creating reading materials is flexible, universities can choose the content, so these materials are focused and appropriate.

3. *Enhanced learning for students:* Learning should improve because many current students do not purchase traditional textbooks because they can cost more than $200 each. Now, they will have access because this is covered by tuition. Also, high-tech reading materials help students learn better and faster because they are interactive and can pinpoint problem areas for each student.
4. *Better business model for publishers:* When universities buy for all students, sales are more predictable; the used book market is eliminated; revisions happen when needed and are cheaper; and unauthorized use of learning materials is easier to control. In addition, selling expenses should be reduced as an army of salespersons, who earn commission on each book sold, are replaced by a smaller group of account managers who work directly with universities.

13.3 CREATING HIGH-TECH READING MATERIALS: THE PRODUCTS

High-tech reading materials are more than transforming a textbook into an e-book that can be read online, because this simplistic approach does not fully use the technology. The following list has important components that can make the learning package better. These items are part of an approach to set learning goals, measure performance, provide feedback, refine knowledge, and repeat the cycle.

1. *Interactive questions, answers, and referrals:* Each segment of the e-book would have an electronic content test/study guide that would ask students about important information that they should learn from reading the book. This mechanism not only lets the students know if their answer is correct, it takes them to the point or points in the e-book that discuss the information, so learning is improved. This tool can assess fact-based knowledge as well as measure students' understanding of concepts, ideas, and the relationships among ideas.
2. *Computer-generated problems:* For courses with quantitative material, students would be presented with problems to solve. They would solve the problem and submit their answer, be informed if the answer is correct or given feedback about why the answer is wrong,

and could be presented with a similar problem that has new data. This could happen over and over at the student's request. This mechanism, which can be thought of as part of a study guide, would do more than provide the correct answer and responses to frequently asked questions. This tool would take the student to the place in the e-book that describes how to work the problem, show the steps in the solution, and have a link to an online video that shows how to solve the problem, including common errors.

3. *Sample tests:* Using the mechanisms from items 1 and 2 in this list, timed tests can be generated that students could take to assess their overall knowledge.
4. *PowerPoint slide deck:* These are usually available with traditional textbooks, but the new versions would be heavily noted so students seeking better explanations could find them as part of the PowerPoint slides. In addition, there would be links from the PowerPoint slides to the e-book that would provide more insights and explanations.
5. *Mechanisms for reading to students:* Students must be able to listen to e-books on a variety of mobile devices. This can be organized by topic so students can pick topics in any order or in the recommended sequence.

13.4 CREATING HIGH-TECH LECTURES

Like creating high-tech reading materials, changing how knowledge is transferred from faculty to students must be done so it costs less and, more importantly, so students learn more. Overall cost declines because the upfront investment to digitized lectures is far less than continuing savings from higher faculty productivity. In the process, less expensive instructional faculty and graduate teaching assistants are used to staff general education and disciplinary core courses that do not require the skill, knowledge, and experience of tenured and professional faculty. The notion of using less expensive faculty is part of the current system, but universities often rely too heavily on these substitutes and/or use them inappropriately by assigning them to teach upper-level undergraduate and graduate courses.

The essence of efforts to use tenured and professional faculty more productively is centered on the creation of downloadable, electronic lectures featuring top scholars discussing key topics and shaping important ideas. This is an effective way for students in general education and disciplinary core courses to gain access to the best faculty. At some point, interactive avatars may present ideas and solve problems. There are also opportunities to utilize 3D graphics to make points that are difficult to make in a 2D textbook, PowerPoint slide, or other traditional tools. A key for making successful video lectures and video vignettes, which is discussed in Chapter 12, is to carefully integrate the lecture with high-tech reading materials. The videos should use concepts, graphs, and problems from the book, even going so far as to mention chapters, section titles, and figure designations, so students see a consistent message.

Students should be able to ask questions and get customized answers, but that may be difficult with the current technology. However, it should be possible for faculty experts to anticipate where students may have trouble and allow them to pause the video and ask questions. If the question was anticipated by the designers, students may get an answer immediately, but if not, the question would pass electronically to a faculty member, who would answer the question and suggest reading materials that might clarify their concerns. The questions would go to instructional faculty and graduate teaching assistants first and be handed off to tenured and professional faculty as needed. Student questions would be compiled and used to improve the videos by addressing the most common questions.

13.5 WHAT MIGHT BE IS UNCLEAR

The ideas in the prior sections and the ideas discussed in Chapter 12 offer good first steps in efforts to electrify and digitize learning while reducing costs and improving outcomes. Publishers are creating some of these electronic tools. Also, there are efforts to provide video presentations to supplement and replace face-to-face lecturing as well as other mechanisms to enhance learning. The journey toward better teaching materials has begun.

The challenge in the early phases of technology development is that efforts are bounded by the context in which people live and work, which is determined by their life experiences. For example, approximately 80 years ago, the Englander, Alan Turing, invented what is commonly called the Turing Machine, which was a theoretical computing machine—a forerunner of the modern-day computer.[8] He and others, working in England and the United States, faced substantial resistance from government and industry. They often found it difficult to get the funding needed to do research and make important and necessary enhancements. Even among the true believers in this technology, it would have been impossible for them to predict accurately its long-term capabilities and applications. Hand-held devices that are a million times more powerful and have a million times more storage than these early devices as well as space travel, satellite communications, the Internet, and dozens of other applications that depend on computing technology would have been impossible to foresee.

Higher education has been slow to adopt technologies that move education beyond traditional textbooks and lecture-discussion sessions. Part of this resistance is caused by the success of higher education and a hesitancy to fix something that administrators and faculty do not feel is broken. Faculty may feel other aspects of universities need to change, but many are comfortable with the current textbook and lecture model. When fundamental change is needed and there is no compelling reason, such as the looming downfall of the current system, there is strong support for the status quo, especially by those who benefit from the current structure. In addition, administrators and faculty are no different from the scientists of 80 years ago, who found it difficult to foresee the long-term application of technology. The next generation of administrators and faculty who have been raised on computer and information technology should have a different perspective and be more likely to embrace and develop new applications.

13.6 DRIVING FORCES FOR CHANGE

State government supported by federal and local governments should use its leverage to encourage public universities (boards of trustee and administrative leadership) to seek high-tech learning materials and require universities, not students, to be financially responsible for these costs. Students, parents, other family members, and friends should contact governments, voicing approval for these reforms.

Curriculum design and execution is within the purview of tenured and professional faculty, and it is not something that administration should force faculty to do because, given the current acrimonious environment, faculty members are likely to resist. To begin, there must be a dialogue with and among faculty to discuss how higher education can improve the quality of instruction and lower costs. *Both issues must be on the table*; otherwise, faculty members will seek smaller class sizes and lower teaching loads so they have more time for developing high-quality teaching tools, and administrators will seek larger class sizes and greater teaching loads to lower cost. University leadership should do the following:

1. Reduce administrative cost to demonstrate that it is serious about cost reductions
2. Provide faculty with more input and governance in university planning and budgeting processes
3. Commit to an upfront investment for creating and implementing high-tech learning materials. These investments should be rolled out over multiple years
4. Consider ways for faculty to share in the benefits from being more productive.

13.7 IMPACT OF CREATING HIGH-TECHNOLOGY LEARNING MATERIALS ON HIGHER EDUCATION OUTCOMES

Creating high-tech learning materials is essential to improve the quality and lower the cost of higher education. Universities can negotiate price more effectively with publishers and other entities, and they should make better choices about what tools are needed. Plus students will no longer have to agonize about finding the money to buy books. The following list examines how this element of the solution impacts the root causes, which are discussed in Chapter 4:

1. *Limited productivity improvements for universities (root cause 4):* Having effectively design learning materials should make faculty more productive and make students better learners.
2. *Rapidly growing costs for books and supplies (root cause 5):* High-tech learning materials and the university's ability to negotiate with publishers should reduce the cost of "textbooks" substantially.

13.8 SUMMARY OF RECOMMENDATIONS

Following is a list of the key recommendations that comprise this element of the solution.

1. Universities become responsible for paying for all learning materials.
2. Universities must create high-tech reading materials that are interactive and help students identify and address knowledge gaps. These should have lower cost, better content coverage, enhanced learning for students, and better outcomes for publishers.
   a. Interactive questions, answers, and referrals to the correct information make these superior learning tools.
   b. Computer-generated problems allow students to learn better by generating an unlimited number of attempts at the same problem with feedback about error.
   c. Sample tests allow students to gauge their ability and provide insight on how to improve.
   d. PowerPoint slide decks are annotated and electronically connected to the e-book.
   e. Mechanisms for reading e-books to students over different devices are available.
3. Universities must create high-tech, digitized lectures and video vignettes that allow students to have access to tenured and professional faculty even in general education and disciplinary core courses. The cost to create these digitized lectures should be offset by lower faculty costs.
4. High-tech learning materials are appropriate for large classes with relatively stable knowledge content, which includes general education and disciplinary core courses.
5. It is essential to continuously improve these tools because technology changes and innovative thinking provide new insight on how to use technology.
6. To implement high-tech learning materials, university leadership must create a cooperative working relationship with faculty who are responsible for curriculum design. To convince faculty of the university's commitment to these efforts, it is important to reduce administrative costs, provide faculty with more governance responsibility, commit to invest in high-tech learning materials, and consider ways for faculty to benefit from being more productive.

REFERENCES

1. Bellis, M. 2017. Johannes Gutenberg and the printing press. *Inventors.about.com*. http://inventors.about.com/od/gstartinventors/a/Gutenberg.htm (accessed February 12, 2017).
2. Wikipedia. 2017. *Printing Press*. https://en.wikipedia.org/wiki/Printing_press (accessed February 12, 2017).
3. Wikipedia. 2017. *Computer-Aided Design*. https://en.wikipedia.org/wiki/Computer-aided_design (accessed February 12, 2017).
4. Wikipedia. 2017. *Computer-Aided Engineering*. https://en.wikipedia.org/wiki/Computer-aided_engineering (accessed February 12, 2017).
5. Wikipedia. 2017. *Computer-Aided Manufacturing*. https://en.wikipedia.org/wiki/Computer-aided_manufacturing (accessed February 12, 2017).
6. Elliot, D. 2014. Amazing 3D simulation of human heart could change medical care. *CBS News*, May 27. http://www.cbsnews.com/news/amazing-3d-simulation-of-human-heart-could-change-medical-care/ (accessed February 12, 2017).
7. The University of Toledo. 2015. *Interprofessional Immersion Simulation Center*. http://www.utoledo.edu/centers/iisc/ (accessed February 12, 2017).
8. MathWorld. 2017. *Turing Machine*. http://mathworld.wolfram.com/TuringMachine.html (accessed February 15, 2017).

14

Revamping Relationships among High Schools, Community and Technical Colleges, and Universities

It seems obvious to say that the performance of institutions of higher learning depends on the quality and preparation of the students they admit, which depends on the quality of high school graduates. One difficulty in writing this chapter is avoiding the trap of trying to describe and fix problems that exist in primary and secondary schools. When scores for math literacy are examined, the United States is below average; in fact, it is ranked 21st among 34 countries in the Organisation for Economic Co-operation and Development (OECD). Its scores are comparable to Norway, Portugal, Italy, Spain, Sweden, Hungary, and the Slovak Republic, and the United States is significantly behind Estonia, Finland, Poland, Ireland, Slovenia, and the Czech Republic.[1] This is not where the United States should be!

In addition, the high school graduation rate for the U.S.'s biggest urban districts, which serve large numbers of disadvantaged students, is only about 50%. For African American males, the number is even lower.[2] The National Center for Education Statistics reported that U.S. public school teachers and principals claim that a lack of parental involvement and poverty are serious problems. Public school teachers state that student apathy and absenteeism are significant issues as well.[3] Describing these interconnected problems and creating and implementing an effective solution is contentious and complex and would require considerable time to resolve.

To avoid shifting attention from the challenges facing higher education to the root causes of the problems with primary and secondary schools, actions are needed to (1) address curricular overlap among universities, community and technical colleges, and primary and secondary schools, (2) prepare students better for higher education, and (3) create lifelong learning opportunities so adults, even those without a high school diploma, have access to knowledge. These three points are summarized here.

1. *Curriculum overlap:*
   a. Unlike the well-defined, curricula demarcation line between primary and secondary schools, the line between high schools and institutions of higher learning is poorly articulated. As a result, there are gaps and redundancies that make the transition from high school to higher education more difficult and more expensive than it needs to be.
   b. There are also problems when students choose to attend a community and technical college for a year or two to save money and possibly earn the first half of a two-plus-two degree. The courses from the two-year institution are likely to transfer to the university, but they may not count toward graduation, so students lose the financial benefit they are seeking.
2. *Unprepared students:* Applicants are unprepared when they (1) fail to earn their high school diploma, (2) graduate but do not take the right courses, or (3) take the right courses but are given passing grades, even though they did not learn what they should have. When applicants are unprepared, students, parents, other family members, friends, and governments pay the high cost of remedial courses at colleges and universities.
3. *Pathways to lifelong learning:* Government is urging higher education to create pathways for learning that allow high school graduates, including graduates from the vocational track, to pursue undergraduate and graduate degrees. Lifelong learning is essential because (1) the refresh cycle for knowledge is becoming shorter, (2) education is becoming more important for personal and societal success, and (3) 15- to 16-year-old high school students, who feel that a degree in higher education is unnecessary, may change their thinking in a few years.

14.1 CLARIFYING RELATIONSHIPS BETWEEN HIGH SCHOOL AND HIGHER EDUCATION

A high school education provides the foundation for success, including the basic knowledge and skills for a career that provides a living wage and becoming a responsible citizen.[4] High schools offer two tracks:

1. *College preparatory track:* The key subject areas are four years of language arts (reading, writing, and speaking English), four years of mathematics, and at least three years of science. In addition, three to four years of social studies (government, history, and geography), two years of world language, and one year of the arts is recommended.[5]
2. *Vocational track:* This track is more hands-on with less traditional academic content. It typically requires four years of language arts, three years of mathematics, three years of science, and three years of social studies.[6] Upon graduation, this track could lead to apprenticeships in building trades or manufacturing, specialty training schools for good jobs such as dental or veterinary assistants, and two-year technical degrees in fields such as automotive service and childcare.

High school curricula for college preparatory tracks are generally well defined and similar across states, but problems arise because there are big differences among the requirements for university majors. For example, engineering students should take four years of high school math, and many universities would like high school graduates to complete calculus. At the university, engineering students take four semesters of calculus and differential equations. Students, seeking to be physicians, need as much science as possible in high school—five or even six courses are desirable—and calculus is less important. Students studying to be elementary school teachers are well served with thorough coursework in algebra and basic geometry; calculus and extra science courses are not necessary. On the other hand, grammar, reading, writing, and speaking skills are essential for elementary school teachers, but they may be less important, or at least different, for engineers engaged in research and development, who write technical reports, or physicians, who must write precise and accurate medical diagnoses.

There are two more problems. First, high school juniors and seniors in college preparatory tracks are considering universities and selecting majors, but they may have already made decisions that prohibit them from taking the high school courses they need, including calculus as a senior or extra science courses. Second, high school students may have taken courses in calculus, chemistry, or other subjects and received a good grade, but their knowledge is insufficient. Grade inflation at the high school level is a significant problem.[7] These problems are addressed in the following sections.

14.2 ADDRESSING CURRICULUM OVERLAP

It is unclear what determines if a course is a high school or a higher education course because these entities offer many courses with the same or similar titles and contents. For example, high schools teach world history and American history, and so do two- and four-year institutions. Both entities offer English composition. Higher education teaches college algebra, which tends to cover the content of first- and second-year high school algebra. At the same time, many high schools offer calculus, which is generally regarded as a higher education course. Both institutions offer foreign languages, biology, chemistry, and physics, yet there is minimal effort to coordinate curriculum to avoid repetition.

This is further complicated as universities parse the same topic to create specialized courses that are designed for specific audiences. For example, universities may offer: Introduction to Physics (for nonmajors), General Physics (for majors), Technical Physics (noncalculus), and Physics for Science and Engineering Majors (using calculus). These courses cover many of the same topics but with different applications and different mathematical rigor. This can cause problems for students who transfer from majors that require general physics to majors that require physics for science and engineering majors.

14.2.1 Transition from High School to Higher Education

It seems clear that students should not spend time and money in higher education repeating coursework taken in high school. The question is: How do we address this overlap? Institutions and their faculty would argue that high school courses in world history, algebra, economics, and other fields are simply not rigorous enough to meet their standards.

Decades ago, advanced placement (AP) courses were established for high school students to address this concern. These are specially identified classes with limited enrollment for only the best students. Credit for higher education courses could be earned by passing an exam administered by the College Board.[8] This opportunity, which is still available today, has not reached the breadth of courses and numbers of students that it should.

In response, many states have established additional programs for high school students, which allow them to get a jump-start on the pursuit of a two-year or four-year degree. Some examples are as follows:

1. *College tech-prep:* This blends college preparation with technology as students in grades 11 and 12 enroll in high school courses as well as college equivalent courses. Students can get a head start on two-year and four-year degrees as they prepare for jobs in high-demand technical fields.
2. *Early college high schools:* Students enroll in special high schools with curriculum that blends high school and higher education. In grades 9 and 10, they take the usual college preparatory classes, and in the last two years, they take college-level classes, in most cases, without cost.
3. *Postsecondary enrollment options (PSEOs):* High school students take classes at a local two-year college or four-year university usually with no cost. These courses earn credit toward a high school diploma and a two-year or four-year degree. Eligibility can begin in the ninth grade.[9]

Although these options have value, they are incomplete because they are only available to students who meet certain criteria, are in school districts that have these programs, and are close by institutions of higher learning. Even if these programs are available, there is still a need to simplify handoffs between high schools and higher education, so students do not waste time and resources repeating courses. This coordination occurs naturally between primary and secondary education because one entity plans and manages both. States should work with their high schools, public community and technical colleges, and public universities to rationalize and routinize this process. Private universities may find it helpful to participate, or they may face a competitive disadvantage.

This task should become part of the mission for the HEC, which is proposed in Chapter 9. The HEC would coordinate efforts with state agencies that oversee primary, secondary, and higher education. The following principles would guide a process to determine whether high school courses also count for credit at community and technical colleges and universities.

1. *Earn dual credit:* Courses in English, math, science, social studies, foreign language, art, music, and possibly others would be eligible for dual credit.
2. *Content and standards:* To earn higher education credit, content and performance standards in high school courses must meet contents and standards *for community and technical college and university courses.* The HEC would oversee a process to determine the courses that can earn dual credit and create a mechanism for implementation. This reduces the cost and time for high school graduates who are seeking advanced degrees, and it simplifies transfers between community and technical colleges and universities.

As a final piece of advice: when high school students are uncertain about their higher education major, they are best served to take as many rigorous high school courses as possible, especially in language arts, mathematics, and science.

14.2.2 Transferring from Community and Technical Colleges to Universities

High school students and their parents face difficult options: pursue an advanced degree, seek a two-year technical degree, attend a community college to save money and then transfer, take the two-plus-two option, or go directly to a four-year degree. These options are laced with pitfalls because relationships between community and technical colleges and universities are difficult for students and their parents to understand. It can be risky to try to save money by attending a community and technical college with the intent to transfer to a university. Figure 14.1 describes these hurdles.

1. *Transferability:* Will a university accept a course taken at a community and technical college?

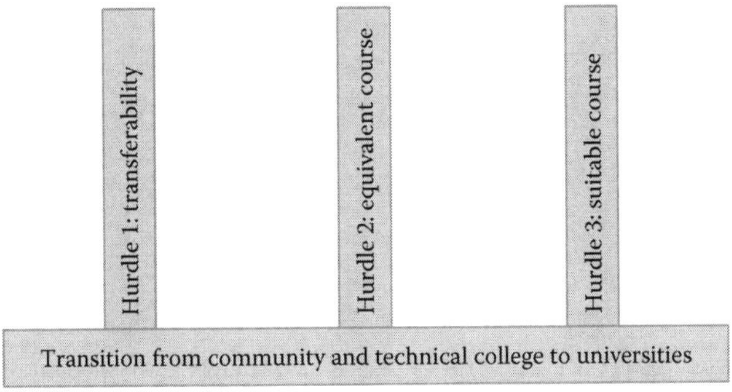

Hurdle 1: transferability

Hurdle 2: equivalent course

Hurdle 3: suitable course

Transition from community and technical college to universities

FIGURE 14.1
Overcoming hurdles: transferring courses from community and technical colleges to universities. Transferability: University will not accept this course, which was taken at a community and technical college. Equivalent course: Course content and rigor are not sufficient, so it cannot be used as part of a degree. Suitable course: Content and rigor may be equivalent to a university course, but the course is not part of the degree.

2. *Equivalent course:* Is the course content and rigor sufficient so it fulfills the requirement of a course that is part of the degree?
3. *Suitable course:* The content and rigor may be equivalent to a university course, but is the course part of the degree?

Community and technical colleges and universities have made efforts to simplify their relationships by creating articulation agreements. These agreements define a pathway that students can follow to eliminate or at least reduce the risk of losing credits when students transfer from community and technical colleges to universities. However, there are fundamental problems with these agreements. They are typically negotiated one at a time, between a community and technical college and a university, and they are specific for each program. Therefore, each university program, such as engineering, business, and education, must negotiate separate articulation agreements with each community and technical college in the state. This takes considerable time and effort, so it is easy to understand why agreements may not exist between all pairs of institutions for all programs, especially in large states with many institutions.

To support the execution of articulation agreements, states typically require public universities to give transfer credit for courses taken at public community and technical colleges, thereby overcoming the first hurdle in Figure 14.1. This ensures acceptance of these courses for university credit. Formulating articulation agreements is further complicated by the fact that there are courses at community and technical colleges and universities such as economics, statistics, and sociology that have the same titles but different content, so they are not equivalent. The second hurdle is shown in Figure 14.1. Different content and performance standards may preclude universities from counting these courses toward graduation for a specific program. This may happen because courses at community and technical colleges have less content and/or lower performance standards than comparable university courses. To eliminate this risk, students and their parents must take actions to ensure that their community and technical college coursework counts toward their four-year degree.

Resolving these problems means unifying content and performance standards for courses taught by both types of institutions, which saves time and money. This begins by standardizing college preparatory classes offered in high school, so high schools, community and technical colleges, and universities could offer the same courses with the same content and performance expectations. Wrestling with this is a task for the HEC. There would be agreement on content, maybe even common learning materials, as well as uniform performance expectations. The coordination of curriculum and rigor would make the transfer between community and technical colleges and university easier, less risky, and less costly.

Once these things are done—so transfer is assured and content and rigor are equivalent—some courses still may not accelerate graduation because a specific major may consider it a prerequisite or may not require the course for graduation. This is the third hurdle in Figure 14.1. For example, completing algebra and trigonometry in high school or at a community and technical college does not count toward an engineering degree because these courses are prerequisites to calculus, which is the entry-level math course for engineers. German courses taken in high school may not count toward a business degree because foreign language may not be a requirement or an elective.

14.3 HIGHER EDUCATION: DROPOUTS AND UNPREPARED STUDENTS

Many students drop out of primary and secondary school and never have the opportunity to pursue degrees in higher education unless they complete their General Educational Development (GED) certification.[10]

In addition, too many high school graduates are unprepared for higher education because they have taken the wrong courses or have taken the right courses but do not have the necessary depth of knowledge. Two-year and four-year institutions have responded by offering remedial courses in mathematics, English, chemistry, and other subjects to fill gaps for high school graduates. Some institutions of higher learning are requiring placement exams to ensure that students have the proper knowledge and skill rather than having them take courses that on paper they are qualified to master but subsequently fail. There are more effective and better ways to cope with these problems.

14.3.1 Supporting Students Who Drop Out

The National Center for Educational Statistics boasted in 2016 that the graduation rate for 2013–2014 "for public high schools rose to an all-time high of 82 percent." This does not include students who dropped out prior to ninth grade, took more than four years to graduate, or earned a GED.[11] Roughly speaking, one in five students who began high school in the Fall of 2010 dropped out.

In a society that promises opportunity and seeks substantial economic growth and prosperity, this performance is not acceptable. Preventing this problem is overwhelmingly complex; there are big differences of opinion on what to do; and the solution is beyond the scope of this book. But it does make sense to discuss alternatives to the GED. There are private educators like Penn Foster High School and James Madison High School that provide adults with opportunities to earn their diploma, but they charge fees for their services.[12,13] There should be public school options for adults learners.

In most states, public schools are mandated to provide free primary and secondary education for students until the age of 20 or 21. A few states end free schooling at 19 years of age, and a few states end at 22.[14] Many states offer virtual high school options for their students, which parents can use to support their efforts at home schooling. States can offer this through "K-12," which provides a framework and access. K-12 online schools do not charge tuition, serve students in kindergarten through 12th grade, use state-certified or licensed teachers, follow state requirements, and lead to a high school diploma.[15]

It seems reasonable to offer this online learning option to adults who are U.S. citizens and permanent residents, have dropped out of school, and are interested in returning to earn a diploma. The infrastructure and relationships exist, so the marginal cost of adding additional students should be modest. Some modification may be needed to accommodate adult learns, but those should be modest as well. Adult learners would gain the same knowledge as if they had completed high school. There would be no extracurricular activities such as sports, band, and choir. It seems positive for society to help adults move from welfare or menial work to jobs with living wages.

14.3.2 Dealing with Unprepared Students

Some high school graduates from the college preparatory track may not take the courses they should. This error can be greatly reduced or eliminated because the college preparatory track provides clear direction about what courses to take, and students' schedules should be monitored by counselors and parents. Students who are missing one or more courses from the college preparatory list would be required to go to the K12-School website,[15] or similar, to complete these courses. This allows students to avoid taking remedial courses at public institutions of higher learning and paying high tuition costs for things they should have learned in high school. To ensure this happens, public community and technical colleges and universities would be prohibited from offering remedial/high school–level courses.

Other students may have taken the right courses but did not learn the subject well enough. This group should be helped by recommendations made earlier to have content and standard for college preparatory courses set so they meets the requirements of higher education. If, in spite of these efforts, some students are deficient, they could also learn the content from the K12-School website,[15] or similar.

14.4 PATHWAYS TO LIFELONG LEARNING

The mantra of education is lifelong learning, which is appropriate. A knowledge-based economy requires continuous learning, and in many jobs, professional development is an integral part of the work. Nurses, psychologists, and many others require continuing education to maintain certification and licensure. Community college degrees can lead to bachelor's degrees and graduate degrees, as well as certificates and training programs that improve knowledge and skills.

Originally, many people thought a two-year technical degree was a terminal degree where students gained specific knowledge about processes and procedures related to hands-on vocations. These people were not expected to shift to fields like management (business), design (engineering), research (science), or government (political science). States are pressing institutions to provide educational opportunities to these very capable technical specialists without asking them to start over and spend four years of full-time study earning a bachelor's degree. However, universities are encountering resistance to counting two-year technical degrees as the first two years of a bachelor's degree.

To provide flexibility for all students as well as to cope with relationship problems between two-year and four-year institutions, many universities have developed individual study programs that allow students to design personalized degrees with unique titles. In many of these programs, students can count up to 60 credit hours from their two-year degree toward an individualized bachelor's degree. For example, someone with an associate degree in computer technology could agree to take additional courses in art and graphics, as well as fill in gaps in the general education requirement, and create an undergraduate degree in computer-based graphic design. A maintenance engineer could add basic business courses and have an undergraduate degree in maintenance management.

The next step is to bring these technical experts into the mainstream by finding degree programs that are familiar to both students and potential employers. The most promising of these paths may be through business because businesses—especially manufacturers, information systems firms, and design companies—often use technology and hire technicians with two-year degrees. By having graduates with a two-year technical degree take the businesses common body of knowledge (business's disciplinary core) and fill in their general education requirements, colleges of business provide a solid undergraduate experience and stay within their accreditation guidelines. With this degree in hand, graduates qualify for admission to a master's in business administration (MBA). Once that is completed, they can opt for a PhD, if they are inclined. There should be other opportunities to develop similar programs in other fields like engineering and science, which have large technical components.

14.5 DRIVING FORCES FOR CHANGE

Government, especially state government, should drive this change because it is the one entity that has direct control over primary and secondary education, public community and technical colleges, and public universities. The first step is to persuade leadership at these institutions, especially the flagship university in the state, that the ideas discussed in this chapter are important and achievable. Unity among state government, boards of trustees, and institutional leaders is essential to set goals and get these entities to work together to design and implement a solution. State agencies, including the HEC, provide leadership and direction for the working group. Students, parents, other family members, and friends are the beneficiaries as completion time and cost for bachelor's degrees decline. These activities may not have a direct impact on private universities, but as public institution find ways to address these problems and lower costs, private universities will be forced to respond.

14.6 IMPACT OF REVAMPING RELATIONSHIPS AMONG HIGH SCHOOLS, COMMUNITY AND TECHNICAL COLLEGES, AND UNIVERSITIES ON HIGHER EDUCATION OUTCOMES

Rationalizing the relationships among these entities is good for students, governments, and potential employers who are the customers of higher education. Lower costs, shorter completion times, lower failure rates, and better quality benefit everyone. The following list examines how this element of the solution impacts the root causes, which are discussed in Chapter 4:

1. *Lack of understanding—Who is the customer? (root cause 1):* Recognizing the problems with these relationships and working on solutions indicates an understanding of the customers' needs and expectations. Students, governments, and potential employers benefit from lower costs and faster completion time.

2. *Eroding standards (root cause 8):* When content and performance standards are set across public high schools, community and technical colleges, and universities, standards are maintained or enhanced and the quality of graduates improves.
3. *Lack of student preparation (root cause 9):* When educational gaps are addressed, students have the knowledge they need, universities no longer require remedial courses, graduation rates should improve, and potential employers should have better employees.

14.7 SUMMARY OF RECOMMENDATIONS

Following is a list of the key recommendations that comprise this element of the solution.

1. When students are preparing for a degree in higher education, they should take as many rigorous high school courses as possible.
2. States should work with high schools, public community and technical colleges, and public universities to create meaningful college preparatory and vocational tracks and to ensure that students get the best education at the lowest cost. This includes the use of the HEC to coordinate course offerings among these entities and eliminate redundancies and gaps.
3. Many states offer virtual high school options to young students. This capability should be extended to adults who dropped out of elementary or high school so they can complete their degree and have the opportunity for a better life, including access to higher education.
4. Universities would be prohibited from offering remedial/high school–level courses. Students who are missing courses would go to their state-supported website to complete them.
5. Students using community and technical colleges to lower the costs of higher education should make sure that their coursework transfers to universities and meets graduation requirements.
6. It is vital to standardize college preparatory classes offered in high school with similar offerings in public two-year colleges and four-year universities so students do not waste time or money.

7. Beyond these courses, community and technical colleges and universities should identify common courses and agree on content and performance standards—even common learning materials. This would simplify transferring to universities and reduce the risk of having courses taken at the community and technical college not counting toward a four-year degree.
8. States should work with universities to create pathways to learning for all students, including graduates from technical programs, so they have ample opportunities for advancement.

REFERENCES

1. National Science Foundation. 2012. *How Do U.S. 15-Year-Olds Compare with Students from Other Countries in Math and Science.* https://www.nsf.gov/nsb/sei/edTool/data/highschool-08.html (accessed February 21, 2017).
2. Guryan, G., and Ludwig, J. 2014. Why half of urban kids drop out. *CNN*, March 12. http://www.cnn.com/2014/03/12/opinion/ludwig-guryan-chicago-education/index.html (accessed July 14, 2016).
3. National Center for Education Statistics. 1993. *What Are the Most Serious Problems in Schools?* https://nces.ed.gov/pubs93/web/93149.asp (accessed February 20, 2017).
4. Taylor, J. 2010. Education: Two-track high-school system a must for education reform. *Psychology Today*, September 12. https://www.psychologytoday.com/blog/the-power-prime/201009/education-two-track-high-school-system-must-education-reform (accessed February 20, 2017).
5. Minnesota Office of Higher Education. 2017. *Recommended High School Classes.* https://www.ohe.state.mn.us/mPg.cfm?pageID=307 (accessed February 21, 2017).
6. Education Commission of the States. 2007. *Standard High School Graduation Requirements (50 States).* http://ecs.force.com/mbdata/mbprofall?Rep=HS01 (accessed February 21, 2017).
7. Huffington Post. 2017. *Grade Inflation.* http://www.huffingtonpost.com/news/grade-inflation/ (accessed February 21, 2017).
8. College Board. 2017. *AP Courses.* https://apstudent.collegeboard.org/apcourse (accessed February 21, 2017).
9. Ohio Department of Education. 2017. *College Prep and Early College Programs for High School Students.* http://education.ohio.gov/Topics/Ohios-Learning-Standards/Career-and-College-Planning/College-Prep-and-Early-College-Programs-for-High-S (accessed February 21, 2017).
10. Wikipedia. 2017. *General Educational Development.* https://en.wikipedia.org/wiki/General_Educational_Development (accessed February 23, 2017).
11. National Center for Education Statistics. 2016. *Public High School Graduate Rates.* http://nces.ed.gov/programs/coe/indicator_coi.asp (accessed August 18, 2016).
12. Penn Foster High School. 2017. *Earn Your On-line High School Diploma.* https://www.pennfoster.edu/ppc/tfa-landings/highschool/index.html?semkey=q486802&cvosrc=ppc.bing.ged&matchtype=e&jadid=155758294&jk=ged&jkid=mc:a8a8ae4cd3fd557e3013fe50919e156b3:i25659936599:te_be&js=3&jsid=35150&jt=1 (accessed February 23, 2017).

13. James Madison High School. 2017. *On-Line High School Diploma*. https://www.jmhs.com/online-high-school-diploma-program/??code=B018&kw=ged&mkwid=rCy7ypCP_dc|pcrid=4582537719|pkw=ged|pmt=be (accessed February 23, 2017).
14. National Center for Education Statistics. 2017. *State Education Reforms*. https://nces.ed.gov/programs/statereform/tab5_1.asp (accessed February 23, 2017).
15. K-12 Schools. 2017. *Tuition-Free On-line and Virtual Public Schools*. http://www.k12.com/k12-schools/free-online-public-schools.html (accessed February 23, 2017).

15

Framing and Implementing a Practical Solution

Chapter 1 begins by describing how institutions of higher learning have evolved and responded to demand from its customers—students, their parents, other family members, and friends who pay the largest portion of the expenses, governments that also pay a significant amount, and employers who hire their graduates. Chapter 1 provides an understanding of higher education, including insights about the differences between higher education and other organizations that offer goods and services. It also described a key turning point as institutions of higher learning began unprecedented growth after World War II, which lasted for decades. During this time, institutions strove to meet growing demand by building new facilities, hiring more administrators and faculty, and developing new programs with little attention to accelerating costs and other concerns.

The method used to investigate the pending crisis begins by describing the underlying problems, which are discussed in Chapters 2 and 3. These problems have a set of root causes, which are explained in Chapter 4, and the root causes can be addressed by implementing the elements of the solution, which are discussed in Chapter 5. This process is illustrated by the backward arrows in Figure 15.1. The solution must be comprehensive and integrated because of the magnitude and complexity of the problems. This is evident by examining the relationships among and within the (1) elements of the solution, (2) root causes, and (3) underlying problems.

1. *Relationships among the three factors:* As indicated in Figure 15.1, Table 5.1 in Chapter 5 provides an overview of the relationships

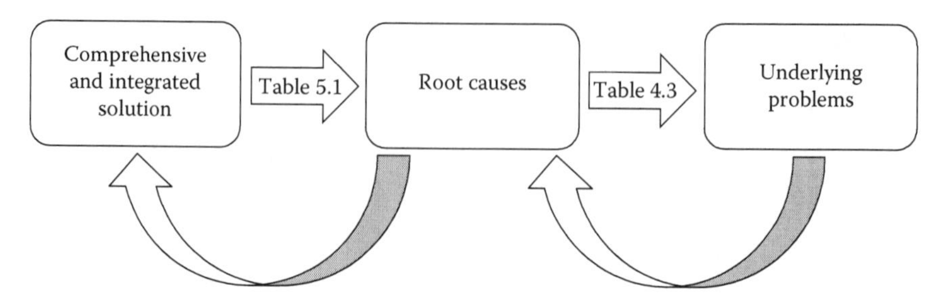

FIGURE 15.1
Relationships among the comprehensive and integrated solution, root causes, and underlying problems.

between the elements of the solution and the root causes, and Table 4.3 offers an overview of the relationships between root causes and underlying problems. Both sets of relationships are dense, so the relationships are many. Table 5.1 also shows that each element of the solution affects more than one root cause, and each root cause is affected by multiple elements of the solution. Similarly, Table 4.3 shows complex relationships between root causes and underlying problems.

2. *Relationships within the three factors:* These relationships are also important and abundant, and they are illustrated by the following examples. Within the elements of the solution, if universities desire to have student-centered learning, they are more likely to redesign curriculum and pedagogy. Within the root causes, if universities do not fully understand who their customers are, their performance standards are more likely to erode. Within the underlying problems, if tuition continues to increase, student access becomes more difficult.

The solution is comprehensive because the problems and root causes are many and complex. The solution is integrated because there are no one-to-one relationships among the problems, root causes, and the elements of the solution, so the solution should be implemented in total rather than piecemeal. To facilitate implementation, the following sections provide insights about the relationship between the elements of the solution and the underlying problems.

15.1 SUMMARY OF THE UNDERLYING PROBLEMS

The discussion begins by reviewing the six interconnected pieces of the underlying problems. These are discussed in Chapters 2 and 3 and are summarized here.

1. *High cost:* Costs for tuition, fees, and textbooks and other learning materials have increased much faster than the rate of inflation. Tuition and fees at public, four-year universities, after *adjusting for inflation*, increased substantially from a baseline of 100 in 1985–1986 to 322 in 2015–2016.[1] Thus, $1 spent on tuition and fees in 1985–1986 would cost $3.22 in 2015–2016, after *adjusting for inflation*.[1] More recent data (2003–2013) show that the rate of increase is unabated as tuition jumped 79.5% during this period, nearly doubling the rate of increase in medical care at 43.1% and growing three times faster than (CPI) at 26.7%. During the same time period, textbook costs have risen by 79.4%, almost matching the increase in tuition.[2] These values are shown in Figure 15.2.

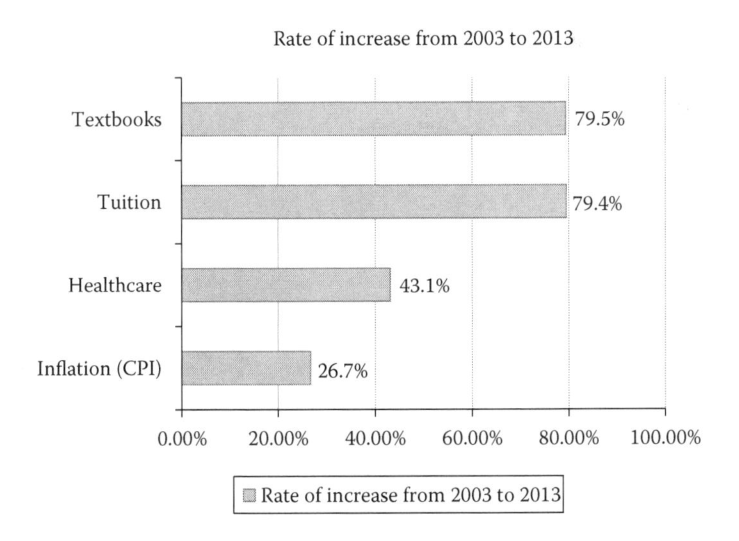

FIGURE 15.2
Comparing rate of inflation in higher education, healthcare, and the Consumer Price Index (CPI) from 2003 to 2013. (From Kurtzleben, D., *Charts: Just How Fast Has College Tuition Grown? US News World Report*, October 23, 2013. http://www.usnews.com/news/articles/2013/10/23/charts-just-how-fast-has-college-tuition-grown)

2. *Quality concerns:* Universities in the United States are performing well, but other countries are closing the gap. The Universitas 21 study, which is the only international ranking of university systems as opposed to individual institutions, has the U.S. system first overall, but it is a different story when the rankings are adjusted for the stage of economic development. When this is done, the U.S. system ranks 16th behind Serbia, China, Finland, and India, among others.[3]
3. *Limited access:* Data indicate that in the 1980s, financial constraints did not determine who attends universities, but today family income and parental wealth do matter.[4] About 78% of high school graduates from high-income families enroll in college and 53% graduate, but the numbers for middle-income families are only 64% and 25%, respectively. Many low- and some middle-income families routinely eliminate a university education as an option because of high costs.[5] See Figure 15.3. On top of financial constraints, many students are simply not prepared or worse yet drop out of primary or secondary schools. The average graduation rate for urban high schools is only about 50%, and it is lower for African American males.[6]

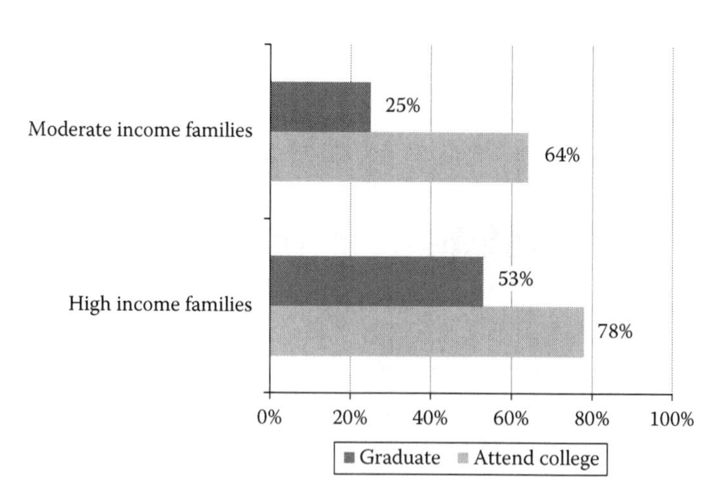

FIGURE 15.3
Percent of high school graduates from moderate- and high-income families attending and graduating from college. (From Middle Class Task Force: The Vice President of the United States. *White House Task Force on Middle Class Families STAFF REPORT: Barriers to Higher Education*, 2010. https://www.whitehouse.gov/assets/documents/MCTF_staff_report_barriers_to_college_FINAL.pdf)

4. *Low graduation rates:* For all four-year institutions, only 39.4% of students complete a bachelor's degree in four years. Public universities are at 33.5%, and private, not-for-profit universities are at 52.8%. The graduation rate at private, for-profit universities is very low at 22.5%.[7] See Figure 15.4.
5. *Long completion time:* When the six-year graduation rate is examined, it increases significantly to 59.4% for all four-year institutions, meaning about one-third of graduates take five or six years to earn a degree. The breakdown by university types are 57.7% for public, 65.3% for private, not-for-profit, and 31.9% for private, for-profit universities.[7] Thus, private, for-profit universities fall short of graduating one-third of its students in six years. See Figure 15.4.
6. *Poor job placements:* In some fields, especially technical fields requiring math and science, there are shortages of qualified applicants, and companies seeking employees often hire international workers to fill the gaps. But in other fields, there can be a shortage of jobs and low wages, making it difficult for students to repay their loans.[8] The Bureau of Labor Statistics reports that about five million university graduates hold jobs that require less than a high school degree.[9]

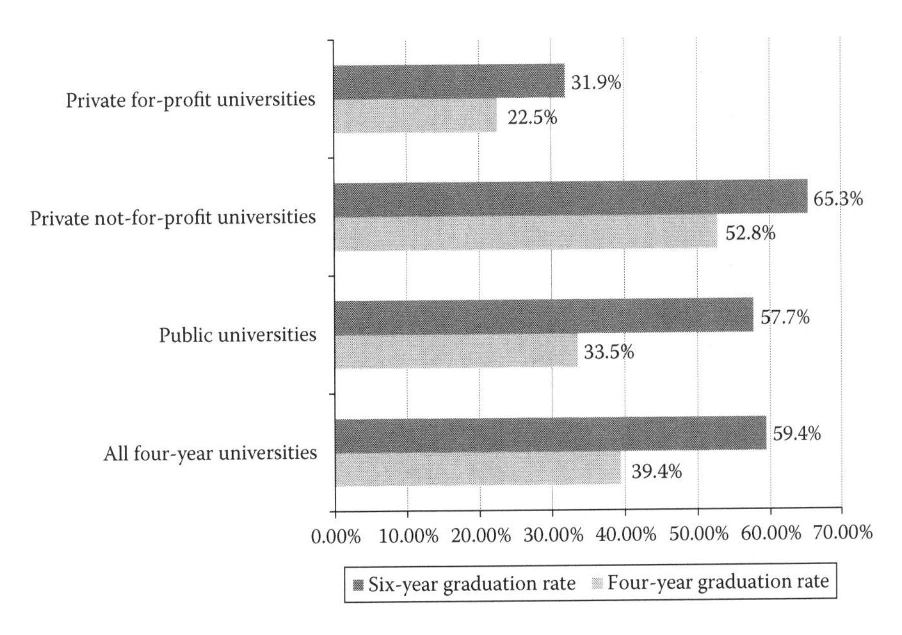

FIGURE 15.4
Four- and six-year graduation rates by university type. (From National Center for Education Statistics, *Graduation Rates*, 2015. https://nces.ed.gov/fastfacts/display.asp?id=40)

15.2 OVERVIEW OF THE COMPREHENSIVE AND INTEGRATED SOLUTION

These problems are systemic, and they directly and negatively impact the mission of institutions. Elements of the solution, which are described in detail in Chapters 6 through 14, focus on customers, curriculum, and resources. As Figure 15.5 illustrates, needs of the trifurcated customer determine curriculum content, standards, and pedagogy, which, in turn, determine what resources to acquire and how to use them. Each element in the solution has a set of recommendations, which is summarized at the end of each chapter, compiled in Appendix A, and organized by underlying problem in Appendix B.

To get the attention of institutions of higher learning, customers must take an active role. It is essential for students, parent, other family members, and friends to change their attitude and treat colleges and universities like they would any other producer of goods or services. They must consider cost, seek the best deal, and press institutions to improve effectiveness and efficiency. They should develop a long-term plan for spending on higher education; pursue ways to improve earnings; save more money; hunt for scholarships; and work toward a goal of graduating debt-free.

Universities must become student centered, which means treating students with respect and working with them to develop a detailed plan of study, so they graduate in four years. But it also means demanding the highest level of performance from students, limiting investment in facilities to keep costs low, not requiring students to live in campus dormitories even as first-year students, and making student activity fees optional.

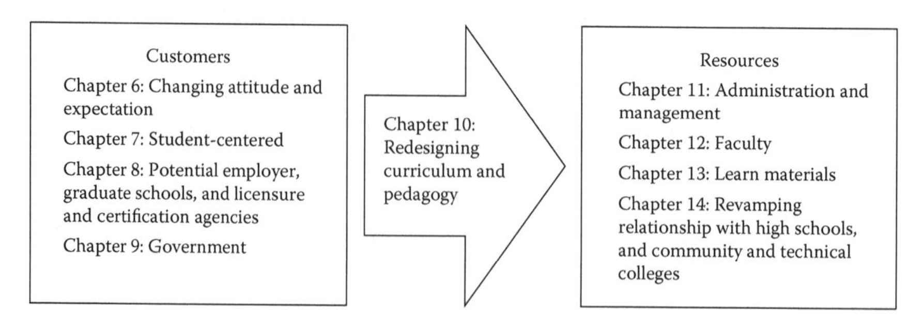

FIGURE 15.5
Customer needs determine curriculum and pedagogy that drive resource acquisition and allocation.

It also means changing the process for and the use of student evaluations of teaching, so instructional faculty feel less pressure from students to reduce content and lower learning standards. Tenured and professional faculty would become responsible for setting course content, preparing tests, and determining grades.

Governments have roles as customer and overseer. State and local governments fund public higher education and have important legislative power over them, and federal government provides significant funding for students to attend public and private universities and can use its power to control behavior. Governments can reexamine how they allocate funds and use future funding as incentives for making improvements. Potential employers, graduate schools, and licensure and certification agencies, and not students, should have the role of defining curriculum content and setting performance standards.

As shown in Figure 15.5, the pivotal issue that connects customers to resources is curriculum and pedagogy. Content and standards are set by tenured and professional faculty, working closely with potential employers and others. Curriculum must be redesigned, so full-time students can graduate with a bachelor's degree in four years, so no student faces closed classes because course offerings are limited, and all students have a professional development course to prepare them for finding a job. Designing pedagogy is developing multiple teaching methods that meet the learning needs of individual students, and creating online courses and programs that are rigorous, secure, and well-staffed.

Universities must acquire and use their resources to achieve the most benefit for their trifurcated customer. Growth in the number of and compensation for administration has been a primary driver of costs in higher education. Actions are necessary to reverse this trend, including administrative budget declines that take place over several years. In addition, faculty must be willing to rethink their roles and responsibilities in ways that use their skills most effectively and enable improvements in productivity. Technology must be brought to the classroom in various forms, especially in the form of high-tech reading materials and high-tech videos that enhance student learning and lower costs. Finally, the relationships among high schools, community and technical colleges, and universities must improve, eliminating curriculum overlap and filling gaps. Too much time and money are wasted because the transition among these parts of the educational system is fraught with errors and inefficiencies.

15.3 IMPLEMENTATION

The first step in successfully resolving any problem is recognizing and admitting that a problem exists. When a system or organization is in crisis mode, like General Motors (GM) as it faced bankruptcy and dissolution, it is easy to get the attention of leadership because closing the business and selling assets to pay creditors is disastrous for the organization and the reputation of its leaders. They are willing to do almost anything to avoid these outcomes. Outsiders who followed GM understood that its problems began more than 40 years ago, becoming more apparent as GM came closer to bankruptcy. Like a stationary object on a railroad track with its back turned to an oncoming, high-speed freight train, GM's leadership was caught off guard even as the train came closer and closer. By the time top management heard the train, it was too late. Universities are facing such a crisis. It is not important to speculate how many years it might be before the crash, but it will come.

An indication of the problems is the success of private, for-profit universities at grabbing market share. These institutions had about 11% of the full-time and 12% of the part-time students enrolled in undergraduate programs in 2009,[10] which indicates dissatisfaction with the traditional product. For-profit institutions have attracted students seeking less expensive, online universities, and they tend to price their offerings well. Their tuition is much less than private, not-for-profit universities but more than public universities. Their students want online convenience and do not have to pay room and board to live on campus, so the pricing is well suited to "nontraditional" students. These institutions would present an even bigger threat if their graduation rates and completion times, which are currently very poor,[7] improve. Even if for-profit universities are unable to make these adjustments, other competitors will take advantage of the problems facing traditional universities and find ways to offer high-quality programs at lower cost. Even if these competitors do not emerge, traditional universities will face increasing pressure as larger and larger segments of the U.S. population cannot afford advanced degrees. Like GM executives, leaders of higher education either do not understand or choose to ignore the long-term implications of these problems. The question is: How do we get their attention?

Substantial effort is required to implement a comprehensive and integrated solution in a large market with many competitors. This is further complicated by the fact that there are fundamental problems with cost, quality, access, graduation rate, completion time, and job placement, which are essential attributes of higher education. For public institutions, this requires bold actions from their customers: (1) government; (2) students, parents, other family members, and friends; and (3) employer, graduate schools, and agencies that offer licensure and certification.

15.3.1 Role of Government

Unless boards of trustees and public university leaders recognize that substantial changes are needed, the implementation rests with state government. States provides significant and direct subsidies to public, two-year community and technical colleges and public four-year universities, which accounts for more than 70% of the enrollment in higher education (see Table 1.2 in Chapter 1),[10] so state governments have considerable influence. Subsidies from local government are small and are directed at relatively few institutions. Federal support is portable and associated with students, who may use it at different institutions. Certainly, the federal government can prohibit funding this or that university and can have a role, but state governments have direct legislative authority over public institutions.

The process begins with state governors meeting as a group to discuss the underlying problems with higher education and making commitments to address them. This step is necessary because it shows unity and the importance of these problems, which are essential to convince institutions that dramatic changes are inevitable, even if the changes are somewhat different among states. Each state would form a HEC or other such-named entity that would coordinate actions within the state and keep open communications with other states. Governors and legislatures would formulate charges for the HECs, which would work closely with institutions of higher learning to set goals for substantial cost reduction and improvements in quality, access, graduation rates, completion time, and job placements. Within a state, these may be different for different universities depending on their mission. For example, research universities may have higher expectations for graduation rates and job placements than open enrollment universities in the same state.

Each public institution would prepare a five-year improvement plan to meet these initial goals. The planning process would roll forward, maintaining its five-year horizon and adjusting its goals to seek even greater improvements. University leadership must engage tenured and professional faculty in these efforts to gain their buy-in and implement changes to curriculum design and instructional delivery. University leadership must show that it is committed to change by making significant cuts in administration, especially to top managers and their direct reports, because administration has grown much faster than tenured faculty positions and enrollment.[2]

If these efforts are successful, market forces should compel private university, both not-for-profit and for-profit, to respond with similar programs. Success would cause administrators to think differently about their expectations, practices, and outcomes. Only well-endowed, private, not-for-profit universities would be insulated from these changes, at least as long as wealthy parents are willing to pay substantially more to educate their children. Smaller, less well-funded, private, not-for-profit universities would be forced to change, consolidate, or close. Private, for-profit universities are having serious problems with graduation rates and completion time. They must improve or face backlashes from the federal government as it denies funding and from applicants who choose not to enroll.

15.3.2 Role of Students, Parents, Other Family Members, and Friends

When state subsidy is excluded, this group pays about 48% of the cost of higher education, making it the largest payer. This does not include loans taken and repaid by student and parents, which represent another 11% and 6%, respectively.[11] To the extent this group pays state and federal taxes, they pay a portion of those subsidies as well. This group must play a prominent role in driving change in two ways.

First, as citizens and taxpayers, they have a right as well as a responsibility to demand that state government take action to address the problems with higher education through their letters, phone calls, votes, and other methods of communication. Governors and members of the state legislature need their support to push back against the institutions and their "well-heeled" alumni who can pressure politicians on behalf of colleges and universities. Second, as customers, this group can contact university presidents and boards of trustees to let them know their concerns about cost, completion time, and other factors that impact higher education. In addition, they can choose educational options that offer the best value. Creating statewide parent groups that can act as a voice directed toward state government on issues related to higher education gives this group a unified and strong message.

15.3.3 Role of Employers, Graduate Schools, and Agencies Offering Licensure and Certification

The third group of customers does not make direct payments for services to institutions of higher learning, but they do have an important stake in the process because they depend on the output of colleges and universities. Employers can have input to both institutions and governments. Employers should interact with programs, colleges, and institutional leadership, including the board of trustees, to make sure that programs educate high-quality graduates while keeping costs low and improving access. As economic development engines that need top-quality employees and that pay local, state, and federal taxes, these organizations can offer important insights on why change must take place. Graduate schools and agencies that offer licensure and certification also depend on the quality of graduates. Even though these entities may be unlikely to contact politicians or institutions of higher learning directly, they can issue reports and provide information on the qualifications of graduate school applicants and how graduates are performing on licensure exams.

15.4 FINAL WORD

For years, higher education has been a competitive advantage for the United States that enabled it to achieve a standard of living and an environment for business success that attracts millions of immigrants each year. Given that manual labor is being reduced by robotics, automation, and computer-based decision support systems, it is vital for the United States to have the best educated workforce in the world. This is more than having a handful of universities that lead the world in research; it means having the best education system from kindergarten through postdoctorate learning. This is not achieved by opening the checkbook and spending whatever it takes to fund higher education. Experience indicates that adding on subsidies increases complacency, ensures the status quo, and takes performance improvements off the table. As shown in Figure 5.1 in Chapter 5 as well as Figure 15.1, improving higher education requires understanding customers' needs and expectations, designing curriculum and pedagogy to meet those needs, and acquiring and managing resources to reach those outcomes. This task faces the United States, and its future depends on how well it is accomplished.

REFERENCES

1. College Board. 2015. *Published Tuition and Fees Relative to 1985–86, by Sector.* https://trends.collegeboard.org/college-pricing/figures-tables/published-tuition-and-fees-relative-1985-86-sector (accessed July 8, 2016).
2. Kurtzleben, D. 2013. *Charts: Just How Fast has College Tuition Grown?* US News World Report, October 23. http://www.usnews.com/news/articles/2013/10/23/charts-just-how-fast-has-college-tuition-grown (accessed July 5, 2016).
3. Universitas21. 2016. *U21 Ranking of National Higher Education Systems.* http://www.universitas21.com/news/details/220/u21-ranking-of-national-higher-education-systems-2016 (accessed July 14, 2016).
4. Science Daily. 2011. *Limited Access to Higher Education May Harm Society,* December 15. https://www.sciencedaily.com/releases/2011/12/111214102926.htm (accessed July 14, 2016).
5. Middle Class Task Force: The Vice President of the United States. 2010. *White House Task Force on Middle Class Families STAFF REPORT: Barriers to Higher Education.* https://www.whitehouse.gov/assets/documents/MCTF_staff_report_barriers_to_college_FINAL.pdf (accessed July 14, 2016).
6. Guryan, G., and Ludwig, J. 2014. Why half of urban kids drop out. *CNN,* March12. http://www.cnn.com/2014/03/12/opinion/ludwig-guryan-chicago-education/index.html (accessed July 14, 2016).
7. National Center for Education Statistics. 2015. *Graduation Rates.* https://nces.ed.gov/fastfacts/display.asp?id=40 (accessed July 5, 2016).
8. Goodman, L. M. 2015. Millennial college graduates: Young, educated, jobless. *New York Times,* May 5. http://www.newsweek.com/2015/06/05/millennial-college-graduates-young-educated-jobless-335821.html (accessed July 5, 2016).
9. The Center for College Affordability and Productivity. 2013. *Underemployment of College Graduates.* http://centerforcollegeaffordability.org/research/studies/underemployment-of-college-graduates/ (accessed July 5, 2016).
10. United States Department of the Treasury and Department of Education. 2012. *The Economics of Higher Education,* December. https://www.treasury.gov/connect/blog/Documents/20121212_Economics%20of%20Higher%20Ed_vFINAL.pdf (accessed June 23, 2016).
11. SallieMae 2015. *How America Pays for College 2015.* http://news.salliemae.com/files/doc_library/file/HowAmericaPaysforCollege2015FNL.pdf (accessed June 16, 2016).

Appendix A: Compilation of the Recommendations

The nine elements of the solution are discussed in Chapters 6 through 14, and the specific recommendations, which are summaries at the end of each chapter, are compiled here for the convenience of the reader. This allows a quick review of the ideas that comprise the solution. Because the solution is comprehensive and integrated, some recommendations are discussed in more than one chapter, so they may appear in the list more than once.

A.1 CHAPTER 6: CHANGING ATTITUDES AND EXPECTATIONS OF STUDENTS, PARENTS, FAMILY MEMBERS, AND FRIENDS

1. Students, parents, other family members, and friends should change their attitude toward universities from benevolent dispensers of knowledge to providers of a key service. They must:
   a. Press universities for improvements in effectiveness and efficiency.
   b. Hold universities accountable for high costs, limited access, and the other problems facing higher education. This is relevant for sports programs, which can consume tuition dollars.
   c. Universities should not participate in outreach and engagement using tuition dollars. Government or other sources must provide special funding if universities are to participate.
   d. Make their feelings known to government and other oversight groups, so additional pressure is brought to bear.
   e. Shop around, pursue discounts, and pick their university base on finding the best value.
   f. Consider and evaluate ways to earn and save more money as well as keep educational costs low, so borrowing is greatly reduced or eliminated.

2. Government should create a database of Higher Education Pricing and Outcomes (HEPO) that offers information about costs, graduation rates, completion time, passing rates for licensure and certification exams, and job placement. This should help applicants make informed choices.
3. Universities should be responsible to pay for textbooks and learning materials as part of the tuition payment. Universities have more leverage with companies who provide this material and can negotiate better prices.
4. Students and their supporters should change their expectation so they graduate debt-free. Long-term financial planning is a vehicle to identify appropriate levels of earning and saving as well as spending funds wisely and making good investments.
   a. Prepare and follow a budget for a university education so spending is targeted on essential items. Those who did spent 40% less.
   b. Students and their support group can earn more, save more, and borrow less. The key is to start early.
5. Students should demand a rigorous curriculum so they have a more valuable education.
6. Students should pick their major bases on both interest in the work and the opportunity to secure a job that pays well. Too often students pick majors with limited job opportunities.

A.2 CHAPTER 7: BECOMING STUDENT CENTERED: THE RIGHT WAY

1. Being student centered means that students get more respect, better treatment, and services that are courteous, responsive, effective, and efficient.
2. Building new dormitories must be carefully examined given the trend toward distance learning, and outsourcing the ownership, construction, and operation of dormitories must be considered.
3. Universities that make students a priority should not require them to live on campus.
4. Universities must examine future trends in higher education to determine how changes in the pedagogy, size of administration, and other factors impact the need to build new facilities.

5. After this careful examination, if universities need more buildings, they must find ways to design and build them to be functional, attractive, and cost less.
6. Student fees must be spent for nonacademic purposes and paying fees is at the option of the students. Funds for academic purposes and nonacademic purposes must not be comingled.
7. Students deserve fast and easy access to services. It is important to use technology, lean thinking, and value stream mapping to design and implement new and innovative processes.
8. Every student must have a plan of study that identifies which courses to take and when they should take them to graduate in the shortest possible time.
9. Universities must diversify their pedagogy to cope with the various learning styles of students. Efforts to do so should enhance learning, reduce costs, and change the roles and responsibilities of faculty. Universities must investment in the upfront cost to create this new pedagogy.
10. The process for students to evaluate faculty must change so instructional faculty are under less pressure to reduce course content and lower learning standards.
    a. Take instructional faculty out of the line of fire by making tenured and professional faculty responsible for course content, test creation, and grading.
    b. Assess teaching effectiveness of contractual faculty and tenured faculty by evaluating them based on what students learned in their courses, using pretesting and posttesting.
    c. Student evaluations assess the (1) availability and use of learning tools to help students learn faster and easier and (2) performance of faculty, which emphasize how students were treated.

A.3 CHAPTER 8: BUILDING BRIDGES TO POTENTIAL EMPLOYERS

1. Universities should create program advisory boards (PABs) for each area of study by reaching out to potential employers, graduate schools, and certification and licensure agencies. PABs are vehicles that tenured and professional faculty can use to determine

curricula and set performance standards so graduates are well prepared. PABs also provide a point of contact between students and employers.

2. Universities should provide placement and job data for applicants to evaluate. Universities currently invest considerable effort and large amounts of money to track alumni for the purpose of fundraising. This mechanism can be used to collect placement and job data.
3. Universities should provide students with easy access to the *Occupational Outlook Handbook* prepared by the U.S. Bureau of Labor Statistics, which provides employment information about hundreds of jobs.
4. Universities help to build strong relationships between students and employers.
   a. Cooperative education and internship programs are ways for students to achieve appropriate professional behaviors, learn how to apply theory and techniques to real problems, and become more interested and motivated to learn. In return, employers can evaluate the talents of students.
   b. Potential employers can work directly with students as mentors or in small groups to offer advice and counsel about various aspects of professional life.
5. As students move toward graduation, programs and colleges within the university must provide better mechanisms for placing students in good jobs. In addition to traditional placement services, programs and colleges should be proactive in finding potential employers and bringing them to campus for job fairs and other interactions with students, including job interviews.

A.4 CHAPTER 9: GOVERNMENT'S ROLE IN HIGHER EDUCATION

1. Governments' role in higher education should be somewhere in the middle between the extreme positions of making higher education tuition-free and eliminating or dramatically reducing government support. The status quo is an appropriate place to begin.

2. State and local governments should use their funding as a mechanism to pressure public colleges and universities to lower costs and improve outcomes. Public colleges and universities would be required to:
   a. Prepare a five-year rolling plan to reduce administrative expenses.
   b. Use fees for nonacademic expenses, make fees payable at the students' option, and require learning-related activities to be paid by tuition dollars.
   c. Take financial responsibility for providing books and other learning materials.
3. State and local governments can condition their funding for higher education on meeting mission-appropriate goals for graduation rates, time to completion, and job placements.
4. States have a hodgepodge of financial aid grants that seem to be politically motivated. Unless there are compelling reasons, state funds that support these grants should become part of the state's general appropriation.
5. States also make appropriations for research as well as agriculture and medical education. These appropriations must have careful oversight with specific outcomes identified.
6. Universities should disengage from outreach and engagement until and unless there is a specific funding source to support it. States provide no funding. Funds for tuition, fees, research, room, and board are intended for these activities and not for outreach and engagement.
7. Federal Pell Grants and other grants should be maintained, but hopefully demand for them declines as the economy improves, saving for education increases, and universities find ways to reduce costs.
8. Student loans must be reduced substantially by reining in demand so students would want and need to borrow less. Students need to understand their repayment obligation, so they must prepare a student borrowing and repayment plan (SBRP) that specifies how much they will borrow, the use of these funds, and what they are willing to forego to make payments.
9. Work-study jobs often do little more than put money in students' pockets. Universities must provide evidence that students are learning something and/or doing work that has value or close the program and roll the funds into the Pell Grant program.

10. Federal funds are used to support private, for-profit universities that have very poor performance outcomes. The poor performers must be disqualified from receiving federal aid.
11. Higher Education Committee (HEC) should be established to examine the cost and benefits of government regulations and eliminate regulations that have gone too far.
12. Government regulations and actions by accreditation agencies should focus on outputs to reduce the amount of regulation and make it easier to spot and resolve problems.
13. When performance is below expectations, governments, accreditation agencies, and employers that hire graduates have the power to cut funding, deny accreditation, and not hire graduates, respectively.

A.5 CHAPTER 10: REDESIGNING CURRICULUM AND PEDAGOGY

1. Bachelor's degrees should be limited to 120 credit hours to lower tuition costs and enable students to graduate in four years.
2. Universities should engage in effective long-term and short-term planning to ensure that students do not face closed classes that prohibit them from graduating in four years.
3. Potential employers work with tenured and professional faculty to set curriculum content and performance standards so graduates learn more and are prepared for the job market.
4. Students should have short courses in professional development to prepare for their job search.
5. Student-centered learning, which is customized to meet individual learning needs, should make it easier and faster to learn. This may be more challenging in general education courses, but it can be accomplished using technology.
6. Online programs and courses can become a low-cost way to deliver a quality education and make it more accessible. Universities should do the following:
   a. Make the upfront investments to develop high-quality programs and courses.
   b. Invest in technology to deliver program content effectively.

   c. Start with high-enrollment courses, where it is possible to enjoy economies of scale.
   d. Offer complete programs so that online students can graduate without setting foot on campus.
   e. Create educational programs that are secure so the person who received the grade is the person actually doing the work.
   f. Share online offerings with other universities to spread the fixed costs of course development.
   g. Have no activity fees for students enrolling in online learning.

A.6 CHAPTER 11: REFORMING ADMINISTRATION AND MANAGEMENT

1. Universities must reconfigure the strategic plan and the strategic planning process. This means:
   a. Recognizing there are multiple customers and goals—students want good jobs and less debt; governments and potential employers want lower costs and better quality graduates.
   b. Increasing faculty involvement in managing universities and the strategic planning process.
2. Universities should change their culture in regard to customers, books and learning materials, organizational structure, relationships between administration and faculty, and state funding.
3. To make change, students, parents, other family members, and friends must support state government as it convinces boards and presidents, who must, in turn influence top and middle management at universities.
4. As culture changes, management practices must change.
   a. Decentralize decision making, so colleges have more freedom to pursue innovative and entrepreneurial activities.
   b. Hire more faculty members for administrative posts and create a faculty resource committee (FRC) to participate in strategic planning and university-level budgeting.
5. Executive leadership must achieve higher productivity by identifying work that is unnecessary, setting targets for reducing administration that can be met over several years, and providing management tools and training as well as information technology that improves productivity.

6. Professional managers and specialists must increase productivity by focusing on systems thinking and process improvements. This involves lean thinking, quality improvement efforts, value stream mapping, seeking process redesign, and implementing continuous improvement efforts.
7. The productivity of nonexempt support staff should improve as processes are redesigned and specific IT projects are implemented.
8. Increases in administrative salaries can be moderated by eliminating benchmarking in salary determination and creating more competition for high-level administrative jobs.
9. Change organizational structure, lower costs, and enhance quality through mergers, closing branch campuses, and most importantly by outsourcing activities.

A.7 CHAPTER 12: RESHAPING FACULTY'S ROLE

1. To have better, faster, and more efficient education, it is essential to prepare faculty so they are knowledgeable in content, pedagogy, and assessment of learning.
    a. All types of faculty should be subject to evaluation by students as described in Chapter 7, be supported by centers for teaching, participate in teaching seminars as part of their work requirements, and have access to teaching improvement funds.
    b. Full-time, tenured faculty must have the education and skills to teach effectively and this begins in the PhD program. In addition, the teaching performance of all faculty candidates is assessed during the hiring process, and newly hired faculty members are assigned to master teachers and together they create a continuous improvement plan.
    c. Full-time, contractual faculty would follow a similar process, but adjustments would be made for faculty who have not earned a PhD and have little if any teaching experience.
    d. Part-time contractual faculty, especially those with limited teaching experience and a full-time job that takes priority, may be reluctant to participate in teaching improvement efforts. There are two options, stop hiring part-time faculty with limited

teaching experience or pay them more for the first two or three times they teach to cover start-up costs.

   e. Graduate teaching assistants would participate in an assessment of their communication skills including language, have regular teaching evaluations, and work with mentors. They would be carefully supervised as they teach.

2. It is important to identify the capabilities of different faculty types, know the instructional needs for courses, and match these to get the best outcomes, meaning both high quality and low cost. This is summarized in Table 12.1.
3. General education and interdisciplinary core courses tend to generate substantial surpluses, which are used to subsidize other undergraduate courses as well as courses in master's and PhD programs. State governments should create a HEC to examine these issues.
4. It is vital to improve faculty productivity by investing in sophisticated, top-quality methods for communicating knowledge and supporting faculty so they create innovative and efficient ways to disseminate knowledge to students. Universities and faculty must move away from the notion that a three-credit-hour course requires three hours of face time.
5. Faculty unions have not caused the problems that universities face, but they are the result of poor relationships between university leaders and tenured and professional faculty. State government, boards of trustees, and top management must mend these relationships.

A.8 CHAPTER 13: CREATING HIGH-TECHNOLOGY LEARNING MATERIALS

1. Universities become responsible for paying for all learning materials.
2. Universities must create high-tech reading materials that are interactive and help students identify and address knowledge gaps. These should have lower cost, better content coverage, enhanced learning for students, and better outcomes for publishers.
   a. Interactive questions, answers, and referrals to the correct information make these superior learning tools.
   b. Computer-generated problems allows student to learn better by generating an unlimited number of attempts at the same problem with feedback about error.

   c. Sample tests allow students to gauge their ability and provide insight on how to improve.
   d. PowerPoint slide decks are annotated and electronically connected to the e-book.
   e. Mechanisms for reading e-books to students over different devices are available.
3. Universities must create high-tech, digitized lectures and video vignettes that allow students to have access to tenured and professional faculty even in general education and disciplinary core courses. The cost to create these digitized lectures should be offset by lower faculty costs.
4. High-tech learning materials are appropriate for large classes with relatively stable knowledge content, which includes general education and disciplinary core courses.
5. It is essential to continuously improve these tools because technology changes and innovative thinking provide new insight on how to use technology.
6. To implement high-tech learning materials, university leadership must create a cooperative working relationship with faculty who are responsible for curriculum design. To convince faculty of the university's commitment to these efforts, it is important to reduce administrative costs, provide faculty with more governance responsibility, commit to invest in high-tech learning materials, and consider ways for faculty to benefit from being more productive.

A.9 CHAPTER 14: REVAMPING RELATIONSHIPS AMONG HIGH SCHOOLS, COMMUNITY AND TECHNICAL COLLEGES, AND UNIVERSITIES

1. When students are preparing for a degree in higher education, they should take as many rigorous high school courses as possible.
2. States should work with high schools, public community and technical colleges, and public universities to create meaningful college preparatory and vocational tracks and to ensure that students get the best education at the lowest cost. This includes the use of the HEC to coordinate course offerings among these entities and eliminate redundancies and gaps.

3. Many states offer virtual high school options to young students. This capability should be extended to adults who dropped out of elementary or high school so they can complete their degree and have the opportunity for a better life, including access to higher education.
4. Universities would be prohibited from offering remedial/high school–level courses. Students who are missing courses would go to their state-supported website to complete them.
5. Students using community and technical colleges to lower the costs of higher education should make sure that their coursework transfers to universities and meets graduation requirements.
6. It is vital to standardize college preparatory classes offered in high school with similar offerings in public two-year colleges and four-year universities so students do not waste time or money.
7. Beyond these courses, community and technical colleges and universities should identify common courses and agree on content and performance standards—even common learning materials. This would simplify transferring to universities and reduce the risk of having courses taken at the community and technical college not counting toward a four-year degree.
8. States should work with universities to create pathways to learning for all students including graduates from technical programs, so they have ample opportunities for advancement.

Appendix B: Summary, Impacts of the Elements of the Solution on the Underlying Problems

Chapters 6 through 14 describe the elements in the solution, and at the end of each chapter, a list of recommendations for that element is provided. A compilation of these recommendations is given in Appendix A. To offer the reader more insights on how the elements affect the underlying problems, a summary of these impacts is organized around the problems. Because the solution is comprehensive and integrated, some recommendations impact more than one problem. Low graduation rates and long completion times are combined because they have many of the same causes.

B.1 IMPACTS OF THE SOLUTION ON HIGH COSTS

Cost reduction is a pivotal part of the solution because high cost impacts the other underlying problems. When costs are high, there are fewer funds to spend on improving quality, access for students from low- and moderate-income students is reduced, students are more likely to drop out or take longer to complete their degree, and they may not be able to put in the time to get the grades they need for the jobs they would want. There are nine elements in the solution and all but one, Chapter 8: Bridges to Potential Employers, has a direct impact of cost. Each of the remaining elements has multiple recommendations to reduce costs, which are listed by chapter in the following subsections.

B.1.1 Chapter 6: Changing Attitudes and Expectations of Students, Parents, Family Members, and Friends

1. Change attitudes and expectation: Students, parent, other family members, and friends should:
   a. Hold universities accountable for high costs.
   b. Press universities for improvements in effectiveness and efficiency.
   c. Make government aware that cost reduction and efficiency apply to high education.
   d. Insist that universities not use tuition dollars to participate in outreach and engagement.
2. Change thoughts and actions: Students, parents, other family members, and friends should expect to graduate debt-free, which is supported by the following actions.
   a. Develop a long-term financial plan for students' education that includes appropriate levels of earning and saving as well as making good investments. The key is to start early.
   b. Prepare and follow a budget so spending focuses on essential items.
   c. Shop around, pursue scholarships, and pick a university based on finding the best value.
   d. Make decisions that keep educational costs low.
3. Create a Higher Education Pricing and Outcomes (HEPO) database: This government regulated database would require universities to provide accurate data on price, graduation rates, completion time, passing rates on certification exams, and job placement, so applicants make informed choices. The federal government has leverage on all universities that accept their aid.

B.1.2 Chapter 7: Becoming Student Centered: The Right Way

1. Student-centered universities should take the following actions.
   a. Offer services that are courteous, responsive, effective, and efficient. Technology, lean thinking, and value stream mapping are used to design and implement low-cost, innovative processes.
   b. Change perspective on constructing new building and operational actions, for which students, parents, and taxpayers ultimately pay.
      i. Given the trend toward distance learning, construction of dormitory and classroom facilities must be carefully examined and justified.

ii. Outsourcing the operation of dormitories should be evaluated to determine if outsiders can do a better job at a lower price.
iii. Changes in the pedagogy, reducing the size of administration, and other factors should impact the need to build new administrative facilities.
iv. If, after careful examination, more buildings are needed, universities must find ways to design and build them to be functional, attractive, and cost less.

c. Students should not be required to live in campus dormitories even as first-year students.

2. Paying student fees must be at the option of students, and fees cannot be spent for nonacademic purposes. Funds for academic purposes (tuition) and nonacademic purposes (fees) must not be comingled.
3. Students must have a plan of study that identifies which courses to take and when to take them in order to graduate in the shortest possible time and with the lowest possible cost.
4. Universities must diversity their pedagogy to cope with the various learning styles of students. This should enhance learning, reduce costs, and change the roles and responsibilities of faculty.

B.1.3 Chapter 9: Government's Role in Higher Education

1. State and local governments should use their oversight and funding as mechanisms to pressure public colleges and universities to lower costs and improve outcomes by requiring them to:
   a. Prepare a five-year rolling plan to reduce administrative expenses, substantially, at least 5% per year for the first five years.
   b. Take financial responsibility for providing textbooks and other learning materials.
2. States should reexamine their funding plans to ensure that their:
   a. Financial aid grants, which can be very specific, are not politically motivated. Without compelling reasons, these funds should become part of the state's general appropriation.
   b. Appropriations for research, agriculture, and medical education have careful oversight with specific outcomes identified.
   c. Universities disengage from outreach and engagement until and unless there is a well-defined funding source to support it. Funds for tuition, fees, research, room, and board are not to be used for outreach and engagement.

3. Federal government provides funding directly to students.
   a. Federal Pell Grants and other smaller grants should be maintained as they support students from low- and moderate-income families. Hopefully, demand for these grants declines as universities find ways to reduce costs.
   b. Student loans should continue, but effort must focus on reducing the need to borrow, which means planning, savings, and cost reductions. They must understand their obligation by preparing a student borrowing and repayment plan (SBRP) that specifies the amount to borrow, the uses of these funds, and what they will forego to make payments after graduation.
   c. Work-study jobs often do little more than put money in students' pockets. Universities must provide evidence that students are learning something and/or doing work that has value, or they should close the program and roll the funds into the Pell Grant program.
4. Governments and accreditation agencies have regulations that drive up compliance costs.
   a. The state's Higher Education Committee (HEC) should consider the costs and benefits of federal, state, and local governments' regulations and eliminate those with little benefit.
   b. Regulations by government and accreditation agencies should focus on outputs, not inputs and processes, to make regulations more relevant and useful in identifying and resolving problems.

B.1.4 Chapter 10: Redesigning Curriculum and Pedagogy

1. Bachelor's degrees should be limited to 120 credit hours to lower tuition costs and enable students to graduate in four years, which reduces cost even further.
2. Universities should engage in effective long-term and short-term planning to ensure that students do not face closed classes that prohibit them from graduating in four years.
3. It is critical to separate instruction from testing so there is no pressure on faculty to cover less material and reduce standards.
4. Online programs and courses can become a low-cost way to deliver a quality education and make it more accessible. Universities should:
   a. Make the upfront investments to develop high-quality programs and courses.

b. Invest in technologies to deliver program content effectively.
c. Start with high-enrollment courses, where it is possible to enjoy economies of scale.
d. Offer complete programs so online students can graduate without setting foot on campus.
e. Create educational program that are secure so the person who received the grade is the person actually doing the work.
f. Share online offerings with other universities to spread the fixed costs of course development.
g. Have no activity fees for students enrolling in online learning.

B.1.5 Chapter 11: Reforming Administration and Management

1. Universities must reconfigure the strategic plan and the strategic planning process. This means:
   a. Recognizing there are multiple customers and goals—students want good jobs and less debt; governments and potential employers want lower costs and better quality graduates.
   b. Increasing faculty involvement in managing universities and the strategic planning process.
2. Universities must decentralize decision making so their individual colleges have more freedom to pursue innovative and entrepreneurial activities, appoint more faculty to administrative posts, and create a faculty resource committee (FRC) to give faculty input on high-level resource planning and allocation.
3. It is critical to improve the effectiveness and efficiency/productivity of:
   a. Executive leadership by identifying work that is unnecessary, setting targets for reducing the number of administration, and providing management tools and training as well as information technology-based decision support systems.
   b. Professional managers and specialists by focusing on systems-thinking and process improvements, which involves lean thinking, quality improvement efforts, value stream mapping, process redesign, and continuous improvement efforts.
   c. Nonexempt support staff through processes redesign and specific IT applications.
4. Moderate administrative salaries by eliminating benchmarking in salary determination and creating more competition for high-level administrative jobs.

5. Change organizational structure, lower costs, and enhance quality through mergers, closing branch campuses, and most importantly by outsourcing activities.

B.1.6 Chapter 12: Reshaping Faculty's Role

1. To improve quality and efficiency, all types of faculty must be educated in content, pedagogy, and assessment of learning. Evaluation of teaching performance by students and peers who are master teachers, access to resources, teaching seminars, and other mechanisms are essential.
2. It is important to identify the capabilities of different faculty types, know the instructional needs for courses, and match these to get both high quality and low cost.
3. General education and interdisciplinary core courses tend to generate substantial surpluses, which are used to subsidize other undergraduate courses as well as courses in master's and PhD programs. State governments should create a HEC to examine these subsidy issues.
4. It is vital to improve faculty productivity by investing in sophisticate, top-quality methods for communicating knowledge and supporting faculty so they create innovative and efficient ways to teaching students. Universities and faculty must move away from the notion that a three-credit-hour course requires three hours of face time.
5. Faculty unions are not the cause of the problems that universities face but are the result of these problems. University leaders and tenured and professional faculty must mend the relationships that have created the underlying problems and driven faculty to unionize.

B.1.7 Chapter 13: Creating High-Technology Learning Materials

1. Universities must create high-tech reading materials that are interactive and help students identify and address knowledge gaps. These should have lower cost, better content coverage, enhanced learning for students, and better outcomes for publishers.
2. Universities must create high-tech, digitized lectures and video vignettes that allow students to have access to top tenured and

professional faculty even in general education and disciplinary core courses. The cost to create these digitized lectures should be offset by lower faculty costs.

3. High-tech learning materials are appropriate for large classes with relatively stable content, which includes general education and disciplinary core courses, and can lead to lower costs.
4. It is essential to continuously improve these tools because technology changes and innovative thinking provide new insight on how to deliver knowledge better and at a lower cost.

B.1.8 Chapter 14: Revamping Relationships among High Schools, Community and Technical Colleges, and Universities

1. When students are preparing for a degree in higher education, they should take as many rigorous high school courses as possible.
2. States should work with their high schools, public community and technical colleges, and public universities to create meaningful college preparatory and vocational tracks and ensure that these entities provide the best education at the lowest cost. This includes the use of the HEC to coordinate course offerings and eliminate redundancy and gaps.
3. Universities would be prohibited from offering remedial/high school–level courses. Students who are missing courses would go to their state-supported website to complete them.
4. Students using community and technical colleges to lower the costs of higher education should make sure that their coursework transfers to universities and meets graduation requirements.
5. It is vital to standardize college preparatory classes offered in high schools with similar offerings in public two-year colleges and four-year universities so students do not waste time or money.
6. Beyond these courses, community and technical colleges and universities should identify common courses and agree on content and performance standards—even common learning materials. This would simplify transferring to universities and reduce the risk of having courses taken at a community and technical college not counting toward a four-year degree.

B.2 IMPACTS OF THE SOLUTION ON QUALITY CONCERNS

It is essential to focus on cost reduction and quality improvement simultaneously because there are many cases where both can be achieved. For example, investing in technology to support course development can improve faculty efficiency, lower cost, and increase the quality of instruction. Too often, a singular focus on cost reduction leads to lower quality. For example, removing student advisors to save money often results in students making bad decisions about what courses to take, which causes them to waste time and money taking the wrong courses. Following are recommendations to enhance quality, and some are repetitive with recommendations in the cost section.

1. Students should demand a rigorous curriculum so they have a more valuable education.
2. Universities must diversity their pedagogy to cope with the various learning styles of students. This should enhance learning, reduce costs, and change the roles and responsibilities of faculty.
3. Universities must change how students evaluate instructional faculty, so they feel less pressure to reduce content and lower learning standards. This can be done by:
   a. Eliminating instructional faculty's role in setting course content, preparing exams, and assigning grades. These tasks would be done by tenured and professional faculty.
   b. Assessing teaching effectiveness of all faculty members, contractual and tenured, by evaluating them based on what students learn.
   c. Student evaluations would assess (1) how faculty members treat students and (2) the learning environment including the application of student-centered learning so that students learn more quickly and easily.
4. Universities should create program advisory boards (PABs) for each area of study by reaching out to potential employers, graduate schools, and certification and licensure agencies. PABs are vehicles that tenured and professional faculty can use to determine curricula and set performance standards so graduates are well prepared.
5. Federal funds are used to support private, *for-profit* universities that have very poor performance outcomes. The poor performers must be disqualified from receiving federal aid.

6. Potential employers work with tenured and professional faculty to set curriculum content and performance standards so graduates learn more and are prepared for the job market.
7. Student-centered learning, which is designed to satisfy individual learning styles, makes it easier and faster to learn so quality, graduation rate, completion time, and job placement improve.
8. Universities must reconfigure the strategic plan and the strategic planning process. This means:
    a. Recognizing there are multiple customers and goals—students want good jobs and less debt; governments and potential employers want lower costs and better quality graduates.
    b. Increasing faculty involvement in managing universities and the strategic planning process.
9. Universities must decentralize decision making so their individual colleges have more freedom to pursue innovative and entrepreneurial activities, appoint more faculty to administrative posts, and create a faculty resource committee (FRC) to given faculty input on resource planning and allocation.
10. Change organizational structure, lower costs, and enhance quality through mergers, closing branch campuses, and, most importantly, by outsourcing activities.
11. To improve quality and efficiency, all types of faculty must be educated in content, pedagogy, and assessment of learning. Evaluation of teaching performance by students and peers who are master teachers, access to resources, teaching seminars, and other mechanisms are essential.
12. It is important to identify the capabilities of different faculty types, know the instructional needs for courses, and match the two factors to get both high quality and low cost.
13. Faculty unions are not the cause of the problems that universities face but are the result of these problems. University leaders and tenured and professional faculty must mend the relationships that have created the underlying problems and driven faculty to unionize.
14. Universities must create high-tech reading materials that are interactive and help students identify and address knowledge gaps. These should lower cost, provide better content coverage, enhance learning for students, and offer better outcomes for publishers.
15. Universities must create high-tech, digitized lectures and video vignettes that allow students to have access to top tenured and

professional faculty even in general education and disciplinary core courses. The cost to create these digitized lectures should be offset by lower faculty costs.

16. It is essential to continuously improve these tools because technology changes and innovative thinking provides new insight on how to apply technology.
17. States should work with their high schools, public community and technical colleges, and public universities to create meaningful college preparatory and vocational tracks and ensure that these entities provide the best education at the lowest cost. This includes the use of the HEC to coordinate course offerings and eliminate redundancy and gaps.
18. It is vital to standardize college preparatory classes offered in high schools with similar offerings in public two-year colleges and four-year universities so students do not waste time or money.
19. Beyond these courses, community and technical colleges and universities should identify common courses and agree on content and performance standards—even common learning materials. This would simplify transferring to universities and reduce the risk of having courses taken at the community and technical college not counting toward a four-year degree.
20. States should work with universities to create pathways to learning for all students, including graduates from technical programs, so they have ample opportunities for advancement.

B.3 IMPACTS OF THE SOLUTION ON LIMITED ACCESS

Any recommendation that reduces costs increases accessibility for low- and moderate-income students, so the recommendations under cost reduction are not included here with a few key exceptions.

1. Online programs and courses can become a low-cost way to deliver a quality education and make it more accessible. Universities should:
   a. Make the upfront investments to develop high-quality programs and courses.

   b. Invest in technology to deliver program content effectively.
   c. Start with high-enrollment courses, where it is possible to enjoy economies of scale.
   d. Offer complete programs, so online students can graduate without setting foot on campus.
   e. Create educational program that are secure so the person who received the grade is the person actually doing the work.
   f. Share online offerings with other universities to spread the fixed costs of course development.
   g. Have no activity fees for students enrolling in online learning.
2. When students are preparing for a degree in higher education, they should take as many rigorous high school courses as possible.
3. States should work with their high schools, public community and technical colleges, and public universities to create meaningful college preparatory and vocational tracks and ensure that these entities provide the best education at the lowest cost. This includes the use of the HEC to coordinate course offerings and eliminate redundancy and gaps.
4. Many states offer virtual high school options to young students. This capability should be extended to adults who dropped out of elementary or high school so that they can complete their degree and have the opportunity for a better life and advanced education.
5. Students using community and technical colleges to lower the costs of higher education should make sure that their coursework transfers to universities and meets graduation requirements.
6. It is vital to standardize college preparatory classes offered in high schools with similar offerings in public two-year colleges and four-year universities so students do not waste time or money.
7. Beyond these courses, community and technical colleges and universities should identify common courses and agree on content and performance standards—even common learning materials. This would simplify transferring to universities and reduce the risk of having courses taken at the community and technical college not counting toward a four-year degree.
8. States should work with universities to create pathways to learning for all students, including graduates from technical programs, so they have ample opportunities for advancement.

B.4 IMPACTS OF THE SOLUTION ON LOW GRADUATION RATES AND LONG COMPLETION TIMES

As the cost of higher education escalates, students face more pressure to work while attending school, so students are more likely to fail, drop out, or delay graduation. Once again, the cost reduction recommendations are not repeated.

1. Students must have a plan of study that identifies which courses to take and when to take them in order to graduate in the shortest possible time and with the lowest possible cost.
2. State and local governments can condition their funding for higher education on meeting mission-appropriate goals for graduation rates, time to completion, and job placements.
3. Bachelor's degrees should be limited to 120 credit hours to lower tuition costs and enable students to graduate in four years, which reduces cost further.
4. Universities should engage in effective long-term and short-term planning to ensure that students do not face closed classes that prohibit them from graduating in four years.
5. Student-centered learning, which is designed to satisfy individual learning styles, makes it easier and faster to learn so quality, graduation rate, completion time, and job placement improve.

B.5 IMPACTS OF THE SOLUTION ON POOR JOB PLACEMENT

Activities that improve the quality of higher education are likely to increase students' knowledge and capabilities, which should enhance job placement. With a few key exceptions, the recommendations to improve quality are not listed here.

1. Students should pick their major bases on both interest in the work and the opportunity to secure a job that pays well. Too often students pick majors with limited job opportunities.

2. Universities should create PABs for each area of study by reaching out to potential employers, graduate schools, and certification and licensure agencies. PABs are vehicles that tenured and professional faculty can use to determine curricula and performance standards so graduates are well prepared. PABs are points of contact for students and employers.
3. Universities must provide placement and job data for all majors for applicants to consider.
4. Universities should provide students with easy access to the *Occupational Outlook Handbook* prepared by the U.S. Bureau of Labor Statistics, which provides employment information about hundreds of jobs.
5. Universities should build strong relationships between students and employers.
   a. Cooperative education and internship programs are ways for students to achieve appropriate professional behaviors, learn how to apply theory and techniques to real problems, and become more interested and motivated to learn.
   b. Potential employers can work directly with students as mentors or in small groups to offer advice and counsel about various aspects of professional life.
6. As students move toward graduation, programs and colleges within the university must provide better mechanisms for placing students in good jobs. In addition to traditional placement services, programs and colleges should be proactive in finding potential employers and bringing them to campus for job fairs and other types of interaction.
7. State and local governments can condition their funding for higher education on meeting mission-appropriate goals for graduation rates, time to completion, and job placements.
8. Potential employers work with tenured and professional faculty to set curriculum content and performance standards so graduates learn more and are prepared for the job market.
9. Students should have short courses in professional development to prepare for the job market.
10. Student-centered learning, which is designed to satisfy individual learning styles, makes it easier and faster to learn so quality, graduation rate, completion time, and job placement improve.

Index

D

E

F

G

H

I

P

Q

R

S

T

U

V

W

Y